PUBLISHING WOMEN

WOMEN IN CULTURE AND SOCIETY

*A Series Edited by Catharine R. Stimpson*

# Publishing Women

SALONS, THE PRESSES, AND THE
COUNTER-REFORMATION
IN SIXTEENTH-CENTURY ITALY

## Diana Robin

*The University of Chicago Press :: Chicago and London*

DIANA ROBIN is professor emerita of classics at the University of New Mexico and a fellow of the American Academy at Rome. She is the recipient of a Rome Prize, as well as fellowships from the Rockefeller Foundation, the National Endowment for the Humanities, the Delmas Foundation, and the Exxon Education Foundation. Currently, Dr. Robin is a scholar-in-residence at the Newberry Library.

The University of Chicago Press, Chicago 60637
The University of Chicago Press, Ltd., London
© 2007 by The University of Chicago
All rights reserved. Published 2007
Printed in the United States of America
16  15  14  13  12  11  10  09  08  07      1  2  3  4  5
ISBN-13: 978-0-226-72156-9 (cloth) ·
ISBN-10: 0-226-72156-6 (cloth)

Library of Congress Catalog-in-Publcation Data

Robin, Diana Maury.
   Publishing women : salons, the presses, and the Counter-Reformation in sixteenth-century Italy / Diana Robin.
       p. cm.—(Women in culture and society)
   Includes bibliographical references and index.
   ISBN-13: 978-0-226-72156-9 (alk. paper)
   ISBN-10: 0-226-72156-6 (alk. paper)
       1. Publishers and publishing—Italy—History—16th century. 2. Italian literature—Publishing—History—16th century. 3. Women and literature—Italy—History—16th century. 4. Women authors, Italian—Early modern, 1500–1700. 5. Salons—Italy—History—16th century. 6. Counter-Reformation—Italy. 7. Women—Italy—Intellectual life. 8. Italy—Intellectual life. 9. Italy—Imprints. I. Title.
   Z340.R628   2007
   070.5094509'031—dc22

                                                                    2006030913

*For Nancy Robin Jaicks*

# CONTENTS

ILLUSTRATIONS

In 2006, I was a juror for a book prize. Thirteen boxes of candidates for the award—stories and novels—accumulated in my office. Women of all races had written them. Some were daring, some conventional; some unbuttoned, some buttoned up; some memorable, some forgettable. None was in danger of being blacklisted, censored, or banned in the United States.

These boxes rested on the floor behind me as I read *Publishing Women: Salons, The Presses, and the Counter-Reformation in Sixteenth-Century Italy.*

Diana Robin is a formidable scholar. Her narrative—a contribution to the histories of Europe, gender, literature and culture, and the book—is thick with facts, notes, and texts in Italian and English translation. They are often unfamiliar—many not reprinted since the Renaissance. Yet her narrative is charged with drama. For she is exploring a momentous period in Western history in which writing could be dangerous for both men and women and when Italian women writers, despite these dangers, became an identifiable group. Rejecting anonymity, they insisted on being published and read under their own names. In 1538, Vittoria Colonna, a compelling figure, was the first to do so. Simultaneously, and helpfully, the mass-produced book was emerging as a cultural force.

Robin focuses on the literary women of five cities: Rome, the location of the papacy; Florence; Naples and Ischia, off-shore islands; Venice, the center of the Italian printing industry; and Siena. These women were fortunately from elite families that offered them literacy, learning, and affluence. The women of Siena were, however, different. Robin suggests that there a "possibly unbridgeable gulf existed" between bourgeois women and those who were royal or royally connected, "whose tragedies were buffered by wealth and entitlement" (p. 159).

Because history studies change, Robin asks why Italian women writers appeared as public figures in the mid-sixteenth century. Her answers make sense. Although men and women writers might debate the question of gender differences, they shaped a consensus about serious cultural questions, among them the value of women as writers and patrons, the indispensability of Tuscan as a literary language, and, crucially, about the need for religious reform. Among the genres, they were drawn to poetry, especially to the sonnet, and to the dialogue. A favorite format was the anthology, a textual "melting pot in which class, occupational, and gender distinctions went practically unmarked . . . the sons and daughters of artisans mingle with noblewomen, courtesans, ambassadors, soldiers, and royalty . . ." (p. 57). Women also established salons, those very influential sites of discussion and the presentation of new work, which were dynamically connected to the new academies and the presses. Editors and publishers sought and brought out women writers. Interestingly, as the innovation of the woman author took hold, the design of and marketing strategies for books became more innovative. Women also formed networks of familial, social, and literary relationships, some of them erotically charged.

Protected though elite women might have been, Italy in the sixteenth century experienced shifting alliances among families and potentates of church and state; conflicts and struggles for land and power; stress and bloodshed; civil wars and foreign invasions. After a long siege, the Republic of Siena was sacked and destroyed in 1555. Tourists who seek out Italy as the glamorous land of fashion and food miserably forget its history.

In a terrible tension, as women writers were claiming a voice and audience, the Roman Catholic Church was reinvigorating the Inquisition and engineering the Counter-Reformation. The sessions of the Council of Trent began in the late 1540s, finally to end in 1563. The advocacy of religious reform, within the Catholic Church or without as a form of Protestantism, became tantamount to heresy to be sniffed for and snuffed out. The papacy that had supported literature and the arts in the fifteenth century persecuted poets, scholars, and humanism in the sixteenth. In 1559, the Venetian publishing house of Gabriel Giolito brought out the first all-woman anthology of poetry. In that same year, the Roman Catholic Church banned the complete works of 550 authors and many individual titles. On March 18, between 10,000 and 12,000 books were burned in Rome.

After Trent, between 1564 and 1575, the number of secular books by men and women and the number of women writers declined. Moreover, between 1575 and 1577, the plague decimated Venice and its publishing industry. Yet, the Italian women writers had created their legacy. Robin shows that in the last part of the sixteenth century, their books were reprinted. After 1595, for more than two decades, women's writing flourished, if in different and mutually conflicting genres. Feminist polemics were there, but so was devotional work.

Famously, the figure of the woman warrior, the Amazon, has been applied to women of unusual force and strength. It was to the first generation of published Italian women writers, and, I suggest, appropriately so. Vittoria Colonna, Guilia Gonzago, Caterina Cibo, the learned courtesan Tullia d'Aragona—these women and others were courageous, adventurous, talented, generative. Because of Diana Robin, I can now imagine them more richly, feel their ghostly presence, and rank the vitality of their words—brave, brilliant, or cajoling—with those between the covers hard and soft in the boxes in my office.

*Catharine R. Stimpson*
*New York University*

## ACKNOWLEDGMENTS

This book began with the fellowship in gender studies I was awarded by the Rockefeller Foundation for a year's work in residence at the Newberry Library in 1999, and I thank the foundation for that grant. For pushing me to finish the research and writing of the book, I have my friend, colleague, and mentor Paul Gehl—custodian of the John M. Wing Foundation on the History of Printing at the Newberry—to thank. It was Paul who forced me to leave Albuquerque and move back to Chicago four years ago so I could take full advantage of the Newberry's treasures. I am especially grateful to JoEllen Dickie and the Newberry staff for their daily labors in carrying to my carrel and my table in Special Collections the hundreds of rare sixteenth-century editions and almost equally rare nineteenth-century Italian studies of early modern Italian texts. I have also benefited from the superb collections in my field at the Regenstein Library at the University of Chicago. I am hugely grateful to Dale Kent and Jane Tylus for not only combing through the whole manuscript in two successive drafts but also for their suggestions for a reconstruction and clarification of the narrative and their correction of my many errors and omissions. To Susan Bielstein at the University of Chicago Press, I am chiefly indebted, since she first spotted my idea for the book—when it was only a germ, back during my fellowship year at the Newberry—and she encouraged me to see it through from prospectus to its final form. My deepest thanks go also to Margaret King and Al Rabil for their friendship over the years and for inspiring all of us who have participated as authors, editors, and translators in the University of Chicago Press series they inaugurated, the Other Voice in Early Modern Europe.

I am also indebted to the many friends who read pieces of the book at various stages, who made invaluable suggestions, and who often called my attention to key articles and books of which I was unaware: Pat Crain, Lydia Cochrane, Konrad Eisenbichler, Julia Hairston, Nancy Jaicks, Deborah Jenson,

Margaret King, Jules Kirshner, John Marino, Lauro Martines, Tom Mayer, Mary Quinlan McGrath, Letizia Panizza, Sarah Ross, Deanna Shemek, Janet Smarr, James Turner, Elissa Weaver, Lynn Westwater, Jane Wickersham, Betsy Wright, Gabriella Zarri—and above all, Paul Gehl. I must thank especially again Lydia Cochrane, Letizia Panizza, Daria Perocco, Meredith Ray, Deanna Shemek, and Lynn Westwater for their advice and help with my translations. I want also to express my gratitude to Elissa Weaver and Gabriella Zarri for bringing me rare volumes and articles from Italy that I could not have found in the United States. I owe thanks, too, to the British Library and their staff for the assistance they provided to me on my several visits to London to forage for more sixteenth-century Italian books relevant to my project.

Finally, I want to thank Susan Bielstein, Anthony Burton, Yvonne Zipter, and my readers at the press for their elegant transformation of what was an unruly pile of paper into the book you now see.

# INTRODUCTION

*In the first place, a large number of people, machines, and materials must converge and act together for it to come into existence at all. How exactly they do so will inevitably affect its finished character in a number of ways. In that sense a book is the material embodiment of, if not a consensus, then at least a collective consent. . . . So a printed book can be seen as a nexus conjoining a wide range of worlds of work.* ADRIAN JOHNS, *The Nature of the Book*

This book explores the very public emergence of women writers as a group for the first time in Italy, during the years 1530–70. Focusing always on the collective process of publication rather than on the figure of the isolated poet, this study will examine intellectual communities in five cities where women and men were active as writers: Naples, Venice, Rome, Siena, and Florence. I will probe the circumstances of the midcentury literary renascence of urban Italian women, asking why women enjoyed unprecedented visibility as writers, thinkers, and literary patrons at the height of the Inquisition and at a time when civil unrest and foreign invasions plagued the peninsula. The literary salons of Italian city women were never more than a few miles from bloody scenes of war and carnage. Siena, where elite women and men had gathered in the evening for poetry readings and serious debate for decades, was sacked and burned in 1555; and in the battle of Ceresole, not far from Maria d'Aragona's brilliant salon in Milan, twelve thousand men lost their lives.

Since the publication of Elizabeth Eisenstein's *The Printing Press as an Agent of Change* in 1979, a fertile field of inquiry has opened up, inaugurating studies in the history of the book and suggesting other avenues for the further investigation of print culture.[1] But the obvious question still needs raising: To what extent did *women* participate in the European print revolution? Joan DeJean's study of the novel in seventeenth-century France, *Tender Geographies,* has shown that women writers were among the first producers of the modern print behemoth—the novel.[2] And Susan Broomhall, in her recent study, *Women and the Book Trade in Sixteenth-Century France*, has made clear that women took part in every phase of the early printing industry, though only a fraction of the total number of books printed in France were written by women.[3] In my study of women's impact on early print culture in Italy, I will focus on literary authorship, a category dominated by elite men and from which all but elite women were excluded, with some notable exceptions. Nonetheless, during this period a significant number of women—writers and patrons—principally from the elite classes did make a dent in the Italian book market, though their numbers were small relative to their male compatriots'. As Carlo Dionisotti has observed, between the years 1540 and 1560, for the first time in Italian literary history and "never before or since," women writers were numerous enough to be considered a significant group.[4] When in 1538, a book of Vittoria Colonna's *Rime* was published in Parma, the first publication of its kind by a woman under her own name, "it was," Dionisotti wrote, "as though a glowing ember had fallen on tinder."[5] At the end of the sixteenth century the number of women who had published their work in Italy topped two hundred.[6] By midcentury many of their poems were appearing in the new poetry anthologies produced by the Giolito press and several other publishing houses affiliated with Giolito in Venice, the uncontested center of the print industry in sixteenth-century Italy.[7] The rise of women writers in the publishing world—from their early token appearances in the Venetian anthologies in the later 1540s, to the solo editions of such writers as Vittoria Colonna, Laura Terracina, and Tullia d'Aragona—peaked in 1559 with the publication of the first anthology of women poets ever produced in Europe, a volume showcasing the works of fifty-three women writers.

The moral strictures placed on the public appearance of women's names, which caused many writers in early modern France and England to publish their works anonymously, simply do not apply in the commercial print world of sixteenth-century Italy.[8] Editors such as Lodovico Domenichi and the critic Girolamo Ruscelli, who assisted women writers in preparing their manuscripts for the presses, also publicized the patronage of the elite women who financially supported the books the press produced. They thanked their women patrons with florid prefaces to their books and even published lists of their names that circulated as a kind of intellectual social register. Ruscelli, for example, published a twenty-two-page list naming 259 women from thirty-five Italian cities in an appendix to his book, *Lettura sopra un sonetto . . . alla divina signora Marchesa del Vasto* (Lecture on a sonnet . . . for the divine signora).[9]

Domenichi publicized the names of 195 elite women patrons and writers by having the characters in his *La nobiltà delle donne* (1549) cite them and their cities by name in the course of their dialogue on the virtues of women.[10]

In this study, I will follow the lives and works of several loosely connected groups of elite women and men in Italy who not only produced a new vernacular literature but who worked, as well, to disseminate ideas for the reform of the established Church. Departing from earlier studies, I will show that many of the leading writers in Italy between the 1530s and 1560s, whether female or male, were active on two fronts: in the religious reform movement inaugurated by Giulia Gonzaga and Juan de Valdés in Naples and in the literary renewal fostered by the urban academies and high-volume Venetian publishing businesses such as the Giolito press, where publications by women spiked at midcentury.

Up to now scholars of early modern Italy have maintained the separation between women's literary history, the history of the book, and Counter-Reformation studies, the three fields most germane to my study—a separation that has perpetuated the marginalization of women as important actors in European history. Crossing the borders between these fields, my study will attempt to produce a cultural history of the period that considers the significant roles that Italian women played in tandem with men in the literary, political, religious, and social life of the peninsula. Following the lead of Ann Rosalind Jones's theory of "negotiation," my work insists that women's works be read alongside those of their male contemporaries and that they be considered in terms of their appropriation—and in some cases rejection—of the literary and linguistic codes of both their male age-peers and their predecessors.[11] I will argue, moreover, that the woman-led salon was the primary vehicle by which elite women first entered the commercial print world of sixteenth-century Italy. Chapter 1 pictures the birth of one such salon on the island of Ischia, off the coast of Naples. It tells the story of the literary circle that Costanza d'Avalos first established on the island and later moved to Naples with the younger women in her family—Vittoria Colonna, Maria d'Aragona, her sister Giovanna d'Aragona, and eventually, Giulia Gonzaga Colonna. These were women who led their lives independently of oversight by a husband or male relative. Their salon proved a potent matrix, generating from itself five subsequent salons, each directed by one of the founding d'Avalos-Colonna women who shaped the institution and were themselves molded by it. Under the leadership of Giulia Gonzaga and the Spanish theologian Juan de Valdés, these salons, which began as gatherings for poets, later functioned as cells for the dissemination of ideas for religious reform that the

Church would soon criminalize as heretical. The poet Vittoria Colonna and her circle played an essential role in the formation of Cardinal Reginald Pole's *cenacolo* at Viterbo; similarly, Maria d'Aragona d'Avalos's court in Milan and her salon at Pavia were centers where both the new Italian poetry and reform thought were cultivated.

The story of the early women-led salons in my opening chapter and their intense commitment, at first, to post-Petrarchan poetry and, later, to Valdesian theology provides a die for the description of the literary coteries in northern Italy, whose activities and publications I will consider in the chapters that follow. The salon differed from the royal court in sixteenth-century Italy in its insulation from the apparatuses of state or city-state. Without official authorization and lacking a bureaucracy, its meetings were informal and sporadic in nature; it functioned primarily as a social and cultural assembly rather than as an appendage of the state. Nonetheless this informal sixteenth-century institution was deeply embroiled in the politics of church and city. The leaders of the Ischia salon were, in Elizabeth C. Goldsmith's formulation, itinerant women, women economically independent enough to change their residences at will, often moving from city to city in the course of their lives.[12] Presiding over the circles she created wherever she was, Vittoria Colonna lived variously in Ischia, Rome, Naples, Ferrara, Lucca, Orvieto, and Viterbo using a network of convent safe houses as bases for her operations, while Maria d'Aragona moved house from Ischia to Naples, Milan, and Pavia, before finally returning to Ischia.

Unlike the salons in seventeenth-century France, the Naples-Ischia salons did not decline but grew in importance with the rise of the printing industry in sixteenth-century Italy, where reciprocity and dynamism characterized the interaction among salon, academy, and press.[13] In the Italian salons and academies, the works of both new and seasoned authors were performed, while this kind of prepublication cultivated an audience for the works and often led to publication.

The forging of intellectual partnerships of the sort Joan DeJean describes in her study of what she calls "salon writings" in seventeenth-century France, in which women writers from the highest ranks of society allied themselves with lower-ranking men who had literary expertise, dominates my study thematically.[14] While DeJean's female-male literary partnerships represent the obverse of Jones's scene of negotiation, where women writers perceived as socially inferior must win the approval of higher ranking males, in both paradigms, when women enter the alien world of print culture, their authorship involves—in Jonesian terms—an appropriation of received (male) literary and linguistic codes.[15] In both cases, women advance their careers as authors via their collaborations with literary men. In sixteenth-century Italy, partnerships between women and men of unequal rank, such as DeJean describes, characterize sociality and discourse both in the religious reform movement and the poetry salons. My subsequent chapters foreground the bonding of elite women writers with men working at the presses as editors, translators, correctors, printers, and consultants. These so-called male *poligrafi,* known as such because of the broad array of artisanal and scholarly functions they performed at the presses, helped aristocratic women to place their work with reputable firms, while collaboration with a woman from an elite family brought gravitas to an editor's portfolio and prestige to his press. In other cases, elite women acted as literary patrons, providing subventions to a publisher or his editor, in return for which she might be lavishly thanked in the work's preface; her name might also be published in a list of distinguished donors to the press, as I noted above in the cases of Ruscelli and Domenichi's patron rosters.[16]

The poetry anthology, a new genre in sixteenth-century Italian print culture, was closely related to the salon, as I will demonstrate, and the publication of a group of writers constituted a virtual salon, in effect. Investigating the roots of one such anthology, chapter 2 locates its impetus in the suppression of Maria d'Aragona's salon and the banning of the literary academies in Naples in 1547. The city's poets were forced to seek a voice elsewhere. Through d'Aragona's connections at the Venetian presses, writers previously unknown outside the Naples salons were able to win peninsula-wide celebrity by virtue of their publication in the commercially successful Giolito poetry series and through the press's promotion of them as a new group from the south—they were sold under the title *Rime di diversi illustri signori Napoletani, e d'altri nobilissimi ingegni.* Similarly, when women writers and their patrons saw their chances for publication dwindle at the height of the Inquisition—with its blacklisting of poetry judged "lascivious" and its targeting of Venice for increased vigilance—they looked to an editor with connections outside the center of the industry. This chapter describes the first anthology composed almost entirely of women's works ever published, the *Rime diverse d'alcune nobilissime, et virtuosissime donne,* which Giolito's senior editor Domenichi placed with a small printer in Lucca in 1559.[17] As in the case of the print afterlife of the Naples salon, the 1559 anthology amounted to the publishing of a salon for women.

Fully thirty-five of the sonnets in Domenichi's 1559 anthology represent exchanges between women, some in the heated amatory language of Petrarch and Ovid. These erotically edged lyrics might not in themselves suggest the beginnings of a same-sex love lyric tradition in late Renaissance Italy such as Harriette Andreadis has found in early modern England, though at least one mid-sixteenth-century critic, Agnolo Firenzuolo, publicly compared a Sienese gentlewoman, whose poems were addressed to another woman in Domenichi's anthology, to Sappho and the sort of woman who, as he put it, "by nature spurns marriage and flees from intimate conversation with us men."[18] When the 1559 women's anthology came out, the Roman Holy Office was tightening its grip on the publishing industry in Venice, and even poetry was suspect. This explains its publication at a press outside the mainstream. Yet this was also a time, as Ruscelli's and Domenichi's lists show, when every city had its coteries of literary women; and the number of women who participated in intellectual salons, wrote poetry for publication, and acted as patrons of the presses was a matter of civic pride. As icons of local culture, these mid-sixteenth-century anthologies projected images of an egalitarian city of letters: courtesans and the daughters and sons of guildsmen shared space in its pages with aristocrats at the top of the social scale. But these were utopias of an editor's imagining, not documents reflecting real-time sodality.

Other elite women writers and patrons fought the geopolitics of the Church as well as its theology. In chapter 3, I present an account of the first in a series of clashes between the Colonna-d'Aragona women and the popes: the Salt War of 1541. When Pope Paul III (Alessandro Farnese) launched a war against the Colonnas, Vittoria Colonna withdrew from her intense involvement in the *spirituali* movement initiated by Valdés to act as her brother Ascanio Colonna's secretary of state. Colonna's little studied letters to her brother during the Salt War—partnered with the war dispatches of the pope's field commissary, who happened to be Colonna's friend and fellow poet, Giovanni Guidiccioni—portray the changing landscape of a war whose outcome would have an impact on the Colonna-d'Aragona women's future role in the politics of the peninsula. Colonna's letters illuminate her skill at forging alliances and representing her clan both at the ambassadorial level and within her extended family, where solidarity was at issue. This chapter also considers two other little known literary interventions the Colonna women authored during the Salt War, the first a highly embellished Ciceronian oration that Giovanna d'Aragona Colonna sent the pope, begging him to ease the misery of her family; in the second, Vittoria Colonna addresses a pair of sonnets to the pope, starkly depicting the sorrow and the waste of war and calling on the pontiff to shepherd his flocks to peace. Crucial resemblances and repetitions of images and ideas, found in both the Colonna women's writings and their friend Guidiccioni's letters to the pope during the war, document the Colonna-d'Aragona women's talent for maintaining longtime friendships across political fault lines.

In a sequel to the story of the Salt War, I present the second installment of the Colonna women's battles with a sitting pope, this time Paul IV (Gian Pietro Carafa, pope 1555–59). When, for the second time in less than fifteen years, a pope's army marched on the Colonna towns in the Castelli Romani, the d'Aragona-Colonna women and their allies fought back. In chapter 4, I argue that the published writings of the Venetian poets show how closely allied such elite women from the south as Giovanna d'Aragona Colonna and Maria d'Aragona d'Avalos had become to the literary academies, salons, and presses of Florence and Venice and how much the papal court had withdrawn from the vibrant literary culture of the Italian cities in its pursuit of heresy. As soon as Carafa was elected pope, he renewed his attacks on the Venetian publishing industry. The Roman Holy Office banned the complete works of 550 authors, among whom were a number of poets who were the mainstays of the Giolito poetry anthologies and the clients of the d'Aragona-Colonna women. In 1557, the pope ordered the imprisonment of Vittoria Colonna's longtime friend Cardinal Giovanni Morone for heresy. It was in this climate that leading publishers in Venice and Florence brought out two major works celebrating Vittoria Colonna's sister-in-law Giovanna d'Aragona Colonna, each of these volumes presenting itself as a temple in her honor. Coming out in rapid-fire succession, Girolamo Ruscelli's *Del tempio alla divina signora donna Giovanna d'Aragona*, a massive polyglot anthology featuring 277 poets writing in four languages (1555), and Giuseppe Betussi's dialogue, *Le imagini del tempio della signora donna Giovanna Aragona* (1556), constituted a public drawing of a line in the sand between the presses and the Church.[19]

Ruscelli's *Tempio*, like the earlier Giolito anthologies represented a utopian, classless republic of letters, where rank and gender had nothing to do with a poet's placement in the text. But Betussi's *Imagini del tempio,* more in keeping with the temper of the times, published a roster of elite female-male literary couples. Here every elite woman in Betussi's list of *imagini* is paired with a man well known for his work at, or in collaboration with, the Venetian presses. Betussi had, in fact, published the very phenomenon that characterized the dramatic entry of women, and in significant numbers, into the urban literary world of the fifties: the alliances between women from the highest social caste with men connected with the presses.

The mélange of mid-sixteenth-century diaries, documentary-style dialogues, travelogues, and poems I cite in chapter 5 make it clear that the literary scene in the provincial city of Siena was very different from that of metropolitan Naples, Milan, and Venice. Siena shared a number of cultural institutions in common with those cities at mid-century: women-led salons; an active religious reform movement associated with the teachings of Valdés and Bernardino Ochino; a literary academy of peninsula-wide fame; and last but most important, an avant-garde circle that promoted the kind of amatory rhetorics that the Inquisition would criminalize under Paul IV. But Siena and its bourgeois elite coteries remained separate from the high salon culture of the d'Aragona-Colonna women. Though Charles V's daughter Margaret of Austria visited Siena twice in the company of her father, the granddaughters of the king of Naples and their friends did not travel to Siena, nor did they forge connections by letter with the elite women of the small republic, though they could have done so through the intervention of such well-connected men within the Venetian publishing world as Ruscelli, Betussi, and Domenichi, who maintained friendships with the intellectual women of both worlds.

Opening proleptically, this chapter chronicles, in the eyes of two contemporary witnesses, the city's fall to Spanish and Florentine troops in 1555. They depict Siena's last days as a free republic and describe the Sienese poet Laudomia Forteguerri's leadership of a legion of a thousand women who, with picks and shovels, attempt to erect new fortifications while the armies of Cosimo I and Charles V are at the city's gates. I then turn, in that chapter, to the world of the Sienese salons where, a decade and a half earlier, women and men displayed their literary talents at poetry games, dialogue writing, and serious debates about the Christian faith and the viability of Valdesian reform doctrine. The friendship between two leaders of the Sienese *veglie* (evening assemblies), Laudomia Forteguerri and Alessandro Piccolomini, a literary alliance of the sort typical of the era, resulted in the first work of criticism on the poetry of a woman author ever published, the *Lettura del S. Alessandro Piccolomini Infiammato fatta nell'accademia degli Infiammati* (1541).[20] The prominence of literary women in the dual sphere of poetry and theology in Siena, a city already under suspicion in the early forties for its ostensible cultivation of heresy and heretics, is evident in Marcantonio Piccolomini's staging of a dialogue between an advocate of Valdesian reform and an orthodox Catholic as a debate between two elite women.

My closing chapter returns to the story of Caterina Cibo, an adherent of Ochino and Valdés introduced in chapter 1, who fled to Florence when the pope expelled her from her home in Camerino. I trace here the shift in Florence, under the rule of Cosimo I de' Medici, from its reputation by 1548–49 as a magnet for heterodox passions to a city where heresy could no longer be tolerated. In the late forties and early fifties, the fervor of intellectuals for religious reform was still entwined in Florence with the zealous pursuit of a new Italian literary canon, in the form of radical dialogues and the revision of the Petrarchan poetic tradition.[21] Cibo, whom a Domenican friar had publicly denounced as a "heretic and a teacher of heretics," is eulogized by Cosimo's protégée Laura Battiferra in 1560, in an ensemble of four poems, as a leader of women's circles in Florence and as the poet's much admired friend and mentor.

At the core of this chapter, three dialogic works represent intellectual partnerships between a woman and a man, relegating to their female speakers an authority not seen in earlier sixteenth-century dialogues. Two of these exchanges—Ochino's *Dialogi sette,* in which Caterina Cibo is cast as one of the principal interlocutors, and Marcantonio Flaminio's consolatory letters addressed to Cibo—belong to the literature of the Valdesian reform movement, though both works fall within the tradition of the Neoplatonic *dialogo d'amore* in their focus on the dialogic prospect of two souls united in their quest for the highest good and the soul's upward journey to God.[22] A third dialogic work in this group, the courtesan Tullia d'Aragona's *Dialogo della infinità di amore,* a work more Aristotelian than Platonic, is the most daring and dynamic of the three pieces.[23] While d'Aragona's *Dialogo* resembles Ochino's *Dialogi sette* in its line of inquiry—its questioning of the nature and meaning of love, desire, happiness, and the location of ultimate satisfaction—d'Aragona's dialogue differs from Ochino's in her striking omission of the organizing trope of the Neoplatonic love dialogue: d'Aragona's interlocutors reach no moment of truth; they ascend no ladder to the pinnacle of spiritual love where the earthly contemplation of beauty leads finally to the apprehension of the source of all goodness in the cosmos.

D'Aragona's *Infinità di amore* differs most from other sixteenth-century dialogues not only in its female authorial voice but in the sensational nature of the literary partnership it publishes as well. In earlier dialogues, courtesans had been portrayed as interlocutors—d'Aragona herself was the model for Sperone Speroni's character "Tullia" in his *Dialogo d'amore.*[24] But d'Aragona's *Infinità di amore* represents the intellectual alliance of a courtesan who presents herself openly as a sexually experienced woman with a professor whose alleged violation of the sodomy laws had made him the subject of public scandal.[25] Cosimo I's sponsorship of d'Aragona's dialogue and its publication twice within a five-year period, in 1547 and 1552, testifies to the tolerance that prevailed at the Medici court at midcentury.

A major shift marks Cosimo's cultural politics after the siege and occupation of Siena, the departure of Ochino to Geneva, Flaminio's and Cibo's deaths, and finally Cosimo's wife Eleonora's own death in 1562. The end of the possibility of a politics of religious reform in Florence in the early sixties after the closing of the Council of Trent and the execution of Cosimo's longtime client Pietro Carnesecchi signaled the demise of the Valdesian movement in Florence and the rest of Italy as well. Laura Battiferra's first book of collected poems, despite its memorial for Caterina Cibo, represents the end of an era.[26]

Many of the early printed texts I selected for inclusion in this book—letters, poems, dialogues, and other documents—are little known, even to specialists in the field; and many of these have not been reprinted since the Renaissance. Of the primary sources I cite, I continue to find the Giolito poetry anthologies and their extensive prefatory apparatuses the most useful of all materials in their revelations about the women, men, and books at the center of my study. In hopes that the reader will find the anthologies as instructive as I have, I've included two appendixes, the first an alphabetical index of the authors, editors, publishers, and dedicatees of each of the anthologies; the second presents a physical description of each of the fifteen anthologies in the Giolito ensemble.[27] A third appendix provides a chronology of the key events that structure the book's narrative. A final appendix contains biographical and bibliographical data for all the major and many minor figures mentioned in the book; these I included to document, and to emphasize, the extent of women's newfound desire for publication and publicity in sixteenth-century Italy.

## NOTE ON THE TEXTS

The idiosyncratic orthography of the early printed Italian editions cited in this book has been retained. The punctuation of the text has been edited in conformance with modern practice. Diacritics missing in the original editions have only been added where clarification of the sense made them necessary. All the translations are mine unless otherwise noted.

CHAPTER ONE

# Ischia and the Birth of a Salon

My story begins on a small island off the coast of Naples. The years 1530–49 saw a divided Italy, kept so by two rulers and their armies. The Habsburg emperor Charles V finally drove the king of France from his foothold in the peninsula and installed his own men as governors in Milan, Siena, and the kingdom of Naples. In Florence, Charles formed a lasting alliance with Cosimo I de' Medici. Pope Paul III (Alessandro Farnese) consolidated and expanded his empire in the papal states, while he fought to expel the influence of Luther and Calvin from the Italian cities, though their works still circulated widely in printed editions in the 1530s and 1540s. The independent Republic of Venice fostered a free, commercially driven publishing industry that not only inaugurated a renascence of vernacular poetry but also became a large-scale producer of books the pope would outlaw as heretical. In the face of such divisions, a group of elite women worked at forging cultural hegemony on two fronts: they played leading roles in the new literary academies and salons in Italy as well as in the religious reform movement that swept the peninsula.[1]

Four women—the sisters Giovanna d'Aragona and Maria d'Aragona and their in-laws Vittoria Colonna and Giulia Gonzaga—dominated the cultural scene in the kingdom of Naples from the inauguration of Gonzaga's court at Fondi in 1529 to her burial in 1566 at the convent of San Francesco delle Monache in Naples. These women came from prominent clans well-endowed with lands, titles, and influence, and they were friends with much in common, though Colonna was a generation older. All four women, whose husbands were away at war and seldom at home, enjoyed their adult lives virtually as single women; Colonna and Gonzaga, whose husbands died encamped with their troops, were widowed early in their marriages. All four of these women found themselves drawn to the reform movement in Italy and its charismatic leaders Juan de Valdés and Bernardino Ochino.[2] They organized and participated in *cercoli, cenacoli*, or salons, where artists and intellectuals met to discuss literature and philosophy, though soon their salons became forums where spiritual renewal and religious reform were the themes of concern. Each of the four Colonna-Aragona women served as an influential patron to the new groups of women and men whose poetry, plays, essays, and dialogues catered to a public hungry for books that brought them pleasure and solace at a time when their cities were under threat of invasion.

As far back as the Aragona-Colonna women could remember, the island of Ischia had been a place of safety: a refuge from war, siege, and plague—the scourges of the age. It was also a place of new beginnings—of starting over. Vittoria Colonna's father Fabrizio had served King Charles VIII of France during his short-lived conquest of Naples in 1495.[3] But six years later the French sacked the Colonna fortresses and lands in the Castelli Romani and Fabrizio Colonna defected to the Aragonese king of Naples. And when the French took Naples in 1502, the Aragonese court—and with it Colonna and his family—retreated to the fortress of the d'Avalos on the island of Ischia. That year the widowed Duchess Costanza d'Avalos, now chatelaine of the island *fortezza*, took up arms herself and led her Italian and Aragonese soldiers against the foreign intruders.[4] For four months that year the French laid siege to the castello from their galleons anchored in the bay of Ischia, and Costanza fought them off until they withdrew. In 1509, the marriage of Vittoria Colonna and Costanza's nephew Ferrante Francesco d'Avalos, and with it the alliance between the Roman Colonna and the Aragonese d'Avalos families, was celebrated on Ischia in a nuptial mass at the cathedral followed by festivities in the castle.[5] That alliance would be strengthened when Giovanna d'Aragona and her sister Maria, granddaughters of the Aragonese king of Naples, would marry into the Colonna-d'Avalos clan and would return intermittently to the island for many years.[6]

Of the four Colonna-d'Avalos women, Giulia Gonzaga Colonna alone seems not to have spent time on Ischia. Still, the island was so persistently linked to the heterodox culture of the Colonna, d'Aragona, and Gonzaga salons in Naples that a telling fiction circulated soon after Gonzaga's death.

Because Gonzaga had been declared a heretic, it was rumored that her corpse had been removed from the convent of San Francesco delle Monache in Naples and transported to Ischia and that there she had been buried in the garden of the castle of Costanza d'Avalos.[7]

### ❧ ISCHIA AND THE D'AVALOS-COLONNA SALON ❧

As Suzanne Therault has shown, from the time of Vittoria Colonna's marriage on Ischia until the mid-1530s, when she had been a widow for nearly a decade, she and Costanza hosted a succession of literary salons.[8] Sannazaro, Cariteo, Britonio, Capanio, and Galeazzo di Tarsia were among the leading poets in the earliest years of their salon.[9] By the end of the twenties, Paolo Giovio, Antonio Minturno, Giano Anisio, Cosimo Anisio, Bernardo Tasso, Luigi Tansillo, Angelo di Costanzo, and Bernardino Rota had joined the Colonna-d'Avalos circle on Ischia. It was here under d'Avalos's and Colonna's direction that writers, artists, philosophers, clerics, and the best society on the island gathered for discussion and the reading of new literary works. As such, the readings and writings of the Ischia circle would produce a matrix for two emergent phenomena in the peninsula: the woman-led intellectual salon and the poetry anthologies of the 1540s–50s, in which women would play an unprecedented role.[10]

The poetry of the writers associated with the Ischia salon represents a fusion of classical and early modern traditions: the Roman elegiac poets, Virgil, and Petrarch were their models. Their themes were intimate: they eulogized friends; they grieved for lost loves and the mutability of fortune; and they celebrated the views of the bay, pinewoods, and orchards from the d'Avalos castle. Often these themes were combined in a single sonnet, as in this poem by Galeazzo di Tarsia, who evokes the contours and sounds of the sea at Ischia in winter while he mourns the loss of summer and the instability of life:

> Storm-shattered, crashing, shale-dark waves,
> once tranquil, placid, and serene,
> you were like my life, and you
> mirror my deep and swelling pain.
> Painted ships, lovely souls, happy nymphs,
> and all other joys are hidden from you:
> whatever made these days sweet for me
> and happy, and others sad and troubled.
> No matter: A good season will come again,

another time that always brings you cheer,
and then my lot in life may change:
bringing me calm nights and clear days,
whether the sun is near or far away,
nor may my tyrant ever carry me away.

Tempestose sonanti e torbid'onde,
Tranquille un tempo già, placide e chete,
Voi foste al viver mio simili, e siete
Simil alle mie pene ampie e profonde.
    Spalmati legni, alme vezzose e liete
Ninfe ed ogni altra gioia a voi s'asconde:
A me ciò che facea care e gioconde
Queste luci e quest'ore egre, inquïete.
    Lasso! Ei verrà ben tempo che ritorni
Altra stagion che rallegrar vi suole,
Onde diversa fia la nostra sorte:
    A me serene notti e chiari giorni,
O che s'appressi o s'allontani il sole,
Non fia che il mio tiranno unqua m'apporte.[11]

Vittoria Colonna probably heard Sannazaro for the first time when he read from his *Arcadia* at the d'Avalos salon on Ischia. From the 1520s on, Colonna and Costanza d'Avalos begin to appear as the frequent dedicatees of the poets they cultivated. Therault has observed that Colonna's name made its debut in print in Britonio's sonnet "La gelosia del sole," published in 1519 in his *Canzoniere*, in which Apollo, on hearing the brilliant, though younger poet singing, praises her from his balcony, calling her "this gentle new Phoenix in the world" (Questa al mondo, gentil nova Phenice).[12] She would soon occupy center stage again in a eulogy by Capanio, dedicated to Costanza d'Avalos and titled *Tempio d'amore* (ca. 1522).

The figuration of a poetic work as a mausoleum or a temple, though suggested in the graphic design of the title pages of many sixteenth-century books (fig. 1), was relatively rare as a literary trope in Renaissance Italy.[13] As we will see in chapter 4, the emblem of the column and its all-important function in the classical temple, not only as support for the whole structure but also as a source of beauty and balance, would serve some thirty years later as the basis for two very different works: Girolamo Ruscelli's *Del tempio* and Guiseppe Betussi's *Le imagini del tempio*, both books published in honor of Colonna's sister-in-law, Giovanna d'Aragona Colonna.[14] In his dedicatory letter to Costanza d'Avalos, as in Betussi's *Imagini*, Capanio describes his monument: there are thirty columns represented by thirty Neapolitan women, beginning with Isabella de Requesens, wife of the viceroy of Naples. Other women from the Ischia circle such as Lucrezia Scaglione, Giulia Grisone, Vittoria Colonna, and d'Avalos also take their positions in the colonnade. As in Betussi's *Imagini*, the colonnade of women represents the harmony of women joined together in a cultural community whose work is to produce and support poetry:

> [Next to the Viceroy's wife is placed] . . . the proud and grand Colonna,
> above whom is supported the World and Heaven;
> This she carries, in her hair, and on her skirt:
> from Cynthia, the shield and Cupid's bow.
> And on this lovely lady's breast,
> if one can see, a new Apollo in Delos
> and, under the beautiful and famous name Vittoria,
> one sees only the triumph of love, honor, and glory.
> · · · · · · · · · · · · · · · · · · · · · · · · · · · · ·
> Fifteen figures on one side and as many on the other:
> Isabella and Vittoria are the first,
> Then come the others, one after another.

> Appresso a lei l'altiera e gran Colonna,
> sovra la qual s'appoggia il Mondo, il Cielo,
> Questa portava essendo in trezza e in gonna
> De Cinthia il scudo e di cupido il telo.
>     Nel petto che sì lieta e bella donna
> Se può veder un altro Apollo in Delo
> E, sotto il nome chiar d'alma Vittoria
> D'Amor sol il trionfo honore et gloria.[15]
> · · · · · · · · · · · · · · · · · · · · · · · ·
>     Quindici all'una e tante all'altra parte:
> Isabella e Vittoria prime fôrno,
> E l'altre appresso poi di parte in parte.[16]

Bernardo Tasso's funeral eulogy for Vittoria Colonna's husband, Ferrante Francesco d'Avalos, probably performed at the d'Avalos castle in 1525, illustrates the way in which, in the absense of an official state court, the unauthorized salon and the poetry written explicitly for presentation at its assemblies reproduced, in effect, a similacrum of the royal court. For, in spite of all its grandeur, the d'Avalos castle on Ischia housed no head of state, no king or

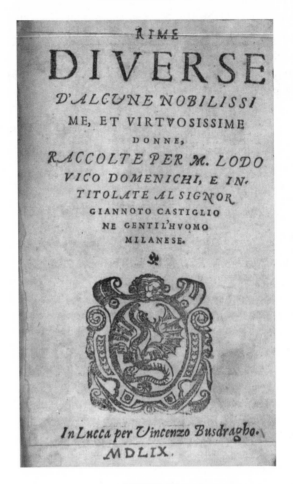

RIME

# DIVERSE

D'ALCVNE NOBILISSI
ME, ET VIRTVOSISSIME
DONNE,

RACCOLTE PER M. LODO
VICO DOMENICHI, E IN-
TITOLATE AL SIGNOR
GIANNOTO CASTIGLIO
NE GENTIL'HVOMO
MILANESE.

*In Lucca per Vincenzo Busdragho.*
MDLIX.

· FIGURE I ·
Title page from Domenichi's anthology of fifty-three
women poets, *Rime diverse d'alcune nobilissime, et
virtuosissime donne* . . . (Lucca: Vicenzo Busdragho, 1559).
Courtesy of the University of Iowa Library.

queen. Costanza ruled her castle, but Ischia was no duchy, and she had no
ministers or standing army. Nor could Charles or his captain, Ferrante Francesco d'Avalos, be called "defenders of all Italy" (*fu d'Italia tutta il defensore*).
Tasso's phrase was rhetorically pleasing, but there was no political reality behind it. Ferrante's sense of loyalty did not extend beyond Naples, nor did that
of the Colonnas. In 1527, the army of Charles V, without opposition from
his d'Avalos or Colonna partisans, would sack and burn Rome—the cultural

capital "of all Italy," and, for some, its political center as well. Nor, from what we know of the Colonna-d'Avalos clan, would Ferrante Francesco have done anything to defend the pope or save Rome's monuments had he lived. His nephew Alfonso d'Avalos left the city when the sack began, and his brother-in-law Ascanio Colonna neither tried to stop Charles's rampaging mercenaries nor offered protection to Pope Clement.

The salon d'Avalos and Colonna led in Ischia exuded cultural and artistic harmony: here a confluence of like-minded women and men came together. But the court they presided over—if we can apply the word "court" to a proxy state of sorts, *in loco civitatis*—was politically divided against itself, as we shall see. Whereas Petrarch had made famous the trope of a fragmented Italy in his poem "Italia mia," Tasso's eulogy for Ferrante Francesco projects the fiction of a unified Italy, a figure that becomes increasingly common in the later sixteenth century.[17]

> You will now see that man, once so dear
> to our emperor, invincible Charles,
> whose death is so bitter to me: Ferrante I say,
> whom a confluence of spiteful stars abruptly
> seized, and he, the undying glory
> of the Avalos clan and defender of all Italy,
> now dwells with the gods in heaven,
> and all my hopes have died with him.
> And gentle Vittoria, mirror of love,
> lofty lady, mirror of virtue,
> his rival, in honor and in valor:
> the untold pain she buries in her heart
> and vents only in her learned poems;
> all other thought she bars and shuns.

> Vedrete ancor colui, ch'un dì sì caro
> Fu al nostro imperator Carlo l'invitto
> E che il suo fin fu a me cotanto amaro,
>     Ferrante intendo dir che 'l reo conflitto
> D'astri maligni colse di repente
> E ch'or fra divi in ciel si vede ascritto.
>     Onore eterno dell'Avala gente
> Che fu d'Italia tutta il defensore,
> E le speranze mie furo in lui spente!
>     E Vittoria gentil, specchio d'amore,

Eccelsa Donna, specchio di virtude,
Emula del suo onor, del suo valore.
   La pena immensa, che nel sen racchiude,
Sfoga soltanto con sua colte Rime,
Et ogni altro pensier fugge ed esclude.[18]

Apart from the fictive construction of a state suggested in this sonnet, what stands out is Tasso's portrait of Colonna, which takes up almost half the poem. Ferrante Francesco's eulogy is not the usual *speculum principis*: it is, to use its own imagery, a mirror of the princess. Colonna is portrayed as her husband's equal in statesmanship and war ("emula del suo onor, del suo valore") and as his superior in literary and moral valence, spinning art from her grief ("La pena immensa, che nel sen racchiude, sfoga soltanto con sua colte Rime").

## ❧c GIOVIO'S LETTER FROM ARCADIA ɔ❧

But where did the fame of the Ischia salon first begin? In the crucible of war, the historian Paolo Giovio would have us believe. In April 1528, Giovio, then bishop of Nocera and personal physician to Pope Clement VII, visited the poet Vittoria Colonna on the island of Ischia, staying as her guest at the d'Avalos castle. He sent the pope a report of the disastrous naval battle fought on April 28, 1528 off the Capo d'Orso and the French army's sack of Naples that accompanied it. Giovio's letter, which circulated widely and was later published in the hugely popular *Diarii* of Marino Sanuto (1533), detailed the horrors of the battle at sea between Genoese mercenaries hired by France and the emperor Charles's fleet. From the battlements of the castle, Giovio and the assembled guests of Costanza d'Avalos heard the cannons rumbling across the bay; they may have seen dim flares from the burning ships.[19] The battle at sea had begun around nine o'clock in the evening on April 28 and had gone on until one in the morning. Charles's fleet was destroyed, and Vittoria's brother Ascanio and Costanza's nephew Alfonso d'Avalos were taken prisoner by the Genoese captains. The previous month, French soldiers had entered Naples pillaging and burning its palaces, convents, and monasteries. Giovio saw it as an act of revenge by the French, in league with pro-papal forces led by the Genoese admiral Filippino Doria, to strike back at the imperial army of Charles V, who had expelled the French from Italy after the sack of Rome in 1527. The damage the French wreaked on Naples, Giovio assured the pope, was no less terrible than Charles's sack of Rome ("Napoli non è manco disfata che Roma.")[20]

Writing from Costanza's castle on Ischia, Giovio told the pope he never would have been able to describe the battle or the fate of its victims unless he had boarded Filippino Doria's ship himself. As he sailed across the bay two days after the battle, he saw the scattered wreckage with his own eyes, and when he arrived at Salerno, where the Genovese had dropped anchor, he interviewed the men.[21] In what was probably one of the earliest formulations of the aims of modern journalism, Giovio pressed home his objective in his letter to the pope: he was publishing a war documentary—a dispassionate presentation of what he and others had seen. "I have had time," he wrote, "to get a very true and balanced account from the men of both sides. I don't believe that anyone could have done this better than me because I visited both the prisoners and the wounded, and because I questioned not just the lords, but the captains and private soldiers as well" (E ho auto tempo de pigliar reguaglio istoriale de l'una parte e de l'altra verissimo, e non credo che meglio di me persona lo abbia potuto fare, per avere io visitato li pregioni e li feriti e essaminati li patroni e prevati soldati, ultra li signori etc). Even so, constructing a "documentary" that would be acceptable to the parties on both sides was not easy. After the sack of Rome the year before when Charles's troops had further humiliated Clement by incarcerating him in the Castel Sant'Angelo, nothing could have pleased the pope more than hearing that the French had crushed Charles's fleet. So Giovio's report to him that, in terms of sheer horror and destruction, the French sack of Naples was every bit the equal of Charles's occupation of Rome, came as news to be savored. But Giovio also had to consider that among Filippino Doria's prisoners was the brother of Vittoria Colonna, his host and literary patron as well as being herself a longtime friend and client of Charles's. In order to take a stand that would not offend the pope or Colonna and her friends on Ischia, Giovio had to keep his report free of language that smacked of partisan loyalty. His account is at times difficult to follow since he steers clear of identifying the combatants as either "our men" or "their men." Only the names of the men and the ships are used. But then, Giovio's "objective" reporting exemplifies not only his own divided loyalty between Colonna and the pope but also the shifting nature of loyalties in sixteenth-century Italy in general. As I observed earlier, Colonna's father Fabrizio was easily able to switch alliances, serving the French one year and the Aragonese the next. The same could be said for Costanza's brother, who suddenly defected to France in 1502. The sense of an "Italy" as a political entity, much less the sense of all Italians as loyal denizens of a single state, was far from a reality.

In the following excerpt from Giovio's letter, the names of the ships and their affiliation, provided in the headnote to the text in Sanuto's *Diarii*, have little importance in comparison to the powerful picture of war painted by Giovio.[22]

Because I know your Holiness usually considers it a good thing to have specific information about important events, and given that talk still persists here on Ischia about the defeat of Charles's fleet and also because there is every cause for mourning here, I wanted you to understand how I reached the decision to go to the ships of Count Filippino Doria because of my friendship with his Lordship, and also, owing to the infinite regard I have for the Marchesa di Pescara, I wanted to assure myself as to the status of the two lords, the Marchese del Vasto and the lord Ascanio Colonna. And so, having been well received by the aforesaid Count and having been awaited with great anticipation by the poor lords, to whom I brought medicine and other useful refreshments to console them in their misfortune, I have had time to get a very true and balanced account of the battle from men on both sides. And I don't believe that anyone would have been better able than me to do this because of my having visited the prisoners and the wounded, and having examined the ship captains and private soldiers, as well as the lords. . . .

Conte Filippino Doria sailed out into the open sea, and all the ships turned back. The Genoese, who understood his signals, suddenly hit on the plan to ram the imperial ships with five galleys while sending their other three ships out toward the open sea as if to flee, with the order that their ships should sail in a circle with the wind at their stern in order to ram our ships through the stern and side. . . . The *Gobba,* the *Sechames,* and Don Bernardo's ship with the galleys and the small boats rammed the *Pelegrina* and the *Donzella* with such great force that the Spanish soldiers jumped up and waved their flags and made a great show; and on the other side the *Perignana* and the *Calabresa* rammed the *Serena,* which was almost carried over to the side of the *Fortuna,*which was in the middle, between the *Serena* and their lead ship, such that already three of Doria's galleons were lost and their lead ship and the *Fortuna* would have been in danger if the ships that had been in the open sea had not come alongside the Spanish lead ship.The *Mora* struck that ship in the middle of its stern; the *Patrona* (carrying the *Nettuno*) struck the lead ship's galley. The *Signora* ran through its ram with its three cannons and the *Patrona* [*la di Nettuno*] demolished its mast, which, when it fell, did untold damage. Don Ugo, who was in the gangway exhorting everyone with his sword and shield, was pierced by a cannon ball in his side and also hit by a harquebus shot in his right arm, and he lept up into the captain's cabin, where due to the infinite numbers of harquebus balls, cook-pots forged in the fires, stones, and halberds, which they launched from the decks, almost all the soldiers and the forced men were overcome, and his Lordship was asphyxiated and died.

The imperial flag was thrown down and the ship of Count Filippino and also the *Mora* remained to finish destroying the imperial fleet. The other two ships pummeled the *Gobba* with a hail of harquebus shots and cannon volleys; Lord Cesare Feramosca was killed; Gobbo was gravely wounded on one thigh; and with the captain Baredo gravely wounded and all his men slaughtered, the Count's men took Baredo's ship. This same Baredo told me that of one hundred and eight of his select harquebus shooters there are no longer living but five, and he said that seven times he had changed his standardbearers and all of them died, one after another, clutching his flag, which I saw full of blood and brains. . . .

The battle lasted from 21 hours to one in the morning, and never was there a skirmish so cruel or so full of horror; and certainly this victory has restored the ancient glory of the Genoese. The Count Doria told me he had lost five hundred of his soldiers and his forced men. He said that on the enemy side there were few survivors, but that more than a thousand men had died, the finest flower of the battlefield and the veteran soldiers. And at this time, the corpse of Don Ugo was buried, which had been left for two days in the captain's cabin, broken and nude between two barrels with a large piece of lard, biscuit, and sacks full of body parts and men's brains.

. . . Naples is no less destroyed than Rome was. They have already sacked some monasteries, and things are going very badly for Charles's partisans, but for the poor Neapolitans it is worse.

Perché so Vostra Santità suole aver care le particulari informazioni delle cose importante, ho voluto farli intender come, perseverando qua in Ischia la fama de la rotta di la armata cesarea, et essendo qui ogni cosa di lutto, io mi determinai andar alla armata del conte Filippino Doria, per la amicizia che io tengo con Sua Signoria, e chiarirme delle persone delli signori marchese del Guasto e del signor Ascanio, per lo infinito obligo tengo con la signora Marchesa de Pescara. E così arivando son stato ben visto dal prefato Conte e bramato da li poveri signori, alli quali ortava medicine e altri refrescamenti opportuni a tanta lora calamità, e ho a[v]uto tempo de pigliar reguaglio istoriale de l'una parte e de l'altra verissimo, e non credo che meglio di me persona lo abbia potuto fare, per avere io visitato li pregioni e li feriti e essaminati li patroni e prevati soldati, ultra li signori etc. . . .

Il conte uscì, e loro se rivoltorno tutti. Li Genovesi, quali se intendevano a cenni, in un subito pigliorono questo partito de investire con cinque galìe e mandare fuora le altre tre al largo mare ad modo de fugire, con ordine che venesseron de giro con il vento in popa ad investire per popa e per traverso . . . La Gobba e qualla di Sechames e la de don Bernardo con le fuste e batelli investirno la Pelegrina e la Donzella con tanto impeto che li soldati Spagnoli saltorno e sbaterno le bandiere e feceron prova grande; e a l'altro canto la Perpignana e la Calabrese saltornono sopra la Serena, quale alquanto era transportata da lato della Fortuna, la quale era in mezo tra essa e la capetania, de maniera che già tre galìe Dorie erano perse, e la capitania e la Fortuna stavano in pericolo se le tre di fuora non fosseron venute per fianco adosso alla capitania. La Mora dette a mezo popa; la Patrona che porta Nettuno dete al fogone; la Signora trapasò lo sperone con tre basiliscate, e la de Nettuno spiantò l'arbore, quale cadendo fece infinito danno. Don Ugo, il qual era in corsia con la spata e la rotella esortando ognuno, fu passato de falconetto in una cossa e de arcobusso nel brazio dritto, e saltò ne; scandolaro, ove la infinita (119–20) moltitudine de archibusi, de pignate de foghi lavorati e de sassi e partegiane, le quale fiocavano dalli gatti, quasi tutti li soldati e sforzati furono opressi, e Sua Signoria, suffogato, morse. Lo stendardo imperiale fu sbatuto, e restorono adosso all capitania quella del Conte e la Mora a finir di ruinarla. Le altre due refrustorno la Gobba con un grandina di archibusate e canonate, e, morto el signor Cesare Feramosca e lo Gobbo ferito gravemente in un coscia, e ferito a morte el capitanio Baredo e amazatoli tutti li soi, la preseron. Me dice el prefato Baredo, de cento e otto soi archibuseri eletti non ne sono rimasi vivi se non cinque, e dice che sette volte la sua bandiera mutò alfieres e tutti morsono ad uno ad uno con la bandiera in mano; la qual ho vista io piena di sangue e de cervella (121). . . .

Durò la battaglia da ore 21 fino ad una ora di notte, né mai più fu sì crudel e così orenda baruffa; e certo questa vitoria ha renovato l'antiqua gloria de' Genovesi. Me dice il Conte che ha perso da 500 tra soldati e sforzati, e che de inimici pochi sono sani, ma morti più di mille, e *maxime* lo fior del campo e delli veterani. In questa ora si sepelisse il corpo dil signor don Ugo, quale è stato dui dì nel scandolaro, nudo fra doi bote, sgambarato a meschio d'un gran pezzo di lardo e biscotto e certi saconi pieni di membri e cervella di omini (121). . . .

. . . E Napoli non é manco disfata che Roma; e già hanno sachegiato alcuni monasterii, e le cose vano malissimo per li cesarei, ma pegio per li poveri Napoletani.

There are no heroes in this dispatch from the front. What prevails in Giovio's narrative is the strong message of the futility of war. His dry account of the four-hour battle at sea relies for its power on the pathos of vignettes. Giovio shows us a captain, whose arm was shattered by harquebus fire and whose side has been opened up by a cannon ball, crawling to the deck to exhort his men not to lose heart. Then there is the officer who said he watched seven of his standard bearers die, one after another, each man clutching his flag as he went down. And the flag, Giovio wrote, was "full of blood and brains." Giovio's report reaches its peak in his account of the way the rotting corpse of Charles's admiral Don Ugo Moncado was found after having been left for two days, "nude and broken between two barrels beside a piece of lard, biscuit, and sacks full of body parts and the brains of men" (121). [In questa ora si sepelisse il corpo dil signor don Ugo, quale è stato dui dì nel scandalaro, nudo fra doi bote, sgambarato a meschio d'un gran pezzo di lardo e biscotto e certi saconi pieni di membri e cervella di omini.] In five hours, the emperor's fleet had lost a thousand men. "Certainly," Giovio wrote with no little irony in his summary statement, "this victory has restored the ancient glory of the Genoese."

## ⸶c ISCHIA, WOMEN, AND THE ITALIAN IMAGINATION ɔ⸶

When it was published in Sanuto's *Diarii*, Giovio's letter established Ischia in the Italian imagination as an Arcadia distant from war and its carnage. Clearly outside the historical narrative, Giovio's Ischia is the antithesis of the state in an age of serial war between the great powers. The island is a utopia where inhabitants receive dispatches from the war zones such as Giovio's report of the battle at Capo d'Orso while remaining safe from peril themselves. In the images projected by such writers as Bernardo Tasso in his eulogy for Ferrante Francesco d'Avalos, women govern the island like the elite female guardians in Plato's *Republic,* a dialogue by no means unfamiliar to the Ischia coterie. In Castiglione's highly popular *Book of the Courtier,* a work the author had given Vittoria Colonna to review in draft long before it went to press, the interlocutors engage in an animated discussion of Plato's ideas about female guardianship.[23] But for Britonio, Capanio, and other writers of the Colonna-Avalos salon, Plato's utopia, from which poets would be banished, represented the antipodes of their Arcadia where poetry was the central concern of the *respublica*.[24]

In 1529–32, the last years that Vittoria Colonna and Costanza d'Avalos led the salon together on a continuing basis, Bernardo Tasso, Luigi Tansillo, Angelo di Costanzo, Bernardino Rota, Antonio Minturno, and Paolo Giovio were the writers most prominent in their Ischia coterie. Their poetry—the works that came out of the Ischia salon—would inform the new poetry anthologies published a decade after the salon on Ischia had reached its apogee.[25] Even as Colonna prepared to follow the call of the reform movement north, Tasso, then secretary to Ferrante Sanseverino, the prince of Salerno, stepped up his involvement in the d'Avalos island circle.[26]

The young Padua-trained Aristotelian and published Latin poet Marcantonio Flaminio, who would play a leading role in the religious reform movement, also visited Tasso in Naples sometime in 1530–31.[27] By then Flaminio had begun to attend the lectures of the Spanish émigré Juan de Valdés, whose call to Christians to "change their lives" drew poets, ordained priests, university students and other intellectuals to him, first in Rome and later in Naples in the 1530s. Therault believes that Flaminio was a member of Colonna's salon on Ischia during these years.[28] Certainly he met her at Giulia Gonzaga's salon at the convent of San Francesco delle Monache in Naples and later in Viterbo, where both she and Flaminio were intimates of Cardinal Reginald Pole and other members of the Viterbo *cenacolo*.[29]

## ❧ VITTORIA COLONNA'S CONVENT SALON IN ROME ❧

In 1530 or 1531, Vittoria Colonna returned to Rome from Ischia.[30] She moved into the convent of San Silvestro in Capite in Rome, where she established the same kind of intellectual circle that she and her aunt Costanza d'Avalos had presided over at the d'Avalos castle on the island, including many of the same personalities. Her life on Ischia had, in a sense, formed the matrix for the community of friends she would gather around herself in Rome in the early thirties and, later, in Naples. Now, at her convent lodgings in Rome she received the Cardinals Pole and Morone, the writers Bembo and Giovio, the sculptor and poet Michelangelo, and other poets, nobles, theologians, artists, and men of the Church. When she settled in Rome, she was already a literary celebrity. Ariosto sang her praises in his bestselling epic *Orlando furioso* (1516); Bernardo Tasso and Berni published poems in her honor, and Castiglione had given her a preliminary draft of his *Il cortegiano* to review (1521). Certainly Colonna's salon at the convent of San Silvestro provided the stage where the two most important reform thinkers in Italy in the first half of the sixteenth century, the Capuchin friar Bernardino Ochino and the Spanish theologian Juan de Valdés, first spread their influence.

Another noblewoman who allied herself with Colonna and her friends in Rome, Duchess Caterina Cibo of Camerino, shared many experiences with the marchesa of Pescara—her humanist education, premature widowhood, and a religious longing that took nothing for granted in its search for truth.[31] Both women descended from humanist scholars and patrons of learning. While Colonna was the granddaughter of the prominent patron of poets and classical learning, Federico di Montefeltro, Duke of Urbino, Cibo's grandfather was Lorenzo (*Il magnifico*) de' Medici, who had sponsored the circle of Ficino and the Florentine Neoplatonists. More learned than Colonna, Cibo read Latin, Greek, and Hebrew. Colonna and Cibo had both married soldiers, and each had been widowed early: Colonna at thirty-three and Cibo at twenty-seven. And while Colonna was left childless, Cibo had a daughter whom she betrothed to the future Duke of Urbino, the court where Colonna had spent her childhood years.

Now, in the 1530s, Colonna and Cibo, both virtually single women, found themselves deeply involved in the politics of religious reform: Colonna with Ochino and Valdés; Cibo, at first bound up solely with Ochino and his Capuchin order, later enmeshed herself, as Colonna did, in the *spiri-tuali* movement. In the wake of the sack of Rome, Ochino's espousal of the radical poverty of the early Church had a potent appeal for Colonna and others in her reform circle such as Cibo. The Capuchins preached the rejection of worldly goods; and they distanced themselves from the preoccupation of the ecclesiastical hierarchy with the acquisition of capital and lands, calling instead for a return to the simple values and faith of the early Church fathers. Caterina Cibo, a widow forced to defend her duchy and its people without a male protector, turned now to her uncle, Pope Clement VII (Giulio de' Medici). She persuaded the pope to sanction the official status of the order and to permit the Capuchins to take vows of Franciscan poverty, and in 1531 she gave Ochino a house near Camerino for the Capuchins' use as a convent. But the order's rough appearance in Rome as hermits and beggars openly mocked the vanity and opulence of the established Church, and in 1534 Clement issued a papal bull mandating the dissolution of the Capuchins and the expulsion of its novitiates from Rome.

Clement's bull against her friend Ochino and the attack on the Capuchins brought Colonna into the conflict. At this point, she allied herself with Cibo in the defense of the order. The two women mounted a letter-writing campaign to help Ochino and the Capuchins. Colonna wrote to Charles V, Cardinal Contarini, and other friends to enlist their support, while Cibo turned again to Pope Clement.[32] Ochino and the Capuchins, Colonna and Cibo argued, were only sending a message of charity and humility to the Church. In 1536, after the new pope, Paul III (Alessandro Farnese) forced Cibo—for other reasons—to abandon Camerino and flee north to Florence, Vittoria Colonna took the lead role in their joint efforts on behalf of the Capuchins.[33] That year, in a move that enhanced both Ochino's and her own prestige in Rome, Colonna convinced Paul III to restore the Capuchins' right to remain as an ordained community under the auspices of the Church and to name Ochino as general of the order.

## ❧ GIULIA GONZAGA'S CIRCLES: FROM FONDI TO NAPLES ❧

Soon after her arrival in Rome from Ischia, Vittoria Colonna met Juan de Valdés for the first time.[34] A Spanish converso, Valdés had fled the Inquisition in Spain to serve as a secretary in Pope Clement's court in 1531. It was through Vittoria Colonna that Valdés was introduced to her cousin Giulia Gonzaga Colonna when he entered the service of Charles V in Naples in 1535.[35]

On November 25 of that year, flanked by his captains Alfonso d'Avalos and Vittoria Colonna's brother Ascanio, Charles made a triumphal entry into Naples. Under d'Avalos's leadership, his troops had crushed an army of eighty thousand Turks in Tunis.[36] The wives of Charles's chief captains, the sisters Maria and Giovanna d'Aragona, and their aunt Costanza d'Avalos were in the city for the festivities. Though Vittoria Colonna did not go to Naples, Giulia Gonzaga chose to attend the parties and ceremonies despite the fact that on August 10 she had watched her closest friend, Cardinal Ippolito de' Medici, die at the age of twenty-four. According to Mario Oliva, she had already accepted Ippolito's proposal of marriage in July, and he had resigned his cardinalate.[37]

Gonzaga had originally come to the Colonna stronghold of Paliano in 1526 to marry Vittoria Colonna's cousin Vespasiano Colonna. She was thirteen at the time, while her bridegroom was forty and suffered from paralysis on one side of his body. Two years after the marriage, Vespasiano died of wounds he sustained in battle, leaving her well-off enough in terms of lands and fiefs as well as disposable income to make her way in the world as a single woman. After her husband's death, Gonzaga had moved to Fondi, a town strategically located on the road between Rome and Naples, resettling her family in the Colonna palazzo. Gonzaga's core household at Fondi in 1529 included her brother Luigi Gonzaga and her stepdaughter Isabella Colonna. Vittoria Colonna was a frequent visitor at Fondi as she traveled between her estates in the Castelli Romani, Naples, and her convent home in Rome. After Vespasiano's death, the seventeen-year-old Cardinal Ippolito de' Medici became a virtual member of Giulia's family. Riding to Fondi at least once a week from his estate at Itri or from Rome, he advised Gonzaga regarding the guests she should invite to Fondi, he recommended artists and poets from his circle in Rome, and he brought in a poet from his own court, Gandolfo Porrino, to serve as her secretary.

Gonzaga's literary salon at Fondi included many of the habitués of the Ischia court: Giovanna d'Aragona Colonna, Maria d'Aragona d'Avalos and her husband Alfonso d'Avalos, the Marchese del Vasto, his aunt Costanza d'Avalos, Vittoria Colonna, Paolo Giovio, Marcantonio Flaminio, Annibal Caro, Bernardo Tasso, Claudio Tolomei, Luigi Tansillo, Francesco Maria Molza, and Ferrante Sanseverino, Prince of Salerno.[38]

While basking in the growing celebrity of her literary evenings at Fondi, perhaps inspired by the powerful female warriors in Ariosto's *Orlando Furioso* (1513–32) and certainly by Vittoria Colonna's aunt, Costanza d'Avalos, Gonzaga also worked at fashioning a name for herself in a different realm: as something of an amazon. On August 8, 1534, two-thousand Turkish sailors, led by the notorious naval commander and former pirate Khair ad-din (Barbarossa), disembarked from their ships at the small port of Sperlonga near Naples and marched northeast until they reached Fondi. According to the tale Gonzaga cooked up for consumption at the urban academies and the popular presses, Barbarossa and his men abducted the duchess after burning her palace and plundering its heirlooms. Had she not escaped in the dead of night, galloping on horseback half-naked across the mountains—so the story went—the Turks would have delivered her to the sultan in Constantinople.[39] A colorful account of her supposed harrowing flight, entitled *The Fugitive Maiden* (*La ninfa fuggitiva*), written by a protégé of Gonzaga's, Francesco Maria Molza, appeared in print soon after the supposed kidnapping and circulated widely throughout the peninsula. In reality, Gonzaga had fled hours before the Turks came even within miles of Fondi. Alerted that a foreign army was headed for Fondi, she had left the town and had taken refuge at Vallecorsa, one of the family's fortified castles a safe distance from Fondi, which Barbarossa and his men did in fact sack, torch, and destroy, slaughtering some townspeople and taking others captive before they sailed away.[40]

## GONZAGA AND VALDÉS LAUNCH A SALON

When Valdés arrived in Naples the following year as part of Charles's retinue, he may have been acting on the advice of Vittoria Colonna, whose convent salon in Rome he had attended regularly.[41] Certainly it was Colonna who introduced him to her cousin by marriage Giulia Gonzaga. Once in Naples, he withdrew from Charles's service in order to devote himself full-time to religious teaching and study.[42] He leased a house at Chiaia, and it was there in his theological *cenacolo* that, assisted by Gonzaga, the *spirituali* movement began. Valdés lectured and held discussion sessions in search of the *vera fede*; and among his hearers were members of Neapolitan society, soldiers, men of the presses, priests, poets, and other intellectuals, many of whom were women. During Lent Valdés and Gonzaga visited the church of San Giovanni Maggiore in Naples where the Capuchin friar Bernardino Ochino was preaching.[43] Costanza d'Avalos and Giovanna d'Avalos also attended Ochino's sermons, which often lasted until late into the night.

In the summer of 1536, Gonzaga obtained papal authorization to move into the convent of San Francesco delle Monache, an order of Santa Chiara, situated in the center of Naples. Taking on the role of the official financier of the community and patron of the house, she lived there but retained the privilege of receiving guests whenever she wished. Here at her convent lodgings,

Gonzaga and Valdés instituted the principal reform salon in Naples. Her evening gatherings drew their conversational format and their participants from the intellectual *cenacoli* held on Ischia in the late 1520s by Costanza d'Avalos and Vittoria Colonna, who now joined Gonzaga's convent coterie. She began to collect disciples of her own, such as Isabella Bresegna and Dorotea Gonzaga, the daughter of Ferrante Gonzaga (later governor of Milan after the death of Colonna's protégé, Alfonso d'Avalos). She also drew poets, literary patrons, editors, translators, and the proprietors of presses to her convent salon just as she had at Fondi. An anonymous contemporary's list of the habitués of her evenings included—in addition to Costanza d'Avalos and Vittoria Colonna—Maria d'Aragona, Giovanna d'Aragona, Clarissa Orsini, Caterina Cibo, Ferrante Sanseverino di Salerno, Galeazzo Carracciolo, Marchese di Vico, Mario Galeoto, Gianfrancesco Alois, Pietro Carnesecchi, Pietroantonio di Capua, Giovanni Tommaso Sanfelice, Bernardino Ochino, Pietro Martire Vermigli, Bernardo Tasso, Annibal Caro, Benedetto Varchi, Jacopo Bonfadio, Scipione Capece, Marcantonio Flaminio, and Marco Antonio Magno.[44]

It was here in Gonzaga's convent lodgings that Giovanna d'Aragona and her aunt Costanza d'Avalos came to hear Valdés and to engage in dialogue with him. It was also a time marked by a deepening of the friendships between the Colonna-d'Avalos women, and in particular between Giovanna d'Aragona Colonna and Vittoria Colonna. Despite d'Aragona's having left her husband Ascanio Colonna, who was Vittoria's brother, the two women's devotion to Valdés and his teachings created a lasting bond between them.

## GONZAGA PUBLISHES THE *SPIRITUALI* METHOD IN THE *ALFABETO CRISTIANO*

Mario Oliva has observed that of all Valdés's writings, the work Giulia Gonzaga cared about most was his dialogue, the *Alfabeto cristiano*, "because they had composed it together."[45] While Valdés testified to having used his conversations with Gonzaga as the basis for the work, there are other reasons for acknowledging Gonzaga not only as the editor and producer of the *Alfabeto* but also as Valdés's coauthor.[46] It was Gonzaga who first brought the manuscript of the *Alfabeto* to the attention of publishers in 1545, and it was she who negotiated the contract with the firm of Nicolò Bacarini to print the work in Venice.[47] By then it had been four years since Valdés's death and perhaps more since her secretary had translated the dialogue from Spanish into Italian.[48] Valdés's will had bequeathed all his manuscripts to Gonzaga to translate, edit, and publish at her discretion.[49] So by the time the *Alfabeto* went to press, anything Valdés may have written in the original Spanish version (which was not then extant) or that her secretary may have translated under her direction, Gonzaga had full permission to revise and could easily have done so.[50] Yet given that Valdés's dialogues would soon suffer the same fate as Ochino's *Dialogi,* the printing and sale of which were outlawed by the Venetian Republic in 1543 under pressure from the Roman Holy Office, Gonzaga's decision not to credit herself on the title page as a coauthor was a wise one.[51] My point is that the *Alfabeto* comes to us in a highly mediated form; the work was edited and managed by Giulia Gonzaga and at least partly composed by her. Finally, the long speeches of the character "Giulia" or "Duchessa" (marked simply "G." in the Bacarini edition), especially at the beginning of the dialogue, are emotionally raw in a way unparalleled in Valdés's other writings.

A comparison between the *Alfabeto* and a dialogue from Ochino's *Dialogi sette* (Venice, 1542) makes clear the radical nature of Valdés's psychological scene painting. Ochino's dialogue, which I discuss in chapter 5, also has as its two main characters a theologian (Ochino) and a noblewoman (Caterina Cibo), who like the "Giulia" character is searching for meaningful action in a life that feels empty. Despite the sameness of the characters' issues and agendas, there is nothing in Ochino's dialogues that rises to the emotional pitch of "Giulia's" speeches or suggests the intimate quality of the friendship that comes to life on the page between Gonzaga and her teacher Valdés. In the *Alfabeto,* the character of the "Duchessa" (Gonzaga) more openly expresses her pain, uncertainty, and the contesting forces, desires, and values—her own and the world's—that pull her apart. Like the real Giulia Gonzaga, Valdés's "Duchessa" has lost her closest friend, her lover, and her reason for living.[52] Because of "Giulia's" constant references to her "inner" self and her "external" cirumstances (*le cose esteriori e queste interiori*), the Gonzaga-Valdés dialogue depicts in psychological detail the pathology of an emotional illness, the origins and species of which Ochino's interlocutors give us mere hints. Over and over, "Giulia" alludes also to the long-term nature of her friendship with "Valdés," which gives their conversation a dimension not present in Cibo's confessional dialogue with Ochino. In the public/private space of the Renaissance dialogue, such an emotional outpouring as "Giulia's" is almost shocking and has no parallel in other dialogues of the period. She brushes aside Valdés's trite protestations, setting the reader up for something more daring:

GIULIA:   I feel so secure in our friendship that I know I can communicate with you freely, even about things one would probably not tell one's confessor. But since I do want to share with you some things I care about more than my life, I beg you—if you don't already have something pressing to do elsewhere—please listen carefully to what I want to say to you. But if you think you won't be able to pay close attention because your thoughts are elsewhere, tell me openly because I can wait until another day.

VALDÉS: No, Signora, I'll gladly do what you ask me to do. You already know I don't have business that could get in the way of my helping you.

GIULIA: Now, putting aside the usual pleasantries, which you and I don't need, I want you to know that ordinarily I am so discontented with myself and with everything in the world that if you saw my heart I know you would have pity for me because in it you would find nothing but confusion, uncertainty and anxiety. And I feel this more or less about my whole situation in life. But in spite of wanting to come to terms with the problem, I never feel I have the peace of mind that what would enable me to come to an understanding of what would satisfy my heart and bring me happiness—which is all I would want. But I can think of nothing that anyone could do for me these days that would have the power to resolve my feelings of confusion, calm my unease with myself, and relieve the sense of uncertainty that plagues me. For many years I've lived in the way I've described to you, and during this time, as you know, so many things have happened that might have thrown even a tranquil spirit into turmoil, but to a mind as despairing and confused as mine they they have been catastrophic. What is more, you know that in the first sermons I heard from our preacher, he persuaded me with his words that through his teachings I would be able to become calm and find peace of mind, but until now the reverse of what I hoped for has occurred. And though I attributed this more to my own imperfection than to his failing, still it gave me pain to see my hopes dashed. I still might have found my situation bearable, but unfortunately, as it turned out, instead of healing my first illness I fell sick with a new malady without ever having been cured of my first illness. This is the greatest and cruelest contradiction: that I feel inside myself so purposeless and exhausted that many times tears come to my eyes over the state of my health because I don't know what to do with myself or where to turn for help. The sermons of the preacher have worsened this contradiction in my mind, and so I feel terribly disturbed and torn—on the one hand, between my fear of the inferno and my love of paradise and, on the other, between the fear of people's slanderous talk about me and my love of honor in this world. So that the two fears and the two loves—or better said the two kinds of fear and the other two of love—are those that are at war in me and those that have kept me in a state of paralysis for some days now. You yourself have sensed what I feel; and you have wondered at how I can go through this and pretend to be just fine. This indeed is my state of mind, and in this confusion that I've described to you, bad or good, stand my affairs as I see them. And then because you have shown such affection and willingness to help and counsel me in practical matters, I pray you will be glad to help me in these emotional ones.

VALDÉS:     Tell me everything you would like me to do for you, Signora, and don't hold back. You can be sure that everything I know and am capable of, I will always do to help you.

DUCHESSA:   Tengo tanta segurtà nell'amistà nostra, che mi pare di poter liberamente communicare con voi anche quelle cose le quali appenda si discuoprono al confessore. Imperò, volendo ora farvi partecipe d'alcune nelle quali mi va più che la vita, vi priego, se non avete cosa che molto v'importi in altro luogo, che siate contento d'udirmi attentamente ciò ch'io vi voglio dire. E mirate che, se non pensate di stare molto attento per tenere il pensiero altrove, ditelomi liberamente, perchioché questo potrò io lasciare per un altro dì.

VALDESSO:   Anzi io, signora, ricevo mercé di quello in che mi comandate ch'io stia. E già sapete che non tengo negoci che mi possano impedire, massimamente in ciò che tocca al servizio vostro.

DUCHESSA:   Ora, lasciando da parte le retoriche vane e le ceremonie inutili, le quali tra noi sono soverchie, voglio che sappiate ch'io per l'ordinario vivo tanto scontenta di me medesima, e similmente di tutte le cose del mondo, e tanto svogliata, che, se vedeste il cuor mio, son certa che m'areste compassione, perciochè in lui non trovereste se non confusione, perplessità e inquietudine. E questo e più e manco, secondo le cose che mi s'offeriscono. Ma non sento mai tanta bonaccia nell'animo mio che, volendo far conto con lui, possa finire d'intendere, che è ciò che io vorrei, che cosa gli soddisfarebbe o con quale si contenterebbe: in modo che non posso pensare che cosa mi si potesse offerire il di oggi che bastasse a togliermi questa confusione ed accbetarmi questa inquietudine e risolvermi questa perplessità. Di questa maniera che io vi dico, sono già molti anni ch'io vivo, nelli quali, come sapete, mi sono intervenute tante cose che basterebbono per alterare uno spirito accbetato, tanto più per inquietare e confondere uno animo svagliato e confuso come è il mio. Oltra ciò, sappiate che nelle prime prediche, le quali udii dal nostro predicatore, mi persuadette con le sue parole, che per mezzo della sua dottrina io potrei serenare e mettere in pace l'animo mio, ma finora mi è avenuto al rovescio di quello, che io pensava. E benchè io attribuisca più questo ad imperfezione mia che a difetto suo, tuttavia mi dà pena il vedere, che la mia speranza non mi accia succeduto, e avenga che questo fusse tolerabile, nondimeno il male è, che in luogo di sanare d'una infermità sono entrata 'n un'altra senza essere uscita di quella. Questa è una grandissima e crudelissima contradizione, che sento dentro di me tanto noiosa e fastidiosa che per mia salute motle volte mi vengono le lagrime agli occhi, per non sapere che far di me, né a cui m'appoggiare. Questa contradizione hanno generato nell'animo mio i sermoni del predicatore, mediante li quali mi veggio fotemente combattuta, da una parte al dallo amore dell'onor del mondo. Di modo che duo timori e duo amori, o per dir meglio duo affetti di timore e altri duo d'amore, sono quelli li quali combattono in me e mi tengono tale alcuni di sono. Che se voi sentiste quel che io sento, vi meravigliereste come io lo possa passare e dissimulare. Questo è ciò che si truova in me, e in questo stato ch'io v'ho detto male o bene, come ho saputo, stanno le mie cose. E poi che voi avete mostrato tanta affezione e volontà d'aiutarmi nelle cose esteriori, vi priego siate contento d'aiutarmi e consigliarmi in queste interiori, poi che io so molto bene, che, se voi volete, avete più parte d'aiutarmi in queste che nelle altre.

VALDESSO: Dite, signora, liberamente titto quello che volete di me e potete esser certa che tutto ciò che io potrò o e saprò, spendereollo in vostro servizio sempre. (*Alfabeto*, 8–9)

Paramount in the message of the *Alfabeto* is that it is not enough to hear the teachings of the Gospels accompanied by a learned commentary on them in daily Mass. There must be follow-up: one-on-one and group discussions of the scriptures and their contemporary significance. Listening to Ochino's sermons, whom she refers to simply as "*nostro predicatore*" (our preacher), has prompted "Giulia" to recognize her suffering but not to remedy it. In the passage below from the *Alfabeto,* it is clear that the Socratic method marks Valdesian teaching as different from the hierarchical preaching and the distance between parishioner and priest prescribed by the Church. While this passage illustrates such recurrent themes in the *Alfabeto* as the Neoplatonist quest for ultimate truth (*camino per il vero*), the road to God (*un camino reale a Dio*), and the Pauline chasm between the ephemeral vanity of this world and the eternal realm of God (*gli occhi di Dio; gli occhi del mondo*), the "Valdés" character's taunting remark—"I don't know what more you want to learn from me that the preacher doesn't tell you daily"—inaugurates a discussion implicitly critical of the rituals of the Church:

GIULIA: All that you say satisfies me, and since I am determined to embark on this journey, I want you to take me by the hand and show me the path you've already walked.

VALDÉS: I don't know what more you want to learn from me that the preacher doesn't tell you every day.

GIULIA: I'm weak and I can't find the mental strength I need if I'm to do everything the preacher counsels.

VALDÉS: What you mean is pretty clear to me now, Signora. But why go to the branches and not the root? I know well what you want.

GIULIA: How annoying! If you know it, why don't you say it?

VALDÉS: Because I was waiting for the words to come out of your own mouth.

GIULIA: If you know what you say you know, please tell me. If you guess, I'll tell you the whole truth and nothing but the truth.

VALDÉS: Alright, fair enough. You, Signora, want to be free from the disturbing things that come to you in your fantasies, and since you know this is truly the way to free yourself from them, you'd like me to show you the true road on which you can come to God without removing yourself from the world. You want to achieve inner humility without showing it on the outside. You want to acquire the virtue of patience without actually having to exercise it in the here and now. You want to reject the world without having the world reject you. You want to clothe your mind in Christian virtue without stripping your body of what you usually wear. You want to nourish your soul with spiritual sustenance without depriving your body of its usual foods; you want to appear good in God's eyes without looking bad in the eyes of the world. And finally, on this walk you would like to be able to pursue a Christian life, but in a way that no one in the world—however many intimate conversations he may have with you—will recognize it in your life any more than he recognizes it now. Have I got it right?

GIULIA: Just about. Or at least, if you haven't got it all, you're definitely on the right road.

GIULIA: Tutto quanto dite mi sodisfà. E poiché io determinatamente voglio entrare in questo camino, resta che voi mi portiate per la mano, insegnandomi quelli passi per li quali credo che che voi abbiate caminato.

VALDESSO: Non so che più vogliate imparare da me di quello che ogni dí dice 'l predicatore.

GIULIA: Io son debile e non posso fare tanta resistenzia al mio animo quanta saria di bisogno per fare tutto quello che dice.

VALDESSO: Già io, signora, v'intendo buon pezzo. Che bisogna andare per li rami? Io so bene ciò che voi vorreste.

GIULIA: Che dispetto! Poiché lo sapete, perché non lo dite.

VALDESSO: Perché aspettava che voi con la bocca vostra lo diceste.

GIULIA: Fatemi questo piacere, poiché lo 'ntendete, che lo diciate, ed io vi dirò la verità, se indovinate, in tutto e per tutto.

VALDESSO: Son contento. Voi, signora, desiderate esser libera dalle cose noise che vi vanno per la fantasia, ed avendo conosciuto che questo è il vero camino per liberarvi da loro, vorreste che io vi mostrassi un camino reale e signorile per lo quale poteste arrivare a Dio senza scostarvi dal mondo, aggiungere alla umiltà interiore senza mostrare la esteriore, possedere la virtú della pazienzia senza che v'accadesse dove essercitarla, disprezzare il mondo ma di tal maniera che il mondo non disprezzasse voi, vestire l'anima vostra di virtudi cristiane senza spogliarvi il corpo delle solite vestimenta, mantenere l'anima vostra con vivande spirituali senza privare il corpo vostro de' soliti cibi, parer bene negli occhi di Di senza parer male negli occhi del mondo, ed infine per questo camino voi vorreste poter fare la vita vostra cristiana, ma di modo che nessuna persona del mondo, per molta familiarità e conversazione ch'avesse con voi, potesse conoscere nella vita vostra piú di quello che conosce al presente. Ho io indovinato?

GIULIA: Quasi quasi, o almeno, se non avete indovinato, potete dire che sete andato alla volta del segno. (*Alfabeto*, 29–30)

The articulation of Valdesianism in the *Alfabeto* is profoundly focused on the interiority of faith. The character "Valdés" dismisses all exterior show of spirituality, not only that of the established church but that of the hermit or the Franciscan as well. True faith is manifested, he explains, not in outward practices but within, in the heart (*nel cuore*). The man who "is moved only by the things he does to the degree that they meet his own interests" cannot love God:[53]

Such a man as this, friar or no friar, because he hoards his love in a way that is misplaced, keeping it invested in himself, nevers knows how or why he has things created with love. Rather, when he wants to prepare himself to love God, because he cannot imagine how to abandon himself, he never finds his way; and because he is continually shifting his opinions, and because he is always confused and awash in his own emotions, whether good or bad, he lives far away from Christian perfection, and will live still further from it the more enamored of himself he becomes—*regardless of how absolutely perfect he becomes in exterior works*, because God wants his heart. (Emphasis mine)

Questo tale, frate o non frate, perché tiene l'amor suo disordinato tenendolo posto in sé, non sagiami come né in che modo ha d'amar le cose create; anzi, quando ben si vuole disponere ad amare Iddio, perché non indovina ad uscire di sé, mai non ritruova la via e perciò continuamente va peregrinando in pareri, e cosí essendo sempre disordinato e svariato negli affetti suoi mali o buoni, vive molto fuori della perfezione cristiana, e tanto viverà piú sarà innamorato di sé, sebbene nell'opre esteriori perfettissimo, perché Iddio vuole il cuore. (*Alfabeto*, 33–34)

Collections of women's letters and the genre of epistolatory self-consolation whether in poetry or prose, which began to be available in print by the 1540s, may have inspired the crafting of some of Giulia's speeches in the *Alfabeto*.[54]

Certainly Gonzaga knew the sonnet that her cousin and friend Vittoria Colonna had addressed to her deceased husband, published in her *Rime*.[55] Here were verses reflecting a sense of interior longing and emptiness that only talk— frank conversation in which feelings are shared, however painful—can begin to relieve:

> I write only to release my inner sorrow,
> to bring the light of the day to my heart,
> not to add splendor to my lovely Sun,
> his shining spirit or honored spoils.
> Just cause encloses me in mourning—
> that I might take away his glory I grieve,
> that another trumpet and wiser speech
> might wrest his great name from death.
> May pure faith, passion, and intense pain
> secure my pardon; my heavy grief is such
> that only time, not reason can constrain.
> Harsh weeping, no sweet song,
> dark sighs, no tranquil voice will give
> me honor: with style no, but misery.

> Scrivo sol per sfogar l'interna doglia
> ch'al cor mandar le luci al mondo sole,
> e non per giunger lume al mio Sole,
> al chiaro spirto e a l'onorata spoglia.
>     Giusta cagion a lamentar m'invoglia:
> ch'io scemi la sua gloria assai mi dole;
> per altra tromba a più sagge parole
> convien ch'a morte il gran nome si toglia.
>     La pura fe,' l'ardor, l'intensa pena
> mi scusi appo ciascun; ché 'l grave pianto
> è tal che tempo né ragion l'affrena.
>     Amaro lacrimar, non dolce canto,
> foschi sospiri e non voce serena,
> di stil no ma di duol mi danno vanto.[56]

As we shall see later in this chapter, when Vittoria Colonna was a member of the Valdesian reform *cenacolo* led by Cardinal Reginald Pole in Viterbo, she sent Giulia Gonzaga a letter that expressed a similar loneliness, a yearning for intimate friendship, and a desire to share feelings and converse at length on philosophical and religious topics of mutual concern. In her letter of December 8, 1541, Colonna thanked Gonzaga for sending the members of the Viterbo circle some writings of Juan de Valdés and hoped that soon she would be able to discuss his work with her face to face. "If the Signora, even when she is absent, is capable of doing so much with her Christian goodness, just think what would happen if, by the grace of God, your Ladyship could be here," she wrote Gonzaga.[57]

In his nearly ten years in Naples, Valdés gathered an ever-widening circle of disciples around him, many of whom would become evangelists of his thought in Italy and abroad. Vittoria Colonna, Giulia Gonzaga, and the Capuchin friar Ochino, whose sermons would rivet congregations in Ferrara, Verona, Lucca, Bologna, Florence, and Pisa, sowed the seeds of a Valdesianism that the Church as early as 1537 would brand as heresy.

## ✤c RENATA DI FRANCIA IN FERRARA: A SALON WITHIN A COURT ꙮ✤

In 1537, while Gonzaga remained in her convent home in Naples, Colonna left the city for Ferrara where she spent some weeks visiting Duke Ercole II d'Este of Ferrara and his wife, Duchess Renata of France, the daughter of the king, Louis XII. She arrived in Ferrara on April 8, 1537.[58] For once, Colonna enjoyed having an apartment in the ducal place for the duration of her stay in Ferrara, departing from her usual habit of taking lodgings at one of the local convents in the city.[59] For independent noblewomen such as Colonna and Gonzaga, the urban residential convents in Italy represented safe houses, providing protection without restriction. They also provided a space for a movable salon such as Gonzaga enjoyed in Naples and Colonna found in Rome and undoubtedly Viterbo. Once settled in their convent lodgings, Colonna and Gonzaga came, went, and received guests as they pleased. And in return, they contributed generously to the daily upkeep of the establishment. Gonzaga's base of operations after 1536 remained the convent of San Francesco delle Monache in Naples, where she served as the convent's treasurer. Colonna, in contrast, traveled with some regularity between convents, stopping at her familiar hostels: the convent of San Silvestro in Rome, the Dominican convent of San Paolo in Orvieto, the convent of Santa Caterina in Viterbo, and the Benedictine convent of Santa Anna in Rome when she returned from Viterbo. On this particular visit to Ferrara, Colonna relished the chance to stay in the Este palace since her cousin Alfonso d'Avalos, whom she and her husband had raised as though he were their own son, would also be a guest of the Duke and Duchess of Ferrara.[60] Charles V had recently made d'Avalos, who was his leading general in Italy and the husband of Colonna's sister-in-law Maria d'Aragona, governor of Milan. The recently elected Farnese pope, Paul III, was threateneing to make war on the Colonna strongholds, and Vittoria was desperately looking for allies.

Duchess Renata, who had come to Ferrara with all the prestige of a daughter of the king of France, made the Este court a destination for artists, poets, and philosophers and a sanctuary for reform thinkers in the 1530s.[61] Calvin, Renata's countryman, spent the summer of 1536 at her court in Ferrara. His opus magnum, the *Institutes of the Christian Religion*, circulated at the Ferrara court in two Latin editions in 1536 and 1539 and, in 1541, in French.[62] In the early 1540s, Renata gathered around her a circle of men and women who met with the duchess to discuss Scripture and translations of the Bible. Among the women who attended were the duchess's two daughters, Anna and Lucrezia, Giulia Gonzaga's protégée Isabella Bresegna, and Bresegna's daughter-in-law, Elisabetta Confalonieri. The men in the group included the Lutherans Gabriele da Bergamo, Don Stefano da Montova, Ambrogio Cavalli, the Este court professor of classics Francesco Porto, and the schoolmaster Franchesino di Lucca.

A participant in Renata's circle, Colonna had originally come to Ferrara in 1537 to hear the reform theologians Claudio Jaio, Simone Rodriquez, and Ochino preach in the city's cathedral. The duchess's reform salon, conducted in the massive Este palace in Ferrara, constituted the home base from which, in February 1538, Colonna embarked to follow Ochino on his preaching tour of Verona, Bologna, and Pisa, where Margaret of Austria, Charles V's daughter, had invited him to speak. Colonna's journey to Lucca to participate in further discussions with her reform friends Carnesecchi, Vermigli, Flaminio, and other Valdesians who were former members of Gonazaga's salon marked the climax of Ochino's speaking tour. That year the small publishing house of Viottis in nearby Parma published the first edition of Colonna's 153 sonnets, comprising both her *rime amorose* and the *rime spirituali*.[63]

Renata's husband, Duke Ercole II, was deeply disturbed by Renata's friends and her reform activities and discussion groups. She had instituted a salon, not sanctioned by her husband, that operated within the court yet outside its purview.[64] Within Renata's coterie, books prohibited by the Church as "Protestant" circulated freely; and men and women the Church condemned as heretics were shown hospitality and welcomed. Celio Secondo Curione stayed in the Este palace for a few months in 1541 and again in the fall of 1542, before he was forced to go into exile in Basel. Finally, in an attempt to purge the court of its Calvinistic cast, the duke expelled the duchess's governess, Michelle de Soubise, who had come with her from the French court and led the reading of the Scriptures and the discussions of reform ideas. Next he sent Clément Marot, Renata's secretary, who translated the Psalms into French and composed a French hymnal, back to France.[65] But the situation in Ferrara for Renata's reform salon would not become dangerous until 1554, when Ercole confined Renata to the ducal palace. That same year the writer and classical scholar Olimpia Morata, who was an active member of Renata's circle and the daughter of a highly respected humanist teacher at the Este court, fled to Germany.[66]

#### ❧ RENATA'S EXTENDED SALON IN FRANCE: COLONNA FORMS AN ALLIANCE WITH MARGUERITE DE NAVARRE ❧

Colonna left Ferrara at the end of 1538, going first to her home base at the convent of San Silvestro in Rome, where for a year she joined her brother Ascanio in his efforts to save the Colonna lands and feudatories even as the pope marshalled an army to occupy them.[67] On February 15, 1540, as she packed to go to Viterbo, where Cardinale Pole and the many of the chief actors from Giulia Gonzaga's convent salon in Naples were convening, Colonna wrote to the Duchess of Ferrara's first cousin Queen Marguerite de Navarre, who had been Renata's first guide to the nascent Protestantism in France. At stake in this new *évangélisme*, as the reform movement was known there, were the same themes that informed the beliefs of the *spirituali* in Italy: the personal nature of one's relationship to God, the doctrine of salvation attained by faith rather than by works, and the primacy of Scripture.

Colonna never encountered Marguerite at the Este court, since the queen was with her brother Francis I in Fontainbleau during Colonna's visit to Ferrara. But the Marchesa's fast-growing friendship with Renata gave her an immediate entrée with Marguerite, and the two women entered into a warm correspondence with one another when Colonna returned to her convent in Rome. Certainly the most visible lay figure in the reform movement in France at the time, sister and confidante of the king of France, Marguerite was arguably one of the most influential women in Europe in 1530s. Colonna's first letter to her is noteworthy on a number of counts. First, it is a signature example of Colonna's talent at forging alliances for herself and her family. In the war that loomed between the pope and the Colonna family, the king of France would be an invaluable friend. At the least, Marguerite's advocacy on behalf of Vittoria and Ascanio with her brother Francis could provide insurance that no French troops would abet the pope's designs on Colonna lands. Second, having aligned herself with Renata and, through her, with the *spirituali* in Ferrara,

Colonna could now reach across linguistic borders to unite with the *évangé-liques* in France, a move that could also prove useful in building a road to asylum in the north if the hunt for "heretics" grew more virulent in the peninsula. Moreover, her mention of the great admiration and respect for Marguerite on the part of such eminent men of the Church as Cardinals Bembo and Pole implicitly suggested Italy as a sanctuary for the queen, should she ever seek it. The reform movement in Italy, by the end of the 1530s already under duress, needed fortification from without as well as within. Colonna proposed a friendship based on reciprocity. Third, in a characteristic move, Colonna employed shared intellectual, literary, and religious values to weave common bonds along political axes. In this and other letters to Marguerite, Colonna strengthened her message not only with Valdesian imagery and citations from Scripture but also with references to the ancient poets and philosophers. And last, she brought in the bond of gender. Earlier in the letter from which an excerpt is cited below, Colonna remarked to Marguerite that in searching for models for her own "difficult journey through life," she always sought out women, judging it more appropriate to imitate her own sex. Now, toward the close of her letter, in a metaphor probably unprecedented in humanist epistolary discourse, Colonna compared the maternal bond she imagined between Marguerite and herself to a mother's love for her baby after a difficult and painful birth:

> I would think it would not displease your Majesty to have a pupil on whom you could exercise your two rarest of virtues: humility, since you would lower yourself greatly in teaching me; and charity, since you would find me slow at learning how to receive your favors. But since it is so often the case that the children most loved come from the most painful births, I hope that your Majesty will be encouraged at having delivered me after such a difficult spiritual birth, and by having made me her new child of God. Nor could I ever imagine how your Majesty saw me before her, if it had not been as a consequence of her most noble nature that she turned back to call me, and thus she was obliged to see me from a distance and in front of her; or perhaps it happened the way the servant John went before the Lord, in whose likeness I could at least serve as the voice crying out in the wilderness of our miseries, to tell all Italy to prepare the way for the long-awaited arrival of your Majesty.
>
> But as long as your arrival is postponed because of your high and queenly cares, I shall expect to talk about it with the most reverend priest in Ferrara, whose fine judgment is demonstrated in everything, and particularly in his respect for your Majesty.[68] And I take pleasure in seeing the virtues of this man, which are so extraordinary that they appear to have the excellence of the ancients, which are novel virtues in our eyes, so used to evil now are we. I converse frequently about these

things with the very reverend Cardinal Pole, who speaks always of heaven, and thinks of earthly matters only for the sake of others. I also often speak with the very reverend Cardinal Bembo, who has so thrown himself into toiling in the Lord's vineyard that, although he was hired late, it is fitting that he should reap every great reward without the grumbling of others.[69] And I am trying to see that all these conversations of mine begin and end with such worthy subjects that they have a little of that light which your Majesty so clearly discerns and honors with the magnitude of her journeys of the mind; and may your Majesty see fit to make illustrious each day so precious a pearl [as Marguerite herself] since she knows how to impart her brilliance to it, and while she treasures it herself, she enriches us also. I kiss your royal hand, and I humbly entrust myself to your long-awaited grace. From Rome. February 15 1540.

From the Marchesa of Pescara, the most steadfast servant of your Majesty, Signora

Et a V.M. penso che non sia discara, per haver dinanzi un subietto, ove possa essercitare le due più rare vertù sue, cioè l'humiltà, perchè s'abbasserà molto ad insegnarmi, la carità, perchè in me troverà resistenza a saper ricever le sue gratie. Ma essendo usanza che'l più delle volte de i parti più faticosi sono i figliuoli più amati, spero che poi V.M. debbia allegrarsi d'havermi sì difficilmente partorita con lo spirito, et fattami di Dio et sua nuova creatura. Non saprei mai immaginarmi come mi vedeva la M.V. innanzi a sè, se non fusse che, essendosi per sua nobilissima natura rivolta indrieto a chiamarmi, è stato necessario che di lontano et dinanzi a sè mi veggia; o forsi nel modo che 'l servo Giovanni precedeva al Signore, a similitudine del quale potesse io almeno servir per quella voce, che nel deserto elle miserie nostre esclamassi a tutta Italia il preparar la strada alla desiderata venuto di V.M.

Ma mentre sarà dalle sue alte et regali cure differita, attendarò a ragionare di lei col reverendissimo di Ferrara, il cui bel giudicio si dimostra in ogna cosa, et particularmente in reverir la M.V. Et mi godo di vedere in questo signore le virtù in grado tale, che paiono di quelle antiche ne l'accellenza, ma molto nuove a gli occhi nostri, troppo homai al mal usati. Ne ragion assai col reverendissimo Polo, la cui conversatione è in cielo, e solo per l'altrui ultilità riguarda et cura la teeerra; et spesso col reverendissimo Bembo, tutto acceso de sì ben lavorare in questa vigna del Signore, ch'ogni gran pagamento, senza mormoratione deli altri, se ben tardi du condotto, gli conviene; et tutti gli miei ragionamenti m'ingegno che habbin pincipio et fine da sì degna materia, per havere un poco di quella luce che, con la mente ne l'ampiezza de'suoi viaggi, V.M. sì chiaramente discerne, e sì altamente honor; la qual di degni illustrare ogni giorno più sì pretiosa margherita, poi che sa sì ben dispendere et impartire gli suoi splendori che, thesaurizzando a sè, fa ricchi noi altri. Baso sua regal mano, et nella sua desideratissima gratia humilmente mi raccommando. Di Roma,alli XV di Febraro del M.D.X.L.

De V.S.M. obligatissima serva La Marchese de Pescara

## ✤c COLONNA'S REFORM *CENACOLO* AT VITERBO ɔ✤

In mid-March 1541, Vittoria Colonna abandoned her convent home in Rome and went to Orvieto.[70] Pope Paul III was threatening to march on the Colonna towns in the Castelli Romani that spring, and Vittoria took refuge at the Dominican convent of San Paolo in that city when the war broke out. During March, April, and May, she advised her brother on a daily basis, acting as his secretary of state from her base in Orvieto, as we shall see in chapter 3. Early in the fall, she followed Cardinal Reginald Pole to Viterbo, moving into the convent of Santa Caterina there, when he was made the papal legate to that city.[71]

In 1541, the deaths of Valdés, the spiritual leader of the reform movement in Naples, and Costanza d'Avalos, the founder of the literary salon in Ischia, spelled the end of an era.[72] And yet when Pole moved to Viterbo and inaugurated his literary and theological *cenacolo,* it was as if Giulia Gonzaga's convent salon had simply been reconstituted in a new city and under new leaders. The core members of Pole's *cenacolo* in Viterbo included the same actors who had formed the nucleus of her convent salon in Naples: Colonna, Flaminio, Carnesecchi, Donato Rullo, Apollonio Merenda, Alvise Priuli, bishop of Brescia, and Giovanni Tommaso Sanfelice, archbishop of Cava. In October, as soon as he was settled in his new office in Viterbo, Pole wrote personally to the two men who had been closest not only to Gonzaga but also to Valdés in Naples, Carnesecchi and Flaminio, asking them to join him. Both men were then in Florence, where since May they had been meeting regularly with Ochino and Caterina Cibo, to discuss Calvin's *Institutione Christianae religionis* and the prospective revision of the *Beneficio di Cristo.*[73] Later that year, Ochino, too, on his way to Rome from Milan and Modena where he had been preaching, must have stopped in Viterbo to see Colonna, but seeing no role for himself in this group, he moved on.

Gonzaga, though she remained in Naples with Isabella Bresegna and other disciples of Valdés, exercised an enormous influence on the direction and shape the discussions took in Pole's reform salon. She had been named heir to all Valdés's writings and papers, with rights to edit, translate, circulate, and publish them at her discretion. As such, she and she alone controlled the flow of his manuscripts and, thus, the preservation and perpetuation of his legacy. And to compound her influence, Gonzaga communicated her thoughts regularly to Pole by letters she sent to Vittoria Colonna and Pietro Carnesecchi, with whom she maintained especially close ties.[74] Convening daily in Pole's residence at the Rocca, the participants of the Viterbo *cenacolo* were divided on many issues but they agreed, for the most part, on one central principle: the Valdesian doctrine that salvation was to be attained through faith rather than works, whether these were acts of monastic self-denial or the rituals of the established Church. Though Valdés himself never articulated the Lutheran proclamation *de justificatione fide sola* in his writings, the primacy of faith over works is a dominant theme in both his *Diálogo de doctrina christiana* and the *Alfabeto*.[75] While Pole maintained his allegiance to the pope as the "true *vicario* of Christ," Gonzaga and Carnesecchi went further than Valdés.[76] They argued not only that faith alone in Christ, God's gift to mankind, was the foundation of the Church but that all other temporal or ecclesiastical claims to authority were false.[77] Still others among the Viterbo *spirituali*, questioned the doctrines of penitence, purgatory, the selling of indulgences, the significance of the Eucharist, and the authority of the pope and the Roman Church.[78]

The *spirituali,* in general, saw themselves as followers neither of Calvin nor of Luther. They believed that open discussion of the doctrine and writings of the Protestant theologians would lead to a rekindling of their faith and a reformation of the Church of Rome. Marcantonio Flaminio, in particular, led Pole's *cenacolo* in discussions of Calvin's magnum opus, the *Institutione*, which had been published in Latin in Venice in 1536 and 1539, and was available in French by 1541.[79] And while Pole warned Vittoria Colonna against giving too much credence to either Calvin or Luther, the group at Viterbo spent considerable time discussing the German theologian since Pole would deliver a "point-by-point refutation of Lutheran doctrine," as Thomas Mayer has characterized the cardinal's speech, at the opening session of the Council of Trent in June 1542.[80] Carnesecchi, in his later years, would recall that his first significant exposure to Luther's writings had dated from his participation in Pole's *cenacolo*. "I began to read books by Luther and others of his persuasion," he testified at his trial, "which I first saw in Viterbo when I was with the cardinal of England, and in the company of Flaminio."[81]

On December 8, 1541, Vittoria Colonna wrote Gonzaga thanking her for sending some of Valdés's last theological works for her to give to Pole. This letter already suggests the pivotal role Giulia Gonzaga would occupy as a member by proxy of the Viterbo circle. It would be she who would send Valdés's writings to the Viterbo group, with Colonna acting as Gonzaga's designated delegate to the assembly. Colonna's letter also makes clear the character of her own place in the circle—as an outsider in some ways: in part because she was a woman and in part because she was neither a priest nor a credentialed theologian, though by 1538 she was an acclaimed author, whose collected poems and verse letters were already in print. And, as Thomas Mayer has remarked, for Pole and many of his circle, literary gravitas was as important as religion.[82] Lesser figures in Pole's entourage at Viterbo, such as Priuli and Carnesecchi, sought her out. But Pole himself and Flaminio, the two chief authors of the new doctrine of the *spirituali* and probably of the widely popular, anonymously published *Beneficio di Cristo* were, at least in the early days of the *cenacolo*, all but inaccessible to Colonna. She had been waiting to learn and draw intellectual sustenance from both these men, but after two months at Viterbo, she let her disappointment be known. She longed for real companionship, and in particular that of her cousin Giulia, whose experiences mirrored her own and whose family and friends were also Colonna's. In short, despite their age and generational distances, these two women shared a considerable history—one that could promise, as Colonna hoped, future collaboration:

> Your Ladyship has always been kind to me; from the time I first saw you at Fondi I knew that I would never find you lacking in graciousness, and now it has been a great consolation to me to pass on so many good things to the Cardinal and the other gentlemen, since in addition to my acting as the intermediary, because of the kindness of the very reverend Monsignor, I am still more gratified because Your Ladyship has helped him begin to rid himself of a strange habit, namely, that of accepting every gift in the worst spirit; for Luigi Priuli told me this morning that the Cardinal has received Your Ladyship's gift with the greatest pleasure, seeing in it much affection and love, without it seeming to his Lordship that there was any purpose in it other than your Ladyship's continuing desire to honor and please him.
>
> Therefore, my Signora, if I long to be able to serve his Lordship—I, who am obliged to the very reverend Cardinal not only for the health of my soul but also that of my body, since the one was endangered by superstition and the other by poor governance—and have never been allowed to do so until now, and only hope he will be a bit more flexible regarding things that are so reasonable, and if the Signora, even when she is absent, is capable of doing so much with her Christian goodness, just think what would happen if, by the grace of God, Your Ladyship could be here? And were I to have the consolation of conversing with you and were I to be able to learn what God imparted to you in the best way possible, I would not have such a great need of them, since I've longed too much for their company—I mean not only that of the monsignor [Pole] who is terribly busy but also that of Monsignor Flaminio, our best spirit, whom I've seen no more than twice since he arrived, so that if it weren't for Monsignor Luigi Priuli and Signor Carnesecchi, I would be unhappy. And certainly it would be a pleasure for Your Ladyship to make a little visit to her home in Lombardy again, now that you know so much about our true celestial home, which can still be helpful to you; and passing through here, if you could stop for a couple of months, it would give the Monsignor [Pole] a chance to actually show you how much he wants to please you and it would give me the opportunity to enjoy your good company. And realizing that everyone else writes to Your Ladyship to convey the Monsignor's

greetings, I won't dare make this letter any longer, since the pleasure of writing you has already made me forget my other responsibilities, and I kiss your hand. From Viterbo, at Santa Caterina on the 8 December.

Your Ladyship's very devoted servant,
Marchesa di Pescara

I have heard that Your Ladyship has sent the commentary on St. Paul, which I desired more than I actually needed; however, thanks very much, and you'll get more of the same when I see you, God willing.[83]

Illustrissima Signora mia. Sempre V.S. mi fece gratia: dalla prima volta che la viddi in Fundi sa che non trovai cortesia se non in lei, et hor mi ha dato molta consolatione a mandare tante et sì buone cose al signor Cardinale et a quelli altri signori, perchè oltre che io ne habbia participato per humanità di monsignor reverendissimo, e ho un'altra maggior satisfattione, cioè che V.S. sia causa che commensi a perdere una certa strana consuetudine che tiene di accettare di malissima voglia ogni presente, perchè questa mattina messer Luigi Priuli me ha detto che ha preso le cose della S.V. con grandissimo piacere, vedendo tanta affettione et charità; senza parere a Sua Signoria di haverneli dato causa con altro che col continuo desiderio di honorarla et compiacerli.

Sì che, Signora mia, io che sono a sua signoria reverendissima della salute dell'anima e di quella del corpo obbligata, chè l'una per superstitione, l'altra per mal governo era in periculo, pensi V.S. se desidero posserlo servire, et nonmi è stato main concesso sin qui, et hor spero che sarà un poco più flexibile a così ragionevol cose, et se la signora absente può tanto con la sua christiana cortesia, hor che sarà se per gratia di potessi esser qui? Massime che havendo io la mia consolatione di conferire con lei, anzi di imparare veramente quel che Dio per ottimi mezzi li ha communicato, non haveria sì gran necessità di loro, che mi bisogna desiderarli troppo, non dico solo monsignor, che è occupatissimo, e lo ho per scusato, ma il nostro ottimo spirito M. Flaminio no lo ho visto se non due volte poi che venne, sì che, se non fusse M. Luigi Priuli et il signor Carnesecchi, io starei male. Et certo saria conveniente che la Signora revedesse un poco la sua patria in Lombardia, hor che della vera celeste patria è sì ben informata, che li potria giovare pur assai, et passando di qui se potria fermare un par di mesi, dando a monsignor occasione di mostrarli in effetto il desiderio che ha di satisfarli et ad me di recevere gratie da lei et pensando che tutti scrivano a V.S. la ottima volontà di monsignor verso lei, non ardirò di far questa lettera più longa, che il piacer si scriverli mi ha trasportato pur troppo, et li bacio la mano. Di Viterbo, in Santa Catharina, a dì 8 dicembre.

Deditissima servir V.S. Ill.ma,
La Marchesa de Pescara

Ho inteso che V.S. ha mandato la espositione sopra San Paolo, ch'era molto desiderata, et più da me, che n'ho più bisogno, però più nella ringratio et più quando la vedrò, piacendo a Dio.[84]

In January of the following year, Giulia Gonzaga received by courier from Pole a draft of a manuscript he and Flaminio were working on together. It is widely believed that it was this manuscript that Gonzaga brought to Venice in 1543 when she negotiated a contract herself with the printer Bernardo de'Bindoni that year to publish an anonymous work titled *Beneficio di Cristo*.[85] Certainly the *Beneficio* represents a distillation of Valdesian doctrine, as articulated both by the Spanish theologian and his disciples at Gonzaga's salon and by the members of Pole's circle at Viterbo.[86]

The years 1541–42 mark the last period of Colonna's and Gonzaga's direct involvement with Pole's circle at Viterbo. In May 1542, Pole, flanked by Flaminio, Carnesecchi, Priuli, and the rest of his circle, left Viterbo for the opening of the first session of the Council of Trent. He probably did not return. In any case, from that year on the members of Pole's group at Viterbo began gradually to disband. Flaminio would recall in his testimony before the Holy Office some years later how firm Giulia Gonzaga's belief in the rightness of the Valdesian doctrine of *giustificazione* had then been.[87] But with the instituting of the Inquisition in Rome in 1542 under the auspices of the Holy Office, the worsening climate for reform thought in Rome, the charges of heresy leveled at so many of Gonzaga's and Colonna's Valdesian friends, and the flight of Ochino from Italy to the Protestant north in August, Gonzaga decided to remain in Naples, occupying herself—so it was said—with the education of her young nephew Vespasiano Gonzaga Colonna.[88] Vittoria Colonna would remain in Viterbo at least until the summer of 1543. In July or August, ill and under suspicion for heresy herself, she left the city she would always associate with not only the presence of Pole but the long shadow of Giulia Gonzaga as well.[89] This time, Colonna retired to the convent of Santa Anna de' Funari in Rome.

## ❧ MARIA D'ARAGONA D'AVALOS'S COURT IN MILAN ☙

In January 1538, in the interim between the end of Vittoria Colonna's long stay in Ferrara and her move to Viterbo, Charles V had named the Marchese Alfonso d'Avalos del Vasto governor of Milan. He and his wife Maria d'Aragona d'Avalos del Vasto gathered up their children and their tutors and their servants, and abandoning their homes at Chiaia in Naples and the d'Avalos castle on Ischia, they settled into the ducal palace in Milan.[90]

No two people could have been better prepared to direct the daily social and military obligations of a major court than Maria d'Aragona and her husband. D'Aragona had grown up observing the ease with which Costanza d'Avalos and Vittoria Colonna entertained literary women and men, scholars, artists, men of the church, and the local nobility at Costanza's castle on Ischia. They had created a salon where new works and ideas were shared, and their evenings drew women and men of talent and means from all over Italy. Like d'Avalos and Colonna, she had read widely and had entered freely into the evening discussions at the island salon. Because of d'Aragona's experience and connections, nothing seemed more self-evident to her than that the responsibility for the organization and leadership of the court of Milan and its cultural program should be hers, not her husband's. Among other things, she was constantly at the court, while he was likely to be in the field with his troops.

Colonna had raised her husband's much younger cousin, Alfonso d'Avalos, as though he were her own son, guiding his studies in Greek philosophy, Roman history, the Augustan poets, Dante, and Petrarch. And like his surrogate mother, Alfonso wrote poetry—an avocation he pursued until his death. Under Colonna's husband, he became skilled in the arts of war, military strategy, and the management of a large army. By the time he was offered the supreme military and civil command of Milan at the age of thirty-six, he had already fought on the front lines at Pavia in 1525, when Charles V had taken the king of France prisoner; he had almost gone down with Charles's fleet in the naval battle at Capo d'Orso in 1528; and he had served as one of the emperor's captains in 1535 at Tunis, where Charles's imperial troops had defeated an army of eighty thousand Turks.

Like other alumnae of the Ischia salon, d'Aragona was intensely involved in the *spirituali* movement in Naples in the 1530s. She attended the salons of Giulia Gonzaga in the convent San Francesco delle Monache in Naples and of Juan de Valdés at Chiaia and heard the sermons of Bernardino Ochino with her aunt. Once in Milan, she remained loyal to Valdés's disciple Pietro Carnesecchi and she continued to correspond with the reform thinker Cardinal Seripando, when he came under attack by the Holy Office in Rome. Her husband Alfonso was also keenly interested in the religious controversies of the 1530s and 1540s, and during the years 1540–42, he tried repeatedly to bring Ochino to Milan, though the Capuchin friar left Italy without preaching in the Lombard capital.[91] Like Colonna and d'Aragona, Alfonso d'Avalos was especially drawn to Ochino's asceticism.[92]

The Venetian Bernardo Capello, a member of d'Aragona's circle of poets and other intellectuals, portrayed the marchesa as the queen of a dazzling court.[93] The habitués of her salon included men who, famous themselves, succeeded in spreading her fame as a patron and learned woman: Paolo Giovio, Girolamo Muzio, Pietro Aretino, Giulio Camillo, and Bernardo Spina, all of whom had taken part in Costanza d'Avalos's salon on Ischia. Other writers and artists whom d'Aragona generously supported were Iacopo Nardi, who dedicated his translation of Livy's *Histories* to her, Aretino, who addressed his *Marfisa* and his *Vita di Santa Caterina* to her, Niccolò Franco whose *Dialoghi della Bellezza* was directed to increasing her glory, and the great Venetian painter Titian. D'Aragona's well-connected secretary Luca Contile chronicled the lives and times of the marchesa, her husband, and her sister Giovanna d'Aragona Colonna in his collected *Lettere*, which circulated widely in manuscript before the volume went to press in 1564.[94]

D'Aragona was alone in her administration of the court and affairs of the city. With the French army encamped outside Milan, Alfonso d'Avalos was constantly on the go. Almost never staying in one place for any period of time, he spent all his days and nights moving between Asti, Coreggio, Vigevano, and Pavia. His army was overextended in every possible way. On April 14, 1544, he suffered a catastrophic setback. In one of the worst disasters in sixteenth-century warfare, twelve thousand of his men died in the battle of Ceresole and three thousand of his men were taken prisoner by the French. Two weeks before the battle, on March 27, Contile had written a letter to his friend Claudio Tolomei in which he painted a scene full of foreboding in Milan. D'Avalos and his captains had virtually transformed the city into an armed camp:[95]

> The incessant roll of drums echoes everywhere in this city day and night. The sound of trumpets pierces the air at all hours, and the streets are full of soldiers. The abundance of horses is such that the deafening sound of their neighing reaches all the way to the ramparts of the city.

> I tamburi giorno e notte rimbombano in questa città, le trombe feriscono l'aria a tutte l'hore, le strade sono piene di soldati, la copia de'cavalli è tanta che con anitrire assordiscono fin le muraglie." (*Lettere*, 1:102v–103r)

After his defeat, d'Avalos retired to his bed. Harquebus balls had shattered his arm and knee. Seeing him disconsolate, Maria tried everything she could think of to nurse him back to health.

Contile wrote to his friend Orlando Marescotti:

> Since the defeat at Ceresole, the good prince is always melancholy, and care is taken to entertain him with various diversions and with discussions of history,

philosophy, and theology since he is a good Christian, or with various games and jousts. And in addition to which always—I mean every day—the gentlewomen of this city come to visit the Marchesa, who then leads them to the Marchese's room where there is virtuous conversation and dancing.

Dalla rotta di Ceresuola in quo questo ottimo principe sempre è vivuto malinconico, e si attende a trattenerelo con diverse maniere, o di ragionamenti istorici, filosofici ed ecclesiastici; essendo egli buon cristiano; ovvero con diverse sorti e giuochi d'armeggiare. Oltrachè sempre, voglio dire ogni giorno, vengono le gentildonne di questa città a visitar la marchesa, la qual poi le mena alle stanze del marchese, dove virtuosamente si ragiona e balla. (*Lettere*, 1:110)[96]

Two years after Ceresole, on March 31, 1546, d'Avalos died, a disgraced man whom Charles had relieved of his duties. D'Aragona moved her entrourage out of the ducal *rocca* in Milan into a palace in Pavia spacious enough for her seven children, her sister Giovanna, their secretaries, and their large staff. There she reestablished her salon and inaugurated the academy of the Chiave d'Oro with Contile, Doni, Aretino, Albicante, Alciato, and many others from her Milan circle.

On February 11, 1547, d'Aragona and her household boarded a ship at Cumae and sailed home to Ischia. Later that month she and her sister reinaugurated their salon at the Castel dell'Ovo in Naples, but on May 13 there was a popular rebellion against Charles's viceroy Pedro di Toledo, and rioting broke out in the city.[97] The viceroy turned his canons on the people, threatened to reinstitute a local office of the Inquisition, and closed the literary academies of Naples. After nine years of war and instability in Milan, d'Aragona left Naples to return to her island birthplace, and there she again received at the d'Avalos castle many of the same poets who had taken part in the Ischia salon of the 1530s.[98]

How then should we assess the significance of the d'Avalos-Colonna salons and their contributions to Italian culture in the third and fourth decades of the Cinquecento?[99] What distinguished these assemblies from later versions of the institution as it evolved in seventeenth- and eighteenth-century Europe? As we have seen, the salon differed from the Italian court in its separation from the apparatuses of the state or city-state, its lack of official authorization, the sporadic rather than daily nature of its meetings, and its primary function as a social and cultural assembly rather than a political institution. Nonetheless this informal sixteenth-century institution was, as I have shown, deeply embroiled in and affected by the politics of church and state.

I have argued in this chapter that the gatherings at the d'Avalos castle on Ischia produced the matrix from which the five subsequent salons discussed in this chapter were derived: Vittoria Colonna's circle at the convent of San Silvestro in Rome; Giulia Gonzaga's at the convent of San Francesco delle Monache in Naples; Renata di Francia's salon within but separate from the Este court in Ferrara; Colonna's powerful shaping of Pole's *cenacolo* at Viterbo; and finally, Maria d'Aragona d'Avalos's court in Milan and her salon at Pavia. The salon that Costanza d'Avalos created on Ischia originated as a place of refuge from war, an arcadia in the Italian imagination not subject to the cities of the peninsula: an anti-state led not by a patriarch but by women, a utopia of sorts—without a prince, a bureaucracy, or a standing army. In his famous letter to Clement VII, Giovio perpetuated this literary image of Ischia, and so it had remained in the minds of the reading public.

The d'Avalos salon proved potent as an institution. Five subsequent salons were generated from it, each instituted, led, or strongly influenced by one of the d'Avalos-Colonna women who were among its founders and were themselves molded by their participation in it. Characteristically, the alumnae of the Naples-Ischia circle were, in Elizabeth C. Goldsmith's formulation, itinerant women: women economically independent enough to change their residences at will, often moving from city to city in the course of their lives.[100] Remarkably, these itinerant salonnières presided over and participated actively in the circles they created wherever they were. Colonna moved from Ischia to Rome and Viterbo, Gonzaga from Fondi to Naples, and d'Aragona from Naples to Milan and Pavia and back to Naples. Further supported by the institution of the convent safe houses, as I have shown, Colonna and Gonzaga were able to travel freely from city to city without the strain of having to maintain a residence themselves.

Historians have speculated as to why these particular women—salon women, as we have portrayed them—were drawn to the reform movement.[101] In the case of the powerful and independent d'Avalos-Colonna women, the idea of having their spiritual lives directed by either of the popes they had known, Clement VII or Paul III, was unacceptable. These were highly educated women accustomed to working at the enigmas of the Scriptures on their own or guided by scholars such as Flaminio and Pole. They were determined to seek God themselves through faith and contemplation. To that end, they sought spiritual mentors and teachers such as Valdés and Ochino, rather than the sanctioned ministers of an institution they knew to be corrupt.

Unlike the salons of seventeenth-century France, illuminated by the studies of Joan Landes and others, the woman-led salon in sixteenth-century Italy did not decline but grew in importance with the rise of the publishing industry.[102] In Italy, reciprocity and dynamism characterized the relationship between the salons, the academies, and the presses. In the salons and academies, works in progress were performed, read, and critiqued in ways that were helpful to both fledgling and seasoned authors, while this kind of pre-publication screening fostered sales as well as interest in the literary works. The Italian salons also served as sites where friendships were forged between writers, editors, and publishers. Social interaction, whether at the salons or the academies of the peninsula, led, as we shall see in the ensuing chapters, to publication.

CHAPTER TWO

# From Naples to Venice:
# The Publication of Two Salons

In 1559, at the height of the Inquisition, the poems of fifty-three women, Vittoria Colonna among them, were published in an all-women anthology in Italy. Lodovico Domenichi, a man who had gone to prison for translating heretical books and who was one of the most prominent figures in the Venetian publishing world, edited the women's anthology for a press in Lucca. Though not the last, the volume was perhaps the grand finale to a wildly successful set of poetry anthologies printed during the years 1545–60 by the prominent Venetian publishing house of Gabriel Giolito, in collaboration with several smaller presses.[1] The story of the 1559 anthology of women authors, the first such collection ever produced in Europe, and its making is the subject of this chapter (fig. 1).[2]

On February 11, 1547, Maria d'Aragona returned to Naples from Milan, where she had ruled the literary scene for ten years.[3] Her husband Alfonso d'Avalos, the governor of Milan, had died the year before, leaving her the single parent of seven children and the matriarch of a large extended family. By late February, she opened the Castel dell'Ovo to the city's leading poets and their patrons. Her aim was to inaugurate a salon like the one her aunt, Costanza d'Avalos, and her sister-in-law, Vittoria Colonna, had hosted on Ischia in the 1530s. In the Castel dell'Ovo, located at the port of Santa Lucia, where boats embarked daily on their way across the bay to Ischia, Maria and her sister Giovanna d'Aragona Colonna welcomed the return of many of the same poets who had frequented the d'Avalos-Colonna salon some twenty years before. Ferrante Carafa, Angelo di Costanzo, Bernardino Rota, Antonio Epicuro, Antonio Minturno, Luigi Tansillo, and Giambattista d'Azzia were among those attending, all of them now members of the leading academy in Naples, the Sereni.[4]

## ❖c CIVIL WAR IN NAPLES AND THE CLOSING OF THE ACADEMIES ᴐ❖

In the beginning of May 1547, rioting broke out in Naples and the nobility mounted, in alliance with the popular classes, an armed rebellion against the Emperor Charles V's viceroy, Pedro di Toledo.[5] By the 1530s, a century of Aragonese-Spanish kings in Naples, intermarriage between the Italian and Spanish ruling classes, and the defection of the pro-French nobility to France had eased anti-Spanish tensions in the kingdom, at least among the aristocracy.[6] Only on one other occasion in sixteenth-century Naples did the elite classes join the *popolo* in an armed revolt against a Spanish regent, and that was in 1510, when an earlier viceroy tried to impose the Spanish Inquisition in Naples, as Pedro di Toledo did now. It was this that touched off the rebellion. In mid-May, with a civil war raging, Maria d'Aragona's secretary Luca Contile wrote another former member of d'Aragona's court in Milan, Bernardo Spina, despairing over the hopeless battle he saw the people of Naples waging against the viceroy's heavily fortified positions, his superior fire power, and his thousands of well-armed Spanish troops.[7]

> The city thunders and two fortresses, San Martino and the Castelnuovo, bombard the Piazza dell'Olmo and the church of Our Lady of the Crown at the same time, but San Martino fires on everything else, though its salvos, coming from high up, do no damage. Yesterday, between the two fortresses, four hundred rounds of artillery were fired. Today it appears that peace might be talked about; the captain of the nobility is the Abbot of Bari of the Caracciola family; and this evening an accord was struck, since the viceroy sent over a *foglio bianco*—thank God. Let's hope the accord holds, since the cause of the insurrection has not gone away. While the viceroy says that the city is stained with heresy, which unfortunately seems to be the truth, . . . he threatens to reinstate the Inquisition, and on this account the rioting in the city continues. We stand to see another round of artillery attacks, perhaps with more death and ruin . . . Naples. 15 May 1547.

> La Città fulmina e le due fortezze, San Martino e Castelnuovo, berzagliano la piazza dell'Olmo e la incoronata, ma San Martino tutto il resto, imperò le sue palle,

venendo d'alto, nulla di danno rendono. Hieri fra i dui castelli, furono tirate quattrocento botte. Hoggi par che si parli di pace; Capo della nobiltà è l'Abbate de Bari
di casa Caracciola. Et questa sera si è fatto l'accordo, perchè il Vicerè ha mandato
il foglio bianco. Laudato sia Dio. Pur che duri tale accordo, perciochè la causa non
cessa. Dicendo il Vicerè esser la città macchiata d'heresia et in vero par che sia
purtroppo la verità, . . . minaccia di metter la inquisitione, per la qual voce la Città
va tumultuando. Staremo a vedere un'altra salva d'artiglieria, forse con maggior
mortalità e ruina. . . . Di Napoli. 15 Maggio MDXLVII. (*Delle lettere*, 1:q3–4)[8]

Contile's prediction in his letter of May 15 was on target. Within two months,
the situation in Naples deteriorated. Even though the leaders of the rebel fac-
tions, Mormillo and Caracciolo, had left town, Toledo remained obsessed with
the threat to the state he saw looming from heretics who had "stained" the
honor of the city ("la città macchiata d'heresia") and he was no more ready to
compromise than he had been before the revolt. For Toledo, there were no real
political differences between the rebelling popular classes in Naples, the poets
from the literary academies, and such academy patrons as Maria d'Aragona
d'Avalos and her sister Giovanna d'Aragona Colonna. As far as he was concerned, the plebs and the intellectuals wanted the same thing: to bring down
his authority and that of the Church. Contile's description of the situation in
Naples captures Maria d'Aragona's recognition of the danger she and the academicians were in as well as that of the powerless people of the city:

There are three thousand foreign soldiers in the city [Contile wrote]. This af-
ternoon the Spanish took over the church of Our Lady of the Crown and they
skirmish using every sort of cruelty. The bloody slaughter has gone on now for
twelve days; artillery fire has leveled all the houses in the Piazza dell'Olmo and its
beautiful fountain is rubble and its pieces scattered, and thus the Spaniards have
chased away the people of Naples . . . ; they batter their way in, going from house
to house, such that the city is more humiliated with each passing day. And it appears that the Abbot of Bari and Mormillo have abandoned the cause and many
other gentlemen and lords have left the city, which yesterday sent a delegation to
the viceroy and he is agreeing now to a peace pact . . . Meanwhile the Marchesa
Maria d'Aragona has gone to Ischia taking with her many lords. . . . From Naples.
15 July 1547.

La città per ciò ha soldati tremila fuorisciti; in questo mezo gli spagnuoli hanno
preso la chiesa della incoronata e scaramucciano con ogni sorte di crudeltà; e
è durata questa mischia sanguinosa gia dodici giorni e l'artigliaria ha sfondate
tutte le case della Piazza dell'Olmo e rotta e dissipata quella bella fontana, così gli

Spagnuoli hanno cacciato i Napoletani . . . ; e forano di casa in casa, di sorte che la città rimane ogni dì più avvilità; e l'Abbate di Bari con quel Mormillo par che habbiano abbandonata l'impresa e molti altri cavalieri et Signori sono usciti della città, la quale mandò Ambasciatore al Vicerè, et egli concede la pace con patto. . . . La Signora Marchesa si è ritirata in Ischia con molte Signore . . . Di Napoli. XV di Luglio MDXLVII. (*Delle lettere*, fols. q4–q4v)[9]

Convinced by the end of 1547 that the literary academies were hotbeds of heresy and sedition, Pedro di Toledo outlawed them, and he imprisoned the poets Ferrante Carafa and Angelo di Costanzo, both leaders in the city's most formidable intellectual enclaves—the academies of the Sereni, the Ardenti, and the Incogniti.[10] After Toledo's suppression of the academies, Maria and Giovanna d'Aragona, whom he suspected of supporting the rebellion, moved their evenings for the reading and discussion of new poetry to Ischia and Pozzuoli, and they traveled less frequently to Naples.[11]

The Neapolitan poets harbored high expectations for Maria's continued cultivation of the Naples coterie when she opened the rooms of the Castel dell'Ovo to them in February. Even after Toledo closed the academies in 1547, Ferrante Carafa, past president of the Ardenti academy and longtime friend of Maria's, expressed the Neapolitan poets' hopes that, between her commitment to them and her connections in Milan and Venice, she would resurrect the Naples salon. In verses dedicated to her, he wrote:

> And because now two famous companies,
> the lofty Sereni and the Ardenti,
> wish to recover their true glory
> and renew their mighty splendor
> from that one whose cruel and evil wishes
> offended our people, they in their gentility
> entrusted me to unite them and to redress
> the common injury that was done to them.
> And therefore since I well know how wrong
> it would be to carry out such work
> without your help, kindly Maria,
> whose strength nourishes every ardent soul:
> so that their names may endure forever
> and honor may abide with me for what
> I shall endeavor, I beg you to give us help,
> with your kindly and infinite grace.

E perché omai le due famose schiere
Degli eletti Sereni e degli Ardenti
Ricovrar voglion le lor glorie vere,
E rinnovare i bei raggi possenti,
Cui le voglie occupar già crude e fiere
Di chi offese ancor più le nostre genti,
Per la lor cortesia commesso m'hanno
ch'io gli unisca e ristori il comun danno.
    Ond'io, che quanto mal per me saria
Esequitar opra simil, ben comprendo,
Senza il soccorso vostro, alma Maria,
Da cui vigor riceve ogni alma ardendo;
Acciocchè il nome lor perpetuo sia,
  meco resti onor di quel che imprendo;
Pregovi che a noi dar vogliate aita,
Con la vostra alma grazia ed infinita.[12]

D'Aragona's ties to poets and the influential men of the presses cut both ways, north and south. Having brought to Naples, as her secretaries, the poets Luca Contile and Girolamo Muzio, Aragona kept in touch with other writers she had supported in Milan and Pavia: men well connected to Venetian editors and printers such as Aretino, Anton Francesco Doni, Paolo Giovio, Francesco Maria Molza, and Bernardo Cappello, who were mainstays of her Milan academy, the Fenici, and the Academy of the Chiave d'Oro, which she established in Pavia.

### ❖C THE VENETIAN DEBUT OF THE NAPLES SALON Ɔ❖

In 1549, the climate looked more promising for the Neapolitan poets in Venice. As Paul Grendler has shown, the Inquisition took effect more slowly in Venice. There were trials in the Republic concerning heretical books that year and the next, and in July 1548, the Venetian Inquisition ordered that some fourteen hundred books be burned in the Piazza San Marco, a portent of the large conflagrations of books that would come later.[13] On May 7, 1549, the prominent Venetian publisher Vincenzo Valgrisi produced a *Catalogo* of prohibited books, which the Republic commissioned him to print.[14] The 1549 *Catalogo* made it a crime to sell or possess a number of books, including two whose contracts Giovanna d'Aragona's cousin by marriage, Giulia Gonzaga, had negotiated herself: Valdés's dialogue—the *Alfabeto*—and the anonymous

· FIGURE 2 ·
A woodcut portrait of Maria d'Aragona d'Avalos from
Ruscelli's *Lettura. . . . sopra un sonetto alla divina signora marchesa
del Vasto* (Venice: Giovan Griffio, 1552), fol. 74.

*Beneficio di Cristo.*[15] But in June the same year the Republic revoked the Valgrisi *Catalogo* and withdrew it from circulation.

Laura Terracina's publication of her *Rime* with Giolito in 1548 made her the first of the Naples academy members to see her collected poems go to press in Venice in a solo-authored edition. Banking on this first connection, Naples academy president Ferrante Carafa, who was not only Terracina's mentor but a close friend of Maria d'Aragona's, approached leading editors and publishers in Venice himself. At a meeting of the academy of the Dubbiosi in Venice in 1551, one of Giolito's senior editors, Girolamo Ruscelli, proposed the collaborative production of a literary monument, a so-called temple (*Tempio*), to honor Maria's sister Giovanna d'Aragona.[16] The nobleman Fortunato Martinengo, founder of the Dubbiosi academy in Brescia, had just inaugurated a new chapter of the organization in Venice.[17] This was one of the many exclusive literary clubs that seemed to spring up spontaneously in the Italian cities at midcentury. Tightly connected to the publishing industry, whose capital was Venice, the academies existed to perform, discuss, and distribute new literary works—and, ultimately, to establish a new canon of modern Italian writers. Among such elite fraternities, the fame of the Neapolitan Incogniti, the Milanese Fenici, the Sienese Intronati, and the Infiammati of Padua spread. Their members represented an array of social classes and professions: poets, printers, translators, editors, historians, teachers, playwrights, and arts patrons, many of whom retained memberships in several academies around the peninsula. Moving freely between academies, members shared information, works, and ideas across cities.[18] Though the poet Laura Terracina was inducted into the Incogniti in Naples, Gaspara Stampa joined the Dubbiosi in Venice, and Laura Battiferra was a Siena Intronati member, women were for the most part excluded from these clubs.

At the opening meeting of the Dubbiosi in 1551, Ruscelli announced that a letter had come to him from Ferrante Carafa, who had requested, as had "many other judicious men" in Naples, that Maria d'Aragona, Marchesa del Vasto, be honored together with her sister Giovanna as the *Tempio*'s dedicatees. In the preface to the academy's decree committing its membership to "erecting a temple" for Maria's sister Giovanna, Ruscelli wrote:

> In the year 1551 as the Academy of the Dubbiosi commences in this ever fortunate city, under the auspices of the blessed memory of the Illustrious Count Fortunato Martinengo and of the most excellent and reverend Doctor Macasciuola, letters have come from the most illustrious and honorable Signor Ferrante Carrafa, in which he has indicated, as many others have also done, that it is the commonly held opinion of the most judicious men that the Temple, which is being built for the divine Signora Giovanna d'Aragona should simultaneously celebrate the equally divine Marchesa del Vasto [Maria d'Aragona].

> L'anno M.D.L.I. facendosi in questa sempre felicissima città, l'Academia de'Dubbiosi, sotto gli auspicii dell'Illustre Signor Conte Fortunato Martinengo, di benedetta memoria e del molto eccellente e Reverendo Signor Dottor Macasciuola: vennero lettere dell'Illustrissimo e honoratissimo Signor Ferrante Carrafa, per quali, sì come haveano ancora fatto molt'altri, significava esser commune parere di tutti i più giudiciosi, che il Tempio, il quale si veniva fabricando alla divina Signora Donna Giovanna d'Aragona, si dovesse far commune alla parimente divina Signora Marchesa del Vasto.[19]

Suppressed in their own city, Carafa and the other members of d'Aragona's coterie wanted desperately to air their works publicly. If they could persuade one of the commercially successful presses in Venice to publish a collective tribute for their patron, the publication of their own poems in the resulting festschrift was virtually guaranteed. As the decree indicates, in 1551 the Dubbiosi had already launched a call for poetic contributions for an anthology entitled *Del tempio alla divina signora donna Giovanna d'Aragona* (The temple for the divine lady Giovanna d'Aragona), which Ruscelli was to edit and his printer Pietrasanta would produce. But that same year, Ruscelli was under separate contract to publish a tribute to Maria d'Aragona (fig. 2), under the title *Lettura di Girolamo Ruscelli sopra un sonnetto dell'illustrissimo signor marchese della Terza alla divina signora Marchesa del Vasto* (A lecture by Girolamo Ruscelli on a sonnet in honor of the divine lady, the Marchesa del Vasto, composed by the Marchese della Terza).[20]

### ✣ GIOLITO'S PROMOTION OF THE NAPLES SALON ✣

With Ruscelli's commemorative volumes for the d'Aragona sisters in the works, the stage was set for the Venetian debut of the Naples salon. Not to be outdone by Ruscelli, on December 9, 1551, Gabriel Giolito's lead editor Lodovico Dolce announced he was putting together a new kind of anthology for his firm's poetry series: the volume would feature writers from Naples. But his project was not only to promote the Neapolitan salon as a new group on the literary circuit but also to call attention to his own role as their producer. With a dedicatory letter addressed to Ferrante Carrafa, dated December 9, 1551, the first of Dolce's four anthologies featuring Neapolitan poets rolled off the presses in 1552 under the title *Rime di diversi illustri signori napoletani e d'altri nobilissimi intelletti; nuovamente raccolte, et non più stampate, Terzo libro* (An anthology of famous Neapolitan poets and other great writers, recently collected and previously unpublished, book 3).[21]

The first work in the Giolito poetry series to promote poets from the Italian south, Dolce's new volume included a wide range of writers, from poets such as Di Costanzo, Epicuro, Galeota, Rota, and Tansillo, who were prominent enough in Naples though they had never been published in Venice, down to the once completely unknown Isabella di Morra, the notorious victim in a triple homicide case.[22] Dolce seems not to have known Carafa before the two collaborated on the Naples anthology. But the warm dedicatory letter he addressed to Carafa in the preface to the *Rime di diversi napoletani* suggests a special bond between the two men that appears to have been a lasting one since Dolce dedicated his second and third editions of the Naples anthology to Carafa as well:

It was not fitting, my Illustrious Signor [Dolce wrote to Carafa], upon publication of the present sonnets and canzoni, born of the genius of many illustrious gentlemen and elevated spirits of your most noble city, that they should have found their way into men's hands without the benefit of some virtuous and learned gentleman, who would add ornament to their nobility. Hence the work is properly dedicated to you so that, just as your lordship honors it with the fruits of his divine intellect, so he may honor it with his name. Now given that you are a man most adorned with all those virtues that belong to a noble cavalier and your distinction both in the study of literature and as a writer merits praise of the first rather than the second order, may it not displease you that these poems will be embellished by your name, to the end that so many noble men, seeing their efforts published under such a name, will appreciate their works and themselves all the more; and they will also recognize the affection which I, who am your servant, together with the magnificent and virtuous M. Gabriello Giolito offer as a tribute to your virtue. I kiss your valorous hand. From Venice on the 9th of December 1551.

Lodovico Dolce

Non era conveniente, Illustre Signor mio, che dovendosi imprimere i presenti Sonetti e Canzoni, parto del ingegno di molti Illustri Signori et elevati spirit di cotesta nobilissima città, essi venissero in man de gli huomini senza il favore di alcun virtuoso e letterato Signore, che alla loro nobiltà accrescesse ornamento. Onde ragionevolmente questa opera s'intitola a voi, acciò che, si come V.S. Ill. l'honora con i frutti del suo divino intelletto, così l'honora col nome. Essendo adunque voi Cavaliere ornatissimo di tutte quelle virtù, che a nobile Cavaliere si appartengono, e nel pregio delle lettere e nel l'opera de gl'inchiostri meritando più tosto le prime, che le seconde laudi, non vi sarà discaro che queste rime si ornino del vostro nome, affine che tanti Signori veggendo le loro fatiche uscire sotto a tal nome, più quelle e se medesimi apprezzino; e conoscono pari mente l'affettione, che il Magnifico e virtuoso M. Gabriello Giolito et io, che a V.S. Ill. Servitor sono, portiamo alle sue virtù. E le bascio la valorosa mano. Di Vinegia a di VIIII di Decembre. MDLI. Lodovico Dolce.

Prior to Dolce's Naples anthologies, two rival publishers secured the rights to follow the first two volumes of Giolito's highly successful poetry anthology series. In 1550, the printer Bartolomeo Cesana brought out what passed for volume 3 of the series, though it was never titled as such; and in 1551, Anselmo Giaccarello produced an anthology he published in Bologna under the title volume 4 (*Libro quarto delle rime*).[23] Unaware of the Cesana and Giaccarello volumes, Dolce brought out his first Naples anthology early in 1552, and publishing it as the sequel to Giolito's volumes 1 and 2, he titled it volume 3 (*Terzo libro*). Later that same year, he published a second edition of the Naples volume, this time calling it volume 5 (*Libro quinto*) to avoid the confusion of there being two volumes billed as volume 3 in the series.[24] Dolce's second edition of the Naples anthology differed significantly from his first, with a revised list of authors and a new dedicatory letter. The second edition sold so well that in 1555 Dolce issued a third edition of volume 5, again with a somewhat different roster of poets and a completely new dedicatory letter.

While not constituting a majority in any of the three versions of Dolce's *Rime di diversi napoletani*, the Neapolitan writers who had frequented Maria d'Aragona's salon dominate these volumes. Poems by Maria's deceased husband, the Marchese del Vasto, lead off both the second and third editions of the *Rime di diversi napoletani*, occupying pride of place there, though not in the first edition. In the fourth and last of Dolce's *Rime di diversi napoletani*, volume 7, published in 1556, Maria's influence remains palpable.[25] Though the Marchese del Vasto has been dropped from the roster of contributing poets and the dedicatee is Matteo Montenero, the lead poem in the book is Ferrante Carrafa's and the members of Maria's old Naples coterie—Angelo di Costanza, Giovam Maria Belprato, Bernardino Rota, Antonio Epicuro, Bernardo Tasso, and Luigi Tansillo—are still very much in evidence.

## ❧ FROM SELLING NAPLES TO SELLING WOMEN ☙

Dolce's Naples anthology served in many ways as the dress rehearsal for the final volume in Giolito's poetry series, the anthology of fifty-three women poets edited by Lodovico Domenichi: *Rime diverse d'alcune nobilissime, et virtuosissime donne*.[26] Domenichi's was perhaps the most daring of the anthologists' attempts to reproduce the image of the salon in an anthology. Dolce, in his four editions of the *Rime diverse di napoletani*, had lifted a previously unknown group of poets from relative obscurity and made men like Bernardino Rota, Angelo di Costanzo, and Ferrante Carafa literary celebrities in Venice. Domenichi hoped to do the same in his *Rime diverse delle donne*. Many of the women he published in this unusual, and in some ways bizarre, anthology were already famous, such as Vittoria Colonna, Veronica Gambara, Isabella di Morra, and Gaspara Stampa. The collected works of Colonna and Stampa, who were both dead by 1559, had gone to press in numerous solo editions, and all four women had previously published their poetry in the Giolito anthology series.

Like Dolce, Domenichi wanted to promote not just individual poets but an entire class of writers. Dolce had brought Naples to Venice. Domenichi's aim was broader. He wanted to show the reading public that a vibrant culture of intellectual women existed not merely in a few select cities but in every part of Italy. Neither women nor the Neapolitan poets were represented in the anthologies in significant numbers until 1551. Both groups had remained outside the cultural mainstream in northern Italy and certainly outside Venetian print culture until roughly that year. It was in 1551 that the Bolognese printer Anselmo Giaccarello published eight women authors—including Lucia Bertana, Giulia Aragona, Virginia Salvi, and Faustina Vallentina, in addition to Colonna and Gambara—in what would widely be considered the fourth volume in the Giolito poetry anthology series. Dolce, as we know, had sent to press his *Rime di diversi napoletani* that year in Venice.[27]

Two years later, Ruscelli published his volume 6 in the series: *Il sesto lbro delle rime di diversi eccellenti autori*.[28] Besides including a representative sample of the Neapolitan poets Dolce had published, Ruscelli's anthology featured nine female authors, the highest proportion of women poets taking part in any one of the Giolito series volumes to that date. Among Ruscelli's women poets in volume 6, Tullia d'Aragona, Ippolita Mirtilla, Coletta Pasquale, Maria Spinola, and Gaspara Stampa were making their first appearance in the Giolito anthologies. Only Vittoria Colonna, Veronica Gambara, and Virginia Salvi had already been anthologized in the series before 1553.

## ❧ THE WOMAN IN THE TEXT: PATRONS, POETS, AND BOOK DESIGN ☙

Sheryl Reiss and David Wilkins have recently called attention to the substantial role elite women played as secular patrons of painters, sculptors, and architects in Renaissance Italy. What forms did women's patronage take in a male-dominated culture, they asked; what, as the historian Kate Lowe has queried, was the "physiognomy of female patronage"?[29] The study of female patronage of the early printed book raises similar issues. Certainly elite women, as I have shown in chapter 1, were no less active as literary patrons and salonnières in the middle of the sixteenth century, and popular books published in Venice reflect the dependence of female writers and patrons on the printing industry for the dissemination of their fame.

In terms of book design, the most innovative literary publications of the 1550s in Italy show a sharp break with manuscript representations both of women's writings and of their activity as patrons.[30] Printed books of essays, dialogues, and poetry introduced literary women to the public for the first time as members of a larger group. Editors now produced women as participants in a collective enterprise. They were showcased as active in literary coteries, urban networks of literary women and men, and the republic of letters in general. The appendix of a new anthology or essay might contain a list of hundreds of patrons grouped under their home city, telephone book style—constituting a kind of intellectual social register. Girolamo Ruscelli's 1552 "Lecture on a Sonnet Dedicated to Maria d'Aragona" (*Lettura sopra un sonnetto alla Maria d'Aragona*), for example, included a ten-page index that named 259 notable women from thirty-five cities in Italy (fig. 3).[31] The highest concentrations of illustrious women, according to Ruscelli's lists, were in Milan (30 women), Venice (28), Savona (26), Novara and Genoa (25 each), Mantua (21), Rome (19), and Pavia (18).[32]

In 1549, Giolito's senior editor Lodovico Domenichi published a similar directory of distinguished contemporary women in his massive dialogue *La nobiltà delle donne* (The nobility of women).[33] But rather than using an appendix, Domenichi slipped the names of 195 Italian women patrons, salonnières, and writers and their cities directly into the discussion his two female and four male interlocutors were engaged in concerning women's achievements. There Domenichi effectively highlighted his notable 195 women by setting their names and those of their cities in capital letters, with Maria d'Aragona d'Avalos's and Giovanna d'Aragona Colonna's names leading off his list (fig. 4).

In both these design formats, editors represented women who were involved in the liberal arts and their cities as partners in reciprocal kudos. The more active literary women a city could boast, the greater its reputation as a magnet for culture and the arts. Even in Ruscelli's *Lettura sopra un sonetto,* a single critical essay devoted to the explication of one sonnet in honor of one woman, the author situated his essay, with his addendum of 259 notable women, within the larger social context of women's urban literary communities. Likewise, Domenichi's emphatic naming of important contemporary women writers or literary patrons in the text of his *Nobiltà delle Donne* graphically advertised the status of women not simply as wealthy donors but as members of exclusive literary coteries.

The aesthetic interest editors and publishers lavished on the paratextual apparatuses of the printed volume—features rarely if ever seen in manuscript books such as the elaborately engraved title page, the numerous indexes even for short books, the lengthy dedicatory letter, and perhaps an epilogue by the editor—further marked the Giolito anthology series and its promotion of such women as Vittoria Colonna and Veronica Gambara, who were not only authors but patrons of the arts.[34] By the 1540s and 1550s, women's names regularly appeared on the title pages of the solo-authored volumes of their writings. Vittoria Colonna's collected poems saw its eighth edition in 1559;

## SECONDA

...di corpo & d'animo vivevano ornate con le doti & felici carte del S. Ortensio Lando.

L.A.S. CATERINA Colonna, Gonzaga.
L.A.S. MARGHERITA Malaspina, Diffusa, degnamente chiamata il Sole.
L.A.S. CONTESSA CAMILLA Gonzaga, de' Rossi, sansonetta.
L.A.S. EMILIA Gonzaga, da Gazuolo.
L.A.S. PORTIA Gonzaga, Massimigliana.
L.A.S. ISABELLA Gattina, Emilia.
L.A.S. GIVLIA Allegretta, Coneggiana.
L.A.S. CAMILLA Pallesa.
L.A.S. LIVIA Cadena.
L.A.S. ISABELLA Rhoa.
L.A.S. MARTIA Nuuolona, gloriosa non meno per la nobiltà & bellezza sua, che per lo splendor della gentilezza & delle virtù del valoroso & saggio signor Cauagliero Nuuolone consorte suo.
L.A.S. MARGHERITA Strozza, de' Strozzi.
L.A.S. CAMILLA Ricciula.
L.A.S. LAVRA Conegiana, Grignana.
L.A.S. CONTESSA MANDELLA, Castigliona.
L.A.S. MARIETTA Strozza, de' Strozzi.
L.A.S. BIANCA Degli Vberti, Gonzaga.
L.A.S. VITTORIA Da Villachiara, Gonzaga.
L.A.S. CAMILLA Volante, Cauagliera.   Con altre infinite.

### A PAVIA.

L.A.S. CONTESSA MARGHERITA Visconti, de' Conti.
L.A.S. CONTESSA PAOLA Beccaria.
L.A.S. CONTESSA LVCRETIA Martinenga, Beccaria.
L.A.S. ALDA Torella, Leuata, glorioso soggetto con le bellezze, con la gentilezza, col valore, & con l'honestà sua, à tutti più rari spirti, che de giumenti con l'essempio di lei provano la perfettione delle Donne, & la felicità & splendor di quella nobilissima città, che la possiede.
L.A.S. LEONORA Beccaria.
L.A.S. OTTAVIA De' Belardi, Beccaria.
L.A.S. BIANCA Bottigella, de' Giorgi.

L.A.S.

---

## PARTE

...forse perfetto splendor suo, non verrà giornalmente mezzendosi, e come Aquile, coloro, che giorno & notte, presenti & lontani un lume lui senti.

### A BERGAMO.

L.A.S. FELICE Della Vicina, Brembata.
L.A.S. EMILIA Brembata, Solza.
L.A.S. CATERINA Carrara.
L.A.S. GIVDITTA Brembata.
L.A.S. LAVRA Brembata.
L.A.S. ISOTTA Brembata, Secca.
L.A.S. MINERVA Rota, Brembata.
L.A.S. MINERVA, Secca.
L.A.S. PACE Gramella, Tassa.            Et altre molte,
laquali io non racconto, perciochè nem le rammento, ne mi pare, poi che io in cominciato à questo potere adurre altre, chè quantunque bellissime, appresso tanta luce appariscono.

### A CREMONA.

L.A.S. LVCRETIA Picenarda, Crotta.
L.A.S. PAOLA Gambara, Trecca.
L.A.S. COLLATINA Da Cassallo Trecca.
L.A.S. CAMILLA Carriola, Stanga.
L.A.S. ISABELLA Picenarda, dalle Torre.
L.A.S. CAMILLA Di Barbo dal pesce.
L.A.S. NOSTRA Da' Borgo.
L.A.S. MARGHERITA Ferrara, Trecca.
L.A.S. LVCRETIA Manna, Crotta.
L.A.S. ANNA Dal Ostron, dal Pesce.
L.A.S. ARTEMISIA Regia de' Moggi.
L.A.S. BARBARA Ferrara, Botta.
L.A.S. PALEMIA Galtrura, Mainolda.        Et molte altre.

### A MANTOVA.

L.A.S. ISABELLA Gonzaga, Signora di Pudino.
L.A.S. LVCRETIA Gonzaga Manfrona, le cui sopr'humani bellezze...

· FIGURE 3 ·
A published "social register" of literary women listed by their cities. From Girolamo Ruscelli's *Lettura . . . sopra un sonetto dell'illustriss. signor marchese della Terza alla divina signora marchesa del Vasto* (Venice: Griffio, 1552), fols. 64v–65. Courtesy of the Newberry Library.

> LIBRO
>
> D. ISABELLA COLONNA *principeſſa di Sulmo-*
> *na, laquale oltra ch'è nobiliſsima, è la piu gentile, &*
> *accorta Signora, c'hoggi uiua* D. CLARICE OR-
> SINA *Principeſſa di Stigliano, ſauia, di ſangue nobi-*
> *le, bella di forma, ornata di coſtumi, di leggiadra ho-*
> *neſtà piena.* D. VITTORIA COLONNA, &
> *la ſorella ſua.* D. GIERONIMA *figliuole del Signo-*
> *re Aſcanio, ambedue per ogni riſpetto digniſsime d'ogni*
> *honore.* D. DIANORA SANSEVERINA *figli-*
> *uola del Principe di Biſignano, non meno nobiliſsima,*
> *che bella, & degna d'immortal gloria, per le infinite uir-*
> *tu dell'animo ſuo. Coſtei è una nuoua Sapho de noſtri*
> *giorni : come hanno fatto fede le dolciſsime rime*
> *Thoſcane prodotte dalla ſua leggiadra uena.* D. ISA-
> BELLA DI TOLLEDO *Ducheſſa di Caſtrouilla-*
> *ri, figliuola del Vicere di Napoli, & ſorella della Signo-*
> *ra Ducheſſa di Fiorenza, nobiliſsima, magnanima, &*
> *prudente.* D. VITTORIA GALIOTTA *Signo-*
> *ra nobiliſsima, & per le rariſsime doti datele da Dio di-*
> *gniſsima d'immortale honore. Et ben meriterebbe che*
> *la mia lingua pareggiaſſe il merito ſuo, e'l deſiderio, il-*
> *quale ho di lodarla.* LA S. CORNELIA DI
> LIGORI, *belliſsima, & gratioſiſsima Signora, oltra*
> *la nobiltà quanto altre, che ſiano hoggi nel mondo.* LA
> S. VITTORIA CAPANNA *moglie del Signor*
> *Hettorre Geſualdo, la cui bellezza uolendo io lodare, ſa-*
> *rebbe un uoler giungere dell'acque al mare. Perche tali*
> *ſono le qualità del ſuo bello, che il giorno pare hauer*
> *ſplendore dal lume de gli occhi ſuoi. L'harmonia mo-*
> *ſtra addolcirſi della melodia delle ſue parole.* La pri-

· FIGURE 4 ·

Publicizing the names of women writers and patrons
in a literary text. From Lodovico Domenichi's dialogue
*La nobiltà delle donne* (Venice: Giolito, 1549), fol. 249v.
Courtesy of the Newberry Library.

and the even more successful Laura Terracina, by 1566, had seen sixteen editions of her poetry go to press, nine of her sonnets, and seven printings of her
*Discorsi*, which Deanna Shemek has characterized as not a commentary but
a feminist response to Ariosto's *Orlando Furioso*.[35] Advertising the name of its
female author, patron, and dedicatee on its title page, a book might frame that
first page with an engraving of a classical temple, suggesting both the sublime
character of the book's patron and the book itself as a shrine (fig. 5). Solo-
authored volumes sometimes displayed their author's portrait on the frontispiece, as does the Valvassorio edition of Laura Terracina's *Quinte rime* (1552),

in which she is shown in profile in a high-necked dress, her hair bound up in a snood. Her portrait is set in an oval frame. The words "La Signora Laura Terracina" encircle the oval frame while crouching satyrs, satyrs' heads, a Muse holding laurel branches and a lyre, and a winged angel fill the rectangular space outside the oval (fig. 6).

The new design practices represented marketing strategies. As such, they suggest the degree to which publishers showcased women authors and their

· FIGURE 5 ·

Title page illustration of a temple shrine to Venus and Minerva,
from Ottavio Sammarco's anthology *Il tempio della divina signora Geronima
Colonna d'Aragona,* honoring Giovanna d'Aragona's daughter (Padua:
Pasquati, 1568). Courtesy of the Newberry Library.

patrons in order to reach out to a new audiences and to tap new readers. Certainly, a working reciprocity between women and their presses drove marketing strategy and book design. While the publishers found that the blazoning of women's names on their title pages and in their indexes sold books, their women authors and anthology patrons enjoyed the publicity they got as authors, intellectuals, and underwriters of culture.

But popular early printed books aimed to appeal to a variety of audiences. Unlike Ruscelli's *Lettura* or Domenichi's *La nobiltà delle donne*, which targeted an elite readership, the Giolito anthologies were great social levelers. From the first volume on, poets from the northern academies dominated the author lists of the anthologies, and many of these writers came from the enormously

· FIGURE 6 ·

A woodcut of Laura Terracina from the frontispiece of her fifth
book of collected poems, *Quinte rime* (Venice: Valvassori, 1552).
Courtesy of the Newberry Library.

influential but socially diverse Infiammati academy in Padua.[36] The early anthologies, like the northern academies, represented a melting pot in which class, occupational, and gender distinctions went practically unmarked and played no role in the organization of the volumes.[37] In author indexes of the anthologies, the sons and daughters of artisans mingle with noblewomen, courtesans, ambassadors, soldiers, and royalty without editorial comment. In volume 1, the son of a scissors maker, Anton Francesco Doni, and the noblewoman Vittoria Colonna share textual space as do the noble governor of Milan, Alfonso d'Avalos, the shoemaker's son Pietro Aretino, the ruler of Correggio, Veronica Gambara, and the courtesan Francesca Baffa. In volume 6, the courtesan Tullia d'Aragona shares space with the Sienese noblewoman Virginia Martini de Salvi, while the jeweler's daughter Gaspara Stampa appears in the same anthology as the Neapolitan nobleman Giovanbattista d'Azzia, who courted the king of Naples' granddaughter, Maria d'Aragona.

After Dolce's Naples volumes, more geographical diversity characterized the anthologies. But the publishers' Tuscanization of Italian—the appropriation of the dialect of Petrarch and Dante as an editor's gold standard in preparing a text for publication—did more than anything else to create a cultural hegemony that stood in stark contrast to the continuing political disunity of the Italian cities. Still, anxiety over such wholesale linguistic and cultural assimilation did not disappear overnight. Dolce's dedicatory letter to Ferrante Carafa, for example, betrays a concern on his part that Carafa and his fellow Neapolitans might be angered by his Tuscanization and perhaps mistranslation of their works. The poems, he told Carafa apologetically, "arrived in my hands without the benefit of a learned gentleman who would have been able to add ornament to their nobility."

## ❧ THE VENETIAN INQUISITION AND THE ATTACK ON LITERATURE ❧

On August 12, 1553, Cardinal Gian Pietro Carafa (later Pope Paul IV) and Fra Michele Ghislieri (later Pope Pius V), then commissioner general of the Roman Inquisition, called on the Venetian Republic to outlaw the printing of Hebrew books in Venice and to condemn the Talmud to public burning.[38] The order was received by the Venetian Inquisition, a magistracy created by the Venetian Republic, consisting of three priests who represented the papacy and three elected members of the Venetian government who sat on the republic's all powerful Council of Ten.[39] On October 18, the Council of Ten ordered all the houses of the Jews in the ghetto searched so that the Talmuds could be collected, and on October 21 a bonfire of Jewish books was made in the Piazza San Marco. Paul Grendler has estimated that hundreds of thousands of Jewish books were burned in cities all across Italy.[40] That year the Jewish publishing firms in Venice moved en masse to Cremona, Sabbioneta, and Riva di Trento.[41]

The following year, the Venetian Inquisition commissioned Giolito to publish a new catalog of prohibited books. In 1553–54, he and his rival publishers flooded the market with new poetry, much of it in the form of anthologies: between Dolce's Naples anthologies, Ruscelli's volume 6 of the *Rime di diversi autori* series, his *Lettura sopra un sonetto alla Maria d'Aragona*, and his massive poetry anthology titled, *Tempio della Giovanna d'Aragona* printed by Pietrasanta, which contained verses in four different languages, poetry appeared to be alive and well in Venice. But the fears of the intellectual community were by no means allayed. The new *Catalogo* Giolito produced in 1554 banned the complete works of some 290 authors, and many standard philosophical works from the humanist curriculum topped the list of books marked for burning: Dante's *De monarchia*, Marsilio of Padua's *Defensor pacis*, Lorenzo Valla's *De libero arbitrio*, and the philosophical and theological works of William of Occam were among them.[42] Within months of its promulgation, the Venetian book guildsmen protested violently, and the Senate withdrew Giolito's *Catalogo* from circulation as they had Valgrisi's index five years earlier.

But it was poetry the Roman Holy Office targeted for prohibition, labeling numerous authors "immoral" and "lascivious" in 1559, when the new *Catalogo* came out banning the publication and sale of the complete works of some 550 authors and many individual titles.[43] Writers, editors, and their publishers had more reason than ever to exercise caution. In addition to condemning the works of Rabelais, Boccaccio, Poggio, and Machiavelli, a number of poets who were the mainstays of the Giolito anthologies were now banned, among them: Aretino, Berni, Nicolò Franco, Bernardino Tomitano, and Giovanni Della Casa, who had authored the 1549 *Catalogo*. The Venetian publishers represented by the priors of the bookmen's guild at first met and agreed to boycott Paul's orders. But when the pope applied economic sanctions to the publishers and booksellers, their will to resist fell apart.[44]

The 1559 index was promulgated that year not only in Venice but Florence, Naples, Bologna, Genoa, Novara, and Rimini, and public bonfires of books were staged in all of those cities.[45] On March 18 of the same year, on the Saturday before Palm Sunday, between ten and twelve thousand books were publicly burned in Rome.[46]

## ⚜ DOMENICHI: CONVICTED HERETIC, PUBLISHER OF WOMEN ⚜

It was in this climate that Giolito's senior editor, Lodovico Domenichi, gave his manuscript of fifty-three women poets' works to Vincenzo Busdragho to publish—not in Venice but Lucca, which had the advantage of being an independent republic and one located at some distance from the bonfires of the Inquisition.[47] In the dedicatory letter he wrote on June 1, 1559, to Giannoto Castiglione, a Milanese friar who had just entered the service of Paul IV, Domenichi emphasized how long he had been developing his anthology of women and noted how important it was to him to find the right venue for his book. At the time, Domenichi was under contract to write an official history of the Medici court, and to facilitate his work, he had been given an apartment in the Medici palace in 1559, so he had no pressing financial need to go forward with the Busdragho anthology.[48] Nor would Cosimo, who was no champion of women as a class, have commissioned the 1559 anthology.

With a prior conviction for having translated and edited books the Roman Holy Office considered heretical, Domenichi was no stranger to the Inquisition. His long imprisonment in the fortezza in Pisa in 1552 for his hand in the publication of the contraband *Nicodemiana,* a book attributed at the time to Calvin, and the *Commentarii* of the German theologian Johannes Sleidanus had made him wary.[49] He wrote Giannoto:

> Many years have passed since I first devoted my whole heart and all my efforts—to the extent that it has been possible for me to do so—to the celebration of the nobility and excellence of women, something of which I have assembled in a book suitable to the project. Ever since I have had this idea, I have placed myself in circumstances that would seemingly best allow me to be able to procure honor and glory for them. And so, with the help of some loving and great minds devoted to feminine valor, I have collected from various parts of the country a reasonable quantity of poetry composed by women. Up to this point in time I have kept these poems with me for that pleasure which only the most beloved and valued things can convey, even though up until the time I began to collect these poems, I was resolved in my desire to publicize them to the world in every way possible making use of the presses to do so, with the object of enlightening those men who still harbor doubts concerning the greatness of the feminine intellect.

> Sono già molti anni passati, ch'essendo Io con l'animo, e con l'opere tutto volto a celebrare quanto per me sì poteva allhora, la nobiltà, et eccellentia delle Donne; la qualcosa Io ridussi poi in un giusto volume; sì come il pensier mi guidava, mi posi

in un medesimo tempo ra[d]unare ciò che mi pareva potere procurar loro gloria e honore. Cosi con l'aiuto d'alcuni amorevoli miei, e grande mente affettionati al valor Donnesco, raccolsi da più part assai ragionevole quantità di rime composte da Donne. Le quali rime sono poi state insino ad hora appresso di me in quel grado tenute, che le più care e pretiose cose si soglion tenere. Et benchè insino allhora, ch'Io cominciai a raccorle, Io fossi fermo di volere in ogni modo publicarle al mondo col mezo delle stampe, per chiarir coloro, i quali stanno in dubbio delle grandezza dell' ingegno feminile.

Domenichi presented himself in his letter to Giannoto as a man who had built his career on the promotion of intellectual women. While this was true enough, he had made a slow start. As not only the first editor but the origi-nator of the enormously influential Giolito anthologies, it is surprising that he chose to publish so few women in the first of the anthologies. Among the ninety some male poets in the three published editions of volume 1 (two in 1546, one in 1549), he included only five women; Francesca Baffa, Vittoria Colonna, Veronica Gambara, Laudomia Forteguerri and Laura Terracina; and in the first edition only Baffa, Colonna, and Gambara were represented.[50]

In his role as senior editor at Giolito, Domenichi also assisted, if not di-rectly, in fostering the fame of the firm's other frontlist authors, such as Tul-lia d'Aragona, whose editor was his friend Girolamo Muzio, and the prolific Vittoria Colonna whose *Rime* Lodovico Dolce shepherded to press at Giolito, after her works had already appeared in solo editions brought out by five dif-ferent publishing houses, four of them among the most prestigious presses in Venice.[51]

The Naples-born and educated poet Terracina can be counted as Domenichi's most successful protégée, though she is absent from his 1559 anthology of women, probably to avoid saturating the market for her work, since by that time her career had reached its apogee.[52] After her debut in volume 1 of the Gio-lito anthologies, Domenichi edited five solo editions of her *Rime* between 1548 and 1565 for Giolito. As a result, in Venice, Lucca, and Naples, publishers soon sought the rights to print the flood of new work she was producing. Valvas-sore published her response to Ariosto's *Orlando furioso*, titled *Discorso* (1550) and her *Quinte rime* (1552); and Giolito, in collaboration with Domenichi, brought out the *Discorso* four more times (1550, 1551, 1559, 1566). Domenichi's friend and publisher Busdragho published her *Sesto rime* in Lucca in 1558, and the Venetian publisher Farri produced her fifth and sixth collections of *Rime* again in 1560.

Considering that the Venetian presses would rerun Terracina's *Discorso*, a thoroughly secular work, five more times before 1608, her remarkable successes would tend to support Paul Grendler's argument that, in the end, the Inquisition failed to derail the course of Italian literary history.[53] Hers is an interesting case in point. Lacking the insulation of a powerful noble family to defend her, Terracina might easily have become the target of the Holy Office at the height of the Inquisition in the later 1550s. She was never identified as a disciple of Valdés, an adherent of the *spirituali,* or a member of any of the numerous reform cells in Naples in the 1540s, but she may have looked like a Valdesian given her intellectual circle. Her mentor and the dedicatee of her first solo publication, the 1548 *Rime,* Vincenzo Belprato was at that time the host and leader of a group that met at his palazzo in Naples to discuss reform theology and to spread the gospel according to Valdés.[54] She also directed an unusually long and warm dedicatory letter, published in both the 1551 and 1554 editions of her *Discorsi,* to another alleged heretic—and friend—Giovanni Bernardino Bonifacio, the Marchese d'Oria.[55] Bonifacio was a celebrated intellectual and a committed exponent of Valdesian thought, who had gone so far as to publicly repudiate the Catholic mass.[56] He emigrated to Basel after being arraigned on heresy charges in Naples. Terracina dedicated numerous cantos in her *Discorso* to the ardent female disciples of Valdés: Costanza d'Avalos, Giulia Gonzaga, Vittoria Colonna, Maria d'Aragona, and Giovanna d'Aragona, the group of women who constitute the primary subjects of the preceding chapter.

But the work Domenichi regarded as the real precedent for his anthology of fifty-three women was his *La nobiltà delle donne,* his own contribution to the *querelle des femmes* (the debate on women).[57] The work was a massive dialogue in five books on the subject of the nature and worth of women. A virtual encyclopedia on the *querelle,* Domenichi's dialogue drew shamelessly, as he admitted in his epilogue, from all the moderns on the subject: he listed Agrippa, Galeazzo Capella, Baldessar Castiglione, Vicentio Maggio, Lodovico Martelli, Sperone Speroni, and Girolamo della Rovere as his models.[58] In book 1, the Milanese noblewoman Violante Bentivoglia presides over three male interlocutors—Francesco Grassi, Pierfrancesco Visconti, and Girolamo Muzio—figures known to some though perhaps not all readers. In books 2–4, Violante officiates among four male speakers, and in the final book, two female speakers and four males debate. In the *Nobiltà,* Domenichi's *querelle* theme, dialogue format, and ensemble of real people as speakers work in tandem to produce a virtual salon, the favored mise-en-scène for sixteenth-century dialogues. Perhaps the most novel section of the work is the catalog of distinguished contemporary women grouped together by their cities in book 5, in which a total of twenty-five cities are represented by the women named.

In his rambling *La nobiltà delle donne,* Domenichi set the stage for the radically different kind of anthology he would produce in his 1559 Busdragho volume: the gathering of women from numerous Italian cities who would address one another across differences of city, rank, profession, age, and occupation, as though they were attending an academy meeting or a salon.[59]

## ❧ ANTHOLOGY AS A VIRTUAL SALON: THE *RÉSEAU* ❧

Literary scholars have observed that the Giolito anthologies introduced two new poetic forms: the cluster or *réseau* (web) of poems composed by a group of friends; and the miniature *canzoniere,* in which the author's personal drama dominates the whole of the poetry book, as with Petrarch's unfulfilled love for Laura in the *Rime sparse.*[60] The mini-*canzoniere* compresses the poet's book-length narrative and dramatizes it within a sequence of five or more poems. Lodovico Domenichi employed both these innovative frameworks in his *Rime di diverse donne* (Anthology of women poets [1559]), but the *réseau* and the mini-canzonière are also strikingly in evidence in Lodovico Dolce's Naples anthologies (Giolito's *Rime di diversi napoletani,* volume 5 [1551–55]). In the *Rime di diversi napoletani,* a model in many ways for Domenichi's anthology of women, Dolce was the first Giolito editor to bill himself as the producer of writers of a particular social group, though the cultural divide in the 1559 volume is one of gender rather than geography.

Observing Domenichi's characteristic habit of grouping poets together who address one another as friends in his anthology of women poets, Marie-Françoise Piejus has coined the term *réseau* to describe the lyric ensemble.[61] She noted that in Domenichi's anthology of women poets the predominance of the dedicatory or choral mode, as Victoria Kirkham has termed it, marks the work as different from Giolito's poetry anthologies prior to 1551: fifty-six of the poems are addressed to friends of the author.[62] One such *réseau* is exemplified in the exchange between four women—three from Pistoia and one from Florence in Domenichi's *Rime di diverse donne:*

> Giulia Braccali de' Ricciardi Pistolese. "Ogni spirto fedel, lasso si doglia"; no addressee (37)[63]
> Giulia Braccali de' Ricciardi Pistolese to Cornelia Brunozzi de Villani. "Veggio coperte sotto un chiaro velo" (37)
> Cornelia Brunozzi de'Villani. "Hor si vedrà, chi più fedele amore"; no addressee (38)

Cornelia Brunozzi de'Villani to Maria Martelli de'Panciatichi. "Se la figlia di Leda hebbe già il vanto" (38)

Cornelia Brunozzi de'Villani again to Maria Martelli. "Lassa, di chi doler mi deggio homai" (39)

Maria Martelli de'Panciatichi Fiorentina to Cornellia de' Villani Pistolese. "Per quelle dolci rime anch' Io m'accorsi" (39)

Maria Martelli again to Cornelia Villani. "Cornelia, mia, ben lode assai conviensi" (40)

Selvaggia Braccali de'Bracciolini Pistolese to Maria Martelli de' Panciatichi. "Ben ti puoi dir felice, e al mondo sola" (40)

Domenichi's ordering of the four speakers in this *réseau* of poems has a symmetry resembling the figures in a dance. But he was not the first of Giolito's editors to use the *réseau*. Dolce displayed the same kind of symmetrical arrangement of speakers in the ensemble he reproduced around Ferrante Carrafa and his circle in his first Naples anthology:

Bernardino Rota to Ferrante Carrafa (78)

Risposta Ferrante Carrafa to Rota (78)

Angelo di Costanza to Ferrante Carrafa (79)

Risposta Ferrante to Angelo di Costanza (79–80)

Luigi Tansillo to Ferrante Carrafa (80–81, the next six sonnets are eulogies on the death of Carrafa's brother and his responses to the eulogies)

Risposta di Ferrante Carrafa to Tansillo (81)

Antonio Epicuro to Ferrante Carrafa (81–82)

Risposta del Ferrante Carrafa to Epicuro (82)

Bernardino Rota a Ferrante Carrafa (82–83)

Risposta of Ferrante Carrafa to Rota (83)

The *réseau* form imitates the salon, whether real or imaginary, in its interactivity, face-to-face style, variety of actors and themes, and mix of personalities. Dolce's *réseau* appears to have come almost unmediated from the meetings of the Ischia/Naples coterie. Not only are the poets the same as those who frequented Costanza d'Avalos's salon, but the Ischian-Neapolitan Petrarchists Rota, Costanza, Carrafa, Tansillo, and Epicuro are all in evidence again in Dolce's *Rime di napoletani* as well. His anthology reproduces the social group and its dialogic performance practices. There are solo songs, duets, quartets, and, even a quintet as in the *réseau* that revolves around the figure of Ferrante

Carrafa, the dedicatee of all Dolce's Naples anthologies and here the impresario of his group.

Anticipating Moderata Fonte's utopian dialogue for women only, *The Worth of Women* (1600), the women poets in Domenichi's Pistoia-Florence *réseau* represent a circle of contrasting female characters captured in conversation with one another. As in the dialogue, the ideology of the anthology privileges the ensemble over the individual speaker. Framing this dialogue between four women are two polemicists, each of whom addresses the group. Giulia Braccali de' Ricciardi articulates religious sentiments characteristic of the *spirituali* or Valdesians, regarded in the high Counter-Reform fever of 1555–59 as bordering on heresy.[64] Her message is clear: only through grace is salvation possible. Happiness and lasting contentment are accessible to sinners not through the offering of good works but by God's suffering and redemption alone.

Selvaggia Braccali, in contrast, calls for solidarity among women and urges her "sisters" to take pride in their sex. In a sonnet addressed to Maria Martelli de Panciatichi, Selvaggia opens her poem with begrudging praise for the city of Florence because it is Maria's hometown. Summoning up images of Minerva and Amor rather than the Christian God, Braccali urges her "faithful companions and sisters" to join with the woodland deity Flora in eulogizing Maria as preliminary to what should be their real purpose:

> And yet my trusted friends and sisters,
> let us celebrate with Flora in this woman,
> the glory and the honor of the female sex.

> Et però fide mie compagne, e sore,
> Rallegrianci con Flora per costei
> Del sesso feminil gloria, et honore.

Cornelia Brunozzi Villani and Maria Martelli cast themselves as a pair of Petrarchan lovers: Cornelia is the pursuer—ardent, hurt, angry by turns—chasing her beloved hopelessly, while Maria Martelli plays the "Laura" role.[65] Employing a major Cinquecento topos for the intellectual woman, Cornelia and Maria describe one another as possessed not only of beauty but of virtue as well.[66] Exemplifying "genius and immortal beauty," as Selvaggia Braccali expresses it, Maria offers Cornelia the excuse for her silence that the winds had blown contrary to her desire but now the storm was over ("Et hebbi un tempo in ciò contrari venti: / Hor sono in porto"). Nothing is known about any of the four women other than the information in the headings to their poems, where their husbands' names and native cities are given. The great eighteenth-century historian of Italian literary women, Luisa Bergalli, reports only that all four women in Domenichi's Pistoia-Florence circle flourished between 1535 and 1540.[67] But the culture of women-led salons was also a feature of the social world of sixteenth-century Tuscany, as we will see in chapter 4, which describes the activities of intellectual women and their groups in Siena. Giulia Braccali leads the dance.[68]

GIULIA BRACCALI DE' RICCIARDI PISTOLESE
(no dedicatee is named, but Braccali seems to address the whole group)

Every faithful weary spirit mourns,
and changes its sweet smile to bitter tears,
gazing intently at the Lord of Paradise,
who left on the cross his mortal veil.
What man is so cruel that he will not wish
to bathe his breast or face with tears today,
seeing the king of heaven taken away, divided
from his soul, having died in such great pain?
O immortal goodness, O steadfast love,
that, with anguish cruel and fresh,
you wished to open to us a path to Heaven!
It pleased you to wash away our sins
with your own blood since, moved by pious zeal,
you wished to bring the sinner happiness.


    Ogni spirto fedel, lasso si doglia,
E in pianto amaro cangi il dolce riso,
Rimirando il Signor del Paradiso
Lasciata in croce haver l'humana spoglia.
    Qual sarà sì crudel, c'hoggi non voglia
Di lagrime bagnarsi il petto, o il viso,
Veggendo il Re del ciel tolto, e diviso
Da l'alma, e morto in tanta pena, doglia?
    O superna bontate, o saldo amore,
Che con un nuovo, e sì crudel tormento
Aprir volesti a Noi la vie del Cielo.
    Lavar co'l proprio sangue il nostro errore
Ti piacque mosso da pietoso zelo
Di voler fare il peccator contento.

*(Rime d'alcune donne, 37)*

GIULIA BRACCALI DE' RICCIARDI TO
CORNELIA BRUNOZZI DE VILLANI

Covered by a bright veil, I see
as many virtues as heaven can bestow.
Truly I wonder how does the earth flood
with light while the heavens must grow dark?
Love, faith, beauty, and zeal for honor
are encompassed in you, showing us
true glory which appears in heaven,
where no fear of heat or cold is found.
And when this lovely body turns to earth
and dark fog engulfs us, it will be bright there:
O fearful day, for whoever remains here!
And so I pray the Lord it will please him
to release my soul, which my body chains,
before I am alone and mourning you.

   Veggio coperte sotto un chiaro velo
Quante virtuti il ciel può mai donare;
Meravigliomi ben come illustrare
s'habbia la terra, e farsi oscuro il cielo?
   Amor, fede, bellezze, e d'honor zelo
chiuse in voi sono, a Noi per dimostrare
La vera gloria, che nel cielo appare,
senza, temer giamai caldo, né gielo,
   Et quando diverrà il bel corpo terra,
oscure nubi havrem, là sù fia chiaro;
O giorno spaventoso, a chi resta.
   Ond' Io prego il Signor, che gli sia caro
L'alma discior, che la mia spoglia serra
Prima, ch' Io dopo voi sia sola, e mesta.

*(Rime d'alcune donne, 37)*

CORNELIA VILLANI (no addressee)

Now we shall see who brings the most
faithful love to this bright star;
now he must not stay hidden, nor should he say,
"I keep my passion closed within."
Now it is time to reveal the heart,
and to speak, though not called upon.

The lover I will call sincere and true
is not that man who says every hour
that he burns; nor will that lover be called
perfect who claims he lives and dies for a "yes,"
nor if he says, "You're my lady and goddess."
But that man who stays constant in troubled times,
from him I'll say that true love comes: and he'll be
that man who'll come before all others.

Hor si vedrà, chi più fedele amore
A questa chiara stella havrà portato;
Hor non deve Egli più restar celato,
Né dir; dentr'hò rinchiuso il fero ardore.

Hor tempo è ben di palesar' il core,
Et risponder anchor che non chiamato;
Et quel dirò sincero, e innamorato,
Non già chi d'arder dice a tutte l'hore.

Nè per mostrar, ch'in un sì muoia, e viva,
Mai chiamerassi alcun perfetto Amante,
Nè men per dir; Tu sei mia Donna, e Diva.

Ma a casi adversi, allhor chi sta costante,
Da lui dirò, che vero Amor deriva;
Et quel sarà, che verrà primo innante.

*(Rime d'alcune donne, 38)*

## Cornelia Villani to Maria Martelli de'Panciatichi

If the daughter of Leda once gained the prize
over all those women who were ever lovely
and charming, you alone, wise Maria,
are among the ones who need not envy them at all—
since the fame of your lovely, charming,
saintly face rises high above the stars.
Nor do I think that Apelles or
Praxiteles ever painted such a face,
or that anyone else has ever known so much.
Vermilion roses in snow set off your amorous eyes
—so well that they make Phaethon's father
jealous: O beauty superhuman, proud,
and quick, who can resist your gaze,
and who will not soon be Love's slave?

Se la figlia di Leda hebbe già il vanto
Di quante furon mai leggiadre, e belle;
Voi sol, saggia Maria, siete di quelle
Da non le invidiar tanto, nè quanto:
    che'l bel vostro leggiadro, unico, e santo
Volto, s'alza per fama oltre le stelle;
Nè credo tal mai ne pingesse Apelle,
O Prasitelle, o s'altri seppe tanto.
    Che le rose vermiglie infra la neve
Son si ben poste a gli amorosi lampi,
Che fanno invidia al padre di Fetonte.
    O beltà soprahumane, altere, e pronte,
Chi sarà quel, ch'a rimirarvi scampi,
Et non resti d'Amor suggetto in breve?

                        *(Rime d'alcune donne, 38)*

### CORNELIA TO MARIA MARTELLI, AGAIN

Alas, whom should I complain of now?
Of heaven, who gave you so much beauty?
Or of your heart, so full of hardness,
    that it delights in keeping me in pain?
The first has shot his darts[69] at you—brilliant rays!
In such a way that each one takes joy in their aim,
The other shows such harshness to anyone who loves you
    that I never thought it could be so cold and hard.
And so, of you alone I must complain:
    the more my trust and ardor for you increase,
    the more your compassion dwindles, lady,
your cruelty instead grows greater,
    and so my heart has no more hope,
since it goes, it seems, from bad to worse.

    Lassa, di chi doler mi deggio homai;
O del ciel, che vi diè tanta bellezza,
O pur del vostro cor pien di durezza
Che sì diletta mantenermi in guai?
    L'un fatto v'hà quadrella: chiari rai,
Talche a mirargli n'hà ciascun vaghezza;
L'altro a chi v'ama mostra tanta asprezza,
ch'aspero, e duro sì, mai no'l pensai.

Doler adunque sol di Voi mi deggio,
Che quanto più mia fè cresce, e l'ardore,
Più và scemando in Voi donna pietate.

Anzi crescendo in Voi vien crudeltate;
Tal che speranza, più non hà il mio core,
Poi che si vede andar di male in peggio.

*(Rime d'alcune donne, 390)*

## MARIA MARTELLI DE PANCIATICHI FIORENTINA TO CORNELIA VILLANI

From those sweet sonnets I've also seen
that your desire is full of ardent tenderness.
And so, to lure you away from cruel suspicion,
I've quickly put my hand to pen.
Since, like a dray with spurs and bits,
I will obey your signs and hints,
and giving you safe haven in my heart,
I have no doubts about your wishes;
If I did not write you gentle verses,
it comes from awful fear that plagues me now
that my allotted time on earth may weary you.
Such was Croesus'[70] happy hour, when Cyrus
freed him from the burning pyre: and in asking
for such mercy, my heart thus honors you.


Per quelle dolci rime anch'Io m'accorsi
Del desir vostro pien d'ardente affetto;
Onde per trarvi fuor di rio sospetto.
A la penna la man veloce porsi.

Com'a destrieri a Me son sproni, e morsi
I vostri cenni, ond'obedir'aspetto;
Et col cor fatto a Voi fido ricetto
Non resto punto a voler vostri in forsi.

Et, se non v'ho versi soavi scritto,
Nasce dal timor rio, ch'è meco anchora,
Che non v'annoi il viver mio prescritto.

Qual fù di Cresso quella felice hora,
Che Ciro il liberò dal fuoco afflitto,
Chiedendo' Io tal mercè; mio cor v'honora.

*(Rime d'alcune donne, 39)*

## Maria Martelli's second sonnet to Cornelia

It's fitting, my Cornelia, to praise her
who can recite the truth in a sweet voice;
but her who portrays it following the model
of the greatest writers, one must adorn.
Thus you, with words and high heart, raise
yourself above the crowd: you can show
that rare virtue, which brings a lovely woman
glory beyond measure and is her crown.
I remember how much I longed to see
the smallest part of your valor;
yet for a time the winds were contrary to me.
Now I am in port and desire no more;
yet it's only right that I should pay you honor,
until these lights of mine go out.


Cornelia mia; ben lode assai conveniensi
A chi sà dolce in voce il ver narrare;
Ma a chi'l descrive, è lecito adornare,
Et a miglior scrittori ogn'hor'attiensi.
    Però Tu con parole, et alti sensi
Ti levi fuor del volgo, e sai mostrare
La virtù rara, che qual gemma appare
In bella donna, e rende i pregi immensi.
    Tornami a mente, quanto Io desiai
Veder del valor tuo la minor parte;
Et hebbi un tempo in ciò contrari venti:
    Hor sono in porto, e più non bramo homai;
Ma sol convenien, ch'attenda ad honorarte,
Fin che saran questi miei lumi spenti.

*(Rime d'alcune donne, 40)*


## Selvaggia Bracali de'Bracciolini Pistolese to Maria Martelli de Panciatichi

You can call yourself happy and the only city
in the world that shelters in its nest Maria,
whose mind and beauty are immortal,
whose eternal fame flies up to heaven,
so that she steals from Minerva her throne and title
since she rivals her in every virtue;

nor does she fear Love's shafts and bow,
since inner virtue makes her law and school.
This woman deserves praise and trophies,
since her grace and bright splendor
conquer this world's men and gods above.
And so, my trusted friends and sisters,
let us celebrate for her, along with Flora,[71]
the glory and the honor of the female sex.

Ben ti puoi dir felice, e al mondo sola
Patria, che nel tuo nido alberghi tale
Maria d'ingegno, e di beltà immortale,
Di cui sù in ciel l'eterna fama vola,
    tal ch'a Minerva il seggio, e 'l nome invola,
A lei d'ogni virtute essendo uguale;
Ne teme di cupido arco, ne strale,
Che pudicità in Lei tien norma, e scola.
    Questa è degna di lode, e di trofei,
Che la sua gratia, e'l chiaro suo splendore
Gli huomini vince al mondo; e in ciel gli Dei:
    Et però fide mie compagne, e sore,
Rallegrianci con Flora per costei
Del sesso feminil gloria, et honore.

*(Rime d'alcune donne, 40)*

Beyond the *réseau* and the miniature *canzoniere*, the 1559 Domenichi anthology reproduced the woman-led salon in other ways. Other gendered genres such as the woman-to-woman duet, addressed and responded to by women, suggested a new kind of salon in women's literary history. Thirty-five poems in the women's anthology were dedicated by one woman to another, while women addressed twenty-three of their poems to men. So, in sum, an evening spent reading or performing pieces from an anthology at home or among friends might have included a women's duet, a quartet or quintet, and a selection of solo pieces from a sample-size *canzoniere*.

## ❧ THE MINI-*CANZONIERE* IN DOMENICHI'S SALON FOR WOMEN ❧

Domenichi's 1559 women's anthology borrowed a second framing device from Dolce that, as Erika Milburn has shown, was a signature feature of the Giolito

Naples anthologies: the miniature *canzoniere*.[72] As Milburn has observed, no printed canzonieri from the Neapolitan Petrarchists appeared between 1530 and 1560, with the exception of the *Rime* by Diego Sandoval de Castro (1542) and the numerous editions of Vittoria Colonna and Laura Terracina's lyric poems.[73] Dolce's volume 5 of the Giolito anthologies (in all three editions) are in fact structured by a series of miniature canzonieri, opening with twenty-three poems by Tansillo, which, though they represented only a small proportion of the poet's lyric opus, nonetheless introduced a representative selection of his work to the public.

To build his own canon of female "greats" for the 1559 anthology of women, Domenichi gathered together for publication a number of small to medium-sized collections of women's lyrics—miniature canzonieri, in effect. Sixteen women's mini-canzonieri, each comprising from six to forty-five poems, largely determined the look of the women's anthology of 1559. In some cases, the mini-canzonieri constituted the first publication ever of these women's collected works. The more substantial of the mini-canzonieri Domenichi published in his 1559 anthology fell into this category: those of Virginia Martini de Salvi (forty-five poems), Olimpia Malipiera (thirty-three poems), Leonora Falletta (twenty-one poems), Veronica Gambara (twenty-one poems), Cassandra Petrucci (eighteen poems), and Isabella di Morra (thirteen poems), all of whom saw the first printing of their lyric oeuvre qua oeuvre in the 1559 anthology.[74] Of the above group, only Morra and Salvi appeared in earlier Giolito anthologies.[75] Salvi belonged to the sizable contingent of Sienese women that Domenichi published in the anthology, but of that group only Salvi, who emigrated to Rome after Cosimo de' Medici's destruction of Siena in 1555, continued to write and publish her work.[76]

A number of the women represented in the 1559 anthology had never before published any of their writings.[77] In other instances, the insertion of a woman's lyric oeuvre within the larger anthology represented a mere sample of her previouly published work. Of the several hundred poems Vittoria Colonna wrote, most had already come out in the eight solo editions that had been printed by 1559. Domenichi chose to publish only twenty of her sonnets in the women's anthology.[78] Perhaps the most distinguished lyricist of the whole group, Gaspara Stampa, whose posthumous solo edition of some three-hundred of her poems was published by Plinio Pietrasanta, had only five poems in the Domenichi anthology.[79] The authors of the much smaller mini-canzonieri in the women's anthology included Suor Girolama Castellana (six poems), Costanza d'Avalos, the sister-in-law of Maria d'Aragona (six poems), Laudomia Forteguerri (six poems, all but one addressed to the Emperor Charles's daughter, Margaret of Austria), and Gaspara Stampa's friend Ippolita Mirtilla (nine poems).[80]

## ✣c ISABELLA DI MORRA'S STORY ɔ✣

Isabella di Morra and her miniature *canzoniere* present a special case.[81] In 1545, the gifted poet (b. 1526) was living with her mother, sister, and five brothers at the Morra castle in Favale, a remote town nearer to Taranto than Naples. Her father, the baron Giovan Michele di Morra, had fled to France where he had joined the court of Francis I at Fontainbleau. Across the valley from Favale, in a neighboring castle, the Spaniard Don Diego Sandoval de Castro lived with his wife Antonia Caracciolo. Someone leaked the story to Isabella's brothers that she was exchanging letters with Castro and that her tutor was acting as the go-between—though it was never clear that she and Castro were lovers. Her brothers Decio, Cesare, and Fabio caught the tutor in the act of delivering Castro's letters and murdered him on the spot. Next they hunted down Isabella. They found her with Castro's letters still unopened in her hands and they stabbed her to death, according to testimony bound over to the viceroy. Castro was more difficult to catch. Several months later, Isabella's three brothers, who were joined by her uncles, Cornelio and Baldassino di Morra, ambushed Castro at Noia, not far from Favale, as he was returning from his fief in Taranto. He was left in the road to die of the multiple wounds he sustained, while his bodyguards were said to have run for their lives as soon as they saw the Morra men coming. Isabella's three brothers and their uncles got away safely to France before the viceroy could arraign them. But the eldest brother Marcantonio, who tesified in the case but had nothing to do with the murders, served a long prison term in Taranto. The real killers remained in France for the duration of their lives.

Isabella di Morra's friend Diego Sandoval de Castro was well connected, to the power structure in Naples as well as to influential literary circles in the north. He was a client and protégé of the viceroy of Naples, Pedro di Toledo, a member of Cosimo I's Academy Fiorentina, and he was a published poet. He may have opened negotiations for the publication of Morra's poems before he was murdered, but they came to nothing if he did. Dolce published Morra's poems in batches in his four successive anthologies of Neapolitan poets.[82] But it was Domenichi who gathered her ten sonnets and three Canzoni together and published them as her complete oeuvre in his anthology of women, though he followed Dolce's ordering of the poems for the most part. While Sandoval de Castro had no trouble publishing his collected *Rime* in 1542, even a partial publication of Morra's opus would have to wait until she had been dead six years.[83] Even then, the story of her murder was still news.[84]

A sample of sonnets from Morra's miniature *canzoniere* indicates how she packed an intense psychological self-portrait into the space of a few lines.[85] She wove several themes into a continuous lament in her ten sonnets: the loss of her father; her struggle with painful circumstances beyond her control (*crudele fortuna*); the ravaged country of her homeland, which mirrored her own inner landscape; her desire to write and live among other poets; and finally, her search for release from her town, her brothers, her state of mind—and, ultimately, her life.[86]

> Grieving my green age, I write
> the fierce assaults of savage Fortune,
> and in country rude and wild,
> I spend my life without all praise.
> Poor though my cradle was, I chase
> the lovely Muses and seek a worthy tomb;
> and I hope to find some pity despite
> her who is bitter, blind, and cruel;
> and with the favor of the holy goddesses,
> and if not in body free at least in soul,
> I hope to find esteem on happier shores.
> Perhaps a lofty King lives in the world,
> who will devote to massive marble,
> this veil, which wraps me in its folds.

> I fieri assalti di crudel fortuna;
> Scrivo piangendo, e la mia verde etade;
> Me, che'en sì vili, e horride contrate
> Spendo il mio tempo senza lod alcuna.
>
> Degno il sepolcro, se fu vil la cuna,
> Vò procacciando con le Muse amate;
> Et spero ritrovar qualche pietate,
> Malgrado de la cieca aspra importuna.
>
> Et col favor de le sacrate Dive,
> Se non col corpo, almen con l'alma sciolta,
> essere in pregio a più felici rive.
>
> Questa spoglia, dove hor mi trovo involta;
> forse tale alto Re nel mondo vive,
> Che'n saldi marmi la terrà sepolta.

> (*Rime d'alcune donne, 86; also vol. 5, all editions*)

7

O valley infernal, look once again,
O alpine rivers, crumbling stones,
O spirits bereft of virtue, empty,
you will hear my pain and grief undying,
Every mountain will hear me, every cave,
wherever I guide my steps or rest,
since Fortune, who is never constant,
swells my sorrow, now eternal,
Ah, while for days and nights I cry,
O beasts, rocks, and fearful ruins,
O pathless forests, and solitary caves,
wail and prophesy my doom:
more piteous than any other: my fate
you must weep, with high and broken cries.

Ecco, che un'altra volta, o valle inferna,
O fiume alpestre, o rovinati sassi,
O ignudi spirti di virtute, e cassi,
Udrete il pianto, e la mia doglia eterna.
    Ogni monte udirammi, ogni caverna
Ovunque arresti, ovunque io muova i passi;
Che fortuna, che mai salda non stassi
Cresce ognora il mio male, ognor l'eterna.
    Deh mentre, ch'io mi lagno, e giorno, e notte,
O fere, o sassi, o horride ruine,
O selve incolte, o solitarie grotte,
    Ulule, e voi del mal nostro indovine,
Piangete meco a voci alte interrotte,
Il mio più d'altro miserando fine.

*(Rime d'alcune donne, 89)*

8

O turbid Siri, puffed up while I weep,
now that I sense my painful end is near,
tell my sorrow to my dear father,
if his bitter fate ever returns him here.
Tell him that in dying, I ease
my harsh fortune and greedy destiny,
and put to sea my unlucky name,
in an example rare and wretched.

As soon as he reaches the rocky shore
(O evil star, why do you cause me to ponder
how lost I am, bereft of every good?),
rile your waves with heartless winds,
and say, "While she lived, not her eyes, no,
but rivers of Isabella's grief made me swell.

    Torbido Siri, del mio mal superbo;
Hor ch'Io sento dappresso il fine amaro,
Fa tu noto il mio duolo al Padre caro;
Se mai qui'l torna il suo destino acerbo.
    Dilli com'io morendo, disacerbo,
L'aspra fortuna e lo mio fato avaro.
Et con esempio miserando, e raro,
Nome infelice a le tue onde serbo.
    Tosto ch'Ei giunga a la sassosa riva,
(A che pensar m'adduci, o fiera stella?)
Come d'ogni mio ben son cassa, e priva.
    Inqueta l'onde con crudel procella,
Et di: m'accrebber si, mentre fu viva,
Non gli occhi no, ma i fiumi d'Isabella.

*(Rime d'alcune donne, 89; also in vol. 5, all editions)*

Each of her poems play on these themes in some way, giving a sense of cohesiveness and unity to the whole ensemble independent of the order in which they appear.[87] While the themes are always the same, and each poem in Morra's miniature *canzoniere* represents a play for one actor, the constant changes of addressee and mis-en-scène provide both variety and a sense of progression. Given that her real life ended with her murder, the dominant theme of her work—the poet's search for a way out—had, and continues to have, a haunting resonance for modern as well as sixteenth-century readers of Morra. As each of her poem shows, Morra the writer is preoccupied with finding an exit from her misery—one way or another:

By achieving fame: poem 1 addressed to the reader.
By marrying: poem 2, to Juno.
By her father's returning: poem 3, to her father.
By a noble patron across the river: poem 4, to the Siri river.
By emigrating to France: poem 5, to the poet Alamanni.
By joining the beasts of Favale: poem 7, to the beasts.

By suicide, which would immortalize the Siri: poem 8, to the Siri.

By delivering her own eulogy: canzone 8, to Fortune.

By suicide, or physically escaping from Favale: poem 10, to Fortune again.

By faith: The last two Canzoni, 11 and 12, address God.

I have suggested in this chapter that the publication of the poetry of two suppressed groups, the Naples salon and women, was not driven alone by the academies, patrons, and the presses who supported them, but by the very measures to outlaw their work that were instituted in Naples and Rome.

Domenichi managed to push to press his anthology of fifty-three women poets, the majority of whom were unknown, at the height of the Inquisition. The 1559 *Index* of prohibited books, which came out almost simultaneously with Domenichi's women's anthology, banned not only Erasmus and Melancthon, Valla and Occam, Boccaccio and Poggio, but many of the modern poets who were the mainstays of the Giolito anthologies.[88] Domenichi, of course, never submitted his anthology to the Venetian Senate for the requisite *privilegio* to publish. Instead, he gave his manucript to the Lucchese printer Vincenzo Busdragho. Perhaps he wondered, in the very year that the new *Index* banned Giovanni Della Casa's poetry as "lascivious," how the officers of the Inquisition would view the scores of sonnets that women in his anthology addressed to members of their own sex, sometimes shockingly in the heated lovers' language of Petrarch and Ovid. As a once convicted heretic himself, Domenichi might have worried about publishing so much work by Vittoria Colonna, a leader in the Valdesian reform movement, who would have been tried for heresy had she lived, and by so many women from Sienese families whose religious leanings made them suspect, but this is the subject of another chapter.[89] Giolito had no trouble reprinting a solo edition of Colonna's poetry in 1559, so beyond matters of "taste" and the red tape it would have taken to publish an all-women anthology in Venice, getting it through would probably not have been difficult. The Holy Office was notoriously unsystematic in its censorship.

That an anthology of women was attempted at all was, as I have suggested, a testimony of the times. Every city, as we shall see in the ensuing chapters, had its coteries of women and men who gathered on a regular basis in informal groups to present their writings and their plans for publication. Since the leading men of the presses such as Ruscelli, Dolce, and Domenichi had come to publishing without social advantage or credentials, it was not surprising that the books they produced—anthologies, among them—suggested a republic of letters where women and men from all ranks of society came together in a Burckhardtian utopia. But these were utopias of an editor's imagination, not documents that reflected lives. The courtier's daughter Laura Terracina dedicated poems to the sisters Maria d'Aragona and Giovanna d'Aragona, but they did not reciprocate. Seeds were sown in the anthologies and the dialogues for a more egalitarian society and, certainly, one in which literary women played an active role. But the leveling of society was a fiction.

If the presses offered the fantasy in print of a more egalitarian society, they sometimes lifted writers from obscurity in a way that was real. When the Naples salon and its academies were threatened with extinction, the Venetian presses stepped in to give the poets who had been silenced a better forum. And when the poets, many of them women hoping to start their careers, saw avenues to publication closing down at the larger publishing firms, they turned to the smaller presses in Lucca, Bologna, and Venice as well and found opportunity there.

In light of the successes of the anthologies, what can be said of the impact of the Inquisition on the popular renascence of vernacular poetry that began in the middle of the sixteenth century in Italy? Challenging the views of Burckhardt, Croce, and Garin that the Counter-Reformation spelled the end of significant literary production after 1555, Paul Grendler has called for a more nuanced assessment of the quality of intellectual life and the practice of the arts in Italy at the end of the sixteenth century.[90] There is no doubt that Protestantism, and religious choice in general, were effectively stamped out. But in spite of the increasing pressure from the Roman Holy Office on the Venetian presses from 1555 to 1559, more poetry books by both men and women were published during this period than ever before. Even the increasingly stringent policies of Paul IV did not yet bring to a halt the production and publication of new poetry on the peninsula or the participation of women in that enterprise.

## CHAPTER THREE

# Rome: The Salt War Letters of Vittoria Colonna

From 1541 to 1557, the Colonna and d'Aragona women of Naples and Rome challenged the power of the popes on territorial as well as intellectual grounds. They fought to maintain their autonomy as landholders and their right to participate in the religious, political, and literary discourses of the times. The diverse political roles the Colonna-d'Aragona women assumed as diplomats, patrons, and writers illustrate how closely allied they were with the academies, salons, and presses of the northern cities and how alienated from the hermetic culture of the Curia they had become. Considered together, chapters 3 and 4 trace the heating up of the sixteenth-century war between the popes and the poets, from the time of the Salt War to the promulgation of one Venetian poet's construction of a mausoleum of words for Giovanna d'Aragona Colonna. The change in the relations between the popes and women and men of learning in Renaissance Italy—from the fifteenth century, when the papacy portrayed itself as the promoter and defender of literature and the arts, to the war the princes of the Church waged on poets and scholars in the mid-sixteenth century—informs my story. In the new world of the popular printed book in Italy, a significant number of women and men of letters gained access to power and privilege such as they had not known in previous times. Very much a consequence of this "Other Renaissance," humanism still flourished in sixteenth-century Italy but without the support of the Church.

The war Pope Paul III moved against the Colonna towns in the Castelli Romani—known as the Salt War of 1541—drew Vittoria Colonna (fig. 7) away from her intense involvement in the reform movement, where she had been a leader since the mid-1530s. Having hosted a reform circle for two years in her lodgings at the convent of San Silvestro in Rome, in 1537 Colonna had followed Bernardino Ochino north to Ferrara where he was preaching at the cathedral. From Ferrara, she traveled with Ochino and his friends to Lucca, where the presiding bishop Pier Martire Vermigli led a reform *cenacolo* that would make Lucca a renowned center of heretical activity long after Vermigli and Ochino fled to Geneva. There in Lucca, Colonna had remained for seven months only returning to her convent home to Rome toward the end of 1538, after trips to

· FIGURE 7 ·
Vittoria Colonna. Portrait by Muziano,
painter in Orvieto and Rome, ca. 1541–47. Galleria
Colonna, Rome. Reproduced courtesy of the Newberry
Library from Johann Wyss, *Vittoria Colonna*
(Fraufeld: Verlag Huber, 1916).

Bologna and Pisa where she heard Ochino preach and again joined in discussion with other intellectuals involved in the reform movement.[1]

When Paul failed to extract the new tax on salt from his subjects in the papal states during the years 1537–40, he decided to make an example of Perugia, the first city to be "tested." On February 7, 1540, the pope issued a brief to the priors of Perugia demanding payment of the tax under the threat of armed retaliation.[2] On April 8, the priors, confraternities, and people of Perugia marched from the church of San Domenico through the main street to the cathedral of San Lorenzo where they stood before the papal envoy, Cardinal Jacobazzi, and demonstrated against the pope's new levy. Ascanio Colonna called together an emergency assembly of delegates from the cities impacted by the pope's promise of a retaliatory war and of the ambassadors of Charles V, whom he sought to rally around Perugia's cause. But the delegates reached no resolution, and on July 4, 1540, the pope's captains entered Perugia with an army of ten thousand men. They took the city by force, terrorizing the citizens and confiscating the town's weapons, armor, and bullion.

Undaunted by the "lesson" of Perugia, Ascanio Colonna again refused the Farnese pope's demands that he pay his share of the salt tax.[3] But when the pope arrested a group of Colonna supporters in Rome, Ascanio ordered the seizure and incarceration of pilgrims and traders traveling through his lands in the Abruzzi on their way to Rome, and he impounded the papal cattle grazing on Colonna lands adjacent to the salt pits at Ostia. On February 25, 1541, the pope demanded that Colonna appear before him in Rome. But banking on reinforcements of matériel and men from Charles V, Colonna refused the pope's invitation to the Vatican and settled in with a company of two thousand men at his *castello* at Genazzano, a pitiful contingent in comparison to the pope's ten thousand.

The onset of the Salt War (*la guerra del sale*) marked Vittoria Colonna's entry into the theater of high-stakes diplomatic relations. While Ascanio, the clan's military commander-in-chief, withdrew from Rome to defend the Colonna strongholds outside the city, Vittoria Colonna acted as his secretary of state. On March 1, 1541, Vittoria Colonna entered into negotiations with the emperor, his ambassador Marchese Manrique d'Aguilar, and his undersecretaries, Conciano and Valanzuola, in an effort to head off the war. Still in Rome herself, she sent letter after letter to her brother. From her accounts of her dealings with Charles V's emissaries, she appears to have met with them face to face whenever she could. Her bullet-like dispatches to her brother, sometimes two a day, were calculated to bolster his spirits and even get him to laugh. "One retaliates when local captains, governors, and cardinals are murdered, but [the pope] hardly needed to go to war for thirty cows," she wrote.[4] [A tante cose grandi de amazzar barricelli, governatori, cardinali se è preso rimedio, però non bisognava tanta guerra per trenta vacche.] At the same time, she fed her brother whatever insider information she could gather, she instructed him on how to win Charles's support, and she told him what to do on a daily basis. She was, as he said in one of his letters, only partly in mockery, his *imperatrice*—his empress and commander in chief. Vittoria Colonna's goal through the month of March was two-pronged: she would keep Ascanio from escalating the conflict; and she would use the emperor, whom she at first believed would intervene militarily if war broke out, to pressure the pope into a negotiated settlement with Ascanio.

Her frontline message concerned the preservation of the honor of the Colonna. When she wrote to Ascanio that "the house of Colonna is always first" [ma Casa Colonna sempre è la prima], she meant it in two ways: the Colonna were first to be targeted in any struggle for power in Rome and, among the great Roman clans, they were regarded as primus inter pares.[5] Her subtext, though, suggests that without Charles V's intervention, war would be suicidal for Ascanio, resulting in irrevocable losses of land and prestige for the Colonna. Yet on March 1, two months away from the war's end, surrender to the Farnese pope still seemed unthinkable. "Defend yourself," she commanded Ascanio. The middle road, she repeated in her letters, was to rely on Charles's long-standing obligation to the Colonna. He could be counted on to come to their defense, and she, Vittoria assured her brother, would be the one to communicate with the emperor:

> Illustrious Signor. From Conciano you will hear what Your Lordship has supposed: that these decisions were made for no other reason than to show good will. I think the reasons for so large an army may be because of someone other than you alone. But the house of Colonna is always the first. Everything has been written to His Majesty. Your Lordship should wait to make sure that everything you will do once the order from His Majesty has come, will be honored. May God in His Goodness watch over you and protect you from all evil. Retaliation is taken in response to such serious acts as the slaughter of local captains, governors, and cardinals; he [the pope] did not, however, need such a great a war for thirty cows.[6] Your Lordship may not ever discover his motive, but you speak the truth that they wanted to arm and used this as a pretext, and that you did not want to be caught sleeping since every day you were seeing good words and sad events. But defend yourself; and may God help you as I hope in his goodness. Signor the Marchese does his job well and in such a way that they will stand ready [estaranno preparati] to act in all the places [in tutti i lochi] in accord with the pope's intentions

and the orders of his Majesty.[7] In the meantime pay attention only to yourself since you tend to trust too much in good words. The marriage negotiations with France [*il matrimonio con Francia*] are concluded, and I have written as much to his Majesty, and these men speak of things not looking well for everyone.[8] Now I will not be able to write too openly as long as God wants them to see what does not concern us alone. Your servant, the Marchesa

Ill.mo S.or. Da Conciano intenderà che V.S. ha indovinato che per altro non se son fatti questi maneggi che per mostrare bona voluntà: penso li motivi de tanta armata sieno per altro che per voi solo: ma Casa Colonna sempre è la prima. Tutto se è scritto a Sua M.tà. V.S. attenda a guardarsi, che ogni cosa che farrà poi de venuto l'ordine de Sua M.tà serrà honorato. Dio per sua bontà vi guardi et estorvi tucti i mali. A tante cose grandi de amazzar barricelli, governatori, cardinali se è preso rimedio, però non bisognava tanta guerra per trenta vacche. V.S. non discovrà mai il suo motivo, ma dica la verità, che hanno voluto armar con questo colore, et che voi non volevate essere preso in letto, poi che ogni dì vedevate bone parole e tristi fatti, però ve defendete; et Dio ve aiuti come spero nella sua bontà. El sig.r Marchese se governa bene, di guisa in tutti i lochi estaranno preparati secondo i motivi del Papa et l'ordin de Sua M. Interim a voi tocca solo, poichè se crede troppo alle bone parole qui: il matrimonio con Francia è concluso, e così ho scritto a Sua Maestà, et questi dicono de non mirare bene a tutto. Ormai non potrò scrivere chiaro troppo, finchè Dio vorrà che deano che non tocca a noi soli. A suo servitio, La Marchesa (March 1, 1541, Vittoria to Ascanio, letter 129)[9]

Vittoria Colonna continued to assure her brother that, in her role as his secretary of state, she and her agents were keeping abreast of all the latest rumors circulating in Rome. The gossip she had been hearing about marriage negotiations being conducted, supposedly behind Charles's back, between the daughter of the pope's son, Pier Luigi Farnese, and a member of the French royal family might easily goad the emperor, she implied, into supporting Ascanio's resistance to the pope. Pope Clement VII's secret alliance with France in 1527 had resulted in Charles's allowing his troops to sack Rome:

Illustrious Signor [Vittoria wrote to Ascanio], I believe that the arrangements with France will soon be made public, and so his Holiness's plan will appear to be not solely about you.[10] Therefore I fear very much that not plans but deceptions will result. But it is good that you may not be the loser if a possible solution is found. I have not given up waiting for this. I would like you, however, write to his Majesty now and give me the letter for Conciano, if it seems fitting to you.[11] It is impossible to understand this pope, but consider well that with the grace of God everything should be done to serve his Majesty, and you should not care about anything else but the service of God, and excusing the wrongs done, with honor however. . . .

Your Lordship should try to see that Signor Conciano, who loves you more than me, is satisfied. A suo servizio, La Marchesa (Dated the beginning of March 1541)

Ill.mo S.or. Io credo che presto si scopriranno cose di Francia, per donde se vedrà che il motivo di Sua S.tà non è per voi solo: per donde temo molto che non riusciranno partiti ma inganni. Però bene è che non manchi per voi, se cosa possibil si trova. Io non ho spacciato aspettando questo. Però vorrei scrivesti a Sua M.tà Voi ancora, et mandatemela per Conciano, se vi pare. Mal se può intendere questo Papa; però considerate bene con gratia di Dio che tutto sia con servitio di Sua M.tà, et non si curi d'altro solo per servitio di Dio et escusar danni, con honore però. V.S. si sforzi che il S.or Conciano venga sotisfatto che ve ama più di me. A suo servizio, La Marchesa (March 1, 1541, letter 128)[12]

Vittoria Colonna did not at first see that Charles V was unlikely to intervene militarily in a territorial or fiduciary dispute between Paul and one of his vassals, even if the vassal requesting the emperor's intercession had laid his life on the line for Charles, as Ascanio had done for twenty years. Charles had already committed himself to the Farnese Pope Paul III in betrothing his own daughter, Margaret of Austria, to the pope's grandson—whose father Pier Luigi Farnese was the pope's military commander in chief in the war he was waging against Ascanio Colonna. Besides, Charles now controlled much of the peninsula. He had installed Alfonso d'Avalos and Diego de Mendozza as his deputies in Milan and Siena, and he had strengthened his alliance with Cosimo I de' Medici by conferring on him the title Duke of Florence. The kingdom of Naples was already his, ruled by his Spanish viceroy Pedro di Toledo; and under Charles's hegemony the French at last had been permanently expelled from Italy. Finally, Charles had put the finishing touches on his own alliance with Florence with his arrangement of the marriage of his viceroy's daughter, Eleonora di Toledo, to Cosimo I. The only large cities Charles did not control in Italy were Venice and Rome, and, as Thomas Dandelet has convincingly shown, Charles would ultimately succeed in making an economic and military partner of Rome by the time of his abdication.[13]

Still, at the outset of the war in March 1541, the Colonna family held some twenty well-placed castles, most of them in the hills of the Castelli Romani and the Abruzzi, some within easy striking distance of Rome. It was these properties that Vittoria Colonna believed Charles V would want to preserve for his own empire as well as for the "Casa Colonna," as she put it. According to what she told her brother, Charles's ambassador, Aguilar, appeared to offer proposals he thought both sides might accept. Direct communication with Charles was slow since he was in Ratisbone, Germany, attending a congress of Protestant and Catholic Church leaders. Moreover, Colonna seems not to have had direct access to Pope Paul III, which was unsurprising given not only her gender but, more important, her status as a Colonna and an enemy combatant.

Full of distrust for Aguilar and concern for her brother, Vittoria's letters in the early days of the negotiations cautiously portrayed the pope's proposals to Ascanio as ranging from the impossible to the absurd—though her advice to him would later change. According to Charles's ambassador, the centerpiece of the pope's proposal was Ascanio's surrender of the Colonna territories in the Castelli Romani, first the walled towns of Nemi and Marino, where Vittoria Colonna was born. Next, Ascanio was to hand over the Colonna stronghold Rocca di Papa—a surrender presented in each of Aguilar's letters as temporary and "in name" only. On March 6, Charles's ambassador, Aguilar, tendered a two-part offer. He first proposed that Ascanio give Nemi and Marino to the pope's general (and son), Pier Luigi Farnese, with the understanding that the emperor would then order the pope to return these lands to Ascanio "without delay." The second part of the proposal was that Ascanio would give the Rocca di Papa "verbally" to Pier Luigi, but "in effect" the property would not change hands since the Colonna men "would remain inside."[14] Colonna wrote her brother that she told Aguilar she would pass the first proposal on in writing to Ascanio, but as to Aguilar's second proposal that they give away Rocca di Papa—this she refused to bring to the table. The condition offered that Ascanio's men would remain in the town of Rocca guaranteed nothing except that he would lose his men as well as the town.

Finally, only when there were no other options for Ascanio except death in battle or surrender to the pope's son Pier Luigi Farnese did Colonna tells her brother that she and others had arranged an escape for him. His cousin Francesco Colonna, archbishop of Taranto and abbot of San Subiaco monastery, awaited his arrival and would welcome him there. Suddenly sounding as if she were truly his commandant, she ordered her brother to accept their cousin's offer of sanctuary, reminding him to show his gratitude to Francesco. Her letter to Ascanio ends with her assurances of the archbishop' continuing respect for him—as if to palliate the proposal that he save his own skin at the expense of his men's lives:

> At this hour Valanzola has arrived, and he says that the Emperor's influence with the pope is paramount, and that the Signor the Marchese [Aguilar], however much

he complains, cannot do anything more.[15] He says that your Lordship should be contented with this final plan for the love of God, that of handing Marino and Nemi over to the Pope with the Marchese's promise that they will be restored to you at an order to come from the Emperor; he also says that the said Signor will command it of you in writing on behalf of his Majesty and that the Pope is not at all contented with this plan but that tonight he will give us this last thing in his power.[16] But that this last thing, which he hopes will satisfy the Pope is that Rocca de Papa be given to the Duke [Pier Luigi Farnese] verbally, but in effect the Signor the Marchese [Aguilar] would let me name those who would be the ones whom your Lordship would write me about.[17] I have responded that the first I will write, but the second I will never say. He [Aguilar] answered that this second is better, because you don't give away anything, your men being inside, and that he will request it of you on behalf of the Emperor, in writing. This evening the post goes to the Emperor who will send the Marchese. Archbishop Colonna says similarly that not only will you have every service from the monastery, but that he will also come to you in person and he says that he would entrust his own cattle and his vassals to you and whatever you want is yours whether you want it or not and that Camillo will serve you with body and soul.[18] Please write to him kindly. Take care to respond in such a way that the Marchese will see it. Today, Sunday, at the 23th Hour.

In questa hora è venuto Valanzola, et dice che la importantia dell'Imperadore è grandissima et che il S.or Marchese per molto che gridi non po più col Papa. Che V.S. per amor di Dio se contenti di questo partito ultimo di dar Marino et Nemi in poter del Papa con promessa del Marchese che vi sieno restitite al venir ordine dell'Imperadore, et che detto signore in scrittis vel commanderà da parte di Sua M.tà, et che di questo partito il Papa non se ne contenta per niente, ma che stasera ce farrà ultimo de potentia: ma che quello, che lui spera che el Papa se contentaria, si è dar Rocca de Papa al Duca in voce, ma in effetto il signor Marchese ce lassasse che io qui li nominassi che sarian quelli che che V.S. mi scrivesse. Io ho risposto che il primo scriverò, ma il secondo non dirò mai. Respose che questo secondo è meglio, perchè non date niente, essendo homini vostri dentro, et che vel commandarà da parte dell'Imperadore in scrittis. Stasera va la posta all'Imperadore che manda il Marchese. L'Arcivescovo Colonna dice similmente che non solo havrete ogni servitio dall'abbadia, ma verria in persona, et che ve raccomanda il suoi bestiami et suoi vassalli e che è vostro vogliate o non, et che Camillo servirà coll' anima et col corpo. Di gratia scriveteli humanamente. Adverite a rispondere di modo che il Marchese la vederà. Oggi domenica a XXIII hore.[19] (March 6, 1541, letter 130)

Though he was being asked, in effect, to surrender Colonna lands and to withdraw himself from his own feudatories, Ascanio's response was deeply restrained. No trace is evident here of the bravado and rage that have come down to us in the historiography of the episode as indelible features of Ascanio's character.[20] Rather, in this letter to his sister he shows himself the perfect courtier. This reply, with its expressions of humility and deference, was clearly for the eyes of both the pope and Charles as well as for Vittoria. Only missing from the proposals in this last letter of his sister's are, as he delicately puts it, the conditions and guarantees necessary to the signing of any such agreements:

> Most illustrious Signora, sister, I have received your letter and it appears to me that your Ladyship has responded well to Valenzuola. In sum, I am wholly at the command and service of his Imperial Majesty. However, I cannot help but be contented with one of the two proposals your Ladyship has sent me to choose from, assuming that all the obligatory and appropriate conditions will necessarily be met, of which your Ladyship makes no mention: matters which, I believe, you perceive as necessary to obtain the peace, on which the Signor Marchese and all these imperial ministers base their service of his Imperial Majesty whose interests I serve and want to come first above all other things. And so if each of these plans should seem very difficult to me, I will comfort myself with doing honor to his Holiness and to obeying his Imperial Majesty, avoiding the wrong and being the cause of good.

> Ill.ma Si.ra sorella. Ho havuta la lettera sua, e mi pare che V.S. habbi ben resposto a Valenzuola. In summa tutta la forza sopra di me è 'l commandamento et servitio de la Ces.a M.tà. Però non posso negar di contentarmi di uno di doi partiti scrittomi da V.S. a mia elettione, presupponendo che debbino intervenire tutte le circumstantie necessarie et convenienti, de le quali V.S. non fa mentione alcuna, credo come di cose che di neccessità ve se intendono per cavarne la quiete, sopra la quale il Si.or Marchese et tutti questi ministri cesarei fundano il servitio di S.M.tà Cesarea, il quale appo me bisogna et voglio che preceda a tutte l'altre cose. Et se ben mi pareno durissimi ognun di questi partiti, mi confortarò con fare honor a Su S.tà et obedir a la Cesarea M.tà, evitando il male et essendo causa di bene. (March 7, 1541, letter 131)[21]

Aguilar understood well enough that Ascanio's polite request for "clarification of the conditions" of the agreement (*circumstantie necessarie et convenienti*) constituted an outright rejection of the offer. That the Colonna family were expected to surrender Nemi and Marino to Pier Luigi Farnese, throwing in Rocca di Papa for good measure, just to save themselves from being attacked was hardly a workable solution in Vittoria Colonna's characterization of the negotiations. Ascanio's epistolary self-control and his mastery of the diplomatic idiom—*circumstantie necessarie et convenienti*—were impressive. Still, sensing that the game was up, in a letter of March 8, Vittoria Colonna urged her brother to accept a subsequent offer from Aguilar, according to which Charles V would give Rocca di Papa to Pier Luigi Farnese, and in return Ascanio would receive one of two Farnese fortress towns, either Nepe or Castro. Aguilar was to hold the Farnese town in escrow until Pier Luigi and his men "entered" (*entragasseno*) Rocca Di Papa. Vittoria's instructions this time were especially nuanced. She cautioned her brother against showing his displeasure with the so-called peace proposals since Aguilar was their only route to Charles. Yet she warned Ascanio that the ambassador was a dissembler. He should be suspicious of Aguilar's professions of anger at Charles and aware of the ambassador's overly cozy relationship with Pier Luigi. She wrote:

> Having already concluded everything, the Signor Marchese [Aguilar] has arrived to speak with me excusing himself and angry because he was not able to say more; he showed me the latest letter he had from his Majesty [Charles V] which tells him that the pope has to be kept happy at all cost. He sees that [Charles] has already given the pope his daughter [Margaret of Austria was given in marriage to the Pope's grandson Ottavio Farnese in 1538], and he says that as long as the Emperor doesn't change his mind, he cannot appear to go against them in any way. He says he has detained his men since they will not be paid until tomorrow morning, and finally he writes to your Lordship saying that he thinks he should give orders in writing on behalf of his Majesty to the effect that [the emperor] will give Rocca di Papa to the Duke of Castro [the Pope's son Pier Luigi Farnese] on the understanding that [Pier Luigi] would return it to the emperor for you. And he repeats his promise that they would give either Nepe or Castro—your choice, either the one or the other—to be held by the Marchese [Aguilar] for you, until such time as they enter Rocca di Papa. Listen well: they will give Nepe or Castro to the Marchese and we will give them Rocca di Papa without using our men or theirs. And as to our not wanting this, do not talk about it any more. Now Signor, I beg you for the love of God, do not move yourself to a fury, keep the Marchese [Aguilar] on your side, above all because it is through him that you can keep his Majesty informed. If you do not want to do this, answer courteously that they should give Nepe or Castro to the said Marchese, and you in turn would give Rocca di Papa to the said Marchese; or if they want the Marchese to contribute men to Castro's army, [speak to the Marchese] so that they will not do this and you will be safe. And if they will do this, it is neither bad nor dishonorable to give everything to the Marchese in the name of his Majesty. For the love of God, consider well that mine is the last chance for a resolution. See how great the dangers are—and may God in his goodness inspire you. Respond immediately and write to his Majesty since it is not a good thing to send post there without a letter from you. I will send the Emperor the copy of your final decision. From Rome, today: Tuesday.

The Marchese has more faith in the Duke than he has in God. These are the times we live in. I responded to him as is fitting. . . . Therefore please, Signor, write sweetly and gracefully since he thinks it's enough that he's made an offer pledging Castro or Nepe. . . . Please, show the Marchese in your writing your respect and let him know that you trust him.

Ill.mo S.or. Havendo già escluso ogni cosa, è venuto il S.or Marchese a parlarmi con collera escusandosi che non pò più: et mi ha mostrata lettera di Sua M.tà freschissima, che gli dice faccia ogni opera per tenere il Papa contento; e che lui vede che li ha data sua figlia, e che non pò mostrarsi in conto alcuno contra loro, finchè l'Imperatore non commanda altro; che lui ha intertenuta la gente che non sia pagata fino in domattina; che per ultimo scriva a V.S. che il parer è, che dia Rocca di Papa al Duca di Castro con fede che dica lui all'Imperatore tornarvela. Et che lui replicò et recluse che dessero o Nepe o Castro a vostra electione de queste due al S.or Marchese, finchè entregasseno Rocca de Papa a V.S. Intendete bene: lor dar Nepe o Castro al Marchese, noi Rocca de Papa senza homini nostri nè loro: et che non volendo noi questo, non se ne parli più. Or, S.or, ve prego per amor di Dio, non ve ne movete a furia, conservative el S.or Marchese, maxime per lo advisar a Sua M. .tà. Se non lo volete far, respondete cortesemente che diano Nepe o Castro al detto S.or Marchese, et voi Rocca de Papa al detto S.or Marchese: o se vogliono che in nome sino del Duca che metta li homini el S.or Marchese che loro non lo faranno et voi restarete bene; et sel faranno non è nè male, nè desonore dare ogni cosa al S.or Marchese in nome di Sua M.tà. Per amor di Dio considerate bene che mo è l'ultima resolutione. Vedete quanti affanni et periculi sono, et Dio per sua bontà ve inspiri. Respondete subito et scrivete a Sua M.tà, chè è mal mandar là una posta senza vostra lettera: et la copia dell'ultima vostra resolutione mandarò allo Imperadore. Da Roma ogi martedì . . .
  El Marchese crede più alle fede del Duca, che se fosse quella di Dio. Li tempi sono così. Da me li fu reposto come conviene. . . . Si che, S.or. Di gratia, scriva dolcemente et in bon modo, chè a lui pare offerir assai pigliando Castro o Nepe. . . . Di gratia, honori molto il Marchese nello scrivere et in mostrarli fede. (March 8, 1541, letter 133)[22]

Vittoria's next letter indicates a gap in Colonna's published correspondence. A lost letter from her brother must have expressed his strong disapproval of Aguilar's proposals, his readiness to go to war, and his need to know from her how many troops they might raise to meet the pope's now imminent attack on Paliano. Vittoria's letter is full of conflicting messages. While she begins by almost admonishing her brother for his lack of enthusiasm for Aguilar's proposals and argues their utility as a means to resolve the conflict, her postscript notes with Colonna hauteur that she has just sent Charles a letter telling him that his ambassador's proposed agreements were "impossible" and that in any case "Rocca di Papa was not *his* [Charles's] to give away."[23] And though she counsels her brother against risking the lives of his men unnecessarily, she fully backs his readiness to go to war and hopes that he will somehow be able to hang onto the Colonna lands and estates:

> Most illustrious Signor: The messenger to His Majesty left yesterday and our letters were on time. I do not know why you don't think the agreement good in every way. It would mean stabilizing things more with the Emperor; I mean the issue of the quarrel. I have the code Pietro Paulo had, but don't put anyone at risk unless it is absolutely necessary.[24] There are enough people here: I believe that there are now close to 5,000 in infantry. I think the agreement to put them under the command of your friend the cavalier is a good one; or if you are waiting for the decision of the Emperor, take good care of yourself and don't let your wishes be revealed in words alone, although I pray that God in his goodness may help you to hold onto the land. Sweeten your relationship with the Marchese again, who enjoys having you as his friend; and may God watch over you.[25] I do not know whether they have mounted a different strategy because I have heard nothing more. From the Marchese del Vasto I do not now have a response, nor will I be able to have one.[26] I do know that the Marchese has written to everyone that they should stand ready at the order of His Majesty.
>
> The Marchesa
>
> [postscript] I wrote to the Emperor saying that the agreements were impossible and that it was not his responsibility to give away the Rocca, which His Majesty gazed at when he was passing through Marino and said: "This is the Rocca de Izo." I believe I have written rightly. Take care of yourself.

> La staffetta a S. M. partì ieri et le nostre furono a tempo. Non so perchè non giudicate bene in ogni tempo quello accordo, saria un stabilirse più con l'imperatore, dico quello della lite. Io ho cifra che haveva Pietro Paulo,[27] ma non arrisicate persone, se non è più che necessario. Qui è gente assai: credo sieno oramai appresso a cinque mila fanti. Io teneva per bene quello accordo dandola in potere di quel cavaliere amico, o se aspettate la risoluzione dell'Imperadore, guardatevene bene, et che non paia la brama solo in parole, benchè a questo tener la campagna Dio ve aiuti per sua bontà. Rendolcite el M.se, che giova haverlo amico; et Dio ve guardi. Non so se di han mosso altro, chè non ho anchor resposta, nè potria haverla. So che 'l M.se qui ha scritto a tutti che stiano in ordine a la resposta di Sua M.
>
> La Marchesa
>
> All'Imperadore ho scritto che li accordi herano impossibili et non suo servitio dar quella Rocca, che Sua M.ta passando per Marini mirò et disse: *esta es la roca de Izo.* Tanto credo haver scritto bene. Attendete pure a voi. (March 7–8, 1541, letter 132)[28]

Vittoria's letters dated March 7–8 and 8, 1541, are the last known letters that she sent her brother from Rome during the Salt War. It had become increasingly clear to Colonna that it was no longer safe for her to remain in Rome. On March 13, 1541, she traveled to Orvieto and entered the monastery of San Paolo, where she lived until August 9 of that year when she again left for Rome.[29]

Ascanio's reply to her letter of March 7–8 makes clear the extent to which she had taken charge of her brother's situation and how much he depended on her advice. Here he alludes to Aguilar's permission, presumably from the pope with whom Charles's ambassador was apparently in close contact, to propose a three-month moratorium on the war. Ascanio shows in this response to Vittoria as well as in previous letters to her that, first, he was willing to defer not only to her but to Charles as well and would be guided in all his actions by the emperor's wishes and that, second, he was by no means averse to a cooling-off period:

Having seen the change in the proposals offered in your Ladyship's letter, notwithstanding their having come from Valensuola, the minister of his Imperial Majesty, I respond that I will wait to defend myself and fight back, according to what the rules of war allow for one's self defense, as your Ladyship advises, nor does it occur to me at this point that I might have to make another plan other than the laying down of arms for three months which has been secured by the very Illustrious Signor Marchese d'Aquilar in the name of the Emperor with restitution later of however much land will be found to be held in the possession of the parties. It is certainly the case that I will accept the will of his Imperial Majesty as dictated by my Empress: when she has shown it to me in his Majesty's writing or via his ministers, I will leave my wishes by the wayside and follow his.

Ill.ma S.ra sorella honorandissima. Vista l'alteration de li partiti per la lettera de V.S. non ostante che sian stati offerti da Valensuola, ministro de la Maestà Cesarea, respondo che io che io attendero a difenderme et offendere, secondo per defenderse la ragion de la guerra permette, da questa matina in lla, siccome V.S. me scrive, ne fin hora me occorre di dover fare altro partito che una suspension d'arme per tre mesi assecurata dall' ill.mo sig.r Marchese d'Aquilar in nome dell'Imperatore con restitutione hinc inde de quanto se troverà detenuto in poter de le parti. E ben vero che la volontà de S.M.tà Ces.a io l'accetto per mia imperatrice, quando me sarrà mostrata per scrittura de S.M.tà o per mezo de suo ministri, lassarò star la mia et seguitarò quella. (March 9, 1541, letter 134)[30]

From the time of the pope's attack on Perugia in May 1540 until March 26, 1541, Vittoria Colonna was in constant touch—by letter, via the intervention of friends, and even through face-to-face meetings—with men close to the emperor and the pope. She exchanged letters with Marguerite de Navarre who was then in France, Duke Ercole II d'Este in Ferrara, the pope's commissary Giovanni Guidiccioni in Rome, and Charles's governor in Milan, Alfonso d'Avalos, who was also Ascanio's brother-in-law. Yet despite the wide net she cast to pull both men back from the brink, despite her partial success in getting Charles to intercede, and despite Ascanio's willingness to compromise and take advice from both his sister and the emperor, neither brother nor sister could move the pope. Paul had no interest in settling peacefully with the Colonna family. As he had shown at Perugia, he had at least three times as many troops as Colonna could muster and a seemingly bottomless war chest to bankroll his ambitions.

From the daily dispatches of Vittoria Colonna's close friend, the poet Giovanni Guidiccioni, who remained the pope's field commissary throughout the war, it is clear that the pope knew at least by March 26, 1541, that Ascanio was amenable to a settlement.[31] Charles wrote the pope from Ratisbone that it was his wish that Ascanio be "graciously pardoned," and since the emperor also promised that Ascanio would "obey," Colonna herself had seen to it that the dispatch gained wide circulation in the papal court. It was also plain that Charles had no intention of intervening if it came to an armed conflict. The pope's commissary wrote:

> Insofar as his Holiness's having taken up arms against Ascanio goes, from what I have understood, the Emperor's intention is that peace be maintained by every means, according to his latest dispatch by messenger; and in this dispatch, which was circulated here by the illustrious Marchesa of Pescara, it is replied to his Holiness that Signor Ascanio will obey: but to the Marchese [Aguilar] it is replied that his Majesty desires that [Ascanio] be generously pardoned for everything without anything being spoken of other than the paying of the salt tax.

> Quanto allo haver Sua Santità prese l'armi contra il signor Ascanio, per quanto ho inteso, l'animo dell'Imperatore è che si quieti in ogni modo, come per l'ultimo corrieri si scrisse; et per questo, il quale fu qua spacciato dalla Illustrissima marchesa di Pescara, si replica a Sua Santità che Signor Ascanio ubidirà: ma al marchese si scrive che Sua Maestà desidera li sia perdonato liberamente ogni cosa senza parlarsi d'altro che di pagare il sale. (April 8, 1541, letter 72)[32]

By mid-March the pope's troops were sitting outside the gates of Paliano waiting to assault the walls. From the front, the pope received a stream of dispatches from Vittoria Colonna's friend Guidiccioni. None of the war correspondence between the pope's commissary and Vittoria Colonna has been preserved. But a lengthy letter from January 1541 by Guidiccioni to Colonna is extant in which he thanks her profusely for her comments on some sonnets he sent her; he tells her how flattered he is that she has read his work and he relays his warm regards. Guidiccioni's daily dispatches, most of which were sent directly to Paul, indicate that, as early as April 2, 1541, when the fall of Rocca di Papa appeared imminent, Ascanio and his men had retreated to the upper town at Paliano, while the papal army under Pier Luigi Farnese's command had set up camp under the walls. From that point on, the town would be battered by Farnese's troops for thirty-eight straight days—first on two sides and finally from three separate base camps—until its surrender on May 9. One of the earliest of Guidiccioni's eyewitness accounts sent to the pope on April 2 depicts the flavor of the deadly firefights and Ascanio's shortages of basic provisions, manpower, and, above all, money to pay the men, all of which made the war an exercise in futility for him and his people. Guidiccioni is likely to have sent a copy of this dispatch to his friend Vittoria Colonna—either directly, as a courtesy to her, or through a third party. He wrote:

A great number of [enemy] harquebusiers came out to help their men whom our men, having captured four of theirs, were chasing with a fury. Thus a large skirmish ensued in which our men were so hot on the enemy's heels that more than a hundred of them threw themselves down those rocky slopes. No one knows how many of our men were wounded. Of the enemy, three or four are dead, many were wounded and about twenty were taken prisoner. Among those was a valiant youth from Valerano sul Sanese who had a dead man with a harquebus and two of our horses in tow. He says that behind him are not more than a thousand infantrymen and perhaps twenty cavalrymen of whom, with four taken captive, only sixteen remain; he also said that signor Ascanio did not willingly allow them to leave the fortress, which is also a sign that he does not have too many people, and he said that in order to get bread, wine and oil, they were bargaining with everything they had—especially shoes, which cost a half a scudo the pair.

Ma essendo incalzati dai nostri, che havevano di già presi quattro di loro, gli uscì in soccorso gran numero d'archibugieri, et così fu attaccato una grossa scaramuccia, nella quale i nimici furono all'ultimo incalzati di maniera che se ne gittorno più di 100 per quelle greppe. De' nostri non si sa ancora che ne sia ferito nessuno: di loro son morti 3 o 4, feriti molti, et fatti prigioni circa XX. Fra' quali è stato un valente giovane da Valerano sul Sanese, il quale ha morto con l'archibugio a due de'nostri i cavalli sotto. Costui riferisce che dentro non son più di mille fanti, et forse XX cavalli, che, scematone i quattro presi, non restano più che 16; et che il signor Ascanio mal volentieri li lassa uscir fuori, che è anche segno che non ha troppa gente, et che, da pane, vino et agli in poi, patono d'ogni altra cosa, et di scarpe massimamente, le quali costano mezzo scudo il paro. (April 2, 1541, letter 67)[33]

On April 6 Guidiccioni wrote the pope to warn him of the local people's desperation and fear of the papal troops, who were looting their towns, shops, and houses and terrorizing their women. In the absence of all security and order, the people of Valmontone and other places were simply abandoning their homes and taking to the road.[34]

Given the ongoing correspondence that existed between Vittoria Colonna and Guidiccioni and the constant contact between Vittoria and Ascanio's wife Giovanna d'Aragona at this crucial time, it seems not at all unlikely that Guidiccioni sent Vittoria and her sister-in-law a copy of his next report to the pope, dated April 6, 1541. This particular dispatch may in fact have furnished both the information and the impetus Giovanna d'Aragona needed for the crafting of her own letter requesting clemency from the pope. Certainly Guidiccioni's references to the "pitiful men and women" in the besieged towns, the "killing of innocent citizens," and his emphasis on the pope's need to show his "compassion and pity" not only resemble d'Aragona's language in her April 8 appeal to the pope, but his dispatch reveals his conflicted feelings about Paul's war. Only at the tail end of this passage does the commissary argue the sheer utility of his own proposal:

> All the towns and villages in and around Valmontone are now under your jurisdiction, your Holiness, yet the local people, fearing our soldiers and not having the protection they need to return to their homes, are simply taking to the road in desperation. And so it has been my thought that your Holiness would do well to station a person of some importance as governor there, who would use his authority to insure the safety of the local people so that they could return to their homes with their wives and he would end the killings that are perpetrated every day. He would order all the towns to deputize people who would be capable of protecting people's property and would promise to banish anyone found without documents, whether from among the soldiers or local inhabitants. This way, there is no doubt that peace and security would be restored to the whole region—beyond the fact that it would be an act of compassion to lead these pitiful folk, wandering and lost, back to their villages and homes—not to mention that such measures would greatly facilitate the movement of troops to and from Rome and the Campo.

> Essendo tutte le terre, da Valmontone in là, sotto l'obbedienza della Beatitudine Vostra, et non s'assecurando le genti per timor de'soldati di ritornarvi, anzi

mettendosi molti di loro come disperati alla strada, ho pensato che la Santità Vostra non poterebbe far meglio che mandarvi in governo una persona di qualche importanza, la quale dopo aver con l'autorità sua assecurati gli uomini et fattili tornare a casa con le lor donne, per ovviare agli assassinamenti che si fanno ogni giorno, commandasse a tutte quelle Terre di deputare genti delle loro che fussero a bastanza per tener securo tutto il lor tenimento, piglianso ciascuno sbandato, che fusse trovato senza bollettino, tanto de'soldati come di quelli del paese. Et non è dubbio alcuno che per questa via—oltra l'atto di pietà che si farebbe raccogliendo quei poveri uomini, che vanno dispersi, a goder la patria et le sostantie loro—si renderìa securo tutto quel paese, et potrebbesi andare et venire da Roma al Campo per quel cammino non senza molta commodità dell'essercito. (April 6, 1541, letter 70)[35]

While Giovanna d'Aragona had been separated from Ascanio for six years and did not plan to return to him, still the pope's attack on the Colonna lands was in her eyes a time for the clan to pull together. When Rocca di Papa fell to Farnese troops, Giovanna, joining forces with Vittoria Colonna with whom she had always enjoyed a close relationship, wrote directly to the pope and then to his grandson, Cardinal Alessandro Farnese. The letter she sent the pope on April 6, 1541, was an eloquent plea for clemency. Structured as a ring composition with its opening theme repeated in the letter's conclusion, the letter reads like a Ciceronian oration. Giovanna portrays herself as a mother surrounded by her children, wretched and alone in the world, who has abased herself as a humble servant, slave, and supplicant at Pope Paul's feet. In the role of a pious daughter, she addresses her "most blessed father" who is the vicar and imitator of Christ. She calls upon Paul to imitate Christ's two principal attributes: pity and infinite compassion. She begs him to end the invasion of the Colonna lands, which is causing the ruin and misery of her people and his poor vassals, and she adds the conciliatory theme obligatory in a humanist oration—the concession that the pope's actions in laying siege to the Colonna lands "depends on a just cause." The vicar of Christ must desist from the war, for who in the world will have compassion, pity, and clemency if not his representatives on earth, she asks, Saint Peter and the popes? The enemies of God must be punished but not mortified (*castigati et non mortificati*).[36] She supplicates Paul for his protection and help, casting him in the character of the shepherd whose obligation it is to tend his flocks. Finally, she repeats her prayer that the pope show compassion, pity, and mercy to her and all her children, who as servants of the holy father prostrate themselves at his holy feet. But to vary the reprise, Giovanna appends to it a request standard in the humanist invocations of divinities, Christian and pagan—that he justify her faith by answering her prayers:

Most blessed Father, not arrogant, not proud of the favors of temporal princes, but with humility and laid low in every land, I—alone with all my children, the servants and slaves of Your Holiness—return to supplicate you at your most holy feet, most devoutly and with those tears that merit and should have a place of compassion in every humble and good heart such as you have. As the vicar and imitator of Christ who is sovereign over all other princes in the world, you are bound to be endowed with that infinite compassion of him whom it pleases to put away anger. And so I beg you to put an end to this great invasion and to this violence suffered by the people and poor vassals, most holy and blessed Father, even though they might have emanated from a just cause. Who then will have pity and compassion, if pity and compassion are not found in the heir and legitimate possessor of the divine and holy keys of the first, most just and good shepherd, Saint Peter? For he must show others the humility and clemency of Christ with living examples in order to be his perfect standard bearer. But, alas, enough of this! Having already shown that it is not possibly to play the part of the subject with his lord, in the name and goodness of Jesus, I beseech you not to allow more blood of the lambs to be shed, whose true shepherd is your Holiness, for you are mindful of those divine words, *castigati et non mortificati*. And all the more so because the lack of prudence in others should not have such power (having relied perhaps more quickly on the kindness of your Holiness in other people's affairs than with a heart that is always turned toward the obedience and satisfaction of his Blessedness) that it can overcome and obliterate the clemency and pity of one who is the vicar and representative of the most clement and compassionate Jesus, which your Holiness surely and deservedly is, or that it should cause the utter ruin of my entire family who are the servants and slaves of your Holiness. Certainly, most holy Father, my faith in him is so closely allied to your Blessedness that if this invasion did not depend on your most just mind and most powerful arm (which you can take away, just as quickly as you now give them), but if it instead depended on other princes in the world, who are inferior to your Holiness, I would fervently hope for your protection and your help so that you would bring peace to the world, however difficult it might be, and my things would be restored to me safe and sound.

And so, with all my very fervent prayers and my humble and abject obedience I beg your Holiness to judge it right to show me I am not mistaken in my great faith in your Holiness, which as your most humble servant, I devoutly adore and revere, kissing the earth at your most holy feet, and awaiting from this the grace and benediction with all these children—the servants of your Holiness, to which, not being contented with kissing and prostrating myself before your holy feet, I send the Reverend Bishop of Ischia, who will supplicate you more eloquently in my name, face to face, humbly beseeching your Holiness to hear him and trust him. And may it please the everlasting Lord to preserve your Holiness in that supreme happiness and triumph that your blessedness desires. From Ischia, April 8, 1541. Your Holiness' most humble servant and slave, Ioanna Aragona de Colonna.

Beatissime Pater. Non tumida, non superbo de gli favori de' principi temporali, ma humile et prostrata tutta in terra dinanti gli soi sanctissimi piedi, una con tutti gli figlioli miei, servi et schiavi de la Santità Vostra, ricorro a quella supplicandogli devotissimamente et con quelle lachrime che meritano et deveno haver loco di pietade apresso de ogni humile et bon core, che, come a ver Vicario di Christo et imitator, ch'è sopra ogni altro potentado, dè essere della infinità misericordia di quello gli piacia deponer l'ire, benchè da giustissima causa quelle deprendessero, et desistere da tanta invasione et ruyna de popoli et poveri vassalli; perchè, Santissimo et Beatissimo Padre, chi serà pio, chi serà misericordioso, se la pietà et misericordia non si trovasse in lo herede et legitimo possessor de le sacrosante et divine chiave del tanto giusto et bon primo pastor San Piero, et che deve mostrar agli altri con vivi esempli la humiltà et clementia di Christo, per esser lui perfetto confaliero di quello? Deh! Basti a Sua Santità, per il nome et virtù de Giesu la supplico, havere dimostrato gia che che mal puo replicare il suddito con il suo signor; ne gli piaccia permettere che si sparga più sangue delle pecorelle, delle quali Sua Santità ne è ver pastore, ricordevole di quelle divine parole, *castigati et non mortificati*: et tanto più che non deve esserli di tanta forza la inconsideratione de altrui (usata forse più presto con alcune cose esteriori, confidandosi in la benignità de la Santità Sua, che con l'animo, il quale gli è tutto volto alla obedientia et satisfatione de Sua Beatitudine), che debia vincere et excedere la clementia et misericordia di quello che gli è sustituto et representador del clementissimo et misericordiosissimo Giesù, come gli è meritamente Sua Santità, et far da quella nascere cosi gran ruina di tutta la famiglia mia serva et schiava di Sua Santità. Certo, Santissimo Padre, la fiducia mia gli è tanta appresso di Sua Beatitudine che, quando questo invasione non dependesse de la justissimamente et potentissimo braccio de la Santità Sua, che come la dà, cosi ancor la può subito togliere, ma dependesse da altri potentadi del mondo che seriano inferiori a la Santità Sua, sperarei fermissimamente tanto in lo presidio et ajuto suo, che ne li porrebbe, per difficil che fosse, silenzio, che le cose mie resterebbeno inviolate et secure. Donche con tutte le ferventissime prece mie et humile et abieta summissione supplico Sua Santità se degni effettualmente dimostrarmi ch'io non sono difraudata de questa mia tanta fiducia in Sua Santità; la quale, come humilissima serva che gli sono, devotamente la reverisco et adoro, basciando la terra dinanzi gli soi santissimi piedi, aspettando da ciò et la gratia et la benedictione con tutti questi figli servi di Sua Santità, alla quale, non contenta con questa de basciarli et prostrarmegli a gli soi santi piedi, li mando il Reverendo Vescovo d'Ischia, il quale supplirà a bocca più amplamente in mio nome, supplicando humilmente la Santità Sua si degni odirlo et darli fede; et piaccia al Signor sempiterno aver sempre la Santità Vostra in quella suprema felicità et triompho, che da Sua beatitudine è desiderata. D'Ischia, a' VIII d'Aprile del 41. De Vostra Beatitudine humilissima serva et schiava Ioanna Aragona de Colonna.[37]

Giovanna d'Aragona Colonna and Vittoria Colonna undoubtedly took care to circulate Giovanna's letter among the urban elites and courts in Naples and Rome, as well as among their friends in the north. In the meantime, Vittoria Colonna sent the Farnese pope a pair of sonnets echoing the main themes of Giovanna's letter. In these two sonnets, Vittoria mourns the tragedy suffered by the people in the town where she was born.[38] Following Giovanna's lead, she calls on the pope, as the shepherd of his flock, to be merciful and wise, clothing himself in the mantle of "the first father" and founder of the Church, Saint Peter. She urges Paul, above all, to banish anger born of pride and to show his flock the leadership that flows from "humble wishes" ("Mostrate . . . le voglie umili," sonnet 22, lines 5–6). Not war and arms but, rather, a rule of justice will bring peace and longed for prosperity, Vittoria concludes (sonnet 23, lines 13–14):

> I see my broad fields glitter with armed men
> and I hear song turned to weeping
> and sweet laughter give way to sorrow,
> where I first touched our ancient mother.
> Ah, show, O Pastor, wise and holy,
> your humble wishes, with high and lovely works.
> As true heir of the first father, clothe
> yourself in his glorious and holy mantle!
> We—if wrath does not hide or dim the truth
> in you—we are the children of your forbears,
> and good men were long wont to love us too;
> our ancestors were born under one sky,
> and they were nurtured together by one
> mother, in the sweet shade of one city.

> Veggio rilucer sol di armate squadre
> i miei sì larghi campi, ed odo il canto
> rivolto in grido, e 'l dolce riso in pianto
> là 've io prima toccai l'antica madre.
> Deh! Mostrate con l'opre alte e leggiadre
> le voglie umili, o Pastor saggio e santo!
> Vestite il sacro glorïoso manto
> come buon successor del primo Padre!

Semo, se 'l vero in voi non copre o adombra
lo sdegno, pur di quei più antichi vostri
figli, e da' buoni per lungo uso amati;
    sotto un sol cielo, entro un sol grembo nati
sono, e nudriti insieme a la dolce ombra
d'una sola città gli avoli nostri.

*("Rime epistolari," no. 22)*[39]

I pray to our Father in heaven that He may
send so great a flame from His fire
to your heart, O earthly father, that no
trace of the heat of human anger
may remain in you: the hapless deer never
fled the fierce lion the way unworthy love
of men's fleeting praise will fly from you,
once heavenly honor inflames your soul.
Then the happy flocks will come
to the sacred bosom aglow from the torch
that Heaven's great Light ignites on earth.
Thus will the divine and glorious nets
be full and the world made peaceful
with the staff, and not the arms of war.

Prego il Padre divin che tanta fiamma
mandi del fuoco Suo nel vostre core,
Padre nostro terren, che de l'ardore
de l'ira umana in voi non resti dramma.
    Non mai da fier leon inerme damma
fuggì come da voi l'indegno amore
fuggirà del mortal caduco onore,
se di quel di là su l'alma s'infiamma.
    Vedransi alor venir gli armenti lieti
al santo grembo caldo de la face
che 'l gran Lume del Ciel gli accese in terra.
    Così le sacre glorïose reti
saran già colme; con la verga in pace
si rese il mondo, e non con l'armi in guerra.

*("Rime epistolari," no. 23)*

While Giovanna's letter and Vittoria's sonnets were surely presented to Paul and perhaps read aloud before the members of the assembled papal court, still the pope did nothing to curb his generals, and conditions worsened for the townspeople penned inside Paliano and the other Colonna lands under siege.

On April 17, Vittoria Colonna's friend Guidiccioni wrote that while Ascanio was said to be marching toward Rome with a company of more than six hundred men, at Paliano there was almost no bread nor were there provisions of any kind, and the men, who still had not been paid, were becoming restive.[40] By April 21, Farnese had set up a third camp, and his troops were mounting an assault on Paliano from the other side of the town. Every day there were more defections from Paliano, and officers from the Farnese camp continued to lure recruits from the citadel with money and promises.[41] Meanwhile twenty-two hundred new infantrymen were encamped on the hill at Anagni, another of the Colonna fortresses nearby, and three aditional companies had arrived to guard the munitions and other supplies at Genazzano. Guidiccioni remarked that the difficulty of the terrain, the dense forests, and steep canyons made it impossible to secure the towns once they captured them.[42] But these were hardships Ascanio's newly recruited troops faced as well.

By May 6, according to Guidiccioni, there were less than nine hundred men left in the fortress in the upper town of Paliano.[43] And on May 8, the remnants of Ascanio's army elected twenty-five delegates from among themselves to conduct the town's surrender.[44] On that day, the last of Ascanio's men held up the spoils of war, dangling them over the battlements of the steep walls. For the benefit of the pope's men who waited below the walls, the soldiers waved the flowing lengths of silk, the cloth of gold, and the heavy silver vessels—perhaps the very plate and rich hangings Giulia Gonzaga had brought from Sabbioneta for her wedding at Paliano in 1526. Guidiccioni described the scene:[45]

> And when Signor Marzio [Marzio Colonna, a cousin of Ascanio in the pope's army] caused them to try to surrender Paliano, they responded that when they had someone to give it to, they would give it to him. But they were men of honor, they said, and they would do nothing not honorable. Today they have shown us from the wall cloths of silk and gold and plates of silver that are believed to belong to Ascanio, which were given to them yesterday evening, as I wrote to your holiness, and these they were dividing among themselves today.

> Et havendoli il signor Martio fatti tentare di renderla, ha risposto che quando l'havessino a dare a nissuno, la darieno a lui; però che lor sono huomini da bene, et non son per fare se non cose honorevoli. Hoggi han mostro dalle mura drappi di seta et d'oro, et piatti d'argento, che si crede sien di quelli del signore Ascanio che fur dati loro hiersera, com'io scrissi alla Santità Vostra, et hoggi gli haveran distribuiti fra loro. (May 8, 1541, letter 87)[46]

The next day at dawn, May 9, all Ascanio's men filed out of Paliano—foot soldiers, captains, standard-bearer, and other officals—and all were paid, counted, and released to go their own way.[47] The fortress was at last in full surrender, with Ascanio long gone from the scene. His cousins, Fabio Colonna and Torquato da Conte, and his chief captains were given letters of safe conduct and allowed to leave. For the time being, the siege of Paliano was over and, with it, the pope's war on Ascanio and Vittoria Colonna.

After the war, Pope Paul III confiscated the extensive landholdings of the Colonna family and razed their fortresses to the ground. Ascanio wandered aimlessly, now plotting to recover his lands, now trying his hand at alchemy in his castle at Marino where it was said he had constructed a *gabinetto alchimistico*.[48] The war affected Vittoria differently. Her reputation was enhanced not only by her diplomatic efforts to thwart Paul's seizure of her family's lands but also by her public exposure of the pope's geopolitical ambitions. She had assumed the moral high ground, and her reform movmement friends rallied around her when she returned to Rome. Among her literary cohort, her continuing friendship with the pope's commissary Guidiccioni demonstrated yet again Colonna's talent at strengthening alliances across political faultlines. Though neither Charles V nor Ercole II d'Este had come to her assistance in her war with the pope, Colonna kept intact her friendships with the emperor and the duke as well as her relationships with her Venetian editors and publishers and the academicians she knew, while she deepened her bond with the most celebrated living artist in Italy, Michelangelo. Colonna continued to show her loyalty to her brother and her in-laws, Giulia Gonzaga, Maria d'Aragona d'Avalos, and Giovanna d'Aragona Colonna, while tightening her ties to the members of Cardinal Reginald Pole's reform circle in Viterbo and the Protestant-leaning Marguerite de Navarre in France.

Six years after the war, Colonna died in Rome, with Cardinal Pole and Marcantonio Flaminio at her bedside. These were the intellectuals who remained closest to her in the aftermath of the fervid meetings of Valdés's followers and other reform thinkers who convened at Viterbo under Pole's direction in 1542–43. Colonna's death came early, when she was only fifty-five, but her legacy was long. Already by 1560, some twelve separate editions of her collected poems had been published in Venice.[49]

CHAPTER FOUR

# Between Rome and Venice:
# The Temples of Giovanna d'Aragona

Eight years after Vittoria Colonna's death, the Venetian poets engaged in a full-throttle public relations effort to promote Giovanna Colonna's reputation as the greatest literary patron of her age, publishing several books between 1555 and 1557 that showcased her name in their titles and celebrated her fame and magnanimity in the works included in those volumes. At the same time, the election of Paul IV (Gian Pietro Carafa) to the papacy in May 1555 ushered in the second act of the wars between the popes and the Colonna family. Already in the late summer of that year, both sides were moving toward war. On August 15, Carafa dispatched envoys to Urbino, Bologna, and Parma in an effort to raise an army of ten thousand men; two days later, Fernandez di Toledo d'Alba, Viceroy of Naples, ordered the boarding and impounding of two of the pope's ships at Civitavecchia.[1] While the pope waited for shipments of men and matériel from France, Giovanna Colonna's son, Marcantonio, and Alba renewed their treaties of alliance with Philip II of Spain, the Sforza of Milan, and Cosimo I de' Medici. Meanwhile, Marcantonio Colonna erected new fortifications at Paliano.[2]

Carafa showed himself not only passionately anti-Spanish; he was also committed to the prosecution of heretics, no matter how tenuous the charge or unlikely the defendant.[3] Giovanna Colonna, her sister Maria d'Aragona d'Avalos, and their sisters-in-law Vittoria Colonna and Giulia Gonzaga Colonna had devoted themselves, in the pope's native Naples, to spreading the reform teachings of Juan de Valdés and Bernardino Ochino, whose books had been banned as heresies in every *catalogo* sponsored by the Roman Holy Office since 1549. Thus Giovanna's associations and activities within the reform movement in Naples combined with her political identity as a dual member of the *casate* Aragona and Colonna—not to mention her long-standing affiliation with Charles V and later his son Philip II—made it dangerous for her to remain in Rome, even before the war broke out.[4]

By December 1555, Carafa had placed Giovanna d'Aragona Colonna under house arrest in the Colonna palace in Rome. He had already thrown her personal secretary and her cousin, Camillo Colonna, into prison and had issued a bull essentially prohibiting her from contracting marriage alliances for her daughters. Around midnight on December 31, 1555, Giovanna d'Aragona, accompanied by her two teenage daughters, Agnesina and Gerolama, her daughter-in-law Felice Orsini, Felice and Marcantonio's baby Giovanna, and their secretaries slipped out of the Colonna palace. Disguised as a peasant woman and wearing a dress of rough cloth, a head scarf and heavy boots, Giovanna led the members of her entourage, similarly disguised, out of the city through the Porta San Lorenzo.[5] Fleeing for their lives, the party traveled from there via Tivoli to the Colonna stronghold at Tagliacozzo, where they settled in until the war's end.[6]

The news of Giovanna Colonna's flight traveled across the peninsula, enhancing the image she already had not only as the ally of the Venetian poets and bookmen, but at the same time as something of a maverick. In 1535, Colonna had left her husband, and taking their six children with her, she lived as an independent woman, setting up apartments for her family in the houses of her aunt and sister. At forty-five, she was still considered a woman of such beauty and charisma, according to the gossips, that her sister Maria's secretary Luca Contile had risked his job—and lost it—when he dedicated a book of his love sonnets to Giovanna.[7] But the poets also sought her patronage because of her connections. A shrewd powerbroker and alliance builder via the marriage market, Colonna had by 1552 arranged unions for her daughter Vittoria with the Viceroy of Naples's son, her son Fabrizio with a daughter of the governor of Milan, and her other son Marcantonio with Paul III's granddaughter.

Some months before Giovanna fled Rome, Girolamo Ruscelli published an international poetry anthology in her honor, featuring works in several languages, titled *Del tempio alla divina signora donna Giovanna d'Aragona* (The temple for the divine signora . . .). Ruscelli's *Tempio* was probably already circulating in Rome in the spring of that year, around the time of Carafa's election as pope.[8] The following year, in the thick of Carafa's war with Spain and its allies in Italy, Cosimo de' Medici's official printer rushed to bring out a still more inflammatory work celebrating Colonna, Giuseppe Betussi's *Le imagini del tempio della signora donna Giovanna Aragona* (Images from the temple of . . .).[9]

Despite Ascanio Colonna's arrest by Charles's agents and his subsequent imprisonment in Naples from 1554 until his death in 1557, conditions in the Campagna were more favorable to the Colonna family under the Carafa pope, Paul IV, than they had been under Paul III. When Carafa excommunicated Ascanio Colonna and his son Marcantonio and seized the Colonna towns of Paliano and Rocca di Papa in May 1556, Marcantonio and the Duke of Alba had no trouble rallying allies to their cause. More was at stake this time than just the Colonna towns; the pope was now fighting to unseat well-entrenched pro-Spanish regimes not only in Naples but in Milan. By the beginning of September 1556, Alba had a disciplined army of twelve thousand Italian and Spanish recruits poised to invade the papal states and Rome.

In late September 1556, Marcantonio Colonna and Alba took Tivoli, Vicovaro, and Nettuno, and with the exception of Paliano and Velletri, they controlled the whole of the Campagna. In November, when Colonna and Alba marched into Ostia, cutting off the pope's access to the sea, the aid Carafa counted on from France still did not come. Hostilities dragged on another year, but when Colonna moved his troops within five miles of Rome, easily occupying Valmontone and Palestrina, the pope at last agreed to come to the bargaining table. With the papal states now in ruins, on September 19, 1557, Alba, accompanied by Marcantonio Colonna, rode into Rome, kissed the feet of the pope, and was pardoned in a ritual enactment of the war's end and the cessation of hostilities.[10]

### ❧ POPE PAUL IV'S WAR AGAINST THE POETS ❧

Giovanna d'Aragona Colonna and her sister Maria d'Aragona d'Avalos had been major literary patrons since mid-1530s when they presided with Victoria Colonna and their aunt Costanza d'Avalos over literary salons in Ischia and Naples, where politics, religion, and literature were discussed with equal avidity. After Charles V made Maria's husband, Alfonso d'Avalos, his governor of Milan in 1538, the d'Aragona sisters led salons in that city and later Pavia where both new poetry and the writings of Valdés, Ochino, and other reform thinkers were subjects of debate. When Maria's husband died, she and her sister returned to Naples and Ischia, where they continued to support many of the same poets during the 1550s who had frequented their houses fifteen years before.

In 1556, the Carafa pope, Paul IV, threatened the sisters' lives and reputations not only by making war on the Colonna towns but by criminalizing the works of the poets who were their clients. During the spring, when Paul IV excommunicated Marcantonio and Ascanio Colonna and seized the Colonna strongholds of Paliano and Rocca di Papa, he ordered the Roman Holy Office to undertake the production of a new *catalogo* of prohibited works. Paul IV was the first pope to ban books of secular poetry, dialogues, and novellas on the sole grounds that the officers of the Inquisition had judged them sexually suggestive or lewd, although these works articulated no dogma inimical to the Church.[11] The new *catalogo*, though slow to go to press since Carafa was preoccupied with the war, was more radical and wide sweeping in its condemnations than any of previous index. Begun in 1556, this index banned the complete works of 550 authors and hundreds of single titles, among which were works of Lucian, Dante, Valla, Poggio, Savonarola, Erasmus, Machiavelli, and Rabelais.[12] Also condemned were a number of poets who were the mainstays of the Giolito anthologies, among them, Aretino, Berni, Niccolò Franco, Bernardino Tomitano, and even the compiler of the Farnese pope's 1549 *catalogo*, Giovanni Della Casa.[13] Forbidden on Carafa's list were all books anonymously published, undated, or printed without ecclesiastical permission; among these were nearly sixty editions of the Bible.[14] Simple expurgation was ordered for such Italian classics as the *Decameron* and many other standard literary titles, but when the pope prohibited altogether the publication of Jewish books and ordered the burning of the Talmud, Cardinal Cristoforo Madruzzo, who was himself a patron of Ruscelli's several poetry anthologies, established a Hebrew press at Riva di Trento, which he kept going until 1562.[15]

## ❧ THE TWO TEMPLES OF GIOVANNA D'ARAGONA COLONNA ☙

It was in this climate that in 1555, 1556, and 1557 three leading publishers in Venice and Florence brought out two major works celebrating Giovanna d'Aragona Colonna, the wife and mother of Paul's worst enemies. In each of these works, Colonna was eulogized as a goddess, while the books themselves were figured as "temples" dedicated to her service. Girolamo Ruscelli's massive anthology *Del tempio alla divina signora donna Giovanna d'Aragona fabricato da tutti i più gentili spiriti, & in tutte le lingue principali del mondo* was published in 1555 by Plinio Pietrasanta who was no stranger to the politics of the index (fig. 8).

· FIGURE 8 ·
Title page from Girolamo Ruscelli's *Del tempio alla
divina signora donna Giovanna d'Aragona* (Venice: Pietrasanta,
1555). Courtesy of the Newberry Library.

In 1554, he had shepherded to press the poems of the well-known salonnière Gaspara Stampa who died suddenly just months before her oeuvre came out: a collection of poems that told the story of her illicit affair with a socially prominent man who had, as she saw it, neglected and abused her—and whose name she made public in her book.[16] Her sister Cassandra Stampa dedicated her work posthumously to their mutual friend, Monsignor Giovanni Della Casa, author of the 1549 *Catalogo*. Similarly motivated to find a protector for his work, Ruscelli prefaced his *Tempio alla Giovanna d'Aragona* with a long dedicatory letter to Cardinal Cristoforo Madruzzo, then the presiding officer over the Council of Trent, the chief organ of the Counter-Reformation and the ongoing Index of Prohibited Books and a man widely respected as one of the Church's most prudent and influential prelates. In his letter to Madruzzo, Ruscelli, in his role as editor and architect of a vast collection of works by other writers, compared the construction of his "temple" for Giovanna Colonna to Homer's monument to Achilles in the *Iliad* and Virgil's celebration of his hero in the *Aeneid*.[17]

The sales of anthologies of contemporary poets probably reached their peak in the 1550s, and certainly Ruscelli's *Tempio* led off with an all-star cast that included Ferrante Carrafa, Girolamo Muzio, Benedetto Varchi, Luigi Tansillo, Domenico Veniero, Lodovico Domenichi, Luca Contile, Alessandro Piccolomini, and Annibal Caro. Among the women poets represented were Gaspara Stampa, Fausta Tacita, Coletta Pasquale, and Laura Terracina—in some ways the dean of women poets since by the mid-1550s six editions of her collected poems and three of her commentaries on Ariosto were in print.[18] Despite the number of subscriptions that were surely sold before the book hit the Rialto booksellers' stands, given that it boasted works by 277 contemporary authors and poems not only in Italian but also Latin, Greek, and Spanish, Ruscelli's phenomenal 524-page anthology was still a flop. It was published only once again, ten years later by the Venetian printer Francesco Rocca.

A year later, Ruscelli's longtime friend and fellow writer Giuseppe Betussi published, in Florence with Cosimo de' Medici's official printer, Torrentino, a work he billed as the sequel to Ruscelli's work: *Le imagini del tempio della signora donna Giovanna Aragona*.[19] Betussi's work was not an anthology but a dialogue between himself and Ruscelli masked as an allegory between the figures Truth (*Verità*) and Fame (*Fama*). While Betussi attacked Ruscelli for the shallowness of his work, he used the *Imagini del tempio*, above all, to launch a thinly disguised attack on the policies of Paul IV. The short dialogue sold well and was published again the next year in Venice, although his publisher, Giovanni de' Rossi, was never able to get from either Venice or the Vatican the obligatory *con privilegio* stamped on the title page, which was required in order to distribute or sell a book. But plenty of booksellers were willing to bend the law.

### ❧ WHY A MONUMENT FOR GIOVANNA COLONNA NOW? ☙

Why was there so much literary agitation around a single female figure, one who, far from being dead, would live another two decades after the poets'

erection of her temple? It was not an uncommon practice in Renaissance Italy for an editor or a well-known literary figure—and Ruscelli and Betussi
played both roles—to assemble a funerary volume to honor the passing of a
prominent statesman or literary figure or to mark the untimely death of one
of her children. In 1555, Francesco Cristiani published such an anthology of
poetry to pay tribute to Livia Colonna, Ascanio Colonna's young ward who
was kidnapped, raped, and murdered.[20] Four years later, drawing on many of
the same poets who participated in Ruscelli's *Tempio alla Giovanna d'Aragona*,
Dionigi Atanagi edited an expansive collection of sonnets to mourn the sud-
den death of the young Friulian painter Irene di Spilimbergo.[21] The notion
of the book as a mausoleum, a temple, a work in marble or metal had been
around at least since Horace's claim that with his lyric opus he had "built
a temple more lasting than bronze" (*Odes* 3.30.1).[22] But in 1555–57 Giovanna
Colonna was still very much alive. Why then did two prominent writers rush
to publish a memorial for this ardent advocate of religious reform and longtime patron of the arts and letters? Compared to her highly visible sister-in-
law, Vittoria Colonna, and her cousin by marriage, Giulia Gonzaga Colonna,
Giovanna cut a less public figure. Still, with Vittoria Colonna's death and
Gonzaga's retirement to Naples, poets saw Giovanna as a major promoter of
Italian literature and patron of humanist values.

In printing and circulating at least a thousand copies of their *Tempio alla
Giovanna d'Aragona* at the outset of Paul IV's papacy, Ruscelli and other leaders in the publishing world had launched a preemptive strike in the broader
forum of Italian public opinion against a pope from whom neither they nor
their patrons could expect anything but aggression.[23] If, as we observed earlier, the poets and bookmen saw in Giovanna Colonna's trials a parallel to
their own burdens under Paul III and later Paul IV, they also saw an analogue
for themselves in Vittoria Colonna. Certainly it was no accident that in 1557,
on the tenth anniversary of her death, Betussi dedicated the first Venetian edition of his *Imagini della tempio della signora donna Giovanna Aragona* to Colonna's
namesake and niece, Vittoria Colonna di Toledo, whose name appears on the
title page of the volume (fig. 9).

## ❧ THE ARCHITECTS OF GIOVANNA'S TWO TEMPLES ❧

"I wanted to become another Ulysses," Giuseppe Betussi wrote in an afterword to his *Imagini del tempio*.[24] For this society journalist with an edge, this
Homeric hero of the pen as he fashioned himself, one military patron seemed
to lead to the next, and it was through his connection with Alfonso d'Avalos

LE IMAGINI

# DEL TEMPIO

## DELLA SIGNORA

### DONNA GIOVANNA

ARAGONA,

Dialogo di M. Giuseppe Betufsi.

# ALLA ILLVSTRISSIMA

## SIGNORA DONNA

### VITTORIA COLONNA

DI TOLLEDO,

*IN VENETIA,*

Per Giouanni de' Rofsi.

M. D. LVII.

D.F.L.

· FIGURE 9 ·

Title page blazoning the names of Vittoria Colonna's
niece and namesake and her sister-in-law Giovanna
d'Aragona. From Betussi's *Le imagini del tempio della signora
donna Giovanna Aragona. Alla . . . signora donna
Vittoria Colonna di Tolledo* (Venice: de' Rossi, 1557).
Courtesy of the Newberry Library.

and his wife Maria d'Aragona in Pavia, where he attended their "evenings"
and was a member of the academy (dei Fenici) they patronized, that he came
in contact with Maria's much admired sister Giovanna d'Aragona Colonna.[25]
Betussi's Italian translation of Boccaccio's famous ancient women's lives,
the *De mulieribus claris*, made him uniquely qualified to compose Colonna's

*Tempio* with its tribute to a roster of contemporary Italian women since he had already appended to his edition of Boccaccio's work his own catalog of over fifty modern Italian women's lives.[26] Moreover, having witnessed the destruction of Siena, which he saw reduced to rubble by Cosimo de' Medici and his ally Charles V in the siege of 1555–56, Betussi spoke with authority in his passionate indictment of the policies of Pope Paul IV and other princes of Italy.[27]

In some ways, Betussi was the perfect choice for the author of a literary "temple" dedicated to one of Italy's most celebrated women in the 1550s. Born the son of a painter in the small town of Bassano in the Veneto and, like Pietro Aretino, largely self-educated, Betussi rose quickly to the top, to the crème de la crème of Italian literary society.[28] He moved in the best circles and knew all the interesting people, mingling with the social and intellectual elites wherever he found himself—Venice, Milan, Rome, Florence, Siena, or Naples—and he traveled a great deal between those cities. He had begun his literary career in Padua, where soon after his arrival he was inducted into the exclusive academy of the Infiammati. But he soon grew bored there and moved on to Venice, where the first two books he wrote—and he was then just thirty-two—were hits: the *Dialogo amoroso*, published by Andrea Arrivabene in 1543, and his second dialogue *Raverta*, which went to press the following year at the most prestigious house in Venice, that of Gabriel Giolito where he was employed as a corrector and translator. But his principal patrons included a string of soldiers who were also prominent literary figures: Camillo Caula, Gian Luigi Vitelli, Alfonso d'Avalos, Vicino Orsini, and Collaltino Collalto, who had been the poet Gaspara Stampa's lover.[29] From 1555 to 1558, Betussi visited the houses of his friends and patrons, Ippolito Gonzaga, the Borromeo family, and the Madruzzi family in Pavia; he stayed with Varchi in Florence and visited Giovanna d'Aragona in Naples and her daughter Vittoria Colonna di Toledo in Rome.[30]

Of the two master architects, Ruscelli was the literary blueblood. He had studied Greek philosophy at the University of Padua and had founded the Accademia dello Sdegno in Rome. He was a noted humanist, Hellenist, linguist, and aficionado of contemporary women writers and literary patrons, whose home base was Venice though he was a native of Viterbo.[31] Primarily a scholar and editor, Ruscelli had been acclaimed for his edition of Plato's *Timaeus* and his translation of Ptolemy's *Geography*, and he had the clout to slam publicly what he saw as a slapdash translation of Ovid's *Metamorphoses* by Giolito's principal editor and pressman, Lodovico Dolce.[32] Like Betussi, Ruscelli traveled frequently between Venice, Rome, and Naples and had many titled patrons, among them the d'Avalos and d'Aragona-Colonna women. Even before the day Ruscelli had rallied the literary community in Venice around his *Tempio* project in 1551, he had given top billing to Giovanna's sister Maria d'Avalos on the title page of Giovambattista d'Azzia's poetic tribute to her, *Lettura sopra un sonnetto dell'illustrissimo Signor Marchese della Terza alla divina signora Marchesa del Vasto* (1552), which he edited.[33] The *Lettura* contains a remarkable list of the names of 259 noteworthy women who came from thirty-five different cities in Italy and were either writers or literary patrons.[34] Ruscelli edited several other poetry anthologies that included works by numerous women and he redacted a posthumous edition of the *Rime* of Vittoria Colonna.[35] He was never arraigned by the Officers of the Inquisition, but his collaboration with such convicted heretics as Bartolomeo Spadafora and his book of letters of the rich and famous, *Lettere di Diversi Autori Eccellenti*, which featured a long list of Valdesians and known reform activists—including Giulia Gonzaga, Vittoria Colonna, and the protestant-leaning Marguerite Queen of Navarre, among others—make it surprising that he was never called to testify.[36]

### ❧ THE CHANGING DIALOGUE OF THE 1550S: WOMEN TAKE CENTER STAGE ☙

Women interlocutors and discussion topics circling around the nature of the sexes, the role of women in promoting culture, love inside and outside marriage, lists of accomplished women of the past and present, and other such topics dominated the dialogues of the period 1540–60 in ways readers of Castiglione's *Il Cortigiano* could not have imagined. During these twenty years, four of the most prominent dialogue and treatise writers—Lodovico Domenichi, Alessandro Piccolomini, Girolamo Ruscelli, and Giuseppe Betussi—repeatedly dedicated their woman-centered works to prominent women writers and intellectuals, not a few of them involved in the reform movement. Lucia Bassani has observed that a stark gap separates even Betussi's early dialogue *Raverta* (1545), which features in the lead role the famous poet and courtesan Franceschina Baffa, from his later work *Leonora* (1557), where the dialogue's most important speeches are delivered not only by a woman but by a writer and socially prominent married woman—Leonora Ravoira di Falletta.[37] In this dialogue, the male characters sit in a circle around Leonora while she discourses on the nature of God, true beauty (*vera bellezza*), and the soul; and, in a passage full of resonances from Proclus's commentaries on Plato's *Timaeus* and perhaps Iamblichus's *Mysteries*, she holds forth on tutelary angels (*angeli* or *demoni*).[38]

## ❧ THE POLITICAL DIALOGUE AT MIDCENTURY ❧

Betussi's *Imagini del tempio della signora donna Giovanna Aragona* treats not theories of love or gender but politics and personalities. The dialogue has only two speaking parts, both female: Truth and Fame (*Verità* and *Fama*), who are introduced at the opening of the work as dialectical opposites without representing masculinity or femininity in any traditional sense, even within the parameters of allegory.[39] Instead, the work confronts the classical dilemmas raised by Plato in book 10 of the *Republic*: What role should the writer play in society? Does imaginative literature pose a danger to the republic? Is philosophy superior to poetry?

Unlike Ruscelli's primarily encomiastic homage to Giovanna, Betussi's *Imagini del tempio* is a dialogue of ideas. Its characters condemn, in general terms, the military and economic policies that describe the programs of Popes Paul III and Paul IV and express sorrow and outrage at the senseless destruction of Siena by "barbarous peoples," alluding, without naming names, to the long bombardment and siege of Siena carried out by Cosimo de' Medici and Charles V's troops in their joint efforts to subdue the city and perpetuate its status as a Florentine protectorate in 1555–56. And even if the subject of the *Imagini's* veneration had not been a victim of the pope's persecution, Betussi could hardly have seen his dialogue as a safe undertaking, particularly since both its first and second editions came out in years when the new enlarged index and the trials conducted by the Holy Office in Rome were aimed at intimidating writers and publishers. In point of fact, unlike Ruscelli's *Tempio*, the *Imagini* went to press without the requisite "permission to publish" (*con privilegio*) on its title page.

But Betussi's dialogue is not a medieval allegory where stock figures represent a contest between antithetical ideas.[40] His Truth and Fame are more complex figures, whose roles overlap and whose characters are susceptible to persuasion and change. Early on in the dialogue, Truth accuses Fame of disseminating lies and truth indiscriminately in her role as the chief organ of public opinion. Exercising her own rhetorical powers, she asks Fame to stop flying from place to place and to walk with feet planted firmly (*piombato piede*, leaden feet) on the ground alongside Time, the "father" of Truth.[41] Fame shows that she is more than mere talk or gossip—that she has some moral views on the state of the world. Growing eloquent in her lament over the wars between the Italian princes, she launches an attack on those responsible for the two wars being simultaneously fought on Italian soil in 1555. She names no names but clearly alludes to Pope Paul IV's initiation of the war against

Spain and her Italian allies and to Cosimo de' Medici and Charles V's siege and sack of Siena. In a trope de rigueur in humanist rhetoric since the fall of Constantinople to the Turks, Fame castigates the most powerful heads of the Italian states for failing to present a unified front against Islam, the real enemy. She inveighs against the political chaos and the abuse of power she sees in Italy, voicing sentiments that Truth finds surprising in Fame—but gratifying. Truth might have given the same speech herself:

FAME:    I will make a conjecture about the present war in Italy, its outcome, and the goals of the princes who initiated it: mainly that some of them can hardly be called men of reason since they are motivated not by the intention to rule justly—because then they would go where the wealth of the orient is located and where fierce and inhuman peoples have destroyed the Empire—not to mention the title Constantine bequeathed to us.[42] But instead, motivated by ambition and evil, these princes go to war with one another while they allow the common enemy of the Christian religion to aggrandize itself, so whatever these princes lose in power and honor, the enemy gains.[43] I see Christianity so abandoned that it now even risks the extinction of its name. And already I have a sense of foreboding that while the princes are at war with one another in Picardy, Piedmont, and beautiful Tuscany (which will remain deserted and left with little praise for anyone), poor Hungary will be assaulted by barbarian armies and proud Scythians, so that now, though she may have more luck than strength, and God may not want it, not only will she be tormented by the Infidels but she will become a ladder and a passageway for them to lay siege to what little has been left untouched after the predations of the Goths, the Vandals and the rest of those first barbarian nations who plundered poor Italy and brought about the decline of the Roman empire.[44] I will go, I say, increasing the din in the ears of anyone and everyone I can, and perhaps I will rouse some noble mind from its torpor so that it will attempt to recover its senses in some lasting and memorable work.

TRUTH:    O Fame, if you always acted in this way and engaged in such worthy works, what a great friend of mine you would be! Now you are not speaking only as yourself. You speak with my voice when you say that the majority if not all the men who now rule this ill-fated Italy of ours are the Gaiuses, the Neros, the Mezentiuses, the Attilas, the Brennuses.[45] To brand them all with one name, they are spirits from Hell in human form, I say.

FAMA:    [fol. 5] Farò fare congiettura dalla presente guerra d'Italia, del successo, e del fino de' Principi, [end fol. 5r; begin fol. 5v] che l'hanno mossa:

tutto che malamente alcuno di loro possa esser chiamato degno di ragione, perciochè mossi, non da giusto animo di signoreggiare, perchè andrebbono la dove sono le Orientali richezze, e dove fiere e in humane genti hanno levato l'imperio—non che il titolo che ci lasciò Costantino. Ma mossi anzi da ambitione e da iniquità, urtano se stessi e lasciano aggrandire il comune nimico della fede Christiana, onde quanto essi perdono di dominio e di riputazione, egli tanto acquistando; chiaramente veggio, così diserta la Christianità che ancho il nome va a pericolo di spegnersi. Et già parmi poter far presagio, mentre nelle guerre di Piccardia, del Piemonti, e della bella Thoscana (la quale rimarrà diserta e abbandonata con poca lode di ciascuno) cozzano insieme, che la misera Ungheria sarà talmente assalita dalle armi barbare e da' fieri Scithi, che se gia hebbe più sorte che forza hora, e Dio no 'l voglia, non pure sarà stranamente travagliata, ma diverrà scala e farassi passo a quelli infideli per opprimere quel poco, che intatto è rimasto dalle reliquie de' Goti, de' Vandali, e del resto di quelle prime barbare nationi, che la misera Italia depredarono e fecero declinare l'imperio Romano. Andrò dico, nelle orecchie di questo e di quello accrescendo irrumori, e destando forse qualche generoso animo mezzo addormentato a cercar di risentirsi con qualche eterna, e memorabil opra.

VERITÀ:    O Fama, se tu sempre facessi i tuoi movimenti con l'essecutione di così degne imprese, quanto amica mi saresti: perchè hora non da te stessa discorri, ma con la propria mia voce parli, atteso che quelli c'hora reggono questa ma l'aventurata Italia—la maggior parte, per non dir tutti—sono Gai, sono Neroni, sono Mezentii, sono Attili, sono Brenni, e per dar loro un solo nome, spiriti infernali sotto humana forma. (Fols. 5–6)

## ❧ BETUSSI'S PLATONIC ATTACK ON RUSCELLI ☙

In the *Imagini*, Betussi draws deeply from his store of knowledge of Latin literature: specifically from the Roman poets Horace, Vergil, Propertius, Lucan, Martial, Apuleius, Gellius, and Statius, where both Truth and Fame are variously personified. As the dialogue progresses, it becomes more obvious that Betussi is using the *Imagini* as a springboard to criticize his classicist colleague for his cowardice in producing a work so bland and so reliant for its effects on formal perfection; the works Ruscelli chose for his anthology volume were reproductions ad nauseam of the Petrarchan sonnet. For the sake of variety, Ruscelli added Spanish, Greek, and Latin poets to the mix, but the work didn't go anywhere: it lacked ideas. Fame (Ruscelli) had made a "beautiful beginning," Truth observed. She had brought together talented men from all over the world, but why had she stopped just at the climactic moment when "so many excellent architects—Greek, Latin, Italian—had already produced so many beautiful pedestals, fine columns, and marvelous perspectives?" (fol. 7v). [Et nel colmo del finire cosi lodevole opra, pare che arresti, e già per lo mondo suona il bel principio di cosi ricca macchina, in cui vi hanno posto le mani tanti eccelenti Architettori, e Greci, e Latini, e Italiani con tanti belli ordini, con tante belle base, con tante degne colonne, e con si mirabili prospecttive.]

"Leave the habit of telling lies and making up stories solely to those who are born in the world to work with rhythm and shading, and take care instead to exalt persons of merit with justice and the truth," she counsels Fame (fol. 6v).[46] [Lascia l'abito delle novelle e delle menzogne a nati solo nel mondo per far numero e ombra. Curati piu tosto d'essaltare le persone di merito col giusto, et col vero.] Truth's advice to Fame against writing poetry suggests that Betussi could count on his readers getting the reference to the locus classicus in book 10 of Plato's *Republic*, where Socrates disparages poets and poetry in much the same way, as incompatible with the representation of truth:

> Shall we, then, lay it down that all the poetic tribe, beginning with Homer, are imitators of excellence and of the other things that they "create," and do not lay hold of the truth, but, as we were just now saying, the painter will fashion, himself knowing nothing of the cobbler's art, what appears to be a cobbler to him and likewise to those who know nothing but judge only by forms and colors? . . . And similarly, I suppose, we shall say that the poet himself, knowing nothing but how to imitate, lays on with words and phrases the colors of the several arts in such fashion that others equally ignorant, who see things only through words, will deem his words most excellent, whether he speak in rhythm, meter, and harmony about cobbling or generalship or anything whatever. (*Republic* 600e–601b)[47]

Beyond objections to mere formalism, Betussi masquerading as Truth wonders whether writing encomia is possible when the subject's good name and that of her family are under attack and even the goddess Fortuna is against her (*contraria Fortuna di lei*). Was the pope's persecution of the Colonna clan deterring Ruscelli (Fame) from publishing a stronger work, Betussi taunted his colleague?

TRUTH:    Why haven't you finished designing the temple as is fitting for so sublime a goddess? Perhaps you are frightened by her enemy Fortuna, who is so bent on persecuting [Giovanna's] lineage that she does not see, being blind and wretched herself, that she is only strengthening the dynasty's hand.

VERITÀ:     Perchè non hai finito di ordinarlo secondo il merito di così sublime Dea?
            Ti spaventa, forse la contraria fortuna di lei, che con l'ingegnarsi di per-
            seguitare il suo lignaggio, misera e cieca, non s'avede che più gli porge
            vigore. (Fol. 7v)

There can be no doubt that the "contraria Fortuna" Truth speaks of refers specifically to the heavy blows Paul IV dealt the Colonna family, just days before Betussi put the last touches on his dialogue—though the pope could not of course be named. It had been on May 4, 1556, as we observed earlier, that Paul had published a bull transferring ownership of all of the Colonna fiefdoms to the pope's own nephew Giovanni Carafa.[48] Six days later in Rome, Betussi penned his dedicatory preface to the *Imagini*, carefully dating it "X di Maggio MDLVI di Roma" and addressing it, with an equal sense of resolve, to Ascanio's daughter Vittoria Colonna di Toledo, whose mother Pope Paul had driven out of Rome in December and whose powerful aunt had now been dead for a decade.

When Fame showers praise first on Ruscelli's sonnets and, then, on the precise roster of celebrated poets who are placed in the front of Ruscelli's *Tempio* anthology—Luca Contile, Giuliano Gosellini, Domenico Venier, Annibal Caro, Alessandro Piccolomini, Tansillo, Giovanni Della Casa, and Lodovico Domenichi—it is equally clear that this character represents Betussi's rival defending his own work. Quoting Horace almost verbatim, Fame (Ruscelli) challenges Truth (Betussi) to come up with a better paradigm for a temple: "Have I not caused a work to be sculpted in marble and stone that will endure forever?" (fol. 8r). [Ho fatto intagliarlo con marmi, con pietre, che dureranno eterne?][49]

Truth's response is negative. Fame's temple has provided a foundation, but now she must do more: she must adorn Giovanna d'Aragona's altar.

### ❧ PUBLISHING FEMALE-MALE LITERARY ALLIANCES ꝫ❧

In her role as temple architect, Truth lays out her plan for a sculpture gallery featuring images of twenty-four contemporary women patrons and poets, paired with the same number of male writers, editors, and academicians who will serve as the women's *conservatori*—their curators and their means of support (fig. 10).[50] According to Truth's blueprint, each woman will represent the virtue that best suits her character. There will be friezes, colossal statues, and columns promulgating the honor of the "most extraordinary women in Europe." But the emphasis will be on the group rather than the single figure. Truth's

· FIGURE 10 ·

Paired rosters representing literary women (le imagini) and their male partners (i conservatori delle imagini) from the Italian academies and presses. From Betussi's Le imagini del tempio della signora donna Giovanna Aragona. Alla . . . signora donna Vittoria Colonna di Tolledo (Venice: de' Rossi, 1557). Courtesy of the Newberry Library.

novel idea of selecting different features from among a group of extraordinary
women to form a composite image of feminine virtue comes, she boasts, from
Pliny's *Natural History*, the ancient encyclopedia cited perhaps more frequently
than any other book in the Renaissance as proof of one's erudition. According
to Pliny, when the Crotonians commissioned Zeuxis to produce a painting of
Venus for the local temple, the painter produced his ideal of beauty by using a
team of rotating girls as his models rather than one girl.[51]

In crossing the modern dialogue of ideas with the classical, though still
popular, catalog of famous women and men, Betussi produced a new hybrid
discourse.[52] But his novel decision to pair women and men's images in his
temple had more important implications since with this format he published
and thereby publicized, perhaps for the first time, a practice that had become
a signal feature of the literary culture of the 1550s: collaboration between elite
women and men of the academies and presses. At the time of the publication
of the *Imagini*, half the women Betussi named were published authors or patrons whose names had either appeared or would soon appear in the popular
poetry anthologies produced and marketed by Giolito and other leading Venetian printers between 1545 and 1559.[53] Among these, Betussi named Gostanza Bonromea, Livia Torniella Bonromea, Alda Torella Lunata, Ottavia
Baiarda Beccaria, Laudomia Forteguerri Petrucci, Francesca de' Baldi, Virginia Salvi, Lavinia Sanvitale Sforza, Lucia Bertana, and Leonora Ravoira
Falletta.[54] And as a kind of coda to the work, Betussi added twenty-three
more literary women to his roster, expanding the ranks of his republic of
women to a total of forty-seven figures.

Most of the women in Betussi's colonnade of twenty-four figures had close
ties to Betussi's "conservators," among whom were literary academy members and editors such as Domenichi, Ruscelli, and Varchi who figured prominently in the Venetian book industry as cultivators of women authors.[55] As we
shall see in the next two chapters, such men as Varchi, Muzio, and Alessandro Piccolomini, though they were never employees at the Venetian presses,
nonetheless acted as important recruiters, readers, mentors, and agents for a
number of women writers on an informal basis. All twenty-four of the men
whom Betussi names as patrons, supporters, and friends (*conservatori*) for the
female *imagini* were well-known literary figures in the period. Nineteen of
these men figure prominently in the highly successful modern poetry anthologies of the 1540s and 1550s published by Giolito, who by this time was the
leading commercial publisher in Venice, and by his imitators.[56] At least two of
Betussi's *conservatori*—Thomaso Porcacchi and Betussi, among others—came
from neither money nor the nobility and lived from time to time in Giolito's

house working as his collaborators, editors, and translators.[57] Porcacchi, Domenichi, Bentivoglio, Muzio, and Lollio, whose books Giolito published, frequented Giolito's home and were considered regular members of his so-called academy.[58] Almost all twenty-four of Betussi's male *lembe* were affiliated with one or more of the prominent Italian academies. Of central importance for this group was an academy Giovanna's sister Maria d'Aragona d'Avalos supported in Milan—the Fenici, where the *conservatori* Giuliano Gosellini, Ruscelli, Luca Contile, Cavalier Giovanni Vendramini, Ferrante d'Adda, Muzio and Betussi were enrolled.[59] Ercole Bentivoglio, though not a member of the Fenici, was an academy kingpin of sorts, holding memberships in four other major academies in addition to Giolito's: the Elevati and the Filareti in Ferrara, the Pellegrini in Venice, and the Infiammati in Padua. Key hubs for intellectual women and men in the smaller cities were the *veglie* (salons or evenings)—attended by such *tempio* icons as Laudomia Forteguerri Petrucci, Giudith Forteguerri Baccinelli, and Virginia Salvi in Siena—and the *cenacoli* (suppers or symposia) hosted by Giovanna and her sister Maria d'Aragona d'Avalos in Milan and Pavia. Betussi's dialogue *Leonora* documents the kinds of discussions that the intellectual circle around Leonora Ravoira Falletti held at her home in Monferrato, where he was a guest for several weeks himself.

Table 1 provides an overview of the geographical distribution of his gallery of women and their academy ties and associations with the men of the presses.[60] While all the women in Giovanna's temple sculpture belong to elite families, the men in Betussi's republic of letters represent, as I note above, a range of classes and occupations. The geographical distribution of Giovanna's colonnade is noteworthy for its complete exclusion of women from Venice and Florence and its near omission of literary women from Rome and Naples, there being only one woman from each of those cities. Five of the women are from Milan and its satellite cities Pavia and Novara; four come from Siena; and four from the northwestern region of Italy—Savona, Genoa, and Monferrato.

The virtues Betussi celebrates in the *Imagini* are courtly, peacetime values—grace, moderation, liberality, magnanimity, beauty, courtesy, kindness, modesty, honor, clemency, and loyalty—while none of the classical martial virtues such as bravery, courage, valor, and fortitude are represented. But this is not surprising since Betussi was living in postwar Siena in 1556, when he was finishing his *Imagini,* and in that work he expressed nothing but disgust for the war and destruction Cosimo and Charles's armies had inflicted on the Sienese townspeople and their once jewel-like city. Chastity and purity are included in Betussi's roster of virtues, but the constant harping on women's promiscuity that marks Boccaccio's catalog of illustrious women, the *De claris*

TABLE I. The Women and Men in Paired Betussi's Sculpture Forum

| Virtue Represented | Participant | Native City | Colaborators, Editors, and Clients | Academy or Other Tie |
|---|---|---|---|---|
| Grace (*Gratia*) | Gostanza Bonromea | Milan | Ferrante d'Adda | Fenici |
| Temperance (*Temperantia*) | Battina Pozzibonella | Savona | Cavalier Vendramini | Fenici[a] |
| Liberality (*Liberalià*) | Livia Torniella Bonromea | Novara | Ottaviano Raverta | Raverta[b] |
| Wisdom (*Sapientia*) | Giulia Lignana Carlina | Bologna | Antonio Terminio | Anthologies |
| Hope (*Speranza*) | Hippolita Gonzaga Carafa | Mantua | Giuliano Gosellini | Anthologies |
| Magnanimity (*Magnanimità*) | Portia Tor' Alta Torniella | Naples | Girolamo Muzio | Fenici |
| Faith (*Fede*) | Lionarda da Este Bentivoglia | Ferrara | Alberto Lollio | Anthologies |
| Beauty (*Bellezza*) | Ginevra Bentivoglia Novata | Bologna | Lodovico Domenichi | Anthologies |
| Prudence (*Prudentia*) | Giustina Trivultia d'Este | Milan | Tomaso Porcacchi | Anthologies |
| Chastity (*Castità*) | Alda Torella Lunata | Pavia | Filippo Binaschi | Anthologies |
| Courtesy (*Cortesia*) | Ottavia Baiarda Beccaria | Parma | Filippo Ziffiri | Anthologies |
| Honor (*Honestà*) | Francesca de' Baldi | Siena | Hercole Bentivoglio | Anthologies |
| Glory (*Gloria*) | Virginia Salvi | Siena | Benedetto Varchi | Fenici |
| Constancy (*Costantia*) | Giulia Farnese Orsina | Rome | Fortunio Spira | Anthologies |
| Humanity (*Humanità*) | Chiara Albignana Gosellini | Milan | Girolamo Ruscelli | Fenici |

| | | | | |
|---|---|---|---|---|
| Religion (*Religione*) | Vavinia S. Sforza | Parma | Alessandro Campesano | Anthologies |
| Reverence (*Reverentia*) | Lucia Bertana | Modena | Lodovico Castelvetro | Modena |
| Humility (*Humiltà*) | Violante Pavese de Savona | Savona | Anibal Thosco | Anthologies |
| Purity (*Pudicitia*) | Leonora Cibo de'Vitelli | Genoa | Bernardo Cappello | Anthologies |
| Clemency (*Clementia*) | Stella Vigera Dalla Rovera | Savona | Giovanni Battista Pizzoni | Ancona |
| Virtue (*Virtù*) | Leonora Ravoira Falletta | Casalasca | Luca Contile | Fenici |
| Benignity (*Benignità*) | Lucretia Pizzinarda Crotta | Cremona | Agostino Rocchetta | Savona |
| Fame (*Fama*) | Laudomia Forteguerri Petrucci[c] | Siena | Alessandro Piccolomini | Anthologies |
| Modesty (*Modestia*) | Giudith Forteguerri Baccinelli | Siena | Monsignor Panthusi Vescovo | |

NOTE. The notation "Anthologies" indicates that the writer published in the Giolito poetry anthology series (1545–60). For a list of the anthologies in which each poet appears, see my appendix A.

[a] Vendramini, Gosellini, Ruscelli, Contile, Betussi, and Muzio, who are listed as Fenici members, also appear in the Giolito poetry anthologies.

[b] Betussi titled his dialogue *Raverta* (Venice: Giolito, 1544) after his Milanese friend and patron Ottaviano Raverta, whom Betussi portrays in conversation with Domenichi and the Venetian courtesan Francesca Baffa in this work. Betussi lists Raverta as Milanese in the *Imangini*; he was probably a member of the Fenici, though Maylender does not list him as such.

[c] Betussi spells Forteguerri's name *Laodamia*; I've changed the spelling to conform to the more common spelling of her name to avoid confusion.

*mulieribus,* has no place in the *Imagini.* Christian values—faith, religion, reverence, and hope—are wedged in, seemingly at random, among the other virtues. But in Betussi's temple, charity, the greatest of all the virtues according to Saint Paul, is nowhere to be found.

The *Imagini del tempio* was a bold experiment in which Betussi not only imagined a community of women and men of unequal rank jointly engaged in the cultivation of the virtues and poetry; in it, he also assumed the role of writer as Horatian *vates*—poet, prophet and truth-sayer—in a time, he argued, of false idols. These were dangerous times both for theologians and writers. By the 1550s, the most influential of Juan de Valdés's posthumous followers—Bernardino Ochino, Pier Paolo Vergerio, and Pier Martire Vermigli—had long since fled to university towns in Switzerland or Germany. While the Holy Office of the Inquisition made it a crime to buy, sell, or own any one of hundreds officially banned books, the pope himself ordered the arrest of Vittoria Colonna's longtime friend Cardinal Giovanni Morone on charges of heresy, despite his reputation as one of the most orthodox churchmen in Rome. Morone's library of sacred and secular books was seized and he was thrown into the Castel Sant'Angelo prison where he remained until Paul's death. Cardinal Pole was also summoned by the pope to answer accusations of heresy, and he too would have been tried as a criminal if he had not died in 1558. During these years, Betussi's not-so-veiled criticism of the pope's war on Spain could easily have been enough to endanger his life, coupled as it was with his doubly brazen dedications—to Giovanna Colonna as the subject of his *Tempio* and to her daughter as its dedicatee and patron, Vittoria di Toledo Colonna, the niece and namesake of Vittoria Colonna. In any case, a book devoted to the promotion of forty-seven literary women and their twenty-four male supporting companions, patrons, and editors might also have been condemned by the Roman Holy Office as impossibly irreverent and morally suspect. Certainly, other iconic women portrayed in Betussi's *Tempio*, notably Laudomia Forteguerri, as we shall see in the next chapter, were associated with the reform movement and the heresies of the Sienese humanist Bartlomeo Carli de'Piccolomini and his wife Girolama.

The temples of Ruscelli and Betussi represented responses to the losses of both Colonna women, Vittoria and Giovanna—in particular, to the papal theft of the Colonna lands, twice in the course of two successive wars. In addressing their volumes to Giovanna Colonna, though, these writers acted,

in a sense, as her *conservatori*. Without alluding specifically to her recent tragedies, they too tacitly mourned the death of her son Fabrizio from his wounds
in war, the pope's expulsion of her and her children not only from their do-
micile in Rome but from Paliano and Marino as well, and finally, the death of
her husband Ascanio, who languished in prison, stripped of honor.[61] The two
"Temples for Giovanna," it could later be claimed, had announced, proleptically, d'Aragona Colonna's eventual triumph in the face of loss. For, when
she reentered Rome to reoccupy the Colonna palace in 1560, her return was
honored, it was said, with a ceremony worthy of an ambassador's entrance
into the city.[62] She was met by a crowd of Roman nobles and welcomed by a
representative of the new pope, Pius IV (Giannangelo de' Medici), by whom
she was received on the following day. She kissed his feet, recapitulating not
only Alba's ritual kiss of obeisance at the end of the Carafa war but also her
own kissing of the Farnese pope's foot, performed by letter, when the Salt
War wound to its end.[63] The poets no doubt saw their fate under Paul IV's
regime as analogous to Giovanna's own. Hindered in their mission to speak,
write, and publish freely under the pall of the Inquisition, they too hoped for
a triumphal return.

CHAPTER FIVE

# Laudomia Forteguerri's *Canzoniere* and the Fall of Siena

When Betussi wrote the epilogue to his *Imagini del tempio della signora donna Giovanna Aragona* in 1556, he was living in postwar Siena. There he saw for himself the wreckage left by thirty-six months of bombardment and the suffering of the city's people in the ensuing invasion and occupation.[1] The attack on the small republic by the combined armed forces of the emperor Charles V and the Duke of Florence, Cosimo I, had ended a year before he arrived. The city lay in ruins and with it the hopes of the Sienese for freedom from foreign rule. The once imposing palazzo pubblico was deserted, and many of the civic buildings facing the Piazza del Campo had been reduced to rubble. For three years Spanish, Italian, and German troops under imperial command lay siege to the city, where some ten thousand citizens held out, penned inside the walls with diminishing supplies.[2] Many who tried to escape were hanged by the soldiers of the imperial forces; others were horribly mutilated and sent back to the city gates. When the Republic of Siena finally surrendered to the emperor on April 17, 1555, and the gates were opened, the diarist Sozzini described the scene of famine, disease, and desolation that met the conquering army:

> There were people in the city, both men and women, at this point who were wholly altered; they were emaciated and gray-faced from their continual hardship and the life they endured. Things had gone so far that it could be said that there were—and it is important to know this—no more than three or four women in the whole city who appeared as they had before the war; all the others were hideously transformed from the women they had once been. A great many people of all ranks and all ages died in a very short time, for they had nothing of sustenance like sugars,

syrups, honey, or preserves, with which a sick man could have been comforted, however much the cost. . . . And because of this, a man necessarily fell sick without having any comfort for himself other than brown bread; he would die, given no more than a little watered-down vinegar, and it was a great pity to see it.[3]

In questo tempo erono le persone in la Città, si uomini come donne, tutti trasfigurati, magri e pallidi per li continui disagi, e per patire del vivere; a tale che si posseva dire con effetto, che in tutta la Città non ci fussero (cosa notabile a sentirla) più che tre o quattro donne nella sua prima effigie e tutte l'altre fatte assai disformi di quello che erono prima. Ne moriva assai di tutti i gradi e di tutte l'età, e con brevissimo male; imperocchè eron mancate alli speziali tutte le cose di sustanza, come zuccheri, giulebbi, mêle e confezione, con li quali un ammalato si posseva alquanto confortare, sebbene erono carissime: per il qual mancamento era necessario che subito chel'uomo ammalava, non avendo da confortarsi con altro che con pane assai bruno, e con un poco di aceto annacquato, si morisse: ed era cosa molto compassionevole a verderla.[4]

A soldier reported that outside Siena, as far as the eye could see, farms and houses had been reduced to rubble and that in the countryside one could not avoid the sight of dead bodies that had become prey to ravening dogs.[5] Beyond the city walls, in the countryside, the once thick forests were gone: both the Sienese and the enemy troops had set about its trees and greenery with axes, turning them into firewood or building material, or else they had bared the hills with conflagrations to deprive one another of hiding places.[6]

In the *Tempio,* Betussi had written a moving elegy in which he grieved over the once beautiful city of Siena, now smoldering and ruined, while he sang the praises of the poet Laudomia Forteguerri Petrucci for her bravery in defending the city throughout the siege:

Among all the other women, look at LAODAMIA FORTEGUERRI PETRUCCI: like an oracle in the world, she is full of every courtesy, she is the summit of every virtue, and she is endowed with enormous honor. Look at this woman, whom everyone deferred to since there, in her, virtue and beauty reside. We should admire anyone who possesses even a pale shadow of her virtue. I will never believe there was a spirit so barbarously and hard-heartedly opposed to the freedom and independence of her city that he could have witnessed her commitment to its defense just once and would still have not yielded to her, been humbled, and been made to retreat. So great is the majesty of her demeanor, so great is her eloquence, and so great is the quickness of her mind.

Vedi fra tutte l'altre LAODAMIA FORTEGUERRI PETRUCCI quasi oracolo nel mondo, piena d'ogni raro costume, colma d'ogni chiara virtù, et dotata d'estrema honestà.

Vedi questa, a cui devriano inchinarsi quanti sanno, che sia virtù, et bellezza. Devria ammirarla chi pure ha compreso una minima ombra delle sue virtù. Non crederò mai, che spirito alcuno fosse stato sì barbaro, et duro verso la libertà della patria sua, il quale una sola volta havesse sentito lei, a pigliare la protettione di quella; che non si fosse piegato, humiliato, e rimosso: tanta e la maestà dell'aspetto. Tanta la facondia del dire, et tanta la prontezza delle ragioni.[7]

Betussi also immortalized Forteguerri as the personification of Fame in a sonnet in the *Tempio*. Like his prose eulogy, the sonnet memorializes not only her physical courage as a defender of her city but her intellectual gifts as well. Having recruited and trained a company of women, she entered the war in 1554 as their captain against the overwhelming forces of Cosimo I and the emperor Charles V. For the better part of two years she faced death, and she may not have survived Siena's fall by much, for the memoirs of her bravery in 1555–56 published by Betussi and others are the last we hear of her:

> Worthy of eternal and glorious FAME—
> she who carries your renown to every land—
> you have won splendid spoils, your lot
> from heaven, which always calls you to it,
> since you, who hold life and also death
> in your lovely gaze, are loved by all:
> this is well and right, since the world is solaced
> only by your grace, nor does it hope for more.
> When will the circling Sun see again
> a searching mind like yours, bejeweled
> with such rare gifts? When will Love own
> a realm more peaceful than your face—
> so like a holy pledge from heaven—whence
> other women have envy and disdain.

> Degna d'eterna, e gloriosa FAMA,
> Ch'il nome vostro in ogni luogo porte;
> Sì bella, e cara spoglia haveste in sorte
> Dal ciel, che sempre a se v'invita e chiama,
>     Ben è ragion s'ogn'un v'honora, e ama,
> Che ne begli occhi havete vita e morte;
> Ne par, che'l Mondo in altri si conforte,
> Che sol la gratia vostra, e più non brama,
>     Quando più vide il Sol girando intorno
> Simile al vostro peregrino ingegno
> Di tante rare qualitati adorno?

Quando hebbe Amor mai più securo regno
Del vostro viso; onde hanno invidia, e scorno
L'altre, come a divin celeste pegno?[8]

Laudomia Forteguerri had led a company of Sienese women in building a fortress to defend the city. On Forteguerri's bravery and the company she headed, the marshal of the French army, Blaise de Monluc, posted dispatches from the Sienese front that reached readers in Paris and London as well as Siena and Florence, as the popularity of the following seventeenth-century English translation of Montluc's *Commentaires* suggests.[9]

All these poor Inhabitants, without discovering the least distaste or sorrow for the ruin of their houses, put themselves their own hands first to the work, every one contending who should be most ready to pull down his own. There was never less than four thousand souls at labour, and I was shewed by the Gentlemen of *Sienna* a great number of Gentlewomen carrying baskets of earth upon their heads. It shall never be (you Ladies of *Sienna*) that I will not immortalize your names so long as the Book of *Montluc* shall live; for in truth you are worthy of immortal praise, if ever women were. At the beginning of the noble resolution these people took to defend their liberty, all the Ladies of *Sienna* divided themselves into three Squadrons; the first led by *Signiora Fortaguerra*, who was her self clad in violet, as also all those of her Train, her attire being cut in the fashion of a Nymph, short, and discovering her Buskins; the second was *la Signiora Picolhuomini* attir'd in carnatian Sattin, and her Troop in the same Livery; the third was *la Signiora Livia Fausta*, apparelled all in white, as also her Train, with her white Ensign. In their Ensigns they had very fine devices, which I would give a good deal I could remember. These three Squadrons consisted of three thousand Ladies, Gentlewomen, and Citizens, their Arms were Picks, Shovels, Baskets, and Bavins, and in this Equipage they made their Muster, and went to begin the Fortifications. Monsieur *de Termes*, who has often told me this story (for I was not then arriv'd at *Sienna*) has assur'd me, that in his life he never saw so fine a sight. I have since seen their Ensignes, and they had composed a Song to the honor of *France*, for which I wish I had given the best horse I have that I might insert it here.[10]

❧ SOCIAL RELATIONS WERE DIFFERENT BETWEEN
THE SEXES IN SIENA: THE *VEGLIE* AND
THE ART OF CONVERSATION ❧

But Sienese women were actively engaged in the public affairs of the Republic long before Cosimo and Charles lay siege to the city. A number of sixteenth-century writers have described social relations between intellectual women and men in Siena at midcentury as characterized by an unprecedented openness. Here was a new and more inclusive city culture not foreseen in Castiglione's *Book of the Courtier* or Bembo's *Asolani*. Looking back on the friendships that were common in Siena at midcentury between elite men and women not married to one another, the author Girolamo Bargagli observed that Sienese men "as a rule were accustomed to visit one or another woman with the liberty with which one visits a sister today. So that leaving the university, or the Academy exhausted, they went as to a peaceful harbor to converse with some woman or other." [Continuamente e in ogni tempo eran soliti or una e or un'altra di quelle donne di visitare, con quella liberté che a vedere una sorella si va oggi. Tal chè ora uscendo dello studio, e dell'Accademia stanchi, or da negozi infastiditi partendosi, se ne andavano, come a tranquillo porto, ad intratenersi con qualcuna di loro.][11]

The members of the Sienese Accademia degli Intronati expressed curiosity about women's intellectual activities. In the early 1540s, they issued invitations to several women to attend their meetings as guests. The letter the Intronati member Alessandro Piccolomini sent Laudomia Forteguerri on August 10, 1539, suggests that in Siena male intellectuals took pleasure in their female compatriots' interest and involvement in literary, philosophical, and religious issues:

> I recently heard that one day this past spring, your ladyship (most noble and beautiful Lady Laudomia) was seen in a garden with other noble women amusing yourselves, and all of you who had congregated at the warmest time of the day in a circle under a laurel tree, were engaged like a celestial choir of angels in the most beautiful, learned, and philosophical dialogues, after which you conversed brilliantly on a variety of themes, turning from one topic to another, until at last you came to the subject of religion.

> Mi e per infin qua venuto all'orecchie (Nobilissima e Bellissima Madonna Laudomia) che trovandosi in questa Primavera passata, la S.V. un giorno con altre nobilissime Donne in un giardino a sollazzo, e essendo tutte insieme, nelle più calde hore del giorno, quasi in un Coro Celeste e angelico ridutte sotto un Lauro in corona; bellissimi, e molto dotti e filosofici ragionamenti accader tra voi, dove doppo che varii e ingegnosi discorsi furon havuti hor da questa, hor da quella, cadute finalmente in proposito de le cose divine.[12]

Commenting on Girolamo Bargagli's *Dialogo de' Giuochi* (1573), modern scholars have called attention to the emergent female public of writers and readers in Siena and to the role the Intronati played promoting women's entrance into the public culture of the Republic.[13] Bargagli's advice to the members of both sexes on playing the conversational games at the *veglie* (as the Sienese called their soirées, salons, or evening parties) show not only that by the 1540s the participation of women in the intellectual life of the city was taken for granted in Siena but that women were expected to set the protocol in their discourse with the men of the city as well. For Bargagli, good conversation was not defined by a succession of long, rambling monologues delivered by men but instead by an exchange of sorts between the sexes. Going beyond the reticence of Castiglione's Emilia Pia, the *De' Giuochi* suggests that women ought to model the art of conversation, in which equal pleasure could be gained from pointed and clever repartee, on the one hand, and extended arguments, on the other. The sexes were given clearly differentiated roles: the women were to demonstrate the art of listening and the making of pithy and amusing comments, while the men were expected to chatter on at length, whatever the subject might be. According to Bargagli, it was up to the women to set a tone of "gravity accompanied by authority" at the *veglie*:

Women, for whom it is fitting to maintain an honorable gravity accompanied by authority, should speak less in offering their judgments since the men do not. Women, on the contrary, should give their opinions in short and sweet statements rather than in long, roundabout orations, leaving it to the men to come up with more arguments, or to their male companions to expand at length about what they [the women] have been saying. Nor should a woman wish to weigh in on every topic. Rather, she should speak only when it is useful for her to say something elegant, and she should show that when she does speak it is because she is being urged to do so by her male companion rather than from any desire of her own to speak or because she presumes some knowledge.

Le donne, alle quali conviene il tenere un'onesta gravità con autorità accompagnata, deono ne'giudicati parlar meno che gli uomini non fanno, e più tosto con un breve e dolce motto dire le loro sentenze, che con un lungo giro di parole, lasciando ad altri il pensar più ragioni, o al compagno l'allungarsi sopra di quello che è stato detto da loro. Non voglia una donna metter bocca in tutte le sentenze, ma parli in quelle solamente dove le sovvenga di dire qualche vaghezza, e ciò anco mostri di fare, più tosto stimolata dal compagno che da desiderio di parlare o da presonzione di sapere.[14]

On a visit to Siena, the Venetian travel writer and author of *novelle* Celio Malespini marveled at the well-established tradition of *veglie* in that city where he noted that women and men met regularly at one another's houses for literary discussions, debates, and also for readings of their own new works:

The *veglie* the Sienese attended in this ancient city, especially those where men and women of rank met for the purpose of conversation, were universally valued for the pleasure of the talk they afforded. Those who came to these gatherings plunged into the consideration of difficult propositions whether it was prudent or not, and often one was left red-faced, since in these beautiful games they heard and offered marvelous propositions and questions and clever traps and inventions as erudite as they were subtle, since it was in the women's power as well as the men's to propose that which pleased them most. But it was necessary to press on with the finest understanding, since all those ladies were extraordinary and divine; and they were similarly endowed in their inventiveness, which caused every man of great intellect to marvel and to be awestruck.

Le veglie che tuttavia si frequentano in questa antichissma città, sono stimate generalmente da tutti per un bellissimo piacere e trattenimento; massime quelle che si fanno fra gentiluomini e dame di valore, nelle quali quegli che non è che prudente nel considerare le difficili proposizioni, che vi si frappongono, sovente egli ne rimane con non poco rossore nel viso, chè in questi bellissimi giuochi vi si odono e dicono quesiti e propositi meravigliosi, et astuzie et trovati non meno dotti che sottilissimi: essendo in potere cosi degli uomini, come delle donne, di proporre quello che più gli piace; ma bisogna istar benissimo in cervello, essendo tutte quelle gentildonne rare e divine in simili invenzioni, le quali fanno stupire e meravigliare chiunque elevato in intelletto.[15]

Bargagli, of course, was Sienese, while Malespini an outsider. Whereas Bargagli wrote prescriptively when he contrasted the operative roles for women and men at the *veglie,* Malespini's guidebook approach aimed simply to describe the local scene. Both works sold widely. The prompt publication of works written by academy members and their friends, the *veglie,* and women's participation in the readings and performances held by the academies were all part of the expanding reading public at midcentury. This broadening of the scene of culture, once limited to the courts and the elites in the large urban centers, was particularly vibrant in some of the smaller cities, such as Siena and Padua, at least until the early 1550s. Later, as we shall see, conditions would change both for the Sienese and the academicians in other cities.

## ❧ SIENESE WOMEN STAGE A DEBATE IN A DIALOGUE BY MARC'ANTONIO PICCOLOMINI (1538) ❧

Rita Belladonna's rediscovery in 1994 of an unpublished dialogue written by a member of Laudomia Forteguerri's circle, Marc'Antonio Piccolomini, sheds further light on the Sienese *veglie* and the participation of elite women in them.[16] It also reveals something of Forteguerri's own intellectual formation and reminds us that the reform or *spirituali* movement had deep roots in Siena, where the charismatic preacher and reform leader Bernardino Ochino began his career. Years before her fame as a battalion captain during the siege of Siena, Forteguerri was not only a leading figure in the literary life of the city, but she also appears to have been involved in the *spirituali* movement, which, by 1542 when Ochino fled Italy, had come under attack as heretical and a danger to the Church.

The performance of Marc'Antonio Piccolomini's new dialogue must have stirred controversy in the academies and the *veglie*. Possibly presented by the author himself in 1538 at a meeting of the reigning Sienese academy, the Intronati, the work documented a frank and wide-ranging discussion of doctrines considered heretical, which three young women well-known in Siena had supposedly conducted in real time, in October 1537.[17] Unlike the Sienese *veglie* but like other literary academies of the period, the Intronati did not recruit women as members—with the exception of the celebrated Florentine poet Laura Battiferri. But her entry into the academy was in 1557, after Siena had come under the rule of Cosimo I de' Medici, who had commissioned her husband, the sculptor Bartolomeo Ammannati, to produce a number of works, including the spectacular Fountain of Neptune in the Piazza della Signoria and the renovation of the Pitti Palace in Florence.[18] The speakers in Piccolomini's dialogue, Laudomia Forteguerri, Girolama Carli de' Piccolomini, and Frasia Marzi, were all prominent participants in the *veglie* and members of the Sienese elite. Forteguerri herself may already have won recognition as a poet since she would recently have circulated among her friends the sonnet cycle she had written for the emperor Charles V's daughter, Margaret of Austria, who visited Siena twice in three years, first in 1535 and again in 1538. All three interlocutors were known in Siena as intellectuals, but it was to Forteguerri that Marc'Antonio Piccolomini's cousin Alessandro Piccolomini had dedicated his scientific and philosophical writings—*La sfera del mondo, Le stelle fisse*, and *L'institutione della tutta vita*. As a character in a documentary dialogue about theological issues, though, the real Girolama presented problems.[19] She was the wife of Bartolomeo Carli de' Piccolomini, an Intronati member who was an intimate of the Sienese heretic or suspected heretic, Aonio Paleario.[20] Moreover, Bartolomeo Carli had authored a tract titled *Regola utile e necessaria a ciascuna persona che cerchi di vivere come fedele e buon cristiano* (A useful and necessary regimen for all who intend to live as faithful and good Christians). The *Regola* bore a dangerously close resemblance to Juan de Valdés's *Alfabeto*

*Christiano,* some academy members feared, given that the *Alfabeto* was widely known by the late 1530s as a profoundly heretical dialogue.[21]

The conversation between Girolama and Laudomia in Piccolomini's dialogue takes place in Girolama's house. It is All Saints' Day and the two women have run into each other "by pure chance" at the cathedral.[22] Girolama has persuaded Laudomia to come home with her to discuss questions of mutual interest. The discussion that ensues moves easily back and forth between socially acceptable topics for debate (What is the nature of woman? Of the sexes?) and the dangerous terrain of religious doctrine (Does free will exist for humans? Are all things in the cosmos preordained?). What is more, since Piccolomini's purpose in writing this dialogue seems to have been to rehabilitate the reputation of Bartolomeo Carli de' Piccolomini after he and other Intronati members were accused of heresy in 1536, as Belladonna has suggested, his wife Girolama Carli de' Piccolomini is portrayed as espousing the orthodox position of the Catholic Church, while Laudomia plays her doctrinal opponent and foil.[23] From Laudomia's lips come the ideas of the *spirituali*—of Valdés, Ochino, Giulia Gonzaga, Vittoria Colonna, and Carnesecchi—while Girolama refuses to be counted a partisan of the heretical Ochino. Alluding to Ochino's preaching tour of the northern cities in 1537, Girolama meets Laudomia's arguments with scathing dismissal: "You," she observes, "must be one of those who presented handkerchiefs to the preacher." As the dialogue continues, the women home in on the question of free will and the role of good works as the means to salvation. Laudomia's thought represents a synthesis of heretical doctrine: she espouses not only the Calvinist doctrine of predestination but the Valdesian teaching that salvation can only be attained through God's grace, not by works alone. Girolama, in contrast, whose views Piccolomini represents as exemplifying the orthodox position of the Intronati and the Church, argues in favor of the freedom of the will, and the importance of both works and faith in attaining salvation:

MAD. LAOD.:  Your argument is very elegant, Madama Girolama, and I am quite pleased with it. But according to your definition of fate, it follows that things which are predetermined by fate in the world below can be changed. Consequently I ask: from where does the Providence of God come? Yours is an argument that must be false since I have heard it said that things which are destined to fall to ruin or that we say cannot be changed because of fate and because God has foreseen these things in his mind are both immutable and predetermined.

MAD. GIR.:  It would then follow that we would not enjoy the freedom God has granted us from his immaculate and pure justice as a most precious and necessary gift.

MAD. LAOD.: But do you think that if God did not grant us grace in our works they would be good and acceptable to him?

MAD. GIR.: Certain preachers today would say no, although they are few and their opinion would be repudiated by everyone, and reasonably so in my opinion.

MAD. LAOD.: But do you believe that as great a gift as God's grace, which guides us to do good, would be denied?

MAD. GIR.: You must have been among those who last year presented handkerchiefs to the preacher. I certainly don't want to see another one of those! The most marvelous and the greatest gift of God, my Madama Laudomia, is his having given us the power to attain that good which is appropriate for our situation in life. The more precious gift is that which you speak of:—that we should desire to be capable of acting on our own rather than according to the will of others. But let us omit this issue from the scope of our present conversation. It ought to be enough to know that fate will not impose its force and constraints on us in every circumstance, and to be aware that it can be impeded, though the providence of God will be necessary.

MAD. LAOD.: Molto sottilmente dite la ragion vostre, Mad. Gir., et me piaccione assai; ma secondo la vostra dichiarazione del fato, ne segue che quel che è disposto dal fato in questo mondo inferiore, possa mutarsi; et conseguentemente, la provvidenzia di Dio, donde egli procede. Il che par che sia falso; perché ho odito dire che le cose che debbono accascare fatalmente o per destino che noi ci volgliam dire, non possono mutarsi et che quel che Dio nella sua mente ha previsto, sia et immutabile et determinato.

MAD. GIR.: Ne seguirebbe adunque che noi non godessemo la libertà dataci da Dio per dono preziosissimo et necessario, da la giustizia sua immaculata et pura.

MAD. LAOD.: Oh, pensate voi che senza ch'egli ci conceda grazia nelle operazioni nostre, le possino esser buone et accette?

MAD. GIR.: Certi predicatori dal dì d'oggi direbber di no, benché pochi sieno e gli sia dato contra da tutti; et ragionevolmente secondo me.

MAD. LAOD.: Oh, volete negarsi un tanto dono di Dio quanto è la grazia sua, la qual ci guidi a far bene? Questa mi pare strana cosa.

MAD. GIR.: Voi dovete esser di quelle che presentorno l'anno passato i fazzoletti al predicatore; io non ne vo' veder altro. Il dono maraviglioso di Dio. Mad. Laod. mia, et molto maggiore è l'averci dato potestà d'avere il bene a nostra posta; et è tanto più prezionso questo di quel che dite, quanto piu si deve desiderare da noi di potere operare a posta nostra che a voluntà d'altrui. Ma lassiamo questo ragionamento che ci menarebbe fuor del nostro proposito; et basti sapere ch'el fato non ci sforza

et non impone alle cose necessità, anzi può essere impedito, benché la
provvidenzia di Dio sia necessaria. (Piccolomini, *Dialogo*, 78–79)[24]

In the concluding section of the dialogue, Girolama plays the passionate
advocate of the official Catholic doctrine of Purgatory, while Laudomia, the
dialogue's supposedly heretical character, attacks the doctrine as pagan and
"contrary to the Catholic faith." Indeed, as Belladonna observes, Girolama's ex-
position of the Church's position on life after death closely resembles accounts
of the migration of souls in Plato's *Republic* and Cicero's *Tusculan Disputations*:

MAD. LAOD.: Do you mean that souls which depart from their bodies must return to
them at a later time?

MAD. GIR.: Many wise men believe this is so.

MAD. LAOD.: Why then would one soul be slower to return than another?

MAD. GIR.: Because many souls, through poor regulation of their bodies, cease to
merit to be in God's presence. Therefore those souls who abandoned
themselves to sin and who grew old in accord with the corruption and
imperfection of their bodies, return more quickly to their bodies because they were less continent. Whether souls return sooner or later to
their bodies depends on the degree to which they have preserved their
simplicity, clarity, and divinity and whether they require a more or
less extended period of time to cleanse themselves. . . .

MAD. LAOD.: If, as you say, souls quickly return to their own nature once they have
been separated from their corporeal mass, why must they be punished
so that they may be cleansed and regain the purity they once had before they came to the body?

MAD. GIR.: This happens to them because things that have been corrupted over
a long period of time cannot suddenly return to their former purity
but are in need of being purged as I could show you through myriad
examples.

MAD. LAOD.: But if such souls, purged as they are, regain the pure being of their
former state, what moves them to want to return again to the world to
be contaminated and to suffer again?

MAD. GIR.: The reason for this is the forgetting they undergo when, in the process
of departing from highest heaven, they pass through the other spheres
of heaven in order to arrive at this lower region.

MAD. LAOD.: I am greatly in awe of you, Madama Girolama, since you speak of
the most profound subjects with such logic and wisdom. And from
this discourse of yours I now understand a passage I heard in a poem
a member of the Intronati wrote on the occasion of the sickness of the
beautiful Madonna Frasia Venturi, who was ill for some days in April
last year. But one thing you say about the return of souls disturbs me.

MAD. GIR.:   And what is that? Tell me.

MAD. LAOD.:   I'm thinking your whole discourse concerning our souls may ultimately be contrary to our Catholic faith.

MAD. LAOD.:   Adonque l'anime che una volta si partono dai corpi, hanno a ritornarvi di nuovo in altri tempi?

MAD. GIR.:   Si, giudicano molti savi.

MAD. LAOD.:   Perché dunque più tardi una che un'altra?

MAD. GIR.:   Peroché per i gattivi lor portamenti nei corpi, molte persano di meritar la presenza di Dio; onde più presto ritornan quella che manco continenti si sono lasciate macchiare et inveschiare da la corruzione et imperfezione dei corpi; et è più o manco il tempo che le ritarda, quanto più o meno s'hanno conservata la simplicità et chiarezza et divinità loro e più o meno fa loro bisogno di purgarsi. . . .

MAD. LAOD.:   Se adonque gli animi, dividendosi da la massa corporea, ritornano subito (come dite) nella propria natura loro; a che fa mestier che con pene si purghino et faccin chiare come eran prima che venissero nel corpo?

MAD. GIR.:   Questo gli avviene perché quelle cose che longo tempo sono state in luogo macchiato, non posson subito ritornare alla candidezza loro; ma fa lor bisogno di purgamento, come per mille esempi vi potrei dimostrare.

MAD. LAOD.:   Ma se tali anime, purgate che sono, racquistano il puro esser di prima, che le muove a voler di nuovo tornare al mondo per macchiarsi et patir nuovamente?

MAD. GIR.:   Di questo è cagione la dimenticanza ch'elle si bevono mentre che, partendosi dal cielo altissimo, passano per gli altri cieli per venire in questa macchina inferiore.

MAD. LAOD.:   Non posso se no molto maravigliarmi, Mad Gir., che parliate di cose tanto profonse con tale ordine et sapere; et da questo vostro discorso intendo ora un passo che ho visto in una canzone che fece uno degl'Intronati sopra l'infermità de la bellissima Madonna Frasia Venturi, la quale ste inferma alquanti giorni nel ultimo di questo aprile passato; ma una cosa mi porge dubbio intorno a quei che dite del ritorno dell'anime.

MAD. GIR.:   Che cosa? Dite su.

MAD. LAOD.:   Dico che mi pare che tutto'l discorso che avete fatto ultimamente dell'anime nostre sia contra la fede nostra cattolica. (Piccolomini, *Dialogo*, fols. 50–53)[25]

Delivered in 1538—in the thick of the Italian academies' often tenuous struggle to survive in the face of Roman charges of Erasmianism and other heresies—Marc'Antonio Piccolomini's dialogue links in complex ways the political, religious, and literary aims of the women of Siena with those of one of the city's major cultural institutions, the Academy of the Intronati.[26] While the dialogue spread abroad the fame of the *Intronati* and the serious nature of the subject matter its members engaged, at the same time it promoted the image of Sienese women as public intellectuals and active producers of culture. It was to three literary women that Piccolomini delegated the job of exonerating the Intronati from charges of heresy. And yet, while Girolama Carli de' Piccolomini's speeches promulgating the Intronati's reputation as impeccably orthodox prevail, Laudomia Forteguerri's siren songs of the *spirituali* continue to haunt it.

### ❧c A WRITER FOR AND ABOUT WOMEN ɔ❧

But Laudomia Forteguerri did not come to public prominence in Siena through the efforts of Marc'Antonio Piccolomini. Her fame was the by-product of her intimate connection with another, more prominent member of the Piccolomini clan: Alessandro Piccolomini (1508–79), whose title as archpriest of Metropolitan Siena and benefices from the Church, which he received in 1525 when he was seventeen, enabled him to pursue a literary career.[27] During the years 1538–42, he immersed himself in his studies at the University of Padua. After 1538, when he held joint appointments as rector of the Church of San Giorgio in Siena and coadjutant of the archbishop of Siena, unlike many of his compatriots, he steered clear of participating in any of the religious reform groups then under investigation by the Holy Office in Rome.

In 1541, Piccolomini, who had been a founding member of the Sienese Intronati, devoted an entire evening to the presentation of Laudomia Forteguerri's poetry before the assembled members of the Academy of the Infiammati in Padua. Benedetto Varchi, the dean of the literary world in Florence, wrote of Forteguerri that she was Piccolomini's *Laura* because of the many works he dedicated to her in which he praised her as the source of his inspiration. Among the works in which he honored her, his magnum opus, the massive *Institutione di tutta la vita de l'huomo nato nobile*, would be published in Venice in 1542.

Before Piccolomini met Forteguerri, he had already had a series of friendships with powerful women in Siena—he had in fact established himself as a writer for and about women. Three works resulting from his early friendships with women and his interest in women's lives were circulating in manuscript by 1538, and each of these books would soon appear in print. First came his translation from the Greek of Xenophon's dialogue guide to household management, the *Oeconomicus*, which he dedicated to the Sienese noblewoman

Frasia Placidi de Venturi.[28] Second was his essay on the virtues of women, his *In lode delle donne*; and third, his parody of a conduct book for women, titled *Raffaella* or *De la bella creanza de le donne*, all three published in Venice.[29] Piccolomini probably presented both works, his essay on women and his dialogue, at Intronati meetings which must have been held within months of one another in 1538.[30]

In 1540, Piccolomini was inducted into the Academy of the Infiammati in Padua. Around this time Lodovico Dolce, who was now the leading editor at the Giolito press in Venice, appears to have joined the Infiammati.[31] Certainly the two men frequented the same circles in Padua. Dolce, who was then editing an Italian translation of Henricus Cornelius Agrippa's eulogy of women, the *Dialogo della institutione delle donne,* for Giolito, appears to have invited Piccolomini to submit his *In lode delle donne* to the press.[32] In 1545, the two treatises came out together in a single volume edited by Dolce. Piccolomini's essay on the female sex diverged sharply from Agrippa's work, which featured a catalog of famous classical and biblical women in the tradition of Boccaccio's *De claris mulierbus (On Famous Women).*[33] Piccolomini took a novel tack. Omitting entirely the lists of illustrious women that were practically obligatory in Renaissance tracts on the nature of woman, he brought his erudition in classical Greek literature to bear. Taking as a given Aristotle's view that women were more susceptible to sensual stimuli than males were, Piccolomini argued that the resistance to temptation that women exercized in their everyday lives was all the more admirable. But the most original feature of the *In lode delle donne* was Piccolomini's appropriation of Aristotle's doctrine of women's emotional susceptibility to support Plato's contention that in the ideal republic highly educated women as well as men should be eligible to govern as philosopher rulers.[34] Since women, by necessity, were endowed with greater mastery over their emotions than were males, they were more suited than men to rule, he argued.

### ❧ SIENESE WOMEN AND THE POETRY GAMES ❧

Despite the insistence of Benedetto Varchi in 1540 that his friend Piccolomini was obsessed with Laudomia Forteguerri and that she was his *Laura*, the Sienese priest in fact exchanged letters, poems, and dedicatory eulogies with several other prominent Sienese literary women. During his Padua years, he was just as active at bringing women into the activities of the leading academy in that city, the Infiammati, as he had been with the Sienese Intronati. Soon after he joined the Infiammati, he wrote Varchi to say that at his invitation two distinguished women, Giovanna Malatesta and Lucretia Pia, would soon attend a meeting of the Infiammati as his guests and that they were looking forward to hearing the reading of a comedy there.[35]

As Florindo Cerreta has noted, group writing and literary game-playing were dominant forms of sociality in the closely interrelated cultures of the Sienese *veglie* and the academies.[36] Women, moreover, were key actors in these games. When Piccolomini returned from a pilgrimmage to Petrarch's tomb at Arqua in August 1540, he circulated a sonnet he had written on the famous tomb and called on other poets to join him in a memorial to the poet by contributing sonnets of their own. His call for sonnets was organized as a highly demanding game of echoing—a game that parodied the literary performances of the academies. Piccolomini began the game himself by offering his own sonnet in memoriam as the template. The rules of the game were that the contributing players had to end each of the fourteen lines in their sonnets with the same words Piccolomini used to conclude his lines. Piccolomini told his friend Pietro Aretino that some twenty-five to thirty contributors—women and men—had participated in the game.[37] The resulting collection of poems was probably performed at a public meeting of the Infiammati in 1540.[38] The Infiammati tomb anthology, later known as *La Tombaiade,* though never printed, is extant in manuscript in the Biblioteca Nazionale in Florence.[39] Among the Sienese women's sonnets included in the *Tombaiade* manuscript, those of Virginia di Matteo Salvi, Frasia Marzi, Virginia di Achille Salvi, Camilla Petroni de' Piccolomini, and Girolama Piccolomini de' Biringucci are now available in a modern edition.[40]

The *Tombaiade* poems by the women and men of Piccolomini's circle indicate that a high level of sophistication flourished in the Petrarchan revival among Siena's elite. The trio of sonnets below, by two women and a man, exemplifies the idiom. All three poems from the *Tombaiade* illustrate a complex weaving of themes from sonnets 185 and 187 in Petrarch's *Rime sparse* and involve layers of imitation. Both of Petrarch's sonnets treat the poets' ability to commemorate beauty in song and to immortalize both their subjects and their own words. The author of the first sonnet is Virginia di Messer Matteo Salvi, perhaps the most prolific of the Sienese poets of the 1550s.[41] Alessandro Piccolomini and Frasia Marzi, who was the third interlocutor in Marc'Antonio Piccolomini's dialogue on reform doctrine, offer the responding sonnets. The resulting trio represents a conflation of themes from Petrarch's two sonnets. Virginia Salvi and her friends' meditations in verse on Petrarch's tomb (*la gran tomba*), their portrayal of the poet's voice as an illustrious trumpet (*la chiara tromba*) that resounds and confers fame beyond this world (*al ciel rimbomba*), and their envy of the trecento poet and his tomb for having a bard to immortalize them (*felice voi*) all derive from Petrarch's reflections on Cicero's famous lament in the *Pro Archia* for Alexander the Great (*Rime sparse*, no. 187). In the same trio of poems initiated by Salvi, the imaging of the breast (*il seno*) as a protective sanctuary from which poetry emanates and to which it ultimately returns, safe from the reach of men's bows and slings (*non . . . arco nè fromba*), and the figuring of sonnets as rare and exotic perfumes (*arabi odori*) echo Petrarch's poem on the mythological phoenix's death and resurrection (*Rime sparse*, no. 185).

### Madonna Verginia di Mister Matteo Salvi

Why can I not see the great Tomb
of that man honored with glorious Laurel,
whose green summits were raised aloft,
where no bow or sling have ever reached?
O fortunate one, since your clear Trumpet
lifts your rich work to the skies and
you sing learned verse in a rare and sonorous
style, your name resounds on high.
Ah, if the shame of Death were far from you,
my gift of Arabian perfumes for your great
and learned breast would not displease you.
And Heaven would favor your desires
and joyous Nymphs would always surround
you, garlanding your hair with lovely blooms.

Perché veder non poss'io la gran Tomba
di quel che celebrò l'amato Alloro,
di cui le verdi cime alzate foro
ove mai non aggiunse arco nè fromba?
Felice Voi, poi che la chiara Tromba
vostra alza al ciel così ricco lavoro,
e in dotti versi, e 'n stil raro e sonoro
cantate, e'l vostro nome alto rimbomba.
Deh, se vi sia lontan oltraggio e scorno
di Morte, non vi spiaccia arabi odori
per me offerir all'almo e culto seno.
E ai vostri desir si mostri ameno
il Ciel' e liete Ninfe sempre intorno
vi stiano, ornando'l crin di vaghi fiori.[42]

## ALESSANDRO PICCOLMINI RESPONDS TO VIRGINIA SALVI

Although the envious slings of fate may forbid
your coming yourself to the grand tomb
of the great cultivator of the noble Laurel
placed aloft, no pines were ever raised for you.
Fortunate is he; since so clear a Trumpet,
the lofty work of your verses, Verginia,
resounds, which honors him in tones so sweet
and sonorous from everywhere to lofty heaven.
For you, I will offer it the same perfumes,
which have come here from your wise breast,
to the shame and disgrace of these Nymphs.
You, Placida and Flori, should sweetly weave
a crown in recompense, with the flowers
you made bloom above the Arbia and Ombron.


Bench'il venir voi stessa a la gran tomba
Del gran cultor di quel ben nato Alloro
Che s'erse v' non mai pini ascesi foro,
Le vieti del suo fato invida fromba;
　　Felice è pur; poi che sì chiara Tromba,
Verginia, in honor suo l'alto lavoro
De i vostri versi, in suon dolce e sonoro
qua d'ognintorno al ciel alto rimbomba.
　　Porgerolle io per voi con onta e scorno
di queste Ninfe i proprii stessi odori
C'arrivan qua da'l vostro saggio seno.
　　Voi in guidardon, con lieto ciglio ameno
cornonate de i fior, ch'aprite intorno,
sopra l'Arbia e l'Ombron, Placida e Flori.[43]

## FRASIA MARZI RESPONDS TO ALESSANDRO PICCOLOMINI

Still proud and fortunate Tomb,
you shade the cultivator of glorious Laurel,
for whom lovely boughs are raised on high,
which neither sling nor bow has ever touched.
One clearest trumpet, Alessandro's, sings
the richest of works for you, making brilliance,
yours and his, clear and sonorous, split
Heaven and resound. Who would pour shame
on both and not do homage with the lofty

perfumes of those who garland your breast
for Alessandro? Stand still above the shade
and pleasing ashes of him for whose sake
you are encircled round and round
by heads crowned with flowers, laurel, and ivy.

Tu pur superba e avventurosa Tomba
cuopri'l cultor del glorioso Alloro
Per cui i bei rami al ciel alzati foro
Che non tanto mai salse arco nè fromba.
D'Alessandro una assai più chiara tromba
ti canta con richissimo lavoro;
Tal che di te e di lui chiaro e sonoro
Splendida folgore il Ciel rompe, e rimbomba.
Chi dunque sia ch'ad ambi faccia scorno
E non esalti con sublimi odori
Di quei ch'ad Alessandro ornano il seno?
Fa soste all'ombra, e al cener grato ameno
Per cui sei est celebrata intorno intorno
da teste cinte di hedra, allori, e fiori.[44]

## ✦❝ WOMEN, MEN, AND SIENESE "NEOPLATONISM" ❞✦

Alessandro Piccolomini's *Raffaella*, the most successful of all his works after
the *Institutione di tutta la vita,* came out in eleven separate editions between
1539 and 1574, ten of them from Venetian presses.[45] A conduct book in dialogue form, the *Raffaella* was written pointedly for an audience of literate
and literary women. Piccolomini addressed his dedicatory letter in this early
work "to those women who will read it"—*a quelle donne che leggeranno.*[46] Because of the sexually suggestive nature of the *Raffaella*'s subject matter and
the complex treatment of its female characters, it is interesting to imagine its
reception first by Piccolomini's female readers and then, at what was probably
its first performance, before an all-male audience at a meeting of the Intronati. Though the *Raffaella* has been called "bawdy," it in no way resembles
Aretino's notoriously pornographic *I ragionamenti* (1534), except that in both
dialogues an older, more experienced woman counsels a younger one.[47] Unlike the characters in Aretino's dialogue, Piccolomini's young protagonist is a
gentlewoman rather than a courtesan or prostitute, and the point of the work
is not to offer graphic instruction in the selling of sex. Instead, the *Raffaella*'s
narrative of seduction makes it closer in spirit to his famous forebear Enea

Silvio Piccolomini's (Pope Pius II) popular erotic novella, *Historia de duobus amantibus* (A tale of two lovers).[48] The love that the older woman Raffaella persuades her young friend Margarita to seek is not exploitive but reciprocal. Both partners belong to the social and intellectual elite: for such lovers, sexual pleasure is not the end goal but, rather, a union of minds, souls, and bodies. And yet this curiously idealized love is a union outside the bonds of marriage, and one that will involve secrecy and deception.

Though the earlier part of the dialogue is taken up with conduct-book trivia—advice on the fabrics, colors, and cut of gowns a gentlewoman should wear, the correct lotions and body washes she should use, and the proper foods and wines she should serve her guests—seen as a whole, the *Raffaella* lays the groundwork for Piccolomini's articulation of his theory of love in his most ambitious work, the *Institutione*. It is as though Piccolomini had crossed Plato's lofty theory of love as a way station to the good, the true, and the beautiful in the *Phaedrus* with Ovid's titillating *Ars amatoria*.

Forteguerri was twenty-seven and newly widowed when Piccolomini brought her a copy of the first printing of his *Institutione di tutta la vita de l'huomo nato nobile* in 1542, with her name emblazoned on the title page of the volume as its dedicatee.[49] After four years at the University of Padua, Piccolomini, who was then thirty-four, had published his first work on ethics—a set of essays on civil and domestic questions loosely modeled on two very different ancient philosophical works: Aristotle's *Nicomachean Ethics* and Xenophon's *Oeconomicus*, a work he had recently translated from the Greek for publication. Piccolomini's *Institutione*, printed by Scoto in Venice in 1542, was designated as a gift to Forteguerri "for the benefit" of her infant son Alessandro, who was not only her friend's namesake but his godson. When she was not yet twenty, she had married the Sienese nobleman Giulio Colombini. Within seven years of the wedding, she was the mother of three children under the age of eight and a widow.

Alessandro Piccolomini had at least an early draft of the *Institutione* in hand when he returned to Siena from Padua for the baptism of Forteguerri's son in 1539 or 1540, according to the dedicatory letter he wrote for Forteguerri.[50] He had by that time established himself as a notable writer in both cities. Among the works he had publicly presented in Siena were his translations of the sixth book of Virgil's *Aeneid* and Xenophon's *Oeconomicus*, his essay *In lode delle donne* and the dialogue *Raffaella*; he was also readying a lecture on a sonnet of Laudomia Forteguerri's for delivery at one of the bimonthly meetings of the Infiammati. It was in these early writings that he developed and experimented with his theory of love. But any hopes he might have harbored toward the newly widowed Forteguerri went up in smoke three years after the publication of his lecture on her work. In 1544, two years after her husband's death, she married Petruccio Petrucci, a man whose wealth and status easily equalled Colombini's.

Part conduct book and part treatise on moral philosophy, Piccolomini's *Institutione* is a curious mix of Platonic love theory, Aristotelian ethics on Alberti-style domestic themes, and stag-party advice clothed in philosophical language.[51] Looking at first glance like a late Renaissance sequel to Leon Battista Alberti's *De familia* (1437), the *Institutione* touches on every imaginable topic in the daily life of the Sienese elite, from the schooling of the young gentleman from infancy to university, to money and finance, justice and the laws, the arts and the sciences, entertainment and polite conversation, and the house and domestic economy.[52] Last, the book treats friendship, love, and marriage.

But Piccolomini's *Institutione* assumes a social ease and freedom between elite Sienese men and women of the same class that Alberti could never have imagined.[53] Judging by its enormous commercial success, which lasted for the rest of the century, the *Institutione* struck a chord with the Italian reading public.[54] This is a serious work, but the instruction Piccolomini offers his readers—women and men—on sex, love, and marriage differs only slightly from his comic and often risqué *Raffaella*. As was the case with the *Raffaella*, the *Institutione* was aimed primarily at a female readership. Certainly both works had dedicatory letters that were explicitly addressed to women, and both works dismissed the idea that one's wife or husband was likely to be the love of one's life. Both works suggest that a true harmony of bodies, minds, and souls—love in the highest sense—may be unattainable within the state of matrimony. Drawing a sharp linguistic distinction between the spouse and the lover, Piccolomini terms the husband or wife the *consorte,* while the man or woman who is the husband or wife's soul mate and spiritual lover he calls the *amata* or *amato.* He not only argues that it is right for a man or woman to have both a *consorte* (spouse) and a lover, but he also speculates that this living arrangement may even be ordained by a higher law (*da miglior legge imposto*). In the following passage, the subject is male and the consort and lover are female; but elsewhere in books 9 and 10, the gender roles are reversed and it is the wife (*moglie*) who is assumed to have a friend (*amato*) who is not her *marito*:

> I know manifestly that most of those who will read my books, when they come to this part about the selection of a wife will assume that I would think it is not right to choose a woman for a wife other than the one with whom . . . one ought to be in love. Thus it would follow that one should love one's consort with one's whole

soul; and having already concluded that one cannot be in love with more than one person at one time, it should necessarily follow that one's wife [*consorte*] and one's beloved [*amata*] would have to be one and the same woman. But this I do not believe. . . . We can conclude, then, that not only is it not necessary for us to take as a wife [*moglie*] the woman who is our soulmate [*amata*]; but it is appropriate that she not be taken as such. It may be that for another purpose and due to a higher law it is imposed on us to love one whom our marriages do not ordain.

Cognosco manifestamente, che la maggior parte di coloro, che legeranno questi miei libri; quando a questa parte de l'elettione de la consorte verrano; terran per certo, che io giudichi, che altra donna elegger per moglie non si convengha, che quella istessa. . . . che amar si debbe; conciò sia che dovendosi amar la consorte con tutto l'animo; e havendo io già concluso, che non si possa amar più persone in medesimo tempo, par che ne segua per sforza, che una medesima donna debbi esser'amata e consorte. La qual cosa io nondimeno non affermo. . . . Concluder dunque potiamo, che non solo non è necessario, che noi debbiam tor per moglie l'amata donna; anzi è cosa convenevole, che non si tolgha. Conciò sia che ad altro fine, e da miglior legge, impostoci sia l'amare, che non si ordinaron le nostre nozze.[55]

In both works Piccolomini challenges the practicality and wisdom of marital fidelity. While the comic character Raffaella reasons that the custom of arranged marriages renders the chances for happiness in a long-term marriage slim and she urges Margarita to find a lover suitable to her rank and interests, in the *Institutione* Piccolomini argues in favor of what Marie-Françoise Piejus has called "spiritual adultery," in which "love and matrimony conserve their prerogatives and co-exist in a precarious equilibrium for the sake of the happiness of individuals and states." [Grazie ad un sorprendente teoria dell'adulterio spirituale, amore e matrimonio conservano le loro perogative e concorrono, in un equilibrio precario, alla felicità degli individuali e degli stati.][56]

There is never any sense that there is a class distinction between Piccolomini's *consorte* and *amata*; rather, it is assumed that both are gentlewomen, as is the case in the *Raffaella*. In the *Institutione*, sex is not brought into the discourse explicitly, but it is implied as a component of the marital relationship since a man and his wife are expected to bear and raise children (bk. 10, chaps. 5 and 6). In the case of the *amata*, the spiritual element, which Piccolomini calls the *union d'animi,* is paramount, and physical pleasure is not a topic in book 10. Throughout book 10, there is a strong sense of Ciceronian, republican mores. A citizen, whom Piccolomini terms *homo civil,* must have a built-in sense of responsibility and allegiance to his republic, which in turn grows out of his duty to his parents, wife, and children. There are many different species of affective attachments, and these have different names: love, friendship, loyalty, devotion, respect, and affective attachment. The affection a husband or wife feels for his or her spouse and children Piccolomini categorizes as filial and matrimonial attachments (*charità filiali e matrimoniali*), not to be confused with higher love (*amore*).[57] These loves and loyalties—for collective entities as well as for individuals—generate feelings of responsibility toward their objects, whether in the public or private sphere, and such emotions exist side by side in the virtuous citizen, the *homo vero civil*. Women and men, he argues, should embrace this more comprehensive understanding of love and the emotions, and not lament it:

> But that I might, for different reasons and in different ways, love more than one person is hardly an impossibility. In fact, it is now appropriate. For example, if I love a woman, I will serve and love some prince at the same time, and in so doing I will do no harm to the woman I love [*amata donna*] since the types of emotional attachments [*maniere di benevolenza*] have different names and forms: that is why we refer to the one sort as "love" [*amore*] and the other as "fondness" and "respect" [*charità e riverenza*] rather than love [*amore*]. . . . And I have more to say to you: the woman who is a man's lover [*amata donna*] should not regret but instead be extremely happy that her lover is not deficient in all the virtuous offices and duties that are the mark of the truly cultivated citizen [*homo vero civil*]: such as loyalty to friendship, the republic, one's family and benefactors, commitment to the learning and the sciences, to honor, and in sum, every activity which pertains to one's virtue and happiness.

> Ma che io ami secondo diversi fini e rispetti, più persone che una in questo non sol non è cosa impossibile, ma è anchor convenevole. Come per essempio, se amand' io una donn servirò e amarò parimente alcun Principe; non questo pregiuditio a l'amata donna; perchè tai maniere di benevolenza han nomi e forme diverse: chiamandosi l'un' amore, e l'altro più tosto charità e riverenza ch'amore. . . . E più vi v'ho dire, che l'amata donna, non sol doler si debba; anzi sommamente goder, che l'amante suo non manchi di tutti quelli virtuosissimi offitii, che ad homo vero civil'appartenghasi, come saria l'osservanza de l'amicitia, de la Republica, de la famiglia, de i benefattori, de le scientie, de gli honori, e i somma d'ogni altra operatione, che a la sua virtù e felicità s'appartengha.[58]

Nothing, not even sin, argues Piccolomini, obviously meaning adultery, is more displeasing to God than discord between husband and wife. [Ne credo io, che sia peccato, che più dispaccia a Dio, che la discordia tra'l marito e la moglie.][59] Since the honor of the woman and the utility of the house, he writes, resides in her respect for her husband and her concord with him, "as on the splendor of the sun" [Poscia che l'honor de la donna, e l'utilità de la casa, ne l'ossservanza del suo marito, e concordia con quello, come lo splendor nel Sole, è riposto (bk. 10, chap. 4, fol. 222.)], much is made of the necessity to preserve, and at all cost, the honor of the marriage and harmony of the house. But nothing is said of the dishonesty to which the spouse having even a "spiritual" affair will have to resort to keep the house afloat. In place of the strategies of subterfuge advised by Raffaella, Piccolomini introduces the doctrine of preemptive suppression:

> A woman should not harbor suspicion of her husband without manifest cause; nor by the same token should she give him any cause to be suspicious of her. For if a suspicion comes between them, the remedy comes too late. For suspicion is like a poisonous plant: so virulent is its power that, out of the depths of Chaos, the Furies brought it to mankind, and so great is its force and nature that wherever it grows and germinates once, it can never be uprooted. . . . Therefore a woman should avoid every occasion to make her husband suspicious; she should behave in a manner that her every act, appearance, and action toward him testifies to her love for him.

> Non prenda dunque la donna senza manifesta cagione sospition del marito: nè parimente porgha occasion'a lui di punto sospicar cosa alcuna, conciò sia che nato che fusse tra loro il sospetto, tardo poi sarebbe il remedio, essendo che così vene-nosa pianta, quanto è quella del sospetto, e de la gelosia, da Megera fin da l'abbisso fu portata tra gli huomini; con questa forza e natura, che dove fiorisce, e ger-moglia un volta, già mai disradicar non si possa. . . . Per la qual cosa la donna sag-gia, per fuggir da 'l canto suo ogni occasion di far sospettoso il marito; viverassi in maniera ch'ogni suo atto, ogni sembianza, e operation sua verso du lui, faccia fede de l'amor.[60]

But whereas the *Raffaella* is explicit both about the pleasures of the body that await the bride who strays from her husband and the many ruses and lies her affair will demand, the *Institutione* keeps the prescribed adultery on a soul-oriented, Neoplatonic plane. Piccolomini's definition of love follows Ficino's commentary on Plato's *Symposium* to the letter in its spiritual and intellectual thrust.[61]

> And listen well to this: although I have said that there are two ways to enjoy the sweetest union of souls for lovers—that is, hearing and sight—nonetheless from these two ways, a third way is born which is more perfect by far than those, and

that is the contemplation of such union. And this we do with our minds, so that suddenly the mind [(*mente*) *ella svegliata*] awakened by the messenger of both sound and sight, beholds and apprehends such bliss. Thus it is well put by Plato who affirms that one enjoys the beauty of the beloved through three means: hearing, seeing, and through the mind, which being itself divine and celestial, cannot know anything without the help of the senses, as long as it is clothed in this corporeal cloak.

Et è d'advertire, che quantunque io habbia detto, che due sono i mezi da far godere la dolcissima union de gli animi de gli amanti; ciò è il vedere e l'odire: nondimeno, da queste due vie ne nasce la terza, molto più perfetta di quelle, et è la contemplatione, che secondo le menti nostre facciam, di tal'unione, subito che per il nuntio de l'odito e del veduto, ella parimente svegliata, una tal felicità contempla e considera. Sì come ben dice Platone: il qual per tre vie afferma, che si fruisce la bellezza de l'amato, per l'odire, per il vedere, e per la mente istessa celeste e divina; la qual mentre che è di questo manto corporeo vestita, senza l'aiuto de i sensi, cognoscere alcuna cosa non puote.[62]

## ❦ PICCOLOMINI'S ROLE AS FORTEGUERRI'S PUBLICIST AND PRESS AGENT ❧

Characteristic of all Piccolomini's work was the interactive nature of his literary friendships with women. He produced the *Tombaiade* with a group of women and men. He wrote the *Raffaella* and the *Institutione* for the Sienese women he knew and he dedicated the latter specifically to Laudomia Forteguerri. In 1541, he took his literary relationships with women a step further. He acted as Forteguerri's agent in presenting a lecture on one of her poems at a meeting of the Padua Infiammati to the assembled membership. His presentation soon led to the poem's publication by two presses, one in Bologna and the other in Venice.[63]

When Alessandro Piccolomini left the Intronati in Siena to enter the Accademia degli Infiammati in Padua, he found that the Paduan literary club was practically a school for aspiring writers. At academy meetings, poets and critics met press men who occupied key posts at the leading publishing businesses in Venice.[64] The florid letters Piccolomini sent his fellow club member Lodovico Dolce, then senior editor at the Giolito press, show how strenuously the Sienese writer courted Dolce.[65] Other members of the Infiammati—whether editors employed by the Venetian presses like Dolce and Domenichi or independent consultants to the presses such as Varchi, Aretino, and Sperone Speroni—figured prominently in a rash of publications in the 1540s and 1550s. Among those new, academy-driven books was the monumental fifteen-volume series of poetry anthologies published by Giolito and his associates between 1545 and 1559, in which sonnets by both Laudomia Forteguerri and Alessandro Piccolomini appeared.[66] The transformation a literary work underwent from the still fluid condition of its airing at an academy meeting to its fininshed state as a published book could be phenomenally quick. The Infiammati's translation of the *Aeneid*, a collaborative effort by several academy members, appeared in print, in book form, only a few months after the work was presented orally in a series of academy meetings.[67]

Early in 1541, Forteguerri brought Piccolomini a manuscript of her sonnets, and it was at that time that she gave him permission to take one of her poems, *Hora te'n va superbo, hor corre altero*, as the text for his lecture at the first meeting of the Infiammati in February of that year.[68] Piccolomini's letters to Varchi about the activities of the Infiammati indicate that women were likely to have been among the crowd on Friday, February 1, 1541, when he delivered his lecture on Forteguerri's *Hora te'n va superbo* at the academy.[69] His lecture, perhaps the first critical essay ever presented at an Italian literary academy on a woman's poetry included a reading and analysis of Forteguerri's sonnet.[70] His critique was a showpiece in its own right, thick with references and quotes from Quintilian's literary theory (*Institutio oratoria*), Aristotle's *Metaphysics*, Claudian's *Rape of Proserpina*, and Tibullus's love elegies.

The full text of Forteguerri's *Hora te'n va superbo*, accompanied by Piccolomini's *Lettura*, appeared in a slim volume published on June 25, 1541, in Bologna.[71] The publication of the *Lettura* had repercussions for both the poet and her critic. In 1546, Lodovico Domenichi, then among the most powerful of the young editors working in Venice, noticed Forteguerri's poem, was impressed by it, and decided to include it in the second edition of Giolito's new anthology of contemporary poets, the *Rime diverse*, which had become an instant bestseller when the first edition came out in 1545.[72] This second edition of the *Rime diverse* included other women, in addition to Forteguerri, who were rising stars on the literary horizon—Vittoria Colonna, Veronica Gambara, Laura Terracina, and the well-known courtesan Francesca Baffa.

Forteguerri dedicated her *Hora te'n va superbo*, and with it a suite of four other sonnets, to the daughter of the emperor Charles V, Margaret of Austria.[73] The two met for the first time, according to Piccolomini, when Margaret and the emperor visited Siena in 1535 en route to Florence, where Margaret's marriage to Alessandro de' Medici, Duke of Florence, would be celebrated.[74] Margaret saw Forteguerri again in 1538 when she was on her way to Rome after the assassination of Alessandro.

## ❧ THE INGRESSO OF CHARLES V INTO SIENA AND THE HONEYMOON PHASE OF THE SPANISH OCCUPATION ☙

On April 24, 1535, the newly crowned Emperor Charles V had staged a triumphal entrance into Siena. According to the Sienese diarist Alessandro Sozzini, the citizens put on a great show.[75] They built triumphal arches, stretched colorful canopies across the Piazza del Campo, staged plays and musical performances, and set off fireworks. An equestrian statue of the emperor was placed on the steps of the cathedral; for days, parties were given in his honor while he and his entourage were guests at the palazzo of Antonmaria Petrucci. This was the beginning of the honeymoon phase between the Sienese and Charles V's imperial occupation. At first Charles's governor in Siena, Alfonso Piccolomini, led the reorganization of the entire administrative structure of the Sienese Republic and put the running of the city wholly in the hands of the Sienese citizens. It would not be until 1548, when Don Diego Hurtado di Mendozza, a bibliophile and a man learned in Greek and Latin literature, of whom both Alessandro Piccolomini and Sozzini spoke highly, came to Siena as Charles's governor that relations between the Spanish and the Sienese began to fall apart. By 1551, there were uprisings and sporadic rioting among the citizens, and by the spring of 1552, the citizens rose up in defiance and burned the Spanish garrison. They killed some one hundred soldiers and threw the rest, including the civil administrators, out of the city.

Laudomia Forteguerri's suite of poems dedicated to Charles' daughter Margaret of Austria was written or at least begun during the first flush of Charles' ceremonial *ingresso* into Siena, his promise to support local republican government, and his pledge to see justice implemented under his protection. While the poems reflect the Italian love lyric tradition from Catullus to Petrarch, they are at the same time politically inspired. Margaret was only thirteen when Charles's party first descended on Siena, but Laudomia, twenty at the time, newly married and perhaps already pregnant, no doubt saw this as a natural opportunity to extend her own patronage and welcome to the daughter of the man who would potentially be the greatest patron that she, her family, and her city could expect to meet in a lifetime.

The poems, though, represent a bittersweet foreshadowing of the tragedy of Siena soon to come, on a national scale as well as on a personal one. While on the surface, Forteguerri's suite of poems dedicated to Margaret represent an offer of friendship, her oeuvre might also be read as a plea to the Habsburg emperor to protect her city from papal and Florentine aggression and to make good on his promises of civic harmony and money to rebuild the state. Socially, of course, there was little common ground that Forteg-uerri and Margaret shared. The Forteguerri were leading members of the nobility but in a city that no longer had a speaking part on the world's stage and was in any case occupied by the emperor's men. Margaret, in contrast, was Duchess of Florence and the wife of Alessandro de' Medici at the time of Charles's *ingresso* into Siena. And after Alessandro's assassination, at the time of Margaret's second visit to Siena, her social status in Italy continued to rise. In 1538, she married Pope Paul III's grandson Ottavio Farnese, acquiring at that time the title Duchess of Parma and Piacenza.[76]

## ❧c FORTEGUERRI'S SONNET CYCLE ɔ❧

In the *Lettura,* Piccolomini tells the story of how Forteguerri and Margaret of Austria met, visited one another, and saw one another again three years later in Siena. To readers unfamiliar with the language of sixteenth-century patronage, such descriptions as Piccolomini's of the first meeting between Charles's daughter and Forteguerri could be misread. "From the first moment she saw Madam [the emperor's daughter Margaret], and was seen by her," he wrote, "both of them immediately burst into the most fiery flames of love." [La qual come prima vidde Madama, e da quella fu veduta altresi sì subito di ardentissime fiamme d'amore, l'una de l'altra su accese.][77] But Piccolomini's own letters to the senior editor at the Giolito press, Lodovico Dolce, make it clear that such language was, certainly in the circles he traveled in, common social currency and not necessarily meant to be taken as a sexual advance. His letter to Dolce after what had clearly been a professional visit was full of talk of the "caldo di quell'amore," "affetto ardentissimo," and "calda affettione" (heat of love; most fiery feeling; and hot emotion) he had felt.[78]

Still, Agnolo Firenzuola's reaction to Piccolomini's lecture, in a dialogue he published in 1541 shortly after the *Lettura* came out in print, suggests, as Konrad Eisenbichler has shown, that an exchange of sonnets between two women in the Petrarchan idiom was bound to raise questions.[79] Firenzuola's interlocutor Celso ponders the nature of Laudomia Forteguerri's love for Margaret of Austria in the context of his discussion of Plato's myth of the origins of same-sex love in the *Symposium.*[80] In Plato's myth of the hermaphrodite (189e), Celso observes, there were two kinds of love between two women: one "lascivious," as in the case of Sappho of Lesbos, whereas the other emanated from "purity and holiness, as the elegant Laudomia Forteguerra loves the most illustrious Margaret of Austria."[81]

The scene Forteguerri paints in her work is suggestive of the erotic tradition in European poetry from Sappho to the Roman elegists, the Nuovo Stil poets, and Petrarch.[82] And yet her own language in the sonnets is tempered.[83] The amatory themes are all there, but the Petrarchan imagery of erotic inflammation, icy chills, bodily pain, and psychological suffering that characterizes the female-male love lyrics of Isabella di Morra, Gaspara Stampa, Domenichi, Varchi, and Tasso is absent in Forteguerri's poetry. Certainly Lodovico Domenichi's anthology of fifty-three women poets demonstrates the existence of a tradition of female literary friendship in Italy.[84] Whether we choose to call this emerging tradition Sapphic or not, sonnet suites dedicated by one literary woman to another and the exchange of groups of sonnets or poem cycles between women were not unusual either in sixteenth-century Italy or elsewhere in Europe, as Harriette Andreadis has recently shown.[85] Virginia de Martini Salvi dedicated such a sonnet cycle to Marguerite de Navarre; Veronica Gambara and Vittoria Colonna addressed a large group of sonnets to one another; Lucretia Figliucci devoted six sonnets to Cassandra Petrucci; Hippolita Mirtilla wrote a suite of four sonnets to Gaspara Stampa; Maria da Sangallo composed sonnets for Bianca Rangona, Silvia di Somma, and Leonora da Este; Cornelia Brunozzi de'Villani and Maria Martelli de' Panciatichi exchanged sonnets, as did Vittoria Colonna and Marguerite de Navarre.[86]

The five poems whose texts, translation, and commentary follow form a miniature *canzoniere*, a story told stage by stage of a lover's investment in an unattainable object of desire.[87] In a diminuative version of Catullus's frustrated desire to possess Lesbia, Phyllis's longing for Demophoon in Ovid's *Heroides*, or Petrarch's for Laura in the *Rime sparse*, each of Forteguerri's Petrarchan sonnets depicts a new phase of the drama:

Fixation on a love object geographically and/or emotionally distant (poems 1–5)

Comparison of the loved one to a god or a force in nature (poems 1, 2)

Request for a love token (poem 3)

Fantasy of the rival's defeat (poem 4)

Silence and rejection on the part of the loved one (poem 5)

Obsessive hope and fantasy that the loved one will return (poems 4, 5)

Recognition, long denied, of the loved one's betrayal (poem 5)

Venting of righteous anger at the betrayal (poem 5)

Prayer for divine intervention to force the lover to return (often addressed to Fortuna as here in poem 5)

1

Why does your Phoebus compete with my Sun,
haughty heaven, if it has won greater glory?
Your Phoebus should return to the forests
or stay buried in the waves, while my Sun gleams
with lovely rays. A small cloud eclipses
your light and thin fog darkens your lovely face:
my Sun, wrapped in clouds and fog,
renders heaven bright with clearer light.
When your Phoebus lifts the day from the sea,
if he did not tear away the veil that dims the air,
he would not illuminate the world. But my Sun
does not remove the veil, nor does she sweep
the air, but making that murk resemble her,
she sets the clouds afire and makes their dimness gleam.

A che il tuo Febo col mio Sol contende,
Superbo ciel, se il primo honor gli ha tolto?
Torni fra selve, o stia nel mar sepolto,
Mentre con più bei raggi il mio risplende.
    Picciola nube tua gran luce offende;
Et poca nebbia oscura il suo bel volto:
Il mio fra nubi (ahi lassa) e nebbie avvolto
Più gran chiarezza e maggior lume rende.
    Quando il tuo porta fuor de l'onde il giorno,
Se non squarciasse il vel, che l'aria adombra,
Non faria di sua vista il mondo adorno.
    Il mio non toglie il vel, né l'aria sgombra;
Ma somigliando a se ciò c'ha dintorno,
Fiammeggiar fa le nubi e splender l'ombra.

2

Now, you go proudly, now you run nobly,
painting both your shores with lovely flowers,
ancient Tiber. Now your bright waters reflect
the image of a sun more clear and true.
Now you carry the scepter, now you rule
over more famous streams; now you have
the power to make your lovely banks grow green,
joyful and more fertile: now you are complete.

Since my fair and pleasing sun is with you,
not far away or near, but always there with you;
and you bathe the fringe of her noble skirt.[88]
And so art, nature, and heaven (and thus
the almighty wishes) make manifest today that
an immortal lady can flourish in the world.

Hora te'n va superbo, hor corre altero[89]
Pingendo di bei fiori ambe le sponde,
Antico Tebro, hor ben purgate l'onde
Rendin l'immago a un sol più chiaro e vero.
    Hora porti lo scettro, hor' hai l'impero
Dei più famosi: hor' haverai tu donde
Verdeggin più che mai liete e feconde
Le belle rive: hor' hai l'esser' intero.
    Poich'egli è teco, il vago almo mio Sole,
Non hor lungi hor vicin, ma sempre appresso,
E bagni il lembo de l'altera gonna.
    Ch'arte, natura, e 'l ciel,' e così vuole
Chi 'l tutto può, mostran pur' oggi espresso,
Che star ben puote al mondo, immortal Donna.[90]

3

Fortunate plant, so welcome in heaven,
for nature invested all her sublimity in you,
when it decided to create such beauty:
I speak of my divine Margaret of Austria.
I know well that she never would have left heaven
except to show us celestial things.
God sculpted her and created with his own hand
this woman he so loved and cherished.
And if he so generously gave us so great a gift,
by showing us the glory of his realm,
it should not anger you to show his glory to me.
And if I have left a pledge from my heart for you,
in exchange you should send me a picture
painted of you, where I have eyes to gaze at it.

    Felice pianta, in ciel tanto gradita,
Ove ogni estremo suo natura pose,

Quando crear tanta beltà dispose,
Dico mia diva d'Austria Margherita.

So ben che mai di ciel non fe' partita,
Ma per mostrarne le divine cose,
Scolpilla Dio e di sua man compose
Questa a Lui tanto accetta e favorita:

S'a noi fu largo Dio di tanto dono,
Di mostrarne la gloria del suo regno,
Non vi sdegnate a me mostrarla in parte.

E s'io del petto v'ho lasciato un pegno,
In cambio un vostro ritratto con arte
Mandate appresso, ove i miei occhi sono.


4

Now triumphant, and still more haughty
walks ancient Rome, possessing every
good that nature and heaven has given:
she reaps it for herself and stows it away.
But if my enemy, who tramples me underfoot,
were sweet to me and bitter to you,
if she took it from you and made me the heir,
no longer would the flowers and meadows
smile on you; no longer would the rich banks
of the wide Tiber glitter with emeralds and rubies.
Only Arbia's brow and breast would be festooned.
No divine *exempla* would you have, no
angelic beauty to enjoy: and if should happen,
then my happiness would be complete.


Hor trionfante e più che mai superba
Sen' va l'antica Roma, che possiede
Tutto 'l ben, che natura, e il ciel ne diede:
Essa in se lo raccoglie e lo riserba.

Ma s'a me fosse dolce, a Te acerba
La mia nimica, che m'ha sotto il piede,
Te lo togliesse e me ne fesse herede,
Più non ti riderian fioretti e l'herba.

Non sarien più di smeraldi & rubini
Le ricche sponde del gran Thebro ornate;
Pur l'Arbia s'orneria la fronte, e 'l seno.

Più non havresti gli esempi divini:

Ne godresti l'angelica beltate:
Se questo avvien, son pur felice appieno.


5

Alas, my lovely Sun will not turn
her divine rays toward me: shall I
then live without my light and joy?
May it not please God for me to live
in this world without her. Ah, cruel fortune,
why do you not allow my body to go
where my heart goes? Why do you hold
me in this cruel prison without hope
of escape from woe? Happy and kind,
turn your face to me now, for it's no
glorious act to abase one of the female sex.
Hear my words, how ready they are
to beg you; for I ask only that you
let me remain at my goddess's side.


   Lasso, chel mio bel Sole i santi rai
Ver me non volgerà: dunque debb'Io
Viver senza il mio ben? Non piaccia a Dio
Che senza questo io viva in terra mai.
   Ahi fortuna crudel, perché non fai,
Che vada il corpo, dove va il cor mio?
Perché mi tieni in questo stato rio,
Senza speme d'uscire unqua di guai?
   Volgi lieta, e benigna homai la fronte
A me; ché non è impresa gloriosa
Abbattere una del femineo sesso.
   Odi le mie parole come pronte
In supplicarti: né voglio altra cosa,
Salvo ch'a la mia Dea mi tenga appresso.


   In the first poem, *A che il tuo col mio Sol contende*, the poet reveals her own perilous hubris.[91] She calls out to Heaven himself (*superbo Ciel*), rebuking him for daring to think that "his sun," referred to here mythologically as Phoebus Apollo, is a rival for *her* lover—*il mio Sol* ("my sun")—which we soon learn is one of her appellations for Margaret: an allusion, Piccolomini notes in his *Lettura*, to Petrarch's adoring references to Laura.[92] In strikingly hyperbolic language, she boasts that her beloved Sun does more than shine down on the world.

> my Sun
> does not remove the veil, nor does she sweep
> the air, but making the murk resemble her,
> she sets the clouds afire and makes their dimness gleam.

> Il mio non toglie il vel, né l'aria sgombra;
> Ma somigliando a se cio c'ha dintorno,
> Fiammeggiar fa le nubi, e splender l'ombra.

> *(#1, lines 12–14)*

*Hora te'n va superbo, ho corre altero,* alone among Forteguerri's sonnet cycle, achieved fame in sixteenth-century Italy, largely because Giolito picked it up for his 1546 anthology, *Rime diverse*, after Bonardo and da Carpi had published it in Piccolomini's *Lettura* in 1541. This second sonnet in Domenichi's edition of Forteguerri's lyric suite places the poet's beloved (Margaret), whom she again calls "il mio Sole," at a distance from her, hopelessly far away in Rome. She addresses the Tiber River as her rival, the classically resonant metonym for the imperial city and a poetic trope she takes from Virgil, Claudian, and Bembo, as Piccolomini reminds his audience at the Infiammati meeting.[93] As Petrarch used the Po River in his *Rime sparse* to portray Laura's power, Forteguerri paints the ancient Tiber (and thus Rome) as rejuvenated by Margaret's presence.[94] But in this most upbeat of the sonnets in her lyric suite, she sees her sorrow at her beloved's absence and thus her writing as productive. In the concluding tercet, Forteguerri links her own fertile portraits of Margaret and the Tiber in her lyric work to the Platonic triad of Art, Nature, and Heaven—*il Ciel*, whom she here describes as "he who is capable of everything." As Piccolomini notes (*Lettura*, fol. 26), Art imitates Nature and Nature imitates the mind of God (*il Ciel*) and he capitalizes the three Platonic concepts in his edition:

> And so Art, Nature, and Heaven (and he who
> is almighty) make manifest today that
> an immortal lady can flourish in the world.

> Ch'Arte, Natura, e 'l Ciel,' e così vuole
> Ch'il tutto può, mostran pur' oggi espresso
> Che star ben puote al mondo, immortal Donna.

> *(#2, lines 12–14)*

Only in poem 3, *Felice pianta, in ciel tanto gradita*, does the poet name her beloved: "Dico mia diva d'Austria Margherita," she writes. Echoing poem 2, Forteguerri returns to the trio of Art, Nature, and God and the theme of reciprocity. God, nature's designer and artist, has given, in Margaret, a perfect being to the world. Women and men should imitate God's magnanimity. In a characteristic Petrarchan move, Forteguerri asks Margaret for a love token, a portrait of her to keep as a memento, in exchange for the gift of her poems: "Et s' io del petto v'ho lasciato un pegno."

The fourth poem, *Hor trionfante e più che mai superba*, takes up Forteguerri's theme of rivalry with Rome for her beloved's presence where the last poem left off. The poet, and bereft lover, again addresses the Tiber River as a character separate from Rome. But the most intriguing lines in the poem introduce ambiguity in the story:

> But if my enemy who tramples me underfoot,
> were sweet to me and bitter to you, . . .
> no longer would the flowers and meadows
> smile on you [the Tiber].

> Ma s'a me fosse dolce, a Te acerba
> La mia nimica, che m'ha sotto il piede, . . .
> Più non ti riderian fioretti e l'herba.

> *(#3, lines 5–8)*

Grammatically and structurally, "la mia inimica" (my enemy) can describe either Fortuna or Rome—or even Margaret? Which is it, though? All three characters would (theoretically, anyway) have the power to reverse the situation and return the object the poet seeks—"tutto 'l ben'" (everything good)—presumably meaning Margaret's return to Siena. The reader can imagine any one of the three characters posed in the classical stance of the conquering soldier, one foot placed on the defeated enemy's chest or back. If Margaret is the *inimica* here and the traditional *amante crudele* trope is appropriated, the narrative deepens. But if the poet's enemy is simply Fortuna or Rome, the danger that the poem might be read as offensive to Charles and his daughter is eliminated.

In poem 5, *Lasso, chel mio bel Sole i santi rai*, all hope for a reunion is gone. As in book 6 of the *Aeneid*, the once beloved girl has turned away from the protagonist; the past cannot be recovered. The poet can only pray to the deity Fortuna. She begs only only to keep Margaret, "la mia Dea" (my Goddess), close to her ("ne voglio altra cosa, / salvo ch'a la mia Dea mi tenga appresso").

Thus in a cycle of five sonnets, we have come full circle, from hope and awe to recrimination and despair. The cycle ends with the lines: "it is not a glorious deed to bring low a woman" [non è impresa gloriosa / Abbattere una del femineo sesso (lines 13–14].

## ✤c THE FAILURE OF TWO COURTSHIPS ᴈ✤

Ten years later, Margaret turned her back on Laudomia Forteguerri and the beautiful Arbia once again. Her father, Charles V, joined forces with Florence to bring Siena to its knees in a siege that began in 1552 and did not end until mid-April 1555. Forteguerri herself directed the construction of fortifications inside the city, commanding a regiment of a thousand women who, armed with picks and shovels, wore the colors of their hometown as they labored. But the Sienese found themselves and their French allies hopelessly outgunned and outmaneuvered. By February 1555, some thirty thousand troops, from the Florentine and Spanish imperial armies combined, were encamped in the hills around Siena and were poised to march on the small city. After the siege, we hear no more of Forteguerri. Only Virginia Martini de'Salvi, of the group of women active in literary affairs in Siena, continued to write poetry after 1555. She moved to Rome, abandoning Siena after the siege. As for Alessandro Piccolomini, while he was named to the chair of civil law at the University of Macerata in 1546, he too left Siena, spending most of the next twelve years in Rome at the papal court. He returned home to Siena in 1558 and remained there in his native city until his death in 1579.[95] The end of the siege and the ensuing settlements between Charles and Cosimo marked the institutionalization of Florentine hegemony in Tuscany and the relegation of Spain to a subsidiary role in the region.

Siena shared a number of cultural institutions in common with Naples, Milan, and Florence at midcentury: women-led salons; an active religious reform movement associated with the teachings of Valdés, Ochino, and Erasmus; a literary academy of peninsula-wide fame; and an avant-garde literary movement that promoted the kind of amatory rhetorics the Inquisition and its Indexes would ultimately criminalize and Piccolomini himself would disavow in the later 1550s.[96] But Siena represents a different case from the other elite cultures I have considered. A possibly unbridgeable gulf existed between the bourgeois elite of Siena and the royalty or royally connected d'Aragona,

Colonna, d'Avalos, and Gonzaga women, whose tragedies were buffered by wealth and entitlement. Charles V's daughter, Margaret of Austria, visited Siena twice, but socially there was little common ground between the Duchess of Parma and Piacenza and the leading women in Siena. The granddaughters of the king of Naples and their friends did not travel to Siena, nor did they forge connections by letter with the elite women of that small republic, though they might have done so through the mediation of such well-connected men within the Venetian publishing world as Varchi, Betussi, and Domenichi, who maintained friendships with the intellectual women of both worlds. Still, in 1559, Domenichi would bring together the poetry of Vittoria Colonna and the Sienese women Virginia di Salvi, Aurelia Petrucci, and Forteguerri in his all-women anthology, *Rime diverse d'alcune nobilissime, et virtuossime donne*. And Betussi, for his part, would immortalize the names of Giovanna d'Aragona and the Sienese poets Francesca de' Baldi and Forteguerri in his *Imagini del tempio*, a work as much a memorial and testament to the courage of Vittoria Colonna as it was to the women of Siena.[97]

## CHAPTER SIX

# Florence: Intimate Dialogues and the End of the Reform Movement

A light rain fell all morning the day the body of Giulia Gonzaga's friend Pietro Carnesecchi was burned. It was said that his headless corpse, stripped of the linen shirt and expensive gloves he wore to the gallows, smoldered for hours in the damp air. The Roman diarist Firmano left a brief memoir of the priest's last hours:

> On the first of October [1567] at dawn the unrepentant heretic, the signor Pietro Carnesecchi, and a relapsed monk of the lesser monastery of the order of Saint Francis, who were handed over to the secular court at Santa Maria sopra Minerva, were decapitated. Their bodies were then burned. They had received the sacrament of the holy Eucharist on the preceding day. The aforesaid signor Pietro would not have been decapitated had he wished to confess his sins. For the queen of France, the Duke of Florence, and a number of other nobles begged for his life. But, as I have said, although he was convicted, since he remained unwilling to confess or show the sign of penitence, he was punished. And before he was beheaded he said nothing. And since the iron ax cut only to the middle of the man's neck, the executioner hacked the rest off with a sword.

> Die mercurii prima octobris summo mane decapitati fuerunt dominus Petrus Carnesicca haereticus impenitens et quidem frater ordinis minorum conventualium Sancti Francisci relapsus, qui in ecclesia Beatae Mariae supra Minervam fuerunt traditi curiae saeculari, et deinde fuerunt traditi curiae saeculari, et deinde fuerunt combusta eorum corpora. Isti die praeterita acceperant summum sacramentum eucharistiae. Praedictus dominus Petrus non fuisset decapitatus, si

confiteri voluisset suos errores, nam regina Franciae, dux Florentiae et infiniti alii nobiles supplicaebant pro vita ipsius; sed quia (ut dixi) licet, ivisset convictus noluit unquam confiteri et ostendere signum penitentiae fuit punitus: et antequam abscideretur sibi caput, nihil dixit, et quia ferrum non abscidit collum nisi usque ad medium, carnifex cum gladio abscidit reliquum.[1]

Gradually, between the deaths of the prominent reform thinkers Caterina Cibo in 1557 and Giulia Gonzaga in 1566, Carnesecchi lost the protection he had enjoyed for over a quarter of a century.[2] He had lived in Rome in the late 1530s, and from there he traveled to Naples to participate in the reform circles that met first at Valdés's house on the Riviera di Chiaia and later at Gonzaga's lodgings at the convent of San Francesco delle Monache in the center of the city.[3] There in her convent salon, Gonzaga and Valdés brought together women and men who would later figure as leaders in the reform movement in Italy and whose friendship would anchor them together for decades to come. Among those who attended regularly were Carnesecchi, Caterina Cibo, Vittoria Colonna, Colonna's sister-in-law Giovanna d'Aragona and her husband's aunt Costanza d'Avalos, the Florentine writer Benedetto Varchi, and the charismatic preacher Bernardino Ochino.[4] Another central figure at the Gonzaga-Valdés salons, Marcantonio Flaminio, a Hellenist trained at Padua, had distinguished himself with the publication of his translation and commentary on perhaps the most difficult and enigmatic of all Aristotle's works, book 12 of the *Metaphysics*.[5] He joined Cardinal Pole's reform circle at Viterbo in 1540–43, together with Carnesecchi and Vittoria Colonna.[6] Flaminio reconnected with Ochino in Rome in 1541, and that year he, Carnesecchi, and Ochino met with Caterina Cibo in Florence, either at her home or Carnesecchi's.

Already in 1540, Carnesecchi found himself among the first to testify in the heresy hearings held by the newly constituted Office of the Inquisition in Rome.[7] Carnesecchi, an ordained priest who had risen to the level of protonotary apostolic, came from an old Florentine family whose descendants had been Medici partisans for generations. After the intervention of Cosimo I, the Medici Duke of Florence and perhaps Caterina Cibo, who was Cosimo's cousin, the inquest ended with Pope Paul III granting the suspected heretic absolution.[8] Carnesecchi stayed on in Rome for several months, after which he shuttled between reform circles in Naples, Viterbo, and Florence, where he was active in Cosimo's Florentine Academy.

In 1547, Cosimo arranged Carnesecchi's transfer to the court of Catherine de' Medici in France, during which time he continued to correspond with Giulia Gonzaga, Flaminio, and probably Cibo. On November 6, 1557, Carnesecchi was called to Rome again by the Office of the Inquisition, but through Cosimo's intervention, the trial was deferred and Carnesecchi remained in Venice. His ecclesiastical benefice and stipend were suspended in 1558, and during this period he was only able to survive through loans from Giulia Gonzaga, who at the same time wrote to her old friends in Rome, the Cardinals Seripando, Morone, Madruzzo, and her uncle, Cardinal Ercole Gonzaga, urging them to support Carnesecchi.[9] At last, under Paul IV's successor, the new Pope Pius IV (Giovanni Angelo Medici), and with continued pressure from Cosimo, Carnesecchi won a sentence of full absolution in July 1561, overriding the wishes of the most fanatical faction of the Roman Inquisition, which was led by its grand inquisitor, Michele Ghislieri.[10] It was in that year that Carnesecchi returned to Naples to work with Gonzaga on an edition of the reform writings of Cardinal Pole. Gonzaga moved out of her convent and took lodgings at the Borgo delle Vergine, where they both stayed during the work.[11]

But in 1567, after the death of Guilia Gonzaga and the confiscation of her papers and correspondence, the former grand inquisitor Ghislieri, now Pope Pius V, reopened Carnesecchi's trial. This time, as Roberto Cantagalli has argued, Cosimo was more than ready to hand over his longtime client to the officers of the Inquisition. There would be a payoff coming, the pope gave Cosimo to understand, if the duke surrendered Carnesecchi to him.[12]

## ✦ CATERINA CIBO ✦

From 1527 on, Caterina Cibo, Duchess of Camerino, widowed and the mother of a young daughter, fought off the yearly armed attacks that neighboring lords mounted against her duchy and the *fortezza* at Camerino.[13] In 1535, she betrothed her daughter Giulia to Guidobaldo Della Rovere, the future Duke of Urbino. But the Farnese pope Paul III, fearing an alliance between the two duchies, confiscated Camerino, taking it for himself, and excommunicated Cibo, her daughter, and her daughter's husband Della Rovere. In 1536, forced to abandon her husband's kingdom, Cibo fled to Florence. Moving into the Pazzi Palazzo with her brother Lorenzo Cibo and his family, she slipped seamlessly into Medici court circles. Born a stone's throw from Florence at Ponzano, she was a granddaughter of Lorenzo (the Magnificent) de' Medici, the niece of two Medici popes, Leo X and Clement VII, and the sister of the reigning primate of Florence, Cardinal Innocenzo Cibo. Cibo was also the first cousin of Cosimo I de' Medici's mother, Maria Salviati. Perhaps the most well-educated of all the women involved in reform thought and politics on the eve of the Counter-Reformation in Italy, Cibo had grown up reading Virgil and Horace in Latin,

Plato and Aristotle in the original Greek, and the Hebrew Talmud; she was a voracious reader used to discussing philosophical and religious ideas.

Cibo's involvement with Bernardino Ochino and the reform movement in Florence went back not only to her participation in Giulia Gonzaga's circle and her attendance at Ochino's sermons in Naples but also to her early association with Ochino's monastic order, the Capuchins, a hermetic community committed to radical poverty. Cibo provided Ochino and his Capuchins with a house and some land near Camerino in 1531. Recently widowed at the time, Cibo still ruled as Duchess of Camerino and was the sole heir to the principality. When Pope Clement VII moved to expel the Capuchins from the Church in 1534, Cibo joined forces with another of Ochino's ardent followers, Vittoria Colonna, to save the order from extinction. Together Cibo and Colonna were able to persuade the pope to rescind his bull disallowing the Capuchins. When Alessandro Farnese succeeded Clement as Pope Paul III and declared null and void all rights to her husband's duchy, Cibo urged Ochino to come with her to Florence. Over a period of several months in 1540–41, Ochino met frequently with Cibo, the Florentine protonotary Carnesecchi, and the Aristotelian scholar Flaminio, whose knowledge of Greek philosophy Cibo shared, at either Carnesecchi's house or Cibo's. It was in Cibo's home in Florence the following year that Ochino took off his friar's robes and changed into lay clothes before he fled to Geneva.

## ✢c SALON DISCOURSE IN FLORENCE ɔ✢

In Florence, Cibo's evenings with Ochino, Carnesecchi, and Flaminio clearly provided the raw material for the Capuchin friar's *Dialogi sette*.[14] This influential work of Ochino's resembles, as we shall see, two other commercially successful dialogues published in Venice soon afterward: the *Alfabeto Cristiano* (1545), a dialogue attributed to Juan de Valdés but edited, translated, and probably cowritten by Giulia Gonzaga, and Tullia d'Aragona's *Dialogo della infinità di amore* (1547).[15] All three authors' works belong to a new species of Renaissance dialogue in which women are cast in the major roles. Even when a female interlocutor occupies center stage in other mid-sixteenth-century dialogues, the impact of her character is often diffused among the several male speakers who converse with her in the work, as in Sperone Speroni's *Dialogo d'amore* and Giuseppe Betussi's *Leonora*.[16] In the dialogues of Ochino, Valdés, and d'Aragona, the effectiveness of the drama depends on the stripped down quality of the exchange: a man and a woman engage in an intellectually and emotionally intense discussion, and there are no other characters to buffer the space between them. These are conversations about ideas; yet all three, because of the female-male casting, are to some degree sexually suggestive—though the traces of it are faintest in Ochino's works. The scene of the encounter in all three dialogues is intimate, private, indoors, in the house of one of the speakers, we assume, though only in Tullia d'Aragona's *Dialogo* is the place, her house, referred to explicitly as such. While the dialogues of Ochino and Valdés belong to the literature of the Italian reform movement and are patently Christian works, both are inflected with the Neoplatonism of their period and thus they resemble many of the nonreligious dialogues on love theory of the mid-sixteenth century. D'Aragona's dialogue, as we shall see later in this chapter, by contrast, exhibits few relics of the Platonism or Neoplatonism so popular in the northern cinquecento courts.

In the first of Ochino's *Dialogi sette,* it is clear from the start that the woman and man who are the speakers have undertaken a *dialogo d'amore* of a different sort.[17] As in other *dialoghi d'amore* of the period, defining "love" is important. The opposition between *amare* and *gustare* in loving God is a key theme in Ochino and represents an attack, as Gabriella Zarri has noted, not only on the excessive regard for ecclesiastical ritual and ceremony but on those mystics and visionaries who reject the intellectual and rely solely on their own personal experience of the divine in their quest for God. To love God (*amare Dio*), Ochino explains, lies not in experiencing him solely in the realm of the senses (*gustare Dio*). It requires an act of the will and the intellect. It demands above all the scorning of the things of this world and the pleasures of the senses:

CIBO: I would always want to love God more than earthly things, but sometimes I find greater pleasure and more sweetness in earthly things than in God.

OCHINO: God does not seek for love from us that is sweet; he wants our love to be strong and unremitting: not sensual but spiritual. Divine love does not reside in the senses; one can love God perfectly without the senses. The love of God resides in our power and authority: not in sensual pleasures, for these are born of self-love.

DUCHESSA: Vorrei sempre amare Iddio, più che le creature, et pur qualche volta trovo maggior gusto nelle cose create et maggiore dolcezza che in Dio.

OCHINO: Iddio non ricerca da noi l'amore dolce, ma il costante e forte, non il sensuale, ma il spirituale. L'amore non sta nei gusti, anzi senza gusto si può perfettamente amore Dio; l'amore è in nostra balìa et potestà, ma non c'è gli gusti, li quali nascono dal proprio amore. (Ochino, *I "Dialogi sette,"* ed. Rozzo, dialogue 1, 47).

In the discussion that follows about the connection between sensual and divine love, Cibo asks the leading question that prompts Ochino to introduce the Platonic trope of the gradual ascent from earthly to divine love, which first circulated widely in Ficino's *Commentary on Plato's Symposium on Love* (1484) and his translations of the *Symposium* and the *Phaedrus*.[18] By the middle of the sixteenth-century the trope had become a commonplace in secular dialogues on love and love theory.[19] Ochino's application of this Neoplatonic trope is unusual in a Valdesian or *spirituali* tract but appropriate to its setting, in Florence, where the Medici-supported Platonic academy took root:

OCHINO: Your ladyship should not stop at this, having gazed at the beauty of earthly things, but being excited by this beauty, you should ascend, raising yourself to divine beauty; you should think that all the beauty of earthly beings is nothing in comparison to divine beauty. We must climb the ladder of earthly beings and on this ladder we shall climb to divine beauty, to ascend with these thoughts to heaven saying, "If one finds such sweetness even in these turbid streams tainted with the bitter corruption of earthly beings, what will it be to taste that infinite sea of love? If we marvel that this one world is governed by his divine wisdom, what will it be for us to see that he is able to govern infinite worlds with that wisdom? O how great is that inexhaustible power and virtue of God, through which he created the universe out of nothing and he preserves it all and he would be able to immediately produce or destroy infinite worlds."

OCHINO: Dovrebbe la signoria vostra, vista la bellezza delle creature, non in essa fermarsi, ma, per essa eccitata, salire, elevarsi alla bellezza divina, pensare che tutte le bellezze delle creature è niente a rispetto della divina. Bisogna farsi delle creature scala e con essa elevarsi alla bellezza divina, salire con gli pensieri insino al cielo, dicendo: "Se nelli rivuli turbidi e di molto amaro aspersi delle creature si trova tanta dolcezza, che sarà dipoi gustare in sé quello infinito pelago dello amore? Che sarà a vedere sé in quella divina sapientia, mediante la quale potrebbe governare infiniti mondi, se ci fa stupire in governare solo questo? O quanta è grande quella infattigabil potestà e virtù di Iddio, mediante la quale di niente ha creato l'universi e preserva il tutto, e potrebbe sì subito produrre er annihilare infiniti mondi. (Ochino, *I "Dialogi sette,"* ed. Rozzo, dialogue 1, 51)

But Ochino's Platonic ladder of love, his version of the Ficinian ascent from the phenomena of the visible universe to the Good, the True, and the One is inextricably connected to the pursuit of grace (*gratia divina*). First you will be able "to contemplate the light of the stars, the sun, and other celestial bodies in your ascent," he tells Cibo, "and then, with the eyes of the mind, you will behold the beauty of the soul, especially when it is clothed in virtue and enriched with spiritual gifts, with light, and grace" (Ochino, I "Dialogi sette," ed. Rozzo, dialogue 1, 52). [Et dipoi ascendendo contemplare la luce delle stelle e il sole e altri corpi celesti: et dipoi alla bellezza dell'anima, massime quando è vestita di virtù e arrichita di doni spirituali, e lume et gratia. Veder dipoi, con li occhi della mente.] Ochino's pairing of the Neoplatonic ascent to God and the Christian doctrine of the gift of God's grace, without which there is no salvation, is in fact a signature feature of the *Dialogi sette*, as in the following passage:

OCHINO:    Whoever ascends to this level in the love of God, knows no further difficulty. On the contrary, for him everything is sweet and delightful. But since everything depends on the love of God, every evil and difficulty emanates from not loving Him. While they were wayfarers, it was difficult even for angels who are pure spiritual essence, to love God more than themselves. For us it is even more difficult. But for the blessed it is easy to give all their love to God and now it is true for many in this life through God's gift of divine grace.

OCHINO:    Però colui che sale a questo grado dell'amor di Dio, in nessun'altra cosa sente difficultà, anzi ogni cosa gli è dolce et suave. Però sì come dall' amor di Dio pende ogni bene, così da non amarlo pende ogni difficultà e male. Anchora gli angioli si ben sono substantie spirituali, mentre che furono viatori, gli fu difficile amare Iddio sopra se stessi, benché molto più difficile sia a noi. Alli beati è facile dare tutto il loro amore a Dio et anchora a molti nella presente vita per il grande aiuto della divina gratia. (Ochino, I "Dialogi sette," ed. Rozzo, dialogue 1, 45–46).

Perhaps most characteristic of this first of Ochino's *Dialogi sette* are the paradoxes the two interlocutors find themselves caught up in. In a powerful speech, Cibo argues for the primacy of the intellect in the pursuit of God's love. In the heavenly hierarchy, she observes, the Holy Spirit presupposes the son of God. Likewise, love presupposes cognition: God cannot be loved by us unless we know how much good there is in him. But the problem, Ochino counters, lies in the human mind and its blindness. In a speech rich in classical and biblical resonances, calling to mind Plato's myth of the cave in *Republic* 7, Cicero's *Dream of Scipio*, and 1 Corinthians 13:12, Ochino warns Cibo:

We are like the owls who cannot see the sun in its brightness. God is infinite, immense, and uncircumscribed. Our intellect is finite and limited: it is closed in the dark prison of the body and infected by the sin of the first parents. And many times through our own malice, which blinds us, we see God imperfectly, in great darkness: he, as it is written, is clothed in light that cannot be approached.[20]

Siamo simili alle nottue, che non possono risguardare al sole nella sua luce. Dio è infinito, immenso et incirconscritto e lo intelletto nostro è finito e limitato et in questo carcere del corpo tenebroso incluso e del peccato delli primi [parenti] infetto. Et anchora molte volte dalla propria malitia, la quale acceca, però in tante tenebre imperfettamente veggiamo Dio, il, sì come è scritto, habita una luce inaccessibile, vestito di lume. (Ochino, *I "Dialogi sette,"* ed. Rozzo, dialogue 1, 49)

For most of the dialogue Cibo is portrayed as the seeker and Ochino as her master and teacher. But curiously, the dialogue ends with Cibo's broaching of the most difficult paradox of all: and it is one that Ochino cannot resolve. Cibo poses the paradox of the coexistence of God's foreknowledge and human free will in the world. "How is it possible," she asks, "that God with certain and infallible foreknowledge from the beginning of time depends on our free will and we are free?" (Ochino, *I "Dialogi sette,"* ed. Rozzo, dialogue 1, 50). [Come è possibile che Iddio con notitia certa et infallibile preveda ab eterno le cose future e contingenti, e dal nostro libero arbitrio depende, e così come siamo liberi."] We are left with the sense that the articulation of the question may be of greater moment than the answer and that ultimately, since we are humans, it may be the seeker who is more blessed than the preacher.

Ochino's second dialogue between himself and Caterina Cibo, "On Happiness," from his *Dialogi sette,* closely resembles the commercially successful *Alfabeto cristiano,* a dialogue whose authorship must be attributed jointly to Giulia Gonzaga and Juan de Valdés, as I have argued in my discussion of the *Alfabeto* in chapter 1.[21] The *Alfabeto* may have been drafted as early as 1536, when Gonzaga's reform circle and her evening gatherings of writers, artists, and religious thinkers in Naples were in full swing. Cibo, Ochino, Carnesecchi, Flaminio, and Valdés were regular participants in her salon that year and afterward.[22] Ochino's second dialogue begins very much the way the *Alfabeto* opens. Cibo is soul-sick, and the preacher Ochino plays the role of her confessor and "doctor." She wants only to find happiness in this life since she has wandered for years in search of relief from the pain, anxiety, and restlessness that plague her (Ochino, *I "Dialogi sette,"* ed. Rozzo, dialogue 1, 61). She hopes only for peace and an end to her misery. Though she makes no specific reference to the death of her husband and her separation from her only daughter Giulia (now wife of Guidobaldo delle Rovere, Duke of Urbino), her move to Florence where she is surrounded by family and friends is no consolation for her sorrow. Ochino's answer is that in this world you may not find permanent *felicità*, but you can pursue happiness that is "fitting" or "appropriate" for a wayfarer ("trovi la felicità conveniente a viatori.") The preacher's conception of "happiness" is Aristotelian and Ciceronian in its definition as that which is *conveniente* (fitting) and Christian in its message that we are simply "wayfarers" in this life.[23] The focus is on the search—on the road to be chosen for the journey.

The soul, unlike the world, is not a sphere (63). It is triangular, says Ochino: a trinity consisting of intellect, memory, and will (*intelletto, memoria, volontà*). We will never be satisfied with earthly things (*creature*): we must fill our hearts not our coffers ("bisogna empire il cuore, non l'arca"). Citing Crates, Cleanthus, Plato, Seneca, and the Gymnosophists, the preacher tells Cibo what she of all people already knows: that the search for earthly goods leads nowhere, that desire begets nothing but desire, and that happiness lies within ourselves—not in things.[24] Cibo's response, more intellectually critical, dismisses even humanist ends: "I have searched for *felicità* in knowledge and eloquence, in the moral virtues, in meditating on truth and in contemplating God, in tasting all things—above all God; and finally, I have tried everything and I have found wretchedness where I believed there would be happiness."[25] Ochino's reply to the duchess, concluding this short dialogue, evokes Caterina Cibo's intellectual roots: her early training in Greek philosophy, particularly in Plato and her legacy from her grandfather Lorenzo de'Medici and the Platonic academy he founded under the aegis of Marsilio Ficino.[26] "According to Plato," Ochino reminds Cibo, "only that man who depends on nothing except God is happy."[27]

OCHINO: Happiness lies within ourselves. There is no need to go outside ourselves. If there were infinite worlds, they could not satisfy a single soul, for its capacity is too great. Nothing less than God can bring contentment to a soul and its desire is infinite because it belongs to God. Likewise, an apple and a spherical body cannot fill a vase which is triangular, since the corners would always remain empty. And so the soul, whose likeness is the Trinity, cannot be satisfied with the world which is a sphere: the intellect, will, and memory will always remain empty. Only God and the highest Trinity can fill and conform to it. As long as we journey with our minds only on worldly things, we will proceed from desire to desire; nor will we ever stop since we will never find anything so perfect in this world that our desire cannot outrun it: our desire passes by and transcends all the things of the world and travels on until it reaches God. And there it stops because it can go no higher, nor can it imagine or desire anything more perfect. Whoever thinks he can be satisfied with the things of this world, thinks that he can satisfy his thirst by eating salt. In this world the more we have, the more we want; but worldly things do not bring calm, they do not satisfy; but rather they arouse and inflame our desires in such a way that those who have more, desire more. We must say that those who are poorer desire less since their desires are born of lack and poverty. It is not then the man who has more who is happy, but the one who desires less. We must fill ours hearts, not our coffers.

OCHINO:  L'è in noi medesimi; non bisogna andare vagando fuora di sé, chi la vuole trovare; se fusseno infiniti mondo non potrebono satirare una anima, è troppo grande la sua capacità; nessuna cosa inferiore a Dio può contentare una anima. E perché l'è di cosa inferiore a Dio può riempire un vaso che sia triangulare, sempre gli anguli resterebbeno vacui. L'anima ad imagine della Trinità non si satia del mondo, il quale è sferico; resta sempre vacuo l'intelletto, la memoria e la volontà; solo Dio e l'altissima Trinità gli è conforme e la riempie. Mentre che colla mente caminiamo per le creature, andiamo di desiderio in desiderio e mai non ci fermiamo e questo è perché non troviamo cosa alcuna in questo mondo tanto perfetta che il nostro desiderio non possi andare più in là. Anchora trascende e passa ogni creatura e va fino a Dio; e lì si ferma, perché non può andare più su, a cosa più perfetta, né col pensiero, né col desiderio. Chi pensa satiarsi delle creature, pensa mangiando sale cavarsi la sete; di questo mondo quanto più ne habbiamo, tanto più ne vorremo, però le creature non quiettano, non satiano, anzi eccitano et accendano gli desiderii nostri, in modo che quelli che più hanno, più desiderano. Bisogno dire che sono più poveri, perché gli desiderii nascano dalla indigentia e povertà; non è adunque felice colui il quale più ha, ma coliu il quale manco desidera; bisogna empire il cuore non l'arca. (Ochino, *I "Dialogi sette,"* ed. Rozzo, dialogue 2, 63)

## ❧ FLORENCE: AN OPEN CITY IN THE 1540S ❧

The late 1540s marked the reemergence of Florence as an important cultural destination in Europe. In 1546, Duke Cosimo I de' Medici opened a new literary academy, the Accademia Fiorentina, dedicated to the advancement of Italian literature and Tuscan as its literary language.[28] That year Cosimo persuaded Benedetto Varchi, who at forty-two had headed the Infiammati academy in Padua and was already considered an intellectual of major importance, to return to Florence to preside over his academy. Cosimo specified that he was to deliver two lectures a month to the membership and write a history of Florence that would immortalize the city's past and present. Soon to play an important role in promoting women writers in Florence, Varchi had already assisted the Sienese writer Alessandro Piccolomini in getting his book on Laudomia Forteguerri's poetry published, the first work of literary criticism ever published on a woman author.[29]

That same year, a senior editor at the Giolito press in Venice, Lodovico Domenichi, put the finishing touches on his translation of the Greek historian Polybius's *Histories* which he had written for Cosimo I and left for Florence, armed with a letter of introduction to the duke from Aretino.[30] That year Domenichi renewed his friendship with Anton Francesco Doni, a colleague almost as well known as Domenichi in Venetian press circles. Doni, whom Domenichi had known as a fellow Ortolani academy member in Piacenza, also hoped to find greener pastures in Florence and together the two men opened a small press.[31] Then a member of Cosimo's Florentine academy, Domenichi continued to translate Greek works such as Xenophon's *Oeconomicus* on commission for the duke, but he left Doni to work for the Flemish publisher Lorenzo Torrentino, a known Lutheran sympathizer and perhaps member of a reform movement cell in Florence. Operating in the shadow of the Giunti press in Florence and the large commercial publishing houses in Venice, Torrentino, whom Cosimo had brought to Florence to serve as his official printer, was phenomenally productive, publishing more than nine new books a year until his death in 1563.[32] Medici protection, however, proved to be a sometime thing. In 1552, Domenichi would be sentenced to life imprisonment in the *fortezza* in Pisa for publishing works by Calvin and Sleidan that had been outlawed as heretical.[33] Cosimo did not intervene to save his client and academy member.[34]

In that same pivotal year, 1546, Florence pulled Tullia d'Aragona, a courtesan and an intellectual of a very different stamp from Caterina Cibo, into its force field (fig. 11). Steeped in Plato's dialogues and the *Nicomachean Ethics* of Aristotle, the Roman elegiac poets Ovid, Propertius, and Tibullus, as well as the writings of her own countrymen Dante, Petrarch, and Boccaccio, Tullia d'Aragona had no use for the dialogues of Valdés and Ochino.[35] Nor was she drawn to the reform treatises and commentaries that interested Domenichi, Cibo, Carnesecchi, and Flaminio.

Three years before Ochino's dialogue with Caterina Cibo was published, d'Aragona's career had begun to take off in Ferrara under the patronage of Girolamo Muzio, one of the few writers who refused to have anything to do with

QVAE S...
CAPVT SALTANDC
OBTINVIT

· FIGURE 11 ·

Tullia d'Aragona. Portrait of the
courtesan posed as Salome, by
Moretto da Brescia, ca. 1540–47;
Salvatore Bongi, *Annali di Gabriel
Giolito de' Ferrari* (Rome: Principali
Librai, 1890), 1:196–98, published
this portrait of Tullia d'Aragona
with extended commentary.
Pinacoteca Tosio-Martinengo,
Brescia. Reproduced courtesy
of the Newberry Library from
Salvatore Rosati, *Tullia d'Aragona*
(Milan: S. A. Fratelli: Treves
Editori, 1936).

the reform movement in the 1530s and 1540s. But when Vittoria Colonna and
Ochino arrived in Ferrara to visit Duchess Renata and Duke Ercole II d'Este
in 1537, d'Aragona was also caught up in the literary swirl around the Protestant-leaning Este court. Battista Stambellino, a courtier of Marchesa Isabella
d'Este of Mantua, who was making the rounds of the aristocratic circles in Ferrara at the time, wrote Isabella about the strong impression Tullia d'Aragona's
appearance made on him and everyone else at the Este court.[36] Stambellino's
letter to Isabella is worth noting not only because of her fame at midcentury
as the greatest living female art patron and collector and her influence as such
on Cosimo's wife Eleonora, but because it suggests as well the allure a learned
courtesan may have had for both an elite woman and her courtiers. Having
employed the painters Mantegna, Perugino, and Costa, among others, to paint
scenes from classical literature for her *camerini* in the Castello di San Giorgio at
Mantua, Isabella d'Este was a model for every ruling woman in Europe with
cultural aspirations. She had acquired works by Leonardo da Vinci, Michelangelo, and Titian while she cultivated the friendship of such writers as Boiardo,

Ariosto, Castiglione, and Equicola. Stambellino's communiqué also suggests that a select number of highly educated courtesans coexisted with elite women in the Italian courts at midcentury. The courtier from Mantua wrote:

A cultivated courtesan from Rome, named Signora Tullia, has just come to stay in this city for a few months, according to what I hear. This lady is educated, modest, and sophisticated, and she carries herself with great elegance: she can perform any motet or canzone from a book singing the melody and all its accompanying embellishments. Her conversation is simply extraordinary and she has such grace that that there is neither a man nor a woman in this land who is her equal, even the illustrious Signora Marchesa of Pescara who is here, as your Excellency knows. This lady shows that she is knowledgeable on every subject. And she speaks eloquently on matters of interest to you. Her house is always full of virtuoso performers and one can always visit her. She has plenty of money and is well-equipped with precious jewels, necklaces, rings, and other beautiful things, and in sum she has been well-provided for.

Gli è sorto in questa terra una gentil cortegiana di Roma, nominata la Signora Tullia, la quale è venuta per star qui qualche mese, er quanto s'intende. Questa è molto gentile, discreta, accorta et di ottimo et divini costumi dotata: sa cantare al libro ogni mottetto et canzone, per rasone de canto figurato; ne li discorsi del suo parlare è unica, et tanto accommodata mente si porta, che non c'è homo nè donna in questa terra che la paregi, anchora che la Illustrissima Signora Marchesa di Pescara sia excellentissima, la quale è qui, come sa V. Ex. Mostra costei sapere de ogni cosa; et parla pur sieca di che materia ti aggrada. Sempre ha piena la casa de virtuosi et sempre si pol visitarla, et è ricca de denari, zoie, colanni, anella et altre cose notabile, et in fine è bene accomodata de ogni cosa.[37]

And hearing about d'Aragona either from other sources or from one of Stambellino's newsy memos to Isabella, the Duchess Eleonora di Toledo of Florence would be among the first of a new group of ruling women to imitate the Marchesa from Mantua.

At ease in the royal courts, Tullia d'Aragona was now confident enough in her own opinion and those of her friends that she sent Ochino a sonnet openly critical of his sermons.[38] He obviously was a gifted orator, but she had no sympathy with his Capuchin asceticism or his puritanical religion if it meant banning poetry, instrumental music, and dancing. She also faulted his rejection of the doctrine of free will (*libero arbitrio*), now a standard charge leveled against the Calvinists and Lutherans. In any case, d'Aragona was clearly striking a rhetorical position in this sonnet, aligning herself with the conservative theologians of the Church: she stood staunchly with men such as her friend and patron Girolamo Muzio in Ferrara and her former lover Filippo Strozzi in Rome. Her subsequent Florentine patron and close friend, Varchi, would walk a fine line between both religious camps. In her sonnet to Ochino, soon to be published by Giolito with her collected *Rime*, she wrote:

Bernardo, it could have been enough
for you to rouse hearts to eternal holy works,
with the sweet voice that nature gave to you,
where the king of the rivers flows with
brightest waters, and if your inner thoughts
are pure and your life befits your fate,
you are a man not frail of flesh or impure
of bone: you come from a heavenly clan.
But why are the masques, the balls, and
the music beloved by our men
and ancient custom forbidden by you?
Not sanctity will it be, but foolish pride
to take away free will, the greatest gift God
gave us in the first abode we had.

    Bernardo, ben potea bastarvi averne
Co'l dolce dir, ch'a voi natura infonde,
Qui dove 'l re de'fiumi ha più chiare onde,
Acceso i cori a le sante opre eterne;
    Ché se pur sono in voi pure l'interne
Voglie, e la vita a destin corrisponde,
Non uom di frale carne e d'ossa immonde,
Ma sète un voi de le schiere superne.
    Or le finte apparenze, e 'l ballo, e 'l suono,
Chiesti dal tempo e da l'antica usanza,
A che così da voi vietate sono?
    Non fôra santità, fôra arroganza
Tôrre il libero arbitrio, il maggior dono
Che Dio ne diè ne la primera stanza.[39]

When Tullia d'Aragona moved to Florence in 1546 she came as a refugee from Siena, fleeing for her life. The hatred of Charles V's governor of Siena, Don Giovanni de Luna, and his corrupt regime had led to a popular revolt, followed by a bloody confrontation between the Sienese supporters of the pro-Spanish Noveschi faction and the rest of the Sienese citizenry. According to the sixteenth-century diarist Sozzini, the citizens' rebellion in February 1545 was the beginning of the end of the peaceful occupation of the city by the Spanish governor, his Noveschi supporters, and his garrison of three hundred Spanish soldiers.[40] The diarist's eyewitness account of the brutal slaughter of pro-Spanish sympathizers that February makes it clear why d'Aragona, who was a Noveschi partisan herself, was in a hurry to leave town.[41]

But d'Aragona had other reasons for wanting to move on. She had presented herself in Siena as the respectable wife of Silvestro dei Guicciardi of Ferrara, a man known to us only through the Sienese city records of her marriage to him, shortly after her arrival in Siena in 1543.[42] But in the enlightened, reform-minded city of Siena where such luminaries as Laudomia Forteguerri and her friend Alessandro Piccolomini presided over avant-garde poetry salons attended by an ever-expanding circle of literary women and men, the now-married d'Aragona remained an outsider, excluded from the *veglie*. Early in 1544, an anonymous informer had denounced her to the Sienese police for not wearing the insignia legally required for a prostitute—the yellow veil.[43] D'Aragona hung on in Siena for another year, but when widespread rioting against the Spanish imperial occupation and their Sienese collaborators with whom d'Aragona was linked brought the city to a standstill, she fled to Florence.[44] Her alliance with the Sienese pro-Spanish, pro-Cosimo exiles from the Noveschi party was an important factor in securing the duke's initial support when she moved to Florence.

In 1546, d'Aragona was living in a villa outside Florence near the Mensola River. There under the patronage of Benedetto Varchi, whom she had met in Siena, she launched her philosophy and poetry salon. As a courtesan, she could not participate officially in Eleonora's poetry academy, the Elevati, or in Cosimo's own Accademia Fiorentina but through Varchi she developed close ties with many members of both academies. But in 1547, she was brought up on criminal charges again, this time with the Florentine authorities for violating the Florentine sumptuary law—a law originally drafted by Cosimo I himself. Throwing herself on the mercy of the duke and duchess, she first wrote to the duchess.[45] Her letter to Eleonora may have had a special resonance with the Spanish-born duchess, as Deana Basile has suggested, not only because it came as a woman-to-woman communiqué but possibly because Eleonora too was treated by the Florentines as a foreigner and an outsider.[46] Even after she had lived in Florence for years, she was characterized by an anonymous diarist in the city as a "Spanish barbarian and an enemy of her husband's homeland."[47] Moreover, a further explanation for her initial patronage of d'Aragona can be seen in Eleonora's demonstrable interest in the culture and history of women: in the books she collected and the paintings of famous women's lives she commissioned for her own apartments in the Palazzo della Signoria, as we shall see later in this chapter.

Eleonora's intercession on behalf of d'Aragona succeeded, and Cosimo granted her an exemption from having to wear the stigmatizing yellow veil on the grounds that she was a poet, not a prostitute.[48] Cosimo's support of Tullia d'Aragona fit easily into his cultural program. Published in 1547 by Giolito, the leading commercial press in Italy, d'Aragona's collected poetry, the *Rime della Signora Tullia di Aragona et di diversi a lei*, demonstrates the overlap between d'Aragona's own literary circle and the elite literary fraternity founded by Cosimo.[49] D'Aragona's paired sonnets in her *Rime*, each of which contains her poem to a friend and his response, include such writers and cultural leaders as Nicolo Martelli, Ugolino Martelli, Girolamo Muzio, Latino Iuvenale (Giovenale), Simone Porzio, Alessandro Arrighi, and Varchi.[50] Among the prominent Florentine figures who did not write poems for d'Aragona's volume but whom she addressed in her *Rime* are Eleonora de' Medici, Cosimo de' Medici, Cosimo's mother, Maria Salviati, Piero Manelli, Ridolfo Baglioni, Colonello Luca Antonio, her Sienese Noveschi friends Emilio Tondi and Francesco Crasso (Grasso), and her friends outside Tuscany, Tiberio Nari, Cardinal Pietro Bembo, Francesco Maria Molza, and Don Pedro di Toledo.[51]

Among the several intimate friendships d'Aragona developed with members of the Florentine academy, Varchi played the role of her official patron and was probably instrumental in introducing her to the editors of the Giolito press in Venice. The gossips, though, may have seen his close friendship with d'Aragona as a cover for his real interests. In a city where sodomy was prosecuted with the harshest punishments, Varchi had been caught more than once in scandals involving young boys.[52] In any case, it was not Varchi but d'Aragona's friend from Ferrara, Girolamo Muzio, who edited her *Dialogo* for publication.

### ❧ D'ARAGONA'S *DIALOGO DELLA INFINITÀ DI AMORE* ☙

Historian of philosophy Lisa Curtis-Wendlandt has recently reassessed Tullia d'Aragona's *Dialogo della infinità di amore*, judging it a unique contribution to Renaissance theories of love that not only departs in significant ways from the Neoplatonism of other contemporary love dialogues but also has an impact on studies in the history of philosophy: "The broad extent to which the problem of communication becomes the actual subject of the text must thus be recognized as a specialty of the *Dialogue on the Infinity of Love*. This coinciding of the semantics of form and content cannot be found in many other love dialogues of the time and highlights the importance the topic must have held for d'Aragona. Her deep concern with the patterns of discourse and the practices of philosophy, we can conclude, were thoughts that would have 'thought' themselves most clearly as a dialogue."[53] But d'Aragona rejects the central trope of Neoplatonism, and this is the point that needs to be made.[54] Deviating strikingly from the path that Plato's Diotima takes in her culminating speech in the *Symposium*, which Letizia Panizza has called "the fountainhead of all later expositions of Platonic love, from Ficino to Bembo to Castiglione to Leon Ebreo," the interlocutors in d'Aragona's *Dialogo* reach no moment of truth, no ladder to the pinnacle of spiritual love, where earthly contemplation of beauty leads finally to the apprehension of the eternal source of all beauty and order.[55]

D'Aragona's *Dialogo* resembles Ochino's more Neoplatonic work, the *Dialogi sette,* and Valdés's *Alfabeto*, which is discussed at length in chapter 1, in a number of ways.[56] All three dialogues come out the milieu of the salon. Conversations like Giulia Gonzaga's with Valdés and Caterina Cibo's with Ochino, held in someone's home in the presence of an appreciative audience of friends, and academy performances like Alessandro Piccolomini's lecture on Laudomia's poetry were quickly turned, as we've seen in the previous chapters, into books that sold. All three dialogues, in which a woman and a man confront one another without the buffer of other characters cannot help but foreground sexual difference, while they consider, or at least suggest, the most fundamental of questions: What is love? What is happiness? What is the meaning of desire? What is lasting? Do men and women want different things? How do the sexes differ from one another? In Ochino and Valdés, the male theologian leads and is presumed to have information the female interlocutor seeks. In the *Dialogo*, Tullia's character is crafted as fully Varchi's match.

The unforgettable portraits in the *Alfabeto* and the *Dialogi sette* of Giulia Gonzaga and Caterina Cibo, each a figure familiar enough to the Italian reading public by 1538–39, made it unnecessary for either Valdés or Ochino to produce a particularized mise-en-scène.[57] Apart from the fact that Gonzaga and Cibo came from celebrated families, the dangers both these duchesses once faced gave them near-legendary status. Gonzaga had narrowly escaped from the pirate Barbarossa (Khair ed-Din), after he and his sailors kidnapped her. That at least was the extravagant fiction that circulated about her.[58] Cibo, for her part, was known first to have fought with two popes to save the order of Capuchin friars from extinction and, then, to have taken up arms herself in defense of her castle and her daughter Giulia when her in-laws attempted to seize Camerino.[59] For her dialogue, d'Aragona needed to craft a storyline for herself that was equally compelling—that of an intellectual courtesan whose interests only ran to things of the mind and who never craved the material elegance that Cosimo's sumptuary law prohibited.

The opening speech by the interlocutor, Varchi, provides a frame for the entire dialogue, setting the scene for the conversation held in the house of a woman who had already been publicly shamed as a courtesan masquerading as a lady and who, if it were not for Duke Cosimo's clemency, would be forced by law to wear, at least in public, the yellow veil of a *meretrice*. D'Aragona takes care not to have the character Varchi allude in any way to the expensive jewelry that Isabella's courtier Stambellino said she customarily wore, nor does he describe the silken gown and lavish furnishings that were commonly associated with a woman of her profession.[60] Instead, in Varchi's opening speech everything is said to paint d'Aragona's home as a place sought after not for its luxuries but for the tranquility of the gatherings she hosted and the high-toned nature of the discourse found there:

VARCHI:    I was afraid, if I hadn't ruined everything, at a minimum I had disrupted the discussion you were having, which can't have been anything but beautiful, I know, and must have dealt with philosophical questions, as is worthy of this place, where the subjects proposed for debate are always edifying and important, and at the same time enjoyable, as are the people who come to your house.[61]

VARCHI:    Io temeva di non forse aver, se non guasti del tutto, almeno interrotti in parte i ragionamenti vostri, i quali so che altro che begli non possono essere, e di cose alte, e degni finalmente cosí di questo luogo, dove sempre si propone qualche materia da disputare non meno utile e grave che gioconda e piacevole, come di cotali persone. (Zonta, ed., *Trattati*, 187)

As in the many dialogues on love published in sixteenth-century Italy, the competitive trading of literary references—classical and contemporary—is very much part of d'Aragona's theater, and allusions to the Greek philosophers as well as to Leone Ebreo's *Dialoghi d'amore* and Bembo's *Asolani* punctuate the conversation. But the point in the *Dialogo* is not simply to entertain but to produce satire: a small-scale *opera buffa* in which the pompous ideas and issues of theologians and philosophers are the object of laughter. D'Aragona, in the passage below, skillfully combines material from Plato and Aristotle—Phaedrus's discussion of the relative merits of beloved and the lover in Plato's *Symposium* (179B), a standard trope in cinquecento love dialogues, with Aristotle's notion of efficient, formal, and final causes from the *Metaphysics*—to make sit-down comedy.[62]

VARCHI: Is it not the case that God loves Himself?

TULLIA: Yes, that is so.

VARCHI: Therefore He is both the lover and the beloved?

TULLIA: He is.

VARCHI: And which one of the two do you consider the nobler, the lover or the beloved?[63]

TULLIA: Without doubt, it is the one who is loved.

VARCHI: Why?

TULLIA: Because the loved one constitutes not just the efficient cause and formal cause of an act, but also the final one. And the final case is the most noble of all causes. It leaves the role of the material cause to the lover, and this is the least worthy form of causation.

VARCHI: That's an excellent and very erudite response. Hence it follows that God, if considered as the recipient of love is more noble than Himself when considered as the agent of love.

TULLIA: Yes.

VARCHI: So it turns out that one single thing can be different from itself if considered in the light of different actualizations?

TULLIA: Yes, but what is that supposed to prove? (*Dialogue*, ed. and trans. Russell and Merry, 63)

VARCHI: Dio non ama stesso?

TULLIA: Ama.

VARCHI: Dunque e amante ed amato?

TULLIA: È.

VARCHI: Chi pensate voi che sia più nobile: o l'amante e l'amato?

TULLIA: L amato, senza dubbio.

VARCHI: Perché?

TULLIA: Perché lo amato è cagion non solo efficiente e formale, ma ancor finale, ed il fine è nobilissimo di tutte le cagioni: onde allo amante non rimane se non la cagion materiale, la quale è men perfetta di tutte.

VARCHI: Bene avete risposto e dottissimamente. E cosi Dio, considerato come amato, è più nobile di se stesso, considerato come amante.

TULLIA: Sí.

VARCHI: Adunque una cosa medesima può essere differente tra sé, considerata secondo diversi atti?

TULLIA: Messer sí. Ma che volete inferir per questo? (Zonta, ed., *Trattati*, 195–96)

As in the other treatises and dialogues of the period, the nature of women is a constant topic of conversation. In d'Aragona's dialogue, questions circling around the theme of sex/gender repeatedly surface, but, as we shall see, the subject is differently manipulated in the hands of this woman author, who ubiquitously identifies herself as such. What is most original, as Curtis-Wendlandt has noted, is d'Aragona's problematizing of the communication process itself. Not only do a man and a woman trade blows here in a dialogue that at times proceeds more in the spirit of a debate than a discussion, but the two speakers are portrayed as constantly misunderstanding one another, as though that were an effect peculiar to communication between the sexes. In keeping with the spirit of the *dialogo buffo* is a profusion of the courtly game themes we saw in the salon writing of Sienese women and men in the last chapter, though d'Aragona, as we noted, had remained an outsider in Siena, excluded from the games and the *veglie*.[64] In d'Aragona's battle of the sexes, the roles of female and male combatants are by no means set. Varchi and Tullia change positions, each shifting from initiate to expert, from pundit to seeker and back again. And in this contest for supremacy, misinterpretations and, consequently, comedy are uppermost:

VARCHI: I don't intend to reply, because unfortunately you'll just try to score points against me. I know what you are like!

TULLIA: Yes, of course. Thank Goodness you won't have much to say. And if you do have a response, speak up.

VARCHI: For that reason too I won't answer!

TULLIA: Please continue the discussion! As I said, you'll be a mighty hero, if you can prove to my satisfaction that love is without end.

VARCHI: Is it then such a heroic feat to defeat a woman?

TULLIA: You're not in a contest with a woman. You're fighting against reason.

VARCHI: And isn't reason female?

TULLIA: I don't know if it is female or male. Now let me do the talking for a while. Let's see if I can catch you by doing the questions my way. (*Dialogue*, ed. and trans. Russell and Merry, 75)

VARCHI: Io non voglio rispondervi, che vi vendichereste pur troppo: tale vi conosco.

TULLIA: Sí, sí gran mercé che non dovete aver che dire; e, se avete, dite pure.

VARCHI: Ed anche per questo non dirò.

TULLIA: Eh, dite, ché, come vi ho detto, sarete valentuomo se mi proverete che amore non abbia fine!

VARCHI: È egli perciò si gran valentigia vincere una donna?

TULLIA: Voi non avete a vincere una donna, ma la ragione.

VARCHI: E la ragione non è femina?

TULLIA: Io non so se ella è feminia o maschio. Lasciate un poco dire a me, per vedere se sapessi anche io coglier voi, col domandare a mio modo. (Zonta, ed., *Trattati*, 207–8)

But new in d'Aragona's *Dialogo* and the woman-centered reform dialogues of Valdés and Ochino is the portraying of emotional states—here both the remembrance and present sensation of pain and unease—as a baseline for serious conversation and the search for happiness. D'Aragona, in the *Dialogo,* in character as a courtesan who is perhaps pushing forty, speaks from experience as she lays out her intimate knowledge of the pain, restlessness, and near psychosis that falling in love entails.[65] Varchi, true to his persona as a man serially trapped by his own dangerous passions, registers not recollections but the presentness of his sufferings in love—as well as the unavoidability of his future misery. He is and has been witness to the power of love. "I wish it were not so now," he says. "For I would not be as miserable and unhappy as I am now, nor would I die a thousand times an hour, as I do, and will do for ever and ever." Tullia and Varchi's speeches make it clear that, while *amore* may be eternal—or not, depending on how you define or limit it—it is desire that is infinite and without end. Here the two speak not of a passion for one another. Rather they share, as friends and not lovers, the emotions they have experienced with others. While Tullia speaks dispassionately about the bizarre behavior of lovers in general, Varchi suffers the agonies of a particular affair that plagues him even as he speaks:

TULLIA: Love is infinite potentially—not in actuality—for it is impossible to love with an end in sight. In other words, the desires of people in love are infinite, and they can never settle down after achieving something. This is because after obtaining it, they long for something else, and something else again, and something more after that. And so it goes on, one thing after the other. They can never be satisfied, as Boccaccio bears witness about himself in the introduction to the *Decameron*. This is the reason why people who are in love can be crying one minute and laughing the next. They can even be found laughing and crying at the same time. This phenomenon is amazing in itself and quite impossible for mere normal mortals! Lovers entertain both hope and fear. Simultaneously, they feel great heat and excessive cold. They want and reject in equal measure, constantly grasping things but retaining nothing in their grip. They can see without eyes. They have no ears but can hear. They shout without a tongue. They fly without moving. They are alive while dying. They say and do the myriad strange things that the poets write about, especially Petrarch, who towers incomparably over all others in the description of the pangs of love.

VARCHI:   It is indeed true. But those people who do not have, and never had, experience of the effects of love, as I have and always shall have, . . . will never believe it and will make fun of it. I know men who experienced love and later reproached it in others, thinking that they would never fall in love again or that they would not be able to. But then they fell in it deeper than before and paid for their pride and ingratitude. Love is god and a great god is Love. Those who are more able, and wiser than others, have always been loyal and obedient to the god. As to myself, I know Love's power well and I can bear strong and true witness to it. I wish it had not been so! In fact, I wish it were not so now! For I would not be as miserable and wretched as I am now and I would not die a thousand times an hour, as I do and will by and by, for ever and ever; for love has no end or limit whatsoever and feeds on lovers' minds, never to tire and become satisfied. (*Dialogue*, ed. and trans. Russell and Merry, 84)

TULLIA:   Che Amore è infinito non in atto, ma in potenze, e che non si può amar con termine: cioè che i disidèri degli amanti sono infiniti e mai non si aquetano a cosa niuna; perché, dopo questo, vogliono qualche altra cosa, e, dopo quella altra, una altra, e cosí di mano in mano successivamente; e mai non si contentano , come testimonia il Boccaccio di se medesimo n el principio della sua *Cento novelle*. E quindi è che gli amanti or piangono, or ridono; anzi (il che è non solo piú meraviglioso, ma del tutto impossibile agli altri uomini) piangono e ridono in un medesimo tempo, hanno speranza e timore, sentono gran caldo e gran freddo, vogliono e disvogliono parimente, abbracciando sempre ogni cosa e non istringendo mai nulla, veggona senza occhi, non hanno orecchie ed odono, gridano senza linqua, volano senza moversi, vivono morendo, e finalmente dicono e fanno tutte quelle cose che di loro scrivono tutti i poeti, e massimamente il Petrarcha, al quale niuno si può comparare, né si dee, negli affetti amorosi.

VARCHI:   Bene è vero. Ma chi non gli ha provati o pruova, come ho fatto e fo io e farò oggimai sempre, . . . non solo non può credergli, ma se ne ride. Ed ho io conosciuti di quegli a cui sono intervenuti, che poscia gli hanno ripesi in altrui; e, credendo di non mai più potersi, non che dovesi innamorare, sono ricaduti assai peggio e dato le pene della superbia, anzi ingratitudine loro. Amore è dio, e grande dio è Amore: e chi ha piú o saputo o potuto, piú gli è stato dedele ed obediente; ed io bene il so e ne posso fare non meno ampia che vera testimonianza. E cosi non fosse stato come fu! Anzi cosi non fosse come è! Ché io non viverei infelice, non mi chiamerei misero, non morrei mille volte ogni ora, come fo e farò piú mai sempre, di mano in mano, posciaché Amore non ha termine né fine niuno, e, pascendosi dell'altrui mente, mai stanco né satollo non se ne vede. (Zonta, ed., *Trattati*, 216)

In a passage that the other members of d'Aragona's salon—whose presence in the room Varchi has already mentioned—had been waiting for and that comes almost at the end of the dialogue, Tullia questions Varchi on what she takes to be Plato's praise of sexual relationsips between men and boys (Phaedrus's speech in *Symposium* 178b–180b). Varchi—a philosopher, a poet, and a man who had Cosimo's complete trust—had been in trouble at least twice in Florence for alleged violation of the sodomy laws.[66] He was arrested for the attempted rape of a boy who was one of his students, and in a notorious incident in Padua he was set upon by the family members of another boy he was alleged to have seduced. The audience must have waited with bated breath as Tullia embarked on this line of questioning, in which she differs from the position taken by Socrates' spirital adviser Diotima in Plato's *Symposium,* who explains that a young man's falling in love with a physically beautiful male is a necessary way station or step on the ladder to attaining knowledge of the one sublime beauty that never dies or fades but is everlasting:

TULLIA:    But . . . here I consider that those men who entertain a lascivious love for youths are not following the true dictates of nature, so they fully deserve the punishments that canon and divine law have imposed on them, as well as the penalties set up by man-made and civil justice. What is more, I can scarcely believe that people who practice such an ugly, wicked and hideous vice . . . are real human beings. I shall be glad if later on you could give me your own view on this, for I know full well that in classical Greece the opposite notion was commmon and that Lucian wrote a dialogue in which he praised this vice, as did Plato.

VARCHI:    . . . You are greatly mistaken if you compare Lucian with Plato, and if you furthermore believe that Plato praised such filthy wickedness.

TULLIA:    Do forgive me. I had understood that not only did Socrates and Plato make a public spectacle of their affairs with young men, but they also took it as something to be proud about, and they wrote dialogues, as we can see in the cases of Alcibiades and Phaedrus, where they speak about love with great beauty and passion.

VARCHI:    I do not say that Socrates and Plato did not show their love for youths in public, that they were not proud of it and did not speak of love with great beauty and passion. I simply maintain that they did not love them the way people commonly interpret and apparently you also believe. (*Dialogue*, ed. and trans. Russell and Merry, 95–96)

TULLIA:    Ma . . . dico che quelli, che amano i giovani lascivamente, non fanno
           ciò secondo gli ordinamenti della natura, e sono degni di quel castigo
           che non solo dalle leggi canoniche e divine è stato loro dato, ma ezian-
           dio dalle civili ed umane. Ed a pena posso credere che chi usa un così
           brutto, scelerato e nefando vizio . . . sia uomo. E di ciò avrò caro mi
           dichiati poi il parer vostro, ché so bene che appreso i greci era tutto
           il contrario, e che Luciano ne fa un dialogo dove loda questo vizio, e
           Platone medesimamente.

VARCHI:    . . . Sète in troppo grande errore se volete aguagliere Luciano a Platone,
           o pensate che Platone lodasse mai cosi lorda scelerazza. . . .

TULLIA:    Perdonatemi. Io aveva inteso che Socrate e Platone non solo amavano
           i giovane publicamente, ma se lo recavano a gloria e ne facevano i dia-
           loghi, come si vede ancora di *Alciabiade* e di *Fedro*, dove parlano di amore
           amorosissimamente.

VARCHI:    Io non dico che Socrate e Platone non amassero i giovani publicamente
           e non si recassero a gloria e non iscrivessero i dialoghi, favellando di
           amore amorosissimamente; ma dico che non gli amavano a quello ef-
           fetto che si pensa il vulgo, e che pare che intendiate ancora voi. (Zonta,
           ed., *Trattati*, 227–28)

When Tullia asks him point-blank whether Socrates and Plato were "lovers" (*amanti*), Varchi taunts her with the answer, "Of course they were lovers!
Very much so." (*Come, se egli erano amanti! Amantissimi.*) Varchi goes on to explain, without ever denying that Socrates and Plato were sexual lovers, that
their goal was not to generate bodies but rather to give birth to souls similar to
themselves. D'Aragona nonetheless seizes on the topic to get Varchi to admit,
as Curtis-Wendlandt has commented, that not only men but women and men
together are capable of generating together that same species of pure, spiritual
love between souls.[67] This advocacy of a purely spiritual love between women
and men, which, as we have seen in the preceding chapter, the Sienese writer
Alessandro Piccolomini espoused in his *Institutione* (1542), departs from the
conventional view put forward in sixteenth-century dialogues on love as well
as from Diotima's speech in Plato's *Symposium*.

D'Aragona's dialogue ends—as no other sixteenth-century Neoplatonic
love dialogue ends—when the child Penelope d'Aragona enters the room and
interrupts the conversation. Born in 1535, the eleven-year-old Penelope is assumed by scholars to have been Tullia's daughter or much younger sister.[68]
Not only has d'Aragona's *Dialogo* been set in a familial setting but the protagonist has cast herself in a domestic role as well. The character Tullia discourses
on Plato and Aristotle when she is not absorbed in household duties or called

on to care for her child. The dialogue had opened with a description of the ambience Tullia created in her own home for the kind of high-flying discussions about love, eternity, and God we have witnessed. Suddenly changing the subject, Penelope's arrival on the scene enriches and expands Tullia's portrait. More than the learned, Diotima-like philosopher of love she has shown herself to be throughout the dialogue, a novel image of the philosopher emerges as progenetrix and guardian of a new generation of females endowed perhaps with intellectual daring equal to hers—a move that suggests the infinitude of at least one species of love.

Despite Benucci Lattanzio's remark at the close of the dialogue that literary experts, aristocrats, princes, and cardinals were accustomed to attend d'Aragona's philosophical evenings as if her house were a "prestigious academy," nonetheless it was soon obvious that there was no place in Eleonora's or Cosimo's academies for d'Aragona, nor did she have allies within the reform circles in Florence. The Jesuits, first Juan de Polanco and Diego Laínz and later Diego de Guzman, became closer to Eleonora than anyone outside her own family and it was through the duchess that Polanco secured support for the founding of a Jesuit college in Florence in 1547.[69] In 1548, one year after the publication of her two books—the dialogue on love and her collected *Rime*, works now far from Eleonora's taste and milieu—d'Aragona left Florence and returned with Penelope to her mother's house in Rome.[70] D'Aragona's departure from Florence, though, by no means signaled her withdrawal from the literary scene. In 1553, she published her poems alongside those of Vittoria Colonna and other elite women writers in an anthology edited by the eminent critic and classical scholar Girolamo Ruscelli in Venice.[71] Seven years later, the Venetian firm Sessa announced their publication of d'Aragona's epic poem, the *Meschino*.[72]

### ❧ CIBO AND RELIGIOUS REFORM DISCOURSE IN FLORENCE ❧

The year Tullia d'Aragona's *Dialogo* and *Rime* were published, Caterina Cibo still occupied center stage among the dwindling group of intellectuals involved in the reform movement in Florence.[73] Cibo's close friendships within the reform circle around Valdés went back to her participation in Giulia Gonzaga's evenings at Fondi and Naples and to her salvaging of Ochino's career and the Capuchin order in collaboration with Vittoria Colonna back in the mid-1530s.[74] It was in Naples that Cibo first heard the sermons of Ochino and came to know Flaminio and Carnesecchi, both of them clerics who were among the Valdesian reform thinkers closest to Gonzaga. Cibo's growing intimacy with the group around Pole dated from her involvement in the frequent discussions with Flaminio, Ochino, and Carnesecchi held at her home in Florence in 1541, the year Ochino had abandoned Italy for good. At the trial of Cardinal Morone in Rome a decade and a half later, Cibo would be denounced by one of the inquisitors as a "heretic, a camp-follower of heretics and a schoolmistress of heretical nuns" [haeretica, sectatrix haereticorum et doctrix monialium haereticarum].[75]

Varchi's friendship with two women as different as Cibo and d'Aragona raises questions about his aims. Within months of shepherding d'Aragona's *Dialogue* to press and helping her secure an exemption from the sumptuary law for prostitutes, Varchi turned to his friend Caterina Cibo, whom he had come to know among the elite circle of humanists in the Medici court. Sending the Duchess a sonnet which was deeply respectful of her and her spiritual mentor and dedicating the work to her, Varchi publicly coupled Valdés's name with the literary Olympians Pietro Bembo and Vittoria Colonna:

> appo 'l gran Bembo luce
> L'alta Colonna e 'l buon Valdesio, a cui
> Fu si conta la via ch'al Ciel conduce.[76]

> Next to great Bembo shines
> Lofty Colonna, and the good Valdés, for whom
> The road which leads to heaven was so well known.

The years 1543–49 had marked a period of doctrinal conflict between the Farnese pope, Paul III, and such Florentine intellectuals who were connected with the ducal court as Cosimo's cousin Caterina Cibo, Varchi, Carnesecchi, and others. Also important in Cibo's ideological formation was her close friendship with another prominent male writer and intellectual who was in Florence in the early 1540s, Marcantonio Flaminio. The clash of values between the pope and Cibo and her Florentine friends crystallized around a clearly Valdesian, anonymously published tract known as the *Beneficio di Cristo,* the only known manuscript copy of which Cosimo's major domo, Pier Francesco Ricco, owned.[77] Cibo's early friend from her Naples days, Giulia Gonzaga had concluded the arrangements for its publication with the Venetian printer Bindoni in 1543.[78] An immensely popular work, selling 40,000 copies in Venice alone in the first six years after its original printing, it was almost instantly declared heretical by the Church. In 1549, the Venetian Republic banned the *Beneficio,* making it a crime to print, distribute, sell, or own the work. The following year the council voted to repudiate formally the central doctrine the *Beneficio* espoused: that faith alone—not works—justified the dispensation of God's grace.[79]

In 1549, the vicar of Florence ordered the holders of "all Protestant books" to present them to him within fifteen days under penalty of 100 scudi and ten years in the galleys. Copies of the *Beneficio,* the *Alfabeto,* and Ochino's *Dialogi sette* were thrown into the fires that burned in the central market places in Florence and cities all over Italy along with the books of Erasmus and Luther. Still, Cibo's friend Varchi wrote a sermon for Good Friday that particular year, which had so much material from the *Beneficio* that it amounted to a public reading and endorsement of the prohibited book.[80] The Flemish publisher Torrentino, brought to Florence by Cosimo I as his official court printer—always under suspicion for heresy because of his northern origins—brought out that year an edition of the poems of none other than the coauthor of the *Beneficio*, Marcantonio Flaminio, under the title *Carmi*, which included a patently heretical epigram accusing the Church of burning and suppressing the vulgate Bible:

> Dum fera flamma tuos, Hieronime pascitur artus
> > Religio, sanctas dilaniata comas,
> Flevit, et o, dixit, crudeles parcite flammae,
> > Parcite; sunt isto viscera nostra rogo.

As long as savage fire feeds on your bones, Jerome, Religion weeps and tears her holy hair; and O, she cries, stop the cruel fires, stop. This is my flesh on that pyre.[81]

Varchi translated Flaminio's epigram into Italian—even spicing it up with a reference to Savonarola.

In 1549, Caterina Cibo, who would soon be denounced as a heretic, received two letters from Flaminio at the end of his life that might have brought her to the executioner's block in Rome, had she lived, in the same way that Giulia Gonzaga's epistles had been instrumental in securing Carnesecchi's conviction for heresy in 1567. Flaminio's 1549 letter ends with a hectic warning. She was not to show the epistle to anyone, and for good reason. It was widely suspected—if not known—in Rome and Florence at the time that Flaminio was at least a coauthor of the *Beneficio*.[82] The Church may have been rightly phobic about the *Beneficio* since recent philological research has made clear the work's extensive borrowings from Luther's *Liberty of the Christian Man* and Melanchthon's *Loci communes theologici,* though the treatise was more Valdesian than Lutheran in its emphasis on the imitation of Christ and the role it gave the Holy Spirit.[83]

Both letters suggest that there existed a surprising degree of intimacy between Cibo and Flaminio, of an emotional as well as intellectual nature. As has been mentioned earlier, both of them were steeped in Greek philosophy and classical literature to a degree that could be said of few if any of their compatriots. Cibo had grown up in the milieu of her grandfather Lorenzo de'Medici, reading and perhaps even speaking classical Greek as well as Hebrew.[84] Flaminio was a Paduan-trained philosopher who had edited and published commentaries both on Aristotle's *Physics* and the *Metaphysics*, a text considered perhaps the most abstract and difficult in all of ancient philosophy. The second letter has the kind of detailed physical description of his agony in the course of his malaria that one would only expect in a letter to an immediate family member, a lover, or one of his closest male friends. From each of Flaminio's two extant letters to Cibo, I have excerpted not only those passages that illustrate the state of mind and body he wished, or perhaps needed, to convey to Cibo but also those that exemplify the Valdesian doctrines that poured so easily from his pen. Both letters would have been read as deeply heretical in the atmosphere of fear and suspicion cast over the peninsula at the height of the Council of Trent in the late 1540s.

The first letter to Cibo, dated February 25, 1547, consoles the duchess on the death of her married daughter on February 17 at age twenty-four and ends with the description of the death of Vittoria Colonna, at whose bedside Flaminio and Pole sat during her last hours.[85] The rest of Flaminio's letter is thick with doctrines associated with the Valdesians and condemned as heretical: the emphasis on the first-hand reading and citing of Scripture (*solo scrittura*); the belief in the foreknowledge of God, predestination, and the existence of persons who are "elect" (*persone elette*) or "chosen" by God for salvation; the weight placed on God's grace (*divina gratia*); and finally, the doctrine of justification through faith alone (*giustificazione per fede*):

The one who thinks of you in the world, my signora, sees you terribly unhappy; but the one who thinks of you in Christ, sees you as so blessed and so favored by God that the more your trials and sorrows increase the more you become like Jesus Christ crucified. In this way I assure myself more every hour that you are among those of whom the Apostle says, God in his foreknowledge of them, predestined them to be made in the likeness of his son who carried always the cross in this world; and he said clearly that whoever wants to be his disciple let him take up his cross every day, and let him follow it[86] if he wants to arrive at the prize of the high calling of God,[87] which purifies you in the furnace of your tribulations, so that being purified by the love of yourself and that of all other living creatures you may become the bride worthy of his son.

. . . Although, if you want to compare the pain you have experienced in losing your daughter in this world with the gain she now has in having the blessed vision of God in paradise, you will see your mistaken respect for the good she had, which was by comparison only the tiniest drop of all water in the ocean, and as a consequence, not only the spirit but the flesh exults in the living God, for he in his compassion is the giver of infinite grace. And this compassion has transported this person chosen by him [*questa sua eletta*] out of the darkness of this wretched world into the light of his most happy kingdom.

But these and all the other reasons I can name have the power to console the faithful in proportion to the strength of their belief, which revealing God to us as the kindest father makes us so superior to all human events that no adversity can weaken our constancy, because, if God is our God, what can be lacking for our happiness now, even if we had nothing else?

Chi vi considera nel mondo, signora mia, vi vide infelicissima, chi vi può considerare in Christo vi vede beata et tanto più favorita da Dio, quanto più crescono le tribulationi per ciò che tanto più diventate conforme a Iesu Christo crocifisso; di maniera che mi cerifico ogni hora più che voi sete nel numero di coloro de' quali dice l'apostolo che, avendogli Dio preconosciuti, gli ha anco predestinati ad essere conformi all'imagine del suo figliolo, che portò sempre la croce in questo mondo; et dice chiaramente che chiunque vole essere suo discipolo, toglia la sua croce ogni giorno, et la seguiti se vuole pervenire alla palma della superna vocatione de Dio, il quale vi affina nella fornace delle tribulationi, acciò che purificata dall'amor di voi medesima et di tutti l'altre creature diventiate sposa degna del suo figliolo.

. . . Benché, se vorrete parragonare il danno che havete fatto voi perdendo in questo mondo vostra figliola col guadagno che ella ha fatto acquistando in paradiso la visione beatifica d'Iddio, vederete il vostro male rispetto al suo bene haver quella proportione che ha una picciolissima goccia con tutta l'acqua del mare, et per conseguente non pur lo spirito, ma la carne essalterà a Dio vivente rendendo infinite gratie alla sua misericordia, la quale ha trasferito questa sua eletta dalle tenebre di questro misero mondo alla luce del suo regno felicissimo.

. . . Ma queste et tutte l'altre ragioni ch'io potessi dire hanno forza di consolare le persone pie secondo la proportione della fede la quale, mostrandoci Dio in forma di patre benignissimo, ne fa tanto superiori a tutti gli accidenti humani che nessuna adversità può debilitare la nostra costantia, perciò che, se Dio è nostro Dio, che ci può mancare alla felicità ancora che tutte altre cose ci mancassero?

The second of Flaminio's two letters to Cibo is dated May 4, 1549.[88] Though gravely ill, he hovered close to death until February 17, 1550, when he died in Pole's house. The letter that follows returns to the Valdesian themes of the earlier letter but lays more stress on the compassion (*misericordia*) of Christ and the personal nature of the Christian's relationship with God. Heretical perhaps, and certainly suspect, would be Flaminio's description to Cibo of his "vision."[89]

Although I may not be very weak in the head and my entire body, nonetheless, knowing the great desire your Excellency has to know what the favors [*favori*] are that our lord God has given me in my gravest bodily infirmity, I have readied myself to narrate them briefly. And I say that the lord God has not favored the interior man in me but the exterior man as well, because I remained more than thirty days and as many nights without being able to sleep as much as six hours during this period of time. And nonetheless my mind never weakened, and I had my wits more completely about me than I ever had when I was well. And this circumstance is all the more amazing since when I was healthy and I stayed up all night, the next day I was lethargic and melancholy all day; and I will say that it was amazing that when the fever and bloodletting had caused me to become terribly weak and devoid of energy, I suddenly felt a vigor spreading over all my limbs accompanied by such sweetness that I seemed to be in a more gentle bath than there could be anywhere in the world, and I felt this great sensation of comfort throughout my body. Attending me I had the best doctors in Rome since I had wanted my . . . [lacuna]. And everyone confessed that they had never had a laying on of hands that was felt so clearly to be the work of God, and this was something that all the principles of medicine dictated that kept me alive. And because it was not possible to attribute this grace [*questa gratia*] to anything other than his Divine Majesty, it caused human events to intervene in my illness that were nonetheless outside of everyday occurrence. Regardless of the interior graces, I say that God suddenly changed my nature and habits because my whole body is full of cholera and burning fevers that continually inflame me for every small thing; and in this malady, to the extent they tell me, I have never made the smallest hint of anger or impatience though the seriousness of the illness would be enough to make the gentlest and most patient man in the world impatient and angry, and this I am certain has been the work of God. . . .

Next, with the illness proceeding, . . . . the eyes of my mind have always seen God who caresses me as a tender mother does when her child is ill. I always saw Christ who led my soul to paradise, and this interior vision gave me such joy that I already began to taste the bliss of eternal life. My attention was so riveted on this sweetest spectacle that I could no longer speak of anything and then I learned why Christ called the little children and his chosen sheep to him and why Christ says that every man who believes in him will not die but will have everlasting life. . . .[90]

I am contented now, through his grace, to live and die when and how it will please his divine Majesty, who in this my illness has shown me such kindness, compassion, and sweetness that I can affirm having felt with my own hands the father's care he has for those who, through his grace, have a living faith in Jesus Christ our Lord. Therefore, my signora, let our sweetest father govern us in all and through all, and let us gladly receive from his holy hand both health and illness, life and death, and every other thing. I beg your Excellency that you will not let this letter of mine leave your hand, and you should take care not to show to anyone for many reasons. . . . Rome 4 May, 1549

Bench'io sia anchora molto debole del capo et de tutta la persona, nondimeno, sapendo il gran desiderio che ha vostra excellentia di sapere quali siano i favori che m'ha fatti nostro Signor Dio nella mia gravissima infermità corporale, mi son posto a narrarli brevemente. Et dico che 'l Signor Dio non mi ha favorito solamente nell'homo interiore ma ancho nell'isteriore, perché io stetti più di venti giorni et altrettanti notti senza poter dormire a pena sei hore in tutto questo spatio di tempo; et nondimeno la testa non se debilitò mai, et hebbi i sensi più integri et sani che io havessi mai in sanità, la qual cosa è tanto più maravigliosa perché quando in sanità io passo la vigilia d'una sola notte, mi trovo il si sequente tutto stordito et melancholico; et dirrò quello che è più meraviglioso, cioè che, quando la febbre et la puntura mi conducevano. Ad un'estrema debolezza et mancamento di spiriti, io mi sentiva venire all'improviso un vigore in tutti i membri con tanta soavità che mi pareva di essere nel più delicato bagno che si possa fare al mondo, et insieme mi sentiva tutto confortare. Appresso io ho havuto dei primi medici di Roma alla mia cura, chè così ha voluto il mio . . . et tutti hanno confessato di non haver mai avuto alle mani cura nella quale si vedesse così apertamente l'opera di Dio, il quale contra tutte le ragioni della medicina dicono che m'ha conservato in vita; et perché non si potesse attribuire si altri che a sua divina Maiestà questa gratia, ha fatto intervinire in questa mia infermità accidenti mortali et fuori d'ogni usanza. Quanto ai favori interiori, dico che Iddio subito mi mutò natura et costumi, perché io ho tutto il corpo pieno di colera et di humori adusti, i quali per ogni poca mi sogliono accendere; et in questa malattia, per quanto mi dicono, io non ho mai fatto pure un minimo cenno di ira o d'impatienzia anchora che la gravezza della malattia fosse bastante di far impatiente e colerico il più patiente et mansueto homo del mondo, et questa son certissimo essere stata opera di Dio. . . .

Appresso, procedendo la malattia, . . . . sempre gli occhi della mia mente vedevano Dio, che mi faceva quelle carezze che suol fare una tenera madre ad un suo figliolino infermo: sempre io vedeva Christo che conduceva l'anima al paradiso, et questa visione interiore mi dava tanto giubilo che già io cominciava a gustare il gaudio della vita eterna. Io era tanto fisso in questo soavissimo spettacolo che io non poteva più discorrere di cosa alcuna et allhora imparai perché Christo dimanda i suoi eletti pecorelle et fanciullini, et insieme imparai perché il medesimo Christo dice che chiunque crede in lui non vederà la morte in eterno.

. . . Per la gratia mi contento hora di vivere et morire quando et come piacerà a sua divina Maiestà, la quale in questa mia malattia mi si ha dimostrata tanto benigna, misericordiosa e soave che posso affirmare d'haver palpato con le mani proprie la cura paterna ch'ella ha di quelli che hanno per gratia sua la viva fede di Jesu Christo nostro Signore. Sicché, signora mia, lasciamoci governare in tutto per tutto da questo nostro dolcissimo padre, et riceviamo allegramente dalla sua santa mano sanità et l'infermità, la vita et la morte et ogni altra cosa. Supplico vostra excellentia che non si lasci uscire di mano questa mia lettera né si curi si mostrarla per più rispetti.

With Flaminio's death in 1550, an era was over. Even before Council of Trent ended its third and last session in 1563, imposing new constraints on an already tightly wrapped Catholicism, Pole and Cibo would be dead as well, with Varchi not far behind. Women such as Colonna, Cibo, and the men with whom they were intellectually allied had given the religious reform movement in Italy life and direction. But with the closing of the Council of Trent and the growing inquisitorial zeal in Rome that followed its finale, Flaminio's consoling, almost sanguine, words to Cibo about Colonna's death could no longer be said of the reform movement: "Having left the world with such quickness of spirit and such faith, . . . we ought not honor her death with any tears except those born of sweetness and holy joy." [Partita dal mondo con tanta alacrità di spirito et con tanta fede, . . . non dobbiamo honorare la morte sua con altre lacrime che nate di dolcezza et di gaudio puro et santo.][91]

### ❧ LAURA BATTIFERRA'S FUNERAL SONGS FOR CIBO ❧

Just months after the massive bonfires of books in Florence, the poet Laura Battiferra published four sonnets on the death of the alleged heretic Caterina Cibo.[92] On the orders of Cardinal Michele Ghislieri, the grand inquisitor of the Holy Office in Rome, many thousands of books were burned in Florence, in the Piazza Santa Croce and in front of the Duomo on March 18, 1559. That month, a new index of forbidden books had been published in Florence and Rome, making it a criminal act to print, distribute, sell, or possess any works of blacklisted writers—a roster that had swollen to 550 names. Included in the index were such vernacular classics as the collected works of Boccaccio, Machiavelli, Rabelais, Berni, and Aretino as well as the already outlawed "heretics" Erasmus, Valdés, Ochino, and all anonymous books. Unlike Venice, Florence had no inquisitors of its own. But as Cardinal Ghislieri wrote that year, "It is true that Florence lacks Inquisitors, but

Duke Cosimo zealously does the bidding of this Holy Office in every way he possibly can."[93]

Born a generation after Cibo, Battiferra was intimately connected to the Duchess of Camerino in a number of ways. Arriving in Florence as an outsider from Urbino, where Cibo's daughter lived as wife of the reigning duke, Battiferra came to the Medici court in 1550 on the strength of the connections her husband Bartolomeo Ammannati enjoyed at court as one of Cosimo's principal architects and sculptors. The daughter of the apostolic protonotary Giovanni Antonio Battiferri, Battiferra was briefly married to Vittorio Sereni, the court organist at Urbino, who died in 1549. It was through Cibo's longtime friend Varchi, though, whom Battiferra had first met in Rome since he belonged to her husband's circle—along with such poets and painters as Bronzino, Michelangelo, and Tasso—that the two women met when Battiferra arrived in Florence.[94]

Battiferra dedicated her first book of poetry, *Il primo libro dell'opere toscane*, to Cosimo's wife Eleonora, who had shown a special interest in Italian poetry early in her rule when she established an academy devoted to its cultivation. Eleonora was also drawn to books and art illustrating the lives of famous women in antquity. Domenico Bruni dedicated the book he had written on the same subject, his *Difesa delle donne*, to the duchess.[95] Italian translations of ancient women's lives from Livy, Ovid, and Valerius Maximus were also available to Eleonora in the Medici Library as was Betussi's 1545 translation of Boccaccio's *De claris mulieribus* (*On Famous Women*), which had an addendum with fifty modern women's biographies including those of Eleonora's own compatriots from Naples—Eleonora d'Aragona and Giulia Gonzaga.[96] The year Battiferra's collected poems were published, the duchess commissioned Giorgio Vasari to execute a cycle of paintings and friezes illustrating the literary theme of famous women for her suite of rooms in the Palazzo della Signoria.[97] Postwar Siena may have provided the inspiration for Eleonora's program since a large number of pre-Medicean famous women painting cycles have been found in Sienese palaces that survived the Florentine bombardment and occupation of the city in 1556–60.[98] Vasari's correspondence with his chief collaborator, Vincenzo Borghini, and with Eleonora and Cosimo provides a testimonial of the duchess's own involvement in choosing the figures for her famous women programme and the still extant large inscription with Eleonora's name and title bordering the paintings on all four walls of the Sala di Ester make clear the duchess's wish to identify herself with the women represented in her program.[99] Battiferra's husband Bartolomeo Ammanati had allegorized the duchess's role as the prolific mother of eight children in his marble sculptures of the Roman goddesses of fertility, Juno and Ceres, which Cosimo had commissioned.[100] But by 1560, as Pamela Benson has shown, the duke's primary objective in having Vasari execute the famous women programme for Eleonora's apartments was to represent the duchess as an active political presence in Florence.[101]

Battiferra's tribute to Eleonora, *Il primo libro dell'opera toscano*, eulogizies the life of Caterina Cibo in four sonnets (86a, 126, 127, and 128), which she composed on the Duchess of Camerino's death in 1557. Enrico Maria Guidi has seen traces of Battiferra's interest in reform thought in her encomiastic sonnets on Cibo as well as in her *I sette salmi penitentiali del santissimo profeta Davit*.[102] The bond Guidi posits between Cibo and Battiferra around reform thought in general and Valdesianism in particular is suggestive given Cibo's long friendships with Vittoria Colonna, Ochino, Flaminio, and Carnesecchi.[103] But the supposition of a shared investment, at the height of the Counter-Reformation under Paul IV, in a theology that was specifically branded as heresy by the Roman Holy Office, raises questions. Not only were the Jesuits, who were enthusiastic supporters of Paul's policies and the Inquisition, Eleonora's closest friends in Florence, but Battiferra and her husband Bartolomeo Ammannati were also friends and patrons of Eleonora's Jesuits and their new college in Florence, as Vittoria Kirkham has made clear.[104] Moreover, Battiferra's high praise of Cibo and the sorrow she expresses over her death cannot be interpreted in themselves as evidence of the young poet's heterodoxy. In 1560 when Battiferra's *Il primo libro* came out, Cibo's Valdesianism, if we can call it that, and her loyalty to the exiled Ochino may have been seen as relics of a past era, particularly in Florence where the book was published. By that year not only Cibo but the Valdesians Vittoria Colonna, Flaminio, and Cardinal Pole as well had all long been dead and the much more moderate Pope Pius IV (Gianngelo de' Medici) had taken Paul's place on the papal throne, rescinding many of his harshest policies.

While Battiferra's sonnets for Cibo represent a moving testament to her profound respect and affection for the Duchess of Camerino, there is nothing explicitly incriminating in them, even in the climate of the later 1550s when guilt by association was the primary tool of the Inquisition. True, as long as Paul IV was still pope it might have been dangerous for Barriferra to dedicate a suite of eulogies to a woman who had been publicly denounced in the proceedings of the Holy Office as a "heretic and teacher of heretics."[105] But Battiferra's sonnet, with its erudite reference to the Hippocrene spring, its Propertian shattering of syntax, its Pindaresque architecture with a tower of dependent clauses piled above the one main verb (*cantate*) in the poem, and its final double pun on Varchi's and Cibo's names (*Benedetto inchiostro* and *Cibo immortal*), stands on its own as a tribute to Cibo's intellect and her classical cultivation, not a call to arms:

### To the Same [Benedetto Varchi] on the Death of the Duchess of Camerino[106]

Since I ask in vain for garlands to wreathe
the brow of that lady, so loved by you, and
since both shores of the Hippocrene elude
my arrogant mind, sing, Varchi, you whom
Phoebus and the Muses, who inspire
all our worth on earth, let taste the holy
waters of Parnassus, a short journey for you,
for others long. Of the great lady—
no, earthly goddess—you should sing,
a rare wonder of heaven and nature,
who nourished souls with immortal food,
since no greater subject could be
given to consecrated ink than to make
her lovely name and yours eternal.

    Poi che cinger le tempie indarno chero
di quella da voi tanto amata fronde,
e ch'al mio troppo ardito alto pensiero
si celan d'Ippocrene ambe le sponde;
    Varchi, a cui Febo, a cui le muse diero,
onde nostro valor quaggiù s'infonde,
per corto a voi, altrui lungo sentiero
di Parnaso gustar le sacrate onde,
    della gran donna, anzi terrestre dea,
raro del cielo e di natura mostro,
che di Cibo immortal l'alme pascea,
    cantate voi, ché al Benedetto[107] inchiostro
maggior soggetto dar non si potea
per fare eterno il suo bel nome e 'l vostro.

*(Il primo libro, ed. Guidi, sonnet 86a, 90)*

But this next sonnet, titled "A Messer Vincenzo Grotti, in morte della medesima," referring to the preceding poem on Caterina Cibo's death, contains evocative allusions to Cibo's spiritual leadership and her passion for knowledge. This and the other three sonnets on Cibo's death leave a loving portrait of a woman who was passionate about her beliefs, utterly fearless, and who reached out to protect the less powerful. In her references to menacing storm clouds (*atra nube*), spiritual numbness (*nostro freddo core*), and sea of horror (*questo mar colmo d'orrore*), Battiferra may be alluding to the notorious excesses of the Holy Office under Paul IV. But again, criticism of Paul, whose statue the Roman people tore from its pedestal and mutilated when the news of his death was announced, does not suggest the promotion of a reform theology that would still be judged heretical under Pius IV.

### To Messer Vincenzo Grotti, on the Death of the Same [Caterina Cibo]

Grotti, what shall we do, blind and lost
without her who was our light and guide?
Who will show us heaven now?
Who will bring us from these false waters
to trusted shores? Who, with sweet, high tones,
will notice us there, where she lives and shines?
When will we see again the face that led
us to virtue, when we had escaped a storm?
How will hot and pure desire be stirred
in our cold hearts without her holy fire,
so that she can make us long for heaven?
How, amid such great and just laments,
shall we rise above this tidal wave of horror,
far from the Sirens' songs and reefs?

    Grotti, che farem noi ciechi e smariti
privi di lei, che n'era e scorta e luce?
Chi più ne mostra il ciel? Chi ne conduce
fuor di queste false onde a fidi liti?
    Chi con soavi accenti, alti e graditi,
ne scorgerà là 'v' ella vive e luce?
Quando la vista, ch'a ben far n'induce,
rivedrem mai, fuor d'atra nube usciti?
    Come senza l'ardor de i santi rai
s'accenderà nel nostro freddo core
caldo e casto desio, ch'al ciel l'invogli?
    Come fra tanti e tanto giusti lai

varcherem questo mar colmo d'orrore,
lungi dalle sirene e da gli scogli?

*(Il primo libro, ed. Guidi, sonnet 127, 141)*

Battiferra's last two eulogies for her friend and teacher praise the ideal-
ism and passion for spiritual enlightenment that Cibo has transmitted to a
younger generation of intellectual women. The last of these eulogies (128) is
of particular note since it suggests that Cibo had gathered around her in her
last years diverse circles of women, who respected her life's work and who saw
in her a model of compassion and a path to salvation. Soon after her arrival
in Florence, Cibo had initiated meetings with women's communities from
several convents, while she at the same time met with a group of women at
the Medici court who looked to her as their teacher.[108] In this last poem, addressed to the women who were the duchess's companions, published for the
first time in 1560 when Cibo's friend Carnesecchi had not yet been executed
for heresy, Battiferra celebrates the duchess's ascent to Paradise and articulates
her desire to follow in her footsteps:

### On the Death of the Duchess of Camerino
### [to her blessed soul in heaven]

O three and four times blessed are you,
O soul, since loosed from your mortal veil,
you returned to heaven with angelic choirs
Ah, if I was sweet and pleasing to you here,
since now you burn with amorous zeal,
pray for me, before I leave this skin,
that I will leave my desire to sin.
And then the sorrow that I harbor
in my heart, which steals away my joy
in your repose, will leave my soul
free of its heavy burden, since I dare not
ascend to heaven, without your help:
a heavy task, though I mirror and
polish myself in your lovely light.[109]

O tre, quattro e sei volte alma beata,
che, deposto il mortal terrestre velo,
pur dianzi nuda ritornasti al Cielo
da gli angelici cori accompagnata:

deh, se quaggiù ti fui dolce, né grata,
or, ch'ardi tutta d'amoroso zelo,
prega per me, ch'anzi ch'io cangi 'l pelo,
cangi la voglia a peccar sempre usata.
    E fa che 'l duol, di cui son fatta albergo
e mi toglie il gioir del tuo riposo,
lasci l'interno mio libero e scarco,
    perch'io da terra al cielo alzar non oso,
senza 'l tuo aiuto, questo grave incarco,
se ben nel raggio tuo mi specchio e tergo.

              *(Il primo libro, ed. Guidi, sonnet 126, 140–41)*

## ON THE DEATH OF THE SAME LADY [CATERINA CIBO], TO HER LADIES

You women, who spent time as companions
of that goddess who graced the world
and now illumines heaven, and for you that life
was as sweet and dear as could possibly be.
Now, since envious death has made you
companions of bitter pain, you have learned
to weep and grieve: an ill opposed to good.
But, ah, since you women have given
your hearts and aching eyes the right
to perform the work of love and pity,
and have fulfilled that right in part,
turn rightly to her since she burns
with true compassion to see you,
once again in a place more blessed.

    Donne, che 'n compagnia di quella dea,
che già 'l mondo, ora il cielo orna e rischiara
viveste un tempo, e vi fu dolce e cara
tanto la vita, quanto esser potea;
    or compagne di doglia acerba e rea
morte v'ha fatte, invidiosa e amara
or piangere, or doler da voi s'impara
contrario male al ben, ch'esser solea.
    Deh, poi ch'agli occhi e al cor dolente avrete
renduto il dritto, e sodisfatto in parte
a l'offizio d'amore e di pietate,

con la ragion vèr' lei vi rivolgete,
ch'arde tutta di vera caritate,
di rivedervi in più beata parte.

*(Il primo libro, ed. Guidi, sonnet 128, 142)*

Nine years after the publication of Battiferra's *Primo libro*, a very different man sat on the papal throne, the fanatic grand inquisitor of the Roman Holy Office, Pius V (Michele Ghislieri). Under the aegis of Pope Paul IV in 1558, Ghislieri and the other inquisitors had sentenced Caterina Cibo's longtime friend Carnesecchi to death, but three years later Pius IV had absolved him of all charges. When Ghislieri became pope in 1566 and demanded from Cosimo de' Medici—with promises and threats—Carnesecchi's extradition from Florence, the duke judged it a request he could not refuse. On July 4, 1566, the pope's men led the protonotary away in chains from Cosimo's palace where he had been dining.[110]

Less than twenty-three months after Carnesecchi's execution, the former grand inquisitor Michele Ghislieri, now Pope Pius V, conferred the long-awaited title of Grand Duke of Tuscany on Cosimo I de' Medici. The following year, on March 5, 1570, in a private chapel of the Vatican palace, the pope performed the coronation mass. He placed the heavy crown of gold on his vassal's head, and Cosimo, wearing a crimson mantle trimmed with ermine over a long skirt of cloth of gold, reached out to take the heavy silver scepter from Ghislieri.[111]

EPILOGUE

In 1575–77, the plague came to Venice, leaving some forty thousand people dead in its wake—roughly one-quarter of the population of Italy's print capital.[1] Venice's shopkeepers, among whom were many printers and employees of the presses, closed their stores and abandoned the city. At the Giolito press, production went into a steep decline, sliding from the thirty or forty editions the press published in a good year, to bottom out at seven editions at the height of the plague, in 1576.[2] And all but one of these editions were religious works.[3] The edicts, manuals, and index of prohibited books the Council of Trent disseminated on its closing in 1563 changed the face of Venetian publishing so much so that by 1567, Giolito, the most popular house in the industry, was regularly printing more devotional than secular books. But other factors also had an impact on the print industry in Venice in the last decades of the century. In 1569, heavy rains, severe flooding, and a typhus epidemic ruined many businesses and took thousands of lives. Venice's war in Cyprus, begun the following year, did nothing to alleviate the city's misery. Further crippling the city's ability to recover from its losses, the war dragged on until 1573, draining the city's manpower and its wealth.[4]

In the first decade after Trent, the production of secular books in Italy declined steeply. Women writers lost ground in the years 1564–75, with some notable exceptions: Laura Terracina saw six editions of her *Il discorso* come out and at five different presses in Venice; and Laura Battiferra's *I sette salmi penitentiali del santissimo Davit* went through three printings in that decade (see table 2).[5] The acclaimed lyric poet and courtesan Veronica Franco published her *Terze rime* in the plague year of 1575, but without the name of a publisher or a print date to legitimate her book. No other solo-authored books by women were published in Italy during that period.

The literary legacy of the mid-sixteenth-century subjects of this book would first resurface in women's writings of the next decade, 1581–93, with

TABLE 2. Italian Women's Printed Works: 1564–1654

| Author/Title | Publication Information | | |
| --- | --- | --- | --- |
| | City | Publisher | Dates |
| Laura Teracina: | | | |
|   *Il discorso* | Venice | Rampazetto | 1564 |
|   *Il discorso* | Venice | Giolito | 1566 |
|   *Il discorso* | Venice | Scoto | 1566 |
|   *Il discorso* | Venice | Farri | 1567 |
|   *Il discorso* | Venice | Viani | 1674 |
|   *Il discorso* | Venice | Bonfadino | 1608, 1513, 1619 |
| Laura Battiferra: | | | |
|   *I sette salmi penitenziali del santissimo Davit* | Florence | . . . | 1566 |
|   *I sette salmi penitenziali del santissimo Davit*[a] | Venice | Giolito | 1568, 1572 |
| Veronica Franco: | | | |
|   *Terze rime* | Venice | . . . | 1575 |
| Chiara Matraini: | | | |
|   *Meditazioni spirituali* | Lucca | Busdragho | 1581 |
|   *Considerazioni sopra i sette salmi penitenziali . . .* | Lucca | Busdragho | 1586 |
|   *Breve discorso sopra la vita . . . della B. Vergine . . .* | Lucca | Busdragho | 1590 |
|   *Lettere* | Lucca | Busdragho | 1595 |
|   *Lettere* | Venice | Moretti | 1597 |
|   *Dialoghi spirituali* | Venice | Prati | 1602 |
| Moderata Fonte:[b] | | | |
|   *Tredici canti del Floridoro* | Venice | n.p. | 1581 |
|   *Le Feste: Rappresentazione* | Venice | Guerra | 1581 |
|   *La passione de Christo* | Venice | Guerra | 1582 |
|   *La Resurrezione de Gesù nostro Signore* | Venice | Imberti | 1592 |
| Maddalena Campiglia: | | | |
|   *Discorso sopra l'annonciatione della . . . Vergine . . .* | Vicenza | n.p. | 1585 |
|   *Flori* | Vicenza | Perin Libraio & T. Brunelli | 1588 |
|   *Calisa* | Vicenza | Perin Libraio & T. Brunelli | 1589 |
| Vittoria Colonna: | | | |
|   *Rime spirituali* | Verona | Discepoli | 1586 |
|   *Rime spirituali* | Verona | Valgrisi | 1596 |

*continued*

TABLE 2. *(continued)*

| Author/Title | Publication Information | | |
|---|---|---|---|
| | City | Publisher | Dates |
| *Mirtilla* | Milan | Bordoni & Locarni | 1605 |
| *Lettere* | Venice | Zaltieri | 1607 |
| *Lettere* | Venice | Combi | 1612, 1620, 1625, 1627, 1634, 1638 |
| *Fragmenti di alcune scritture* | Venice | Combi | 1620 |
| *Lettere* | Venice | Minerva | 1647 |
| *Lettere* | Venice | ... | 1652 |
| Lucrezia Marinella: | | | |
| *La colomba sacra. Poema eroica* | Venice | Ciotti | 1595 |
| *Vita del serafico et glorioso San Francesco* | Venice | Bertano | 1597 |
| *Amore innamorato ed impazzato. Poema* | Venice | ... | 1598 |
| *L'Enrico overo Bisantio conquistato. Poema eroico* | Venice | ... | 1635 |
| *La nobiltà et ecellenza delle donne* | Venice | Ciotti Sanese | 1600 |
| *La vita di Maria Vergine imperatrice* | Venice | B. Barezzi | 1602 |
| *Rime sacre* | Venice | ... | 1603 |
| *Arcadia felice* | Venice | Ciotti | 1605 |
| *Vita di Santa Giustina* | Florence | ... | 1606 |
| *De' gesti heroici e della vita meravigliosa della serafica Santa Caterina da Siena. Libri sei* | Venice | ... | 1635 |
| *Le vittorie de Francesco il serafico* | Padua | Crivellari | 1647 |
| *Holocausto d'amore della vergine Santa Giustinia* | Venice | Leni | 1648 |
| Sara Copio Sullam: | | | |
| *Manifesto . . . , nel quale è da lei riprovata e detestata l'opinione negante l'immortalità dell'Anima* | Venice | ... | 1621 |
| Arcangela Tarabotti:[c] | | | |
| *La semplicità ingannata*[d] | Leiden | Sambix | 1654 |

*continued*

TABLE 2. (*continued*)

| Author/Title | Publication Information | | |
| --- | --- | --- | --- |
| | City | Publisher | Dates |
| *Lettere familiari e di complimento* | Venice | Guerigli | 1650 |
| *Il paradiso monacale* | Venice | Oddoni | 1643 |

[a] Printed as part of an anthology compiled by Giolito.
[b] Pseudonym for Modesta Pozzo.
[c] Pseudonym: Galerana Baratotti.
[d] Originally titled *La tirannia paterna*.

the new publication and reprinting of twelve solo-authored works by five women, four of whom—Moderata Fonte, Maddalena Campiglia, Isabella Andreini, and Chiara Matraini—represented a new age in women's publishing.[6] The post-Trent reprinting of two mid-sixteenth-century writers, Vittoria Colonna's *Rime spirituali* (1586, 1596) and Terracina's *Il discorso* (reprints—see above), bear witness to the enduring impact of their publications on Andreini's generation. The literary women of the 1580s and early 1590s moved out of the confined space of the salon and into the theater and the court. Campiglia's published writings include two pastoral dramas in verse, *Flori* (1588) and *Calisa* (1589); similarly Andreini's work, the *Mirtilla* (1588), is a pastoral piece for theater and Fonte's *Le feste* (1581) presents a musical play in verse written for presentation before the doge Niccolò da Ponte and his court in Venice. Also typical of women's publications in the 1580s—and reflective of taste in the post-Trent era—are works on religious themes; six of the women's works published during this decade belong to this category: Matraini's *Meditazioni* (1581), *Considerazioni* (1586), and *Breve discorso* (1590); Fonte's *La passione di Christo* (1582); and Campiglia's *Discorso sopra l'annonciatione* (1585). Together, these works constituted a new wave among turn-of-the-century writers.

These fin de siècle women writers, who flourished from 1595 to 1619 and, in some cases, beyond that date, published, most notably, in genres that were diametrically opposed to one another: feminist polemics, on the one hand, and religious and devotional poetics, on the other.

Fonte's dialogue *Il merito delle donne* and Marinella's treatise *La nobiltà et eccellenza delle donne*, both published in 1600, delivered frontal attacks on patriarchal culture in Venice, presenting a sharp contrast to Marinella's Christian epic poems *La colomba sacra* (1595), her *Vita del serafico et glorioso San Francesco*

(1597), and Fonte's *La resurrezione di Gesù* (1592).[7] The frequently reprinted editions of Matraini and Andreini's collected letters (both titled *Lettere*) indicate that the letter collection, a genre appropriated by women writers since the fifteenth century, was still considered a viable medium by women at the opening of the seicento.[8] Though the publication of women's epistolaries all but disappeared during in the middle of the sixteenth century, the genre continued to cast itself as a major mode for women's publications from the opening of the seventeenth century until the modern era.[9]

A final generation of post-Trent women writers in the peninsula, whose works in print extend from 1600 to 1654, further represents the conflicting publication patterns of seventeenth-century female authorship. While the revolutionary rhetoric of Marinella's *Nobiltà* contrasts starkly with her more traditional heroic poems, *L'Enrico overo Bisantio conquistato* (1635) and the *De' gesti heroici e della vita meravigliosa della serafica Santa Caterina da Siena* (1635), the exuberant feminist vitriol of the Venetian nun Arcangela Tarabotti's *Tirannia paterna* (1654) has no prior parallel.

In sum, the prolific women writers who lived, worked, and published in Italy after the closing of the Council of Trent did so under very different social and political circumstances—and they published under different legal constraints after Trent—from those of their female predecessors. The polemicists Fonte and Tarabotti even found it necessary to publish their works pseudonymously—something almost unknown in cinquecento Italy. A variety of factors brought mid-sixteenth-century literary women and men together in Italy, and in a way that did not happen in the next century. First of all, leading intellectuals in mid-sixteenth-century Italy, both women and men, shared a common involvement in, if not a consensus about, the new theology espoused by such writers as Juan de Valdés and Giulia Gonzaga, Bernardino Ochino and Vittoria Colonna. In Venice, and more specifically at Giolito's press, new writers on the scene, many of whom were women, had a venue that served as a central clearinghouse for the publication of their works. Moreover, the women-led salons of the period, the counterpart of the male academies, also served as a funnel between new writing and the presses. Aspiring women writers could look also to editors whose special interests included the recruitment and publication of new women writers as well as female patrons. And these readers of women were men deeply committed to the cultivation of the Tuscan language and new poetry, such as Domenichi, Ruscelli, and Varchi. Cinquecento writers also had the advantage of being able to coalesce around the performance, production, publication, and even game-playing inspired by two focal forms—the sonnet and the dialogue, which, as we have seen, were both deployed interactively. These were forms not for solo singers but for the group. All these factors brought midcentury Italian literary women and men together, giving them at least the appearance of a culturally hegemonic and coherent group. These, too, were the conditions that enabled Italian women writers at the dawn of commercial print technology to enter, for the first time in European history, the very public world of the mass-produced book.

# The Giolito Poetry Anthology Series: Titles, Printers, Editors, Dedicatees, Poets in Editions 1545–1560

## LIST OF EDITIONS

Volume 1, 1st edition (1a). Venice: Gabriel Giolito, 1545. *Rime diverse di molti eccellentiss. auttori nuovamente raccolte. Libro primo.* Editor's dedicatory letter by Lodovico Domenichi to Don Diego Hurtado di Mendozza. Women poets included: Francesca Baffa, Vittoria Colonna, Veronica Gambara.

Volume 1, 2nd edition (1b). Venice: Gabriel Giolito, 1546. *Rime diverse di molti eccellentiss. auttori nuovamente raccolte. Libro primo, con nuova additione ristampato.* Same editor's dedicatory letter as above. Women poets: Francesca Baffa, Vittoria Colonna (listed as Marchesa di Pescara), Laodomia Forteguerra, Veronica Gambara, Laura Terracina.

Volume 1, 3rd edition (1c).Venice: Gabriel Giolito, 1549. *Rime diverse di molti eccellentiss. auttori nuovamente raccolte. Libro primo, con nuova additione ristampato.* With the same editor's dedicatory letter as above. Women poets: Francesca Baffa, Vittoria Colonna (listed as Marchesa di Pescara), Laodomia Forteguerra, Veronica Gambara, Laura Terracina.

Volume 2, 1st edition (2a). Venice: Gabriel Giolito, 1547. *Rime di diversi nobili huomini et eccellenti poeti nella lingua thoscana. Libro secondo.* With a dedicatory letter by Giolito to Sigismondo Fanzino dalla Torre. No editor named. Women poets: Giuglia,[1] Veronica Gambara.

Volume 2, 2nd edition (2b).Venice: Gabriel Giolito, 1548. *Delle rime di diversi nobili huomini et eccellenti poeti nella lingua thoscana. Nuovamente ristampate, libro secondo.* With the same dedicatory letter by Giolito to S. F. dalla Torre. No editor named. Women poets: Giuglia, Veronica Gambara.

Volume 3, 1st and only edition (3). Venice: Bartolomeo Cesana, Al Segno del Pozzo, 1550. [*Libro terzo*] *delle rime di diversi nobilissimi et eccellentissimi autori nuovamente raccolte.* Mutilated title page is missing top and is pasted onto a new page. Bongi indicates title was *Libro terzo delle rime,* etc., as above. Editor's dedicatory letter by Andrea Arrivabene to Luca Grimaldo. Women poets included: Vittoria Colonna, Veronica Gambara.

Volume 4, 1st and only edition (4). Bologna: Anselmo Giaccarello, 1551. *Libro quarto della rime di diversi eccellentiss autori nella lingua volgare.* Nuovamente raccolte. Editor's dedicatory letter by Hercole Bottrigaro to Giulio Grimanni. Women poets: Giulia Aragona, Lucia Bertana, Gieronima Castellana, Vittoria Colonna, Veronica Gambara, Marguerite de Navarre (listed as La Regina di Navara), Verginia Salvi, Faustina Vallentina.

Volume 5, 1st edition (5).[2] Venice: Gabriel Giolito, 1551–52.[3] *Rime di diversi illustri signori napoletani e d'altri nobiliss. intelletti; nuovamente raccolte, et non piu stampate. Terzo Libro allo illus. S. Ferrante Carrafa.* Editor's dedicatory letter by Lodovico Dolce to Ferrante Carrafa dated December 9, 1551. Women poets: Isabella di Morra.

Volume 5, 2nd edition (5a). Venice: Gabriel Giolito, 1552. Rime di diversi illustri signori napoletani, e d'altri nobiliss. ingegni. Nuovamente raccolte, et con nuova additione ristampate. Libro Quinto. Allo illus. S. Ferrante Carrafa. New dedicatory letter by Dolce, May 10, 1552. Women poets: Isabella di Morra.

Volume 5, 3rd edition (5b). Venice: Gabriel Giolito, 1555. *Libro quinto delle rime di diversi illustri signori napoletani, e d'altri nobilissimi ingegni. Nuovamente raccolte, e con nova additione ristampate, allo illus. S. Ferrante Carrafa.* A third, completely new dedicatory letter by Dolce to Carrafa, May 11, 1555. Women poets: Isabella di Morra.

Volume 6, 1st and only edition (6). Venice: Giovam Maria Bonelli, Al Segno del Pozzo, 1553. *Il sesto libro delle rime di diversi eccellenti autori, nuovamente raccolte, et mandate in luce. Con un discorso di Girolamo Ruscelli. Al molto reverendo, et honoratiss. Monsignor Girolamo Artusio.* Edited by Ruscelli,[4] with a dedicatory letter by Andrea Arrivabene to Monsignor Girolamo Artusio. Women poets included: Tullia d'Aragona, Vittoria Colonna, Veronica Gambara, Ippolita Mirtilla, Coletta Pasquale,

Volume 7, 1st and only edition (7). Venice: Gabriel Giolito, 1556. *Rime di diversi signori napoletani, e d'altri. Nuovamente raccolte et impresse. Libro Settimo.* Editor's dedicatory letter by Lodovico Dolce to Matteo Montenero.[5] Women poets included: Chiara Matraini, Isabella di Morra, Caterina Pellegrina, Lucretia di Raimondo, Laura Terracina.

Volume 8, 1st and only edition (8).[6] Venice: Gio. Battista & Melchior Sessa Fratelli, 1558. *I fiori delle rime de' poeti illustri, nuovamente raccolti et ordinati da Girolamo Ruscelli.* Editor's dedicatory letter by Girolamo Ruscelli to Aurelio Porcelaga. Women poets: Vittoria Colonna, Veronica Gambara.

Volume 9, 1st and only edition (9). Cremona: Vincenzo Conti, 1560. *Rime di diversi autori eccellentiss. Libro Nono.* Editor's dedicatory letter by Vincenzo Conti to Guglielmo Gonzaga, Duca di Montova. Women poets included: Laura Battiferro, Lucia Bertana, Virginia Salvi.

Volume "10," 1st and only edition (10).[7] Lucca: Vincenzo Busdragho, 1559. *Rime diverse d'alcune nobilissime, et virtuosissime donne, raccolte per M. Lodovico Domenichi, e intitolate al Signor Giannoto Castiglione gentil'huomo milanese.* Editor's dedicatory letter by Domenichi to Castiglione, and a second dedicatory letter by the publisher Vincenzo Busdragho to Gerardo Spada, gentilhuomo lucchese. Poets included: fifty-three women; eight sonnets by male poets are included in this anthology, almost all of them responses to a woman's poem.

## AN INDEX OF POETS, EDITORS, PRINTERS, AND DEDICATEES PUBLISHED IN GIOLITO'S ANTHOLOGY SERIES

Note that women's names are in bold in this index.[8]

Trincheri, Giov. Battista—6

Tosco (also Thosco), Annibal—1a, 1b, 1c

Trissano, Gio. Giorgio—3

Tuccio, Dario—9

Ugoni, Gioanni Andrea—8

Valle, Giovan Maria dalla—5, 5a, 5b

**Vallentina, Faustina**—4

**Varchi, Benedetto**—1a, 1b, 1c, 2a, 2b, 3, 4, 5b, 6, 8

Vasio, Marco—5, 5a

Veggio, Francesco—9

Vendramino, Cavalier—5a, 5b, 6

**Veniero, Domenico**—3, 4, 5, 5a, 5b, 6, 8

Vergerio, Aureolio—2a, 2b

Vigerio, Urban—4

Vinciguerra, Conte—5, 5a, 5b, 6

Vitale, Giovan—4

Vitelli, Cardinal

Vivaldi, Michel'Angelo—5b

Volpe, Girolamo—1a, 1b, 1c, 2a, 2c

Volpe, Giovan Antonio—1a, 1b, 1c, 3

Zacco, Bartolomeo—6

Zaffiri, Filippo—6

Zancaruolo, Carlo—2a, 2b, 6

Zane, Bernardo—3, 6

Zane, Giacomo—6

Zenzani—4

Zerbo, Giovanni—1a

Zuccheri, V. G (see Gemma)

# Descriptions of the Fifteen Volumes in the Giolito Anthology Series: 1545–1560

## VOLUME I: THREE EDITIONS

### First Edition of Volume 1 (1a) 1545. Case Y 7184 .7452

**Title page (each line centered):** RIME / DIVERSE DI / MOLTI ECCELLENTISS. / AUTTORI NUOVA- / MENTE RACCOLTE. / LIBRO PRIMO / ★★★★★★ / *Con Gratia &* *Privilegio*

**Underneath the above and centered:** the Giolito *marca* with the phoenix with spread wings reborn from the flames with initials G /G /F and motto on ribbons: DE LA / MIA MORTE / ETERNA / VITA IO / VIVO. / SEMPER EADEM.

**Below crest:** VINETIA APPRESSO GABRIEL / GIOLITO DI FERRARII / MDXLV [1545]

**Dedicatory letter follows the title page:** By Lodovico Domenichi to "Illustriss. S. Don Diego Hurtado di Mendozza."

**Print style:** Both dedicatory letter and *Rime* are set in italic type larger than the italic used for the sonnets.

This six-page dedicatory letter is dated November 8, 1544, Venice. It is signed "Di V.S. Illustriss. Servitore Lodovico Domenichi." It begins: "Molte son le cagioni, Signore, che mi muovano a dover presentarvi questo libro, le quali assecurandomi d'ogni paura, mi porgano ardire sopra le forze mie: et queste sono le divine conditioni, et l'innumerabili gratie del cielo cumulate con mirabil providenza nella persona vostra."

***First poem, first line in the edition:*** The *Rime* begin with sonnets by Pietro Bembo. The first lines of the first sonnet are "Se mai ti piacque Apollo non indegno / Del tuo divin soccorso un tempo farmi."

***Pages:*** The volume contains 370 pages, numbered on both sides of each page.

***"Tavola degli autori" for the first edition (women's names are shown in bold type):*** At the end of the volume there's a "tavola di autori," with names listed in alphabetical order by the authors' first names as follows: the *tavola* includes the first line of each poem listed under the author:

> Andrea Navagero, Antonio Broccardo, Antonio Cavallino, Annibale Caro, Abbate Giovio, Alfonso Davalo Mar. del Vasto [=Alfonso d'Avalos Marchese del Vasto], Annibal Tosco, Aurelio Solico, Antonio Corradi, Anton Francesco Doni, Anton Maria Braccioforte, Bartolmeo Ferrino, Baldessare Stampa, Battista dalla Torre, Bartolomeo Carlo Piccolomini, Baldessar Castiglione, Benedetto Varchi, Bartolomeo Gottifredi, Bernardin Tomitano, Bernardin Daniello, Bernardo Capello [=Bernardino Cappello], Bernardo Tasso, Cornelio da Castello, Cosmo Ruccellai. Camillo Caula, Clario, Collaltino da Collalto, Claudio Tolomei, Emanuel Grimaldi, Francesco Coppetta, Francesco Maria Molza, Francesco Capodilista, Fortuna Spira, Francesco Sansovino, **Francesca Baffa**, Francesco Coccio, Gio. Andrea Gesualdo, Giulio Camillo, Giovan Mozzarello, Giovanni Guidiccione, Giovan Cotta, Giovan Ciorgio [*sic*, but listed over his *Rime* as Giovan Giorgio] Dressino, Gio. Andrea dall'Anguillara, Girolamo Volpe, Giovan Antonio Volpe, Giovanni Brevio, Giovanni dalla Casa [*sic*], Girolamo Mutio [=Muzio], Gabriel Zerbo, Girolamo Parabosco, Girolamo Fraccastoro, Giulio Roselli Acquaviva, Gio. Battista Corradi, Gio. Luca Benedetto, Gandolfo Porrino, Giovanni Battista Susio, Giuseppe Betussi, Giorgio Belmosto, Hippolito Cardinale de [*sic* but de' in text] Medici, Hercole Bentivoglio, Iacopo Marmitta, Iacopo Sellaio Bolognese, Lodovico Ariosto, Luigi Alamanni, Lorenzo de [*sic*, but de' text] Medici, Luigi Raimondi, Lodovico Dolce, Lelio Capilupi, Luigi Cassola, Leone Orsino [=Leone Orsini], Lodovico Domenichi, Marco Cavallo, Marc'Antonio Passero, Nicolo Amanio, Nicolo Martelli, Ottaviano Salvi, Pietro Bembo, Pietro Barignano, Paolo Canale, Pietro Aretino, P. Antonio Chiocca, Scipio Costanzo, Thomas Castellano, Triphon Gabriele, Tiberio Pandola, Vincenzo Martelli, Vincenzo Quirino, **Vittoria Colonna, Veronica Gambara**, Vicino Orsino, Ugolino Martelli. [the end]

IN VINEGIA APPRESSO / GABRIEL GIOLITO/DE FERRARI / ★★★★★

***Last page of volume:*** Giolito's colophon with the motto "Semper eadem."
Errata page is last page of volume.
Of this first volume, Salvatore Bongi, *Annali di Gabriel Giolito*, 1:88–89, writes:

The first and tone-setting volume of a collection of great interest for Italian lit in the 16c. And one of the great works of L. Domenichi. Dedicated by LD to Don Diego Hurtado di Mendozza, a great political and literary leader and one of the chief governors of the Spanish government and empire in Italy. The series was continued and carried on by other editors and published in other places and subsequent years until it comprised nine books in 1560. These books were brought out in a varying number of editions. If one of the editors or presses had wanted to bring together all the presses and books for a complete collection, it would have been a difficult undertaking. The concept the editor-anthologizers had was to publish a representative collection of the best sonnets, whether edited or unedited, of contemporary poets. The volume was received with much acclaim and its sales were so successful that Giolito was obliged to bring out a second and third edition in 1546 and 1549. These books sold for 1 lira and 4 soldi each in Venetian money. Dolce's *Rime Scelte* published by Giolito in 1553 is largely derived from this volume.

### The Second Edition of Volume 1 (1b). 1546. Case Y 7184 .7452

The second edition of volume 1 is bound in the same volume. Its title page is identical except for the date 1546.

*Title page (each line centered):* RIME / DIVERSE DI / MOLTI ECCELLENTISS. / AUTTORI NUOVA- / MENTE RACCOLTE. / LIBRO PRIMO / ★★★★★★ / Con Gratia & Privilegio

Underneath the above and centered: the Giolito *marca* with the phoenix with spread wings reborn from the flames with initials G/G/F and motto on ribbons: DE LA / MIA MORTE / ETERNA / VITA IO / VIVO. / SEMPER EADEM.

Below crest: VINETIA APPRESSO GABRIEL / GIOLITO DI FERRARII / MDXLV [1546]

*Pages:* 400 (including *tavola*)

*Dedicatory letter:* By Lodovico Domenichi to the dedicatee Don Diego Hurtado di Mendozza is the same as the first edition.

*First poem (by Pietro Bembo), first line:* Same as in the first edition ("Se mai ti . . .").

*"Tavola di diversi auttori" for the second edition* has many of the same names, although a number of names from the first edition have been dropped in this edition; new male additions to this edition and all female authors are in bold type.

Andrea Navagero, Antonio Broccardo, Annibal Caro, **Alessandro Piccolhomini, Alessandro** Giovio, Annibal Thosco, **Antonio Mezzabarba**, Anton Francesco

Doni, **Alessandro Campesano,** Bartolmeo Ferrino, Baldessare Stampa, Battista Dalla Torre, Bartolomeo Carlo Piccolhomini, Baldessar Castiglione, Benedetto Varchi, Bartolomeo Gottifredi, Bernardin Tomitano, Bernardin Daniello, Bernardo Capello, Bernardo Tasso, **Camillo Besalio,** Collaltino di Collalto, Cornelio da Castello, Cosmo Ruccellai, Camillo Caula, Claudio Tolomei, Emanuel Grimaldi, Francesco Coppetta, Francesco Maria Molza, Francesco Capodilista, Fortunio Spira, Francesco Sansovino, **Francesca Baffa**, Francesco Coccio, Gio. Andrea Gesualdo, Giulio Camillo, Giovanni Mozzarello, Giovanni Guidiccione, Giovanni Cotta, Gio. Giorgio Dressino, Gio. Andrea dall'Anguillara, Girolamo Volpe, Gio. Antonio Volpe, **Girolamo Mentovato,** Girolamo Mutio (=Muzio), Girolamo Parabosco, Gandolfo Porrino, Gio. Battista Susio, Giuseppe Betussi, Giorgio Belmosto, Hippolito Cardinal de Medici, Hercole Bentivoglio, Iacopo Antonio Benalio, Iacopo Marmitta, Iacopo **Salvi** [was Sellaio in *Libro primo*] Bolognese, Lodovico Ariosto, Luigi Alamanni, **Laodamia Forteguerri,** Lorenzo de Medici, **Lancilotto Gnocco, Laura Terracina,** Luigi Raimondi, Lodovico Dolce, Lelio Capilupi, Lodovico Domenichi, Marco Cavallo, Marchese del Vasto, **Marchesa di Pescara** [listed as Vittoria Colonna in *Libro primo* first ed.], Monsignor dalla Casa [was Giovanni dalla Casa], **Nicolo Thiepolo,** Nicolo Amanio, Ottaviano Salvi, Pietro Bembo, Pietro Barignano, Paolo Canale, **Paolo Crivello,** Pietro Aretino, Pier' Antonio Chiocca, Scipio Costanzo, Thomaso Castellano, Triphon Gabriele, Vincenzo Martelli, Vincenzo Quirino, **Veronica Gambara**, Ugolino Martelli. [the end]

*The Third Edition of Volume 1 (1c). 1549. Case Y 7184 .7452.*

A third edition of the same *Rime diverse di molti ecc. autori* follows the second edition and is in the same modern binding.

*Title page:* The same. This edition is dated 1549. (Each line centered.) RIME / DIVERSE DI / MOLTI ECCELLENTISS. / AUTTORI NUOVA- / MENTE RACCOLTE. / LIBRO PRIMO

*Dedicatory letter:* By Domenichi and is the same.

*Pages:* 400 pages including *tavola degli autori.*

*First poem, first lines in the volume:* The same, by Pietro Bembo ("Se mai ti piacque . . .").

The *"tavola"* at the end of the third edition has most of the same names as in the first edition. Type is bolded for new authors, some of whom appeared in the second edition Women authors are also bolded:

Andrea Navagero, Antonio Brocardo [*sic*], Annibal Caro, **Alessandro Piccolhomini**, Alessandro Giovio, Annibal Thosco, **Antonio Mezzabarba**, Anton Francesco Doni, **Alessandro Campesano**, Bartolmeo Ferrino, Baldessare Stampa, Battista dalla Torre, Bartolomeo Carlo Piccolhomini, Baldessar Castiglione, Benedetto Varchi, Bartolomeo Gottifredi, Bernardin Tomitano, Bernardin Daniello, Bernardo Capello, Bernardo Tasso, Camillo Besalio, Collaltino di Collalto, Cornelio da Castello, Cosimo [*sic*] Ruscellai [*sic*], Camillo Caula, Claudio Tholomei [*sic*], Emanuel Grimaldi, Francesco Coppetta, Francesco Maria Molza, Francesco Capodilista, Fortunio Spira, Francesco Sansovino, **Francesca Baffa**, Francesco Coccio, Gio. Andrea Gesualdo, Giulio Camillo, Giovanni Mozzarello, Giovanni Guidiccione, Giovan Cotta, Giovan Giorgio Dressino, Gio. Andrea d'allanguilara [*sic*], Girolamo Volpe, Gio. Antonio Volpe, **Girolamo Mentovato**, Girolamo Mutio (=Muzio), Girolamo Parabosco, Gandolfo Porrino, Gio. Battista Susio, Giuseppe Betussi, Giorgio Belmosto, Hippolito Cardinale de [*sic*] Medici, Hercole Bentivoglio, **Iacopo Antonio Benalio**, Iacopo Marmitta, Iacopo Salvi Bolognese, Lodovico Ariosto, Luigi Alamanni, **Laodamia Forteguerri**, Lorenzo de Medici, **Lancilotto Gnocco, Laura Terracina**, Luigi Raimondi, Lodovico Dolce, Lelio Capilupi, Lodovico Domenichi, Marco Cavallo, Marchese del Vasto, **Marchesa di Pescara**, Monsignor dalla Casa, **Nicolo Thiepolo**, Nicolo Amanio, Ottaviano Salvi, Pietro Bembo, Pietro Barignano, Paolo Canale, **Paolo Crivello**, Pietro Aretino, Pier' Antonio Chiocca, Scipio Costanzo, Tomaso Castellano, Triphon Gabriele, Vincenzo Martelli, Vincenzo Quirino, **Veronica Gambara**, Ugolino Martelli. [the end]

## VOLUME 2: TWO EDITIONS

*First Edition of Volume 2 (2a). 1547. Case Y 7184 .7452*

*Title page:* RIME DI DI- / VERSI NOBILI HUO / MINI ET ECCELLENTI / POETI NELLA LINGUA / THOSCANA. / LIBRO SECONDO. / ★★★★★ / *Con Gratia & Privilegio* / Giolito logo De la / Mia Morte, etc. / Eagle logo / IN VINETIA APPRESSO GABRIEL / GIOLITO, etc.[1]

*Date:* MDXLVII. [1547]

*Dedicatory letter* set in italic type and written by Gabriel Giolito himself addressed to "AL MOLTO ILLUSTRE S. IL SIGNOR SIGISMONDO FANZINO DALLA TORRE." Letter begins: "Molto Illustre Signore. Si come le buone Pitture collocate in buon lume meglio riescono, et piu interamente dimostrono la eccellenza loro; cosi nel mettere io in publico questo secondo libro di rime di diversi rari et pellegrini intelletti sotto il chiaro nome di V.S. ho pensato non solo di meglio in tal modo mostrar al mondo la bonta delle cose in quello contenute, ma anchora di accrescere a esso libro lume & riputatione." (3½ pages)[2]

*Woodcut:* Two men wrestling or embracing.

*First author, first poem, first lines:* By Messer Claudio Tolmei: "De la belta, che Dio larga possiede, / Si vivo raggio in voi Donna riluce."

*Pages:* 184 pages but paginated only on the rectos. So 368 pages + tavola of 22 pages.

*Tavola:*

Anibal Caro, Antonio Francesco Rinieri, Arsiccio Intronato, Astemio Bevilacqua, Antonio Mezzabarba, Agostino Beatiano, Astratto, Aureolio Vergerio, Amanio, Andrea Conegrano, Alessandro Piccolhuomini, Bartholmeo Ferrino, Benedetto Varchi, Bernardino Tomitano, Bernardo Capello, Bartholomeo Gottifredi, Bernardo Tasso, Benalio, Baldessar Stampa, Claudio Tolmei, Cavalier Gandolfo, Cavalier Harmodio, Carlo Zancaruolo, Commendator Giovio, Camillo Besalio, Christophoro da Canale, Cornelio da Castello, Doni, Francesco Maria Molza, Fedel Fedele, Felice Figliucci, Fabio Benvoglienti, GirolamoVolpe, Gualtieri, Giacomo Cencio, Giovan Paolo Ferraro, Giovan Francesco Lottini, Giovan Francesco Fabri, Giovan Battista Pellegrini, Giovan Battista Susio, Giovanni Petreo, Giovan Giac. dal Pero., Giovan Francesco Torelli, **Guglia,** Giulio Camillo, Giovan Giustiniano, Giulio Avogaro, Giacomo Marmitta, Giovan Michel Bruto, Girolamo Parabosco, Hercole Bentivoglio, Incerti Autori, Lelio Capilupi, Lodovico Ariosto, Lodovico Domenichi, Luigi Alamanni, Lodovico Dolce, Mutio (=Muzio), Mons. di Rossi, Paolo Canale, Pietro Barignano, Paolo Crivello, Pietro Orsilago, Petronio Barbati da Foligno, Remigio Fiorentino, Sannazaro, Vincenzo Quirino, Ugolino Martelli, Unico Aretino, **Veronica Gambara.**

*Gli Errori Page.*

*Colophon:* Last two pages, eagle crowing at the sun and title bane and dare.

*Second Edition of Volume 2 (2b). 1548. Case Y 7184.7452.*

*Title page:* A little different as follows—DELLE RIME / DI DIVERSI NO- / BILI HUOMINI ET EC- / CELLENTI POETI NELLA LINGUA THOSCANA / NUOVAMENTE RISTAMPATE / LIBRO SECONDO / ★★★★ / CON PRIVILEGIO

Giolito logo, phoenix rising from the flames image followed by place and date: VINEGIA APPRESSO GABRIEL / GIOLITO DE FERRARI / MDXLVIII [1548]

**Dedicatory letter:** Exactly the same as the first edition of *Libro secondo*: Giolito to Sigismondo Fanzino dalla Torre. Exact same wording of letter.

**First author, first lines:** Exactly the same as the first edition of *Libro secondo*: Claudio Tolmei.

**Pages:** 177 pages but paginated only on recto so really 354 pages + *tavola*.

**Tavola:**

Anibal Caro, Antonio Francesco Rinieri, Arsiccio Intronato, Astemio Bevilacqua, Antonio Mezzabarba, **Anton Giacomo Corso,** Agostino Beatiano, Astratto, Aureolio Vergerio, Andrea Conegrano, Alessandro Piccolhuomini, Bartholmeo Ferrino, Benedetto Varchi, Bernardino Tomitano, Bernardo Capello, Bartholomeo Gottifredi, Bernardo Tasso, Benalio, Baldessar Stampa, Claudio Tolomei, Cavalier Gandolfo, Cavalier Harmodio, Carlo Zancaruolo, Commendator Giovio, Camillo Basalio, Cornelio da Castello, Doni, Francesco Maria Molza, Fedel Fedele, Felice Figliucci, Fabio Benvoglienti, GirolamoVolpe, Gualtieri, Giacomo Cencio, Giovan Paolo Ferraro, Giovan Francesco Lottini, Giovan Francesco Fabri, Giovan Battista Susio, Giovanni Petreo, Giovan Giac. dal Pero., Giovan Francesco Torelli, **Guglia,** Giulio Camillo, Giulio Avogaro, Giacomo Marmitta, Girolamo Parabosco, Hercole Bentivoglio, Incerti Autori, Lelio Capilupi, Lodovico Ariosto, Lodovico Domenichi, Luigi Alamanni, Lodovico Dolce, Mutio (=Muzio), Mons. d'i Rossi, Paolo Canale, Pietro Barignano, Paolo Crivello, Pietro Orsilago, Petronio Barbati da Foligno, Remigio Fiorentino, Sannazaro, Vincenzo Quirino, Ugolino Martelli, Unico Aretino, **Veronica Gambara.**

Colophon on last page with date MDXLVIII [1548]

## VOLUME 3: FIRST AND ONLY EDITION (3). 1550. CASE Y 7184 .7452

The binding labeled *Libro III* contains only this one edition.

Note that the mutilated title page, which has been glued onto a new blank page, is missing the title text above "DELLE RIME." According to Bongi, the title for this book was *Libro terzo delle rime, etc.* We can assume that the lost title text was "LIBRO TERZO."

**Title page:** DELLE RIME / DI DIVERSI NOBILIS- / SIMI ET ECCELLENTIS- / SIMI AUTORI / NUOVAMENTE RACCOLTE. / *Con Privilegio*

The publisher is not Giolito but it has a different motto and logo image: here a winged man holds a bowl and points into the basin of a fountain. Fountain scene is bordered by a frame of acanthus leaves with fruit and two cherubs, one on each side of the frame. The motto on the banner says: PRIA CHE / LE LABBRA BAGNERAI / LA FRONTE

Above the fountain woodcut is the publisher's logo: IN VINETIA AL SEGNO DEL / POZZO M. D. L. [1550]

*A dedicatory letter by Andrea Arrivabene is addressed:* "AL MOLTO MAGNI- / FICO ET ILL. SIGNORE / IL SIGNOR LUCA / GRIMALDO." The letter, which is set in italic type, begins: "Il gran desiderio, Magno & honorato Signore, ch'io ho sempre havuto di giovare in tutto quello che mi e' stato possibile a le persone studiose, & massimamente a quelle che si dilettano di questa nostra lingua, si come gia ne tempi passati m'indusse dare ale stampe di quelle cose, che allhora mi pervennero a le mani, et che secondo il mio piccolo giudicio di esser vedute & lette non mi parvero indegne" (dedicatory letter is 7½ pages long).

*First author, first lines, first poem:* Messer Francesco Maria Molza: "Poi che le stelle a miei desir nemiche, / Perche da vita a morte acerba io passi, / Fresache acque, verdi colli, e piagge a-priche, Restino almen convoi, che sempre amiche / Hebbi."

*Pages:* 217 pages, but really 434 since pages are paginated only on one side + the pages from the *tavola*, which is not numbered.

*Tavola:*

Agostino Beatiano, Andrea Navagero, Antonio Brocardo, Annibal Caro, Antonio Girardi, Anton Giacomo Corso, Baldessar Stampa, Baldassar Castiglione, Bartolomeo Gottifredi, Bernardo Capello, Bernardo Accolti l'unico Aretino, Bernardo Tasso, Bernardo Zane, Benedetto Varchi, Bernardo Tomitano, Camillo Besalio, Cavalier Gondolfo, Cesare Gallo, Claudio Tolomei, Cola Bruno, Domenico Michele, Domenico Veniero, Duca di Ferrandina, Felice Figliucci, Francesco Maria Molza, Francesco Conterno, Fortunio Spira, Gondolfo Porrino, Giorgio Gradenico, Georgio Merlo, Giovanni Guidiccione, Girolamo Querini, Giulio Camillo, Gio. Battista Susio, Giovanni Mozzarello, Gio. Battista Amaltheo, Girolamo Mentovato, Girolamo Fracastoro, Giacomo Marmitta, Gio. Paulo Amanio, Gio. Antonio Volpe, Gio. Giorgio Trissino, Giacomo Salvi, Girolamo Parabosco, Girolamo Britonio, Gio. Francesco Fabri, Hercole Strozza, Hercole Bentivoglio, Hippolito Capilupi, Incerti authori, Lelio Capilupi, Lenzo, Lodovico Ariosto, Lodovico Dolce, Marchese del Vasto, Malatesta Fiordano, Nicolo Delfino, Nicolo Tiepolo, Nicolo Leonico, Nicolo Amanio, Pietro Aretino, Pietro Orsilago, Rafael Gualtieri, Remigio Fioretntino , Rinaldo Corso, Scipion Castro, Trifon Gabriele, **Veronica Gambara, Vittoria Colonna**, Ugolino Martelli, Vicenzo Martelli.

2¼ pages of *errori.*

**Printer's colophon:** *In Vinetia appresso Bartholomeo Cesano m. d. l. [1550]*

## VOLUME 4: FIRST AND ONLY EDITION (4).
## 1551. CASE Y 7184 .7452

This is the fourth bound volume of *Rime di autori diversi.* This volume contains only one volume labeled *Libro quarto.*

**Title page:** LIBRO QUARTO / DELLE RIME / DI DIVERSI ECCEL- / LENTISS. AUTORI / NELLA LINGUA / VOLGARE / NUOVEMENTE RACCOLTE

**Woodcut logo:** Depicts inside an oval frame of leaves Hercules (?) slayinging the hydra (?). The slogan, written on the left and right sides of the frame, respectively, says: "Vinconsi Con Vertu / Gli Humani Effetti."

**The lettering of the bottom of the title page says:** In Bologna presso Anselmo Giacca-rello. M. D. L. I. [1551].

**Opposite page:** "Dr. Giac. Soranzo owned this book"; the date 1730 is written in his hand. [No "con privilegio" since it was published in Bologna?]

**Dedicatory letter:** Written by Hercol Bottrigaro to "ALLO ILL. ED HON. IL SIG. GIULIO GRIMANNI." It begins: "Lo animo & debito mio fu, & sara piu di giorno, in giorno, Sig. Giulio Honor. Di amare, et honorare, quanto per me si potra, coloro, che donatisi alla vertu, vanno quel poco di tempo, che dal Cielo in questa fragile vita n'e conceduto, hora in questa, hora in quella honoratamente dispensando; & questo ac-cioche morte, continovamente vivano." The dedicatory letter takes up 3½ pages and is set in italic type.

**The woodcut** that embellishes the capital letter at the beginning of the dedication depicts a servant serving a man dinner and his dog is there too.

**Pages:** Both sides of page paginated. This book has 328 pages

**Tavola:**

Andrea Navagero, Abraan Attieri, Antenor Torrella, Antonmaria Alberigo, Anto-nio Broccardo, Aiilio Noal, Alessandro Mellano, Annibal Caro, Accademici Fioren-tini, Bernardo Capello, Benedetto Varchi, Bernardin Baldini, Bernardin Daniello, Cavallier Gandolfo, Cavalier Armodio, Claudio Tolomei, Cavalier Renghieri, Cornelio Magnani, Conte di Monte, Cornelio Zenzani, Daniel Barbaro, Domenico

Michele, Domenico Veniero, Dante Aligeri, Emanuel Grimaldi, Francesco Maria Molza, Francesco Coppetta, Francesco Petrarca, Francesco Milanese, Francesco Strozza, **Faustina Vallentina**, Giacomo Marmitta, Giacomo Sellaio, Gianfrancesco Fabri, Giuseppe Baroncino, Giambattista Berrardo, Giangiorgio Dressino, Galleazzo Gonzaga, Goro da la Pieve, Giambattista Sancio, Giulio Falloppia, Gianfrancesco Bossello, Giampaolo Castellina, Gianandrea Caligari, Giovan Brevio, Gioan Vitale, Girolamo Giustiniano, Gianfrancesco Bellentani, Giuseppe Gualdo, **Giulia Aragona**, Giulio Camillo, Gianfrancesco Arivabene, Girolamo Mentovato, Horatio Diola, Hercole Strozza, Incerti Autori, Latin Iuvenale, Luigi Alamanni, **La Regina di Navara**, **Lucia Bertana**, Lorenzo d'Acquaria, Lazaro Fenucci, Lorenzo de Medici, Luigi Cassola, Lodovico Corsino, Lodovico Ariosto, Monsignor dalla Casa, Marco Cavallo, Maganza, Malatesta da Rimini, Marco Michele, Nicolo Franco, Nicolo Martelli, Nicolo Amanio, Nicolo Delfino, Offuscato Affumato, Odoardo Gualando, Pietro Bembo, Paul Costantino, Pietro Barugnano, Rinaldo Corso, Speron Sperone, Simon Castelvetro, **Sor Gieronima Castellana**, Tomaso Macchiavelli, Tron Bentio, **Veronica Gambara**, **Vittoria Colonna**, Urban Vigerio, **Verginia Salvi**.

*This volume has an afterword* addressed: "Allo Istesso Ill. Sig. Giulio Grimanni, Suo sig. Osservandissimo." The author this time is Horatio Diola. It begins: "Qual fosse, ill. Sig. Mio, il premio di un perfetto Amore dimandato Pitagora esser disse un'altro Amor perfetto. La onde sforzandosi tutto di il Mag. Sig . Cavallier Bottrigaro di fare, che ogni uno chiaramente conoschi, che io infinito Amore, che V.S. le porta, ha il meritevol premio."

*Colophon:* Again the oval frame with Hercules slaying the hydra; the text: IN BOLOGNA PRESSO ANSELMO GIACCARELLO. / M.D.L.I. [1551].

## VOLUME 5: THREE EDITIONS

Bongi (*Annali di Gabriel Giolito*, 1:356–57) notes that Giolito published the first edition of volume 5 in the early months of 1552. He titled this edition *Rime di diversi illustri signori napoletani e d'altri nobiliss. intelletti; nuovamente raccolte, et non piu stampate. Terzo Libro. Allo ill. S. Ferrante Carrafa. Libro Terzo*, not realizing that two other printers—Bartolomeo Cesano in Venice and Anselmo Giaccarello in Bologna—had already brought out their own volumes 3 and 4 for the series Giolito had inaugurated. Giolito's erroneously labeled *Libro terzo* has a dedicatory letter dated December 9, 1551, by Lodovico Dolce to Ferrante Carafa. The edition is dated 1552 on the title page. I refer to this first edition of volume 5 as (5) 1551–52.

To avoid confusion, Giolito put out a second edition of this work, with a new dedicatory letter by Dolce to Carrafa dated May 10, 1552, this time with the title *Libro quinto*. There followed in 1555 a third edition of *Libro quinto*, again edited by Dolce, with a third dedicatory letter to Carrafa. The Newberry Library has bound together the second and third editions of Giolito's volume 5. Their titles are *Rime di Diversi Il-lustri Signori Napoletani e d'altri nobiliss. ingegni. Nuovamente raccolte, et con nuova additione ristampate. Libro Quinto. Allo illus. S. Ferrante Carrafa*, dated 1552; and *Libro quinto delle rime di diversi illustri signori napoletani, e d'altri nobilissimi ingegni. Nuovamente raccolte, e con nova additione ristampate. Allo illus. S. Ferrante Carrafa*, dated 1555. I refer to the second and third editions of volume 5 as 5a and 5b, respectively.

It should be noted that the three editions of Giolito's *Libro Quinto* (5, 5a, and 5b) differ from one another significantly, in the following respects: each of their dedicatory letters is different, though all are addressed to Carrafa; the authors included or excluded vary from volume to volume; the title pages vary slightly for the three editions; only the first edition (5) contains an afterword addressed *Ai lettori*.

### The First Edition of Volume 5 (5). 1551–52. Case Y 7184.7452

*Title Page* (lines centered): ★★R I M E★★ / DI DIVERSI / ILLUSTRI SIGNORI / NA-POLETANI, / E D'ALTRI NOBILISS. / INTELLETTI; / NUOVAMENTE RACCOLTE, / ET NON PIU STAMPATE / T E R Z O L I B R O / ALLO ILL. S. FERRANTE CARRAFA / ★★★ / CON PRIVILEGIO

*Giolito crest and date:* IN VINEGIA APPRESSP GABRIEL / GIOLITO DE FERRARI / ET FRATELLI / MDLII [1552]

*Dedicatory letter:* From Lodovico Dolce to Ferrante Carrafa: "Allo illustre signore il signor Ferrante Carrafa, Non era conveniente, Illustre Signor mio, che dovendosi imprimere i presenti Sonetti & Canzoni, parto del l'ingegno di molti Illustri Signori et elevati spiriti di cotesta nobilissima citta; essi venissero in man de gli huomini senza il favore di alcun virtuoso & letterato Signore, che alla loro nobilta accrescesse ornamento," dated "VIIII di Decembre, M D L I." [December 9, 1551]

*Pages:* 413

*Opening poem one, opening line one:* Sonnetti del Signor Luigi Tansillo: "Amor m'impenna l'ale; & tanta in alto / Le spiega l'animoso mio pensero, / Che d'hora in hora sormontando, spero / A le porte del ciel far novo assalto."

*An afterword, "Ai lettori":* Volume 5 ends with an afterword addressed "Ai lettori." It is not signed or dated and is not contained in the two subsequent editions.

*Tavola:*

Antonio Epicuro, Angiolo di Costanzo, Annibal Caro, Alessandro Flaminio, Alfonso Mantegna, Ascanio Priscianese da Squillace, Anton Francesco Doni, Bernardino Rota, Bernardo Tasso, Bernardo Capello, Bartolomeo Ferrino, Cesare

Alberti, Conte Vinciguerra, Domenico Veniero, Ferrante Carrafa, Fabio Galeota, Giovambattista Agrippa, Giuliano Goselini, Giuseppe Leggiadro Galani, Giovambattista Baselli, Giovan Vincenzo Belprato, Giovan Maria dalla Valle, Girolamo Ruscelli, Giovambattista Amaltheo, Giacomo Mocenico, Giacomo Zane, Gandolfo, Hercole Bentivoglio, **Isabella di Morra**, Incerti, Luigi Tansillo, Landolfo Pighini, Lelio Capilupi, Minturno, Marchese dal Vasto, Merlo, Marco Vasio, Marino de Nordi, Nicolo Spadaro, Pietro Gradinico, Sperone Speroni, Signor, [ Pietro Aretino is listed as having two sonnets, beginning "E' Giulio, e Carlo" and "Iddio, c'hor calchi" but his name is crossed out with brown ink and his poems (323–24) are also crossed out with same brown ink], Pietro Percoto.

## Second Edition of Volume 5 (5a). 1552. Case Y 7184.7452

*Title page (lines centered):* ★★RIME★★ / DI DIVERSI / ILLUSTRI SIGNORI / NAPOLE-TANI / E D'ALTRI NOBILISS. / INGEGNI / NUOVAMENTE RACCOLTE / Et con nuova additione ristampate. / LIBRO QUINTO / ALLO ILLUS. S. FERRANTE CARRAFA / ★★★★★ / CON PRIVILEGIO

Underneath the above comes the Giolito phoenix, reborn with spread wings on flames crest and motto, and below that the usual: IN VINEGIA APPRESSO GABRIEL / GIOLITO DE FERRARI / ET FRATELLI / MDLII [1552]

*Pages:* 448 pages

*Dedicatory letter:* To Ferrante Carrafa. Dedication in italic type but slightly larger than the one used for the sonnets. Bongi (*Annali di Gabriel Giolito*) notes that the author of the dedicatory letter is Lodovico Dolce. This dedication letter also mentions Conte di Aversa, Angelo Costanzo, il Tansillo, and Fabeo Galeoto. This letter begins:

> Quantunque Illustre Signore, le presenti rime: tra le quali quelle di V.S. Illustre; come carbonchi tra molte lucidissime gemme risplendono; dovessero per la loro eccellenza se medesime distringuer dalle altre publicate da altri impressori: nondimeno, perche molti, leggendo il titolo di questo libro; che e il terzo di quegli, che furono per adietro mesi nel publico dalla accurata diligenza del nobile Gabriello Giolito; restavano sospesi, se esso fosse nuovo volume, o il medesimo gia dato in luce da altri, accio che cosi fatto dubbio sia da ciascuno levato, seguitando il numero de'libri pur da altri impressi, di nuovo il medesimo s'e ristampato.

*Opening poem, opening line:* The opening poem in the anthology is by Signor Marchese del Vasto; first line "Signor, che del tuo eccelso empireo cielo."

*Autori* in this volume (new names that were not in 5 are bolded; note also that two authors from 5 are dropped in 5a: Giacomo Mocenico and Giacomo Zane):

Antonio Epicuro, Angiolo di Costanzo, **Alessandro Piccolomini**, Annibal Caro, Alessandro Flaminio, Alfonso Mantegna, Ascanio Priscianese da Squillace, Anton Francesco Doni, Bernardo Rota, Bernardo Tasso, Bernardo Capello, Bartolomeo Ferrino, Cesare Alberti, Conte Vinciguerra, **Claudio Tolomei, Cardinal de Medici, Cavalier Vendramino**, Domenico Veniero, Ferrante Carrafa, Fabio Galeota, **Francesco Sauli**, Giovambattista Agrippa, Giuliano Goselini, Giuseppe Leggiadro Galani, **Giuseppe Giovio**, Giovambattista Baselli, **Gio. Fran. M. . Molza**, Giovan Vincenzo Belprato, Giovan Maria dalla Valle, Girolamo Ruscelli, Giovambattista Amaltheo, Gandolfo, **Giovambattiste d'Azzia**, Hercole Bentivoglio, **Isabella di Morra**, Incerti, Luigi Tansillo, **Luigi Alamanni**, Landolfo Pighini, Lelio Capilupi, **Lodovico Dolce**, Minturno, Marchese del Vasto, Merlo, Marco Vasio, Marino de Nordi, **Navagero**, Nicolo Spadaro, **Novato**, Pietro Mirteo, Pietro Gradinico, Sperone Speroni, Signor, Pietro Aretino, Pietro Percoto, **Caserta, Desiderio Cavalcabo.**

*Colophon:* Last page of the volume: at the end of the *tavola* of names is the Giolito colophon: the phoenix rising from the flames and crowing at the sun with banner that says "SEMPER EADEM" over a small winged ball with G/G/F on it.

This is followed by: IN VINEGIA APPRESSO GABRIEL / GIOLITO DE FERRARI / ET FRATELLI / MDLII [1552]

### *Third Edition of Volume 5 (5b). 1555. Case Y 7174 .7452*

In same binding as the second edition of volume 5.

*Title page:* LIBRO QUINTO / DELLE RIME DI DIVERSI ILLUSTRI / SIGNORI NAPO-LETANI, / E D'ALTRI NOBILISSIMI INGEGNI. / *NUOVAMENTE RACCOLTE, / e con nova additione ristampate.* / ALLO ILLUS. S. FERRANTE CARRAFA. / *CON PRIVILEGIO*

Also includes Giolito crest and motto and at page bottom the following with new date: IN VINEGIA APPRESSO GABRIEL / GIOLITO DE FERRARI / ET FRATELLI / MDLV [1555]

*Pages:* 512 pages

*Dedicatory letter:* To Ferrante Carrafa, this time by Lodovico Dolce. But the letter text, which is in a larger italic type than the one used for the sonnets, is new and begins:

> Con felice augurio si vede essere uscite fuori le presenti Rime, illustre Signore; per cioche nello spatio di tre anni sono state ristampate tre volte. Ilche e da stimare, che avenuto lor sia non solamente per eccellenza loro, ma ancora per essere dedicate a Vostra Signoria. La onde, si come a niun' altro personaggio piu convenivano, che a voi; cosi è degno, che esse portino nella fronte eternamente il

vostro nome: che eterne si puo con ragion giudicare, che le medesime habbiano ad essere. Laqual cosa io disidero sommamente: si perche gli studiosi godano di tempo in tempo questi degni frutti, come perche vivendo questi versi, viva al mondo insieme perpetuo testimonio della divition mia verso le vostre rare virtu; lequali meritano esser celebrate da ogni nobile intelletto.

*Opening poem, opening line:* Exactly the same as the second edition (5a) of *Libro quinto*: sonnet by Signor Marchese del Vasto, Alfonso d'Avalos. First line: "Signor, che del tuo eccelso empireo cielo."

*Tavola:* Only the editor's own name, Dolce, has been deleted from the list of authors in the *tavola* of the third edition. He has, however, added names (in bold) not in 5 and 5a:

**Alessandro Contarini**, Antonio Epicuro, Angiolo di Costanzo, Alessandro Piccolomini, Annibal Caro, Alessandro Flaminio, Alfonso Mantegna, Ascanio Priscianese da Squillace, Anton Francesco Doni, Bernardo Rota, Bernardo Tasso, Bernardo Capello, Bartolomeo Ferrino, **Corfini**, Cesare Alberti, Conte Vinciguerra, Claudio Tolomei, Cardinal de Medici, Cavalier Vendramino, Caserta, Domenico Veniero, Desiderio Cavalcabo, Ferrante Carrafa, Fabio Galeota, Francesco Sauli, Giovambattista Agrippa, Giuliano Gosolini, Giuseppe Leggiadro Galani, Giuseppe Giovio, Giovambattista Baselli, Gio. Fran. M. Molza, Giovan Vincenzo Belprato, **Guidiccione**, Giovan Maria dalla Valle, Girolamo Ruscelli, Giovambattista Amaltheo, Gandolfo, **Giorgio Gradinico**, Giovambattista d'Azzia, Hercole Bentivoglio, **Isabella di Morra**, Incerti, Luigi Tansillo, Luigi Alamanni, Landolfo Pighini, Lelio Capilupi, **Lelio Bonsi, Lucio Oradini,** Minturno, Marchese del Vasto, Merlo, **Michel'Angelo Vivaldi**, Navagero, Nicolo Spadaro, Novato, Pietro Mirteo, Pietro Gradinico, Sperone Speroni, Signor [illegible blur], Pietro Aretino, Pietro Percuoto, **Varchi.**

*Last page of the volume:* The Giolito colophon: a sun, the phoenix rising from the flames with the ribbon banner that says "SEMPER EADEM" over a small winged ball with G/G/F on it.

This is followed by: IN VINEGIA APPRESSO GABRIEL / GIOLITO DE FERRARI / ET FRATELLI / MDLV [1555]

## VOLUME 6: THE FIRST AND ONLY EDITION (6). 1553. CASE Y 7184 .7452

*Title page:* IL SESTO LIBRO / DELLE RIME / DI DIVERSI ECCEL- / LENTI AUTORI, / NUOVAMENTE RACCOLTE, ET / MANDATE IN LUCE. / CON UN DISCORSO DI GIROLAMO RUSCELLI. / AL MOLTO REVERENDO, ET / HONORATISS. MONSIGNOR / GIROLAMO ARTUSIO. / *Con Gratia, & Privilegio*[3]

Underneath and centered: Al Segno del Pozzo *impresa* and motto, CHI BEVERA DI QUESTA / ACQUA NON HAVERA / SETE IN ETERNO. Text surrounds a woodcut of a woman drawing water from a well where Jesus sits.

Below woodcut: IN VINEGIA AL SEGNO DEL POZZO. M. D. L I I I [1553]

*Pages:* 272 (paginated on one side only) = 554, counting both sides of each page, + 36, counting the following front and end matter: the dedicatory letter to Artusio, 6 pages; a verse *epithalamio* by Francesco Turchi, 5½ pages; a partial *tavola degli autori*, 16 pages, which follows the *epithalamio* and precedes the *rime*; plus the rest of the *tavola degli autori* at the end of the volume, 9 pages.

Bongi (*Annali di Gabriel Giolito*, 1:466) notes that this *Libro sesto* was edited by Girolamo Ruscelli. He also notes that *Libro settimo*, which came out in 1556, was edited by Giolito himself.

*Dedicatory letter:* Follows the title page; by Andrea Arrivabene addressed to Girolamo Artusio as follows: "*AL MOLTO RE- / verendo, et honoratissimo Signor-/re, il* S. GIROLAMO AR / TUSIO, *Preposto di Con / cordia, & Canoni- / co di Feltre.* / ANDREA ARRIVABENE." The type of the dedicatory letter is larger than that used for the *Rime* and is in italic type. It begins: "Io non credo, che alcuno sia per negare, che gli huomini di questa eta non restino con infinito obligo tenuti alla schiera a de'buoni scrittori delle passate, poscia, che in ciascheduna scienza, et intorno a ogni proposito scrivendo, & ragionando, lasciarono tanti, & si fatti tesori, di quanti si vede il mondo esser fatto comodo, & ricco" (6 pages). Di Venetia, Il di primo di Decembre. M. D. I I. [1552]

*Epitalamio:* By Francesco Turchi. It is in verse and follows the dedicatory letter. It begins "Sorgi chiraro, & lucente / Febo" and fills six pages.

The the first half of the *tavola* appears in the front of the volume, right after the *epitalamio*; the second half of the *tavola* is at the end of the volume:

### *"Tavola," first half:*

Abbate Dardano, Agostino Cazza, Angelo di Costanzo, Angelo Simonetti, Annibal Caro, Anton Francesco Rivieri, Anton Giacomo Corso, Antonio Guidone, Antonio Placidi da Siena, Antonio Terminio, Aurelio Gratia, Bartolomeo Zacco, Benalio, Benedetto Varchi, Bernardo Capello, Bernardo Zane, Bernardino Rota, Bernardino Tomitano, Buonaccorso Montemagno, Camillo Bracali, Camillo Pellegrino, Carlo Fiamma, Cavalier Vendramini, Cardinale Egidio, Carlo Zancaruolo, Cavalier Gandolfo, Cavalier Vendramini [for the second time], **Coletta Pasquale**, Conte Baldassar Castiglione, Conte Gio. Battista Brembato, Conte Pico dalla Mirandola, Conte Vinciguerra da Collalto, Cola Benedetto di Capua, Domenico Veniero, Dragonetto Bonifatio, Duca di Ferrandina, Ferrante Carrafa, Filippo Binaschi, Filippo Zaffiri, Fermo, Francesco Angelo Coccio, Francesco Davanzati,

Francesco Melchiori, Francesco Maria Molza, Francesco Reveslati, Francesco Abondio Castiglione, **Gaspara Stampa**, Giacomo Bonfadio, Giacomo Marmitta, Giacomo Mauro, Giacomo Mocenico, Giacomo Zane, Giovann'Andonio Carrafa, Gio. Antonio Olivierio, Giovanni Antonio Sacchetto, Giovanbattista d'Azzia, Giovian Battista Brebbia, Giovan Battista Trincheri, Gio. Bernardin de gli Oddi, Giovanni della Casa, Giovan Domenico Mazzarello, Giovanni Evangelista Armenini, Gio. Francesco Arrivabene, Giovanni Ferretti, Giovan Francesco Peranda, Giovan Giacomo Balbi.

*First author, first poem, first lines in volume:* Giovan Battista D'Azzia, Marchese della Terza: "Quando talhor 'l'alto pensier mi mena, / A mirar de'vostr'occhi il vivi Sole, / L'accesa voglia tosto trovar suole / Cosa, che'l suo sfrenato ardire affrena."

"*BRIEVE DISCORSO / DI GIROL. RUSCELLI, / INTORNO AD ALCUNE COSE IN UNIVERSALE, ET / IN PARTICOLARE DI / QUESTO LIBRO*": At the end of all the poetry is a short prose essay (4½ pages) by Girolamo Ruscelli addressed to the readers. This *discorso* is followed by a page of *errori*, and after this page the second half of the *tavola* follows.

*"Tavola," second half:*

Gioan Lucci Riccio, Giorgio Merlo, Gioseppe Ingleschi, Girolamo Altavilla, Girolamo Ferlito, Girolamo Fenaruolo, Girolamo Parabosco, Girolamo Ruscelli, Giuliano Gosellini, Giulio Camillo, Giulio Cesare Caracciolo, **Ippolito Mirtilla**, Lodovico Corsini, Lodovico Domenichi, Lorenzo de' Medici, Luigi Alamani, Luigi Contarino, Luca Contile, Luigi Tansillo, Marc' Antonio Passero, **Maria Spinola**, Marquese d'Aquaniva, Nicolo Amanio, Nicolo Eugenico, Nicolo Franco, Ottaviano dalla Ratta, Paolo Caggio, Petronio Barbato, Pietro Barbaro, Pietro Barignano, Pietro Gradenico, Pietro Novato, Pietro Spino, Rinaldo Corso, Sebastiano Erizzo, Scipione Ammirato, Silvestro Bottigella, Silvio, Pontevico, **Tullia d'Aragona, Veronica Gambara,** Vicenzo Quirino, **Virginia Salvi, Vittoria Colonna**, Zaccaria Pensabene.

*Colophon:* The last page of this volume the printer's colophon, IN VINEGIA / PER GIOVAN MA / RIA BONELLI / M. D. L. I. I. I. [1553]

## VOLUME 7: THE FIRST AND ONLY EDITION (7). 1556. CASE Y 7184. 7452.

*Title page:* R I M E / **DI DIVERSI SIGNORI** / NAPOLETANI. E D'ALTRI. / *NUOVAMENTE RACCOLTE* / ET IMPRESSE. / LIBRO SETTIMO / ★★★★ / *CON PRIVILEGIO*[4]

Underneath the above and centered: Giolito crest with phoenix rsing from the flames with spread wings, perched on a ball with initials G/G/F and motto on ribbons: DE LA / MIA MORTE / ETERNA / VITA I O / VIVO . / SEMPER EADEM.

Below crest: VINEGIA APPRESSO GABRIEL / GIOLITO DI FERRARI, E / FRATELLI. MDLVI. [1556]

*Pages:* 190 paginated on both sides of the pages + dedicatory letter + prefatory sonnets + "Tavola degli autori diversi" + "Tavola delle rime," first lines of each poem.

*Dedicatory letter:* By Lodovico Dolce, addressed to Signor Mattheo Montenero Genovese, in very large italic type after the address, which is in roman type: "AL MAGNIFICO E / VALOROSO SIGNOR / MATTHEO MONTENERO, / *GENTILHVOMO* / G E N O V E S E."[5]

*Printer's ornament*

*Dedicatory letter:* In larger font italics, addressedd to VALOROSO SIGNOR MATTHEO MONTENERO, begins: "Io fui sempre di questo parere, Nobilissimo, e dottissimo Signor Mattheo, come me ricorda in altra epistola haver detto; che la nostra eta nella eccellenza d'ogni virtu si possa ragionevolmente paragonare all'antica. E, per cominciar da quelle arti; lequali considerando la nobilta loro, e di quanto ornamento elle fossero al mondo, levo Aristotele dalle Mecanische, e giudico, che si dovessero nelle citta far publicamente insegnare a fanciulli nelle scuole." It is signed at the end: "Di Venetia il di primo di Genaro 1555. Servitor di V.S. Lodovico Dolce."

*Prefatory verses:* The *Rime* is prefaced by a ten-sonnet collection by S. Duca d'Adri Girolamo Acqua Viva, whose first poem begins: "Io dissi al mio sperar, ben guiderai."

*First author, first poem, first lines in the volume:* The first author is Ferrante Carafa. His first sonnet befgins: "Benche ognihor le tre gratie habbia d'interno / Guivabette leggiadre, & co'crin d'oro, / La Dea che regina e splende al terzo choro; / E"l partir mostra e' l ritornar del giorno."

Underneath the above and centered: Giolito crest with eagle with spread wings perched on a ball with initials G/G/F and motto on ribbons: DE LA / MIA MORTE / ETERNA / VITA I / VIVO. / SEMPER EADEM.

Below crest: VINETIA APPRESSO GABRIEL / GIOLITO DI FERRARII / MDXLV [1555]

*"Tavola" of first lines given in an appendix, but no "tavola" of authors:*

Ferrante Carafa, Mattheo Montenero, Giovam Maria Bernardino Belprato, Antonio Terminio, Bernardino Rota (*risp.* to Terminio), Luigi Tansillo (*risp.* to Terminio), Angelo Costanzo (*risp.* to Terminio, Conte di Mataluni, Marchese di Laino, **Madonna Chiara Matraini Gentildonna Lucchese** [68–150]; Lodovico Domenico, *risp.* to him by Chiara Matraini, Andrea Lori to Chiara Matraini; her *risp.* to him; C. Matraini to Lodovico Dolce; Matraini to Gio. Battista Giraldi, **Lucretia di Raimondo** to Giovambattita di Raimondo, unknown author to Isabetta Marchesana di Massa; Lodovico Dolce to Giovambattista Castaldo General di Cesare in Piemonte nella morte del Marchese di Marignano and *risponse* of same to Lodovico Dolce; Ferrante Carafa [again], including his *epitalamio* addressed to Antonio Carafa, Duca di Mondragone, on his marriage *con la Signora Duchessa Hippolita Gonzaga,* Luigi Sances; Giovanni Antonio Serone; Angelo Costanzo; Bernardino Rota [again], followed by a note indicating a *risp.* by the Duca d'Adri to Rota would follow "a la penultima fac."; Civilio Cesare Caracciolo; M. Antonio Terminio [again]; **Laura Terracina;** Marc'Antonio Plantedio Pirrone; **Isabella di Morra**; Di Sertorio Pepe, followed by a *risp.* by Ferrante Carafa to him, followed by a *risp.* by Bernardino Rota to Pepe, followed by Pepe's *risp.* to him, followed by F. Carafa's *risposta*; Antonio Epicuro; Ottaviano della Ratta Gentil'huomo Capuano, to and from **Caterina Pellegrina**, Fra Vincenzo d'Antignano di Capua; Horatio Marchese di Capua; **Laura Terracina** [again]; *risp.* of Signor Mattheo Montenero to her; Camillo Pellegrino; Lodovico Corfino Veronese to the Reverendiss. Cardinal di Mantova.

*"Tavola" of first lines only follows.*

*Giolito colophon, lettering only no woodcut:* MDLVI [1556]

## VOLUME 8: THE FIRST AND ONLY EDITION 8 (8). 1558. CASE Y 7184 .7452

*Title page:* I FIORI / DELLE RIME DE / POETI ILLUSTRI, NUOVA- / MENTE RACCOLTI ET / ORDINATI / DA / GIROLAMO RUSCELLI / Con alcune annotationi del medesimo, sopra luoghi, che / le ricercano perl'intendimento delle sentenze, / o per le regole & precetti della lin- / gua, & dell'ornamento / CON PRIVILEGII[6]
 New printer logo and woodcut with eagle in oval frame and Latin motto: In Venetia per Gio. Battista & Melchior Sessa Fratelli, 1558.

*Pages:* 605 pages (both sides paginated).

*Dedicatory letter:* By Girolamo Ruscelli to Signor Aurelio Porcelaga in roman type: "Quanto gli Scrittori Greci & Latini, degni pero sempre di eterna gloria, habbiano ne i lor lodatissimi componi, emti, coisi Eroici come Lirici, & come ancor Comici, lasciato luogo di maggior perfettione a i lor posteri" (21 pages).

*Prefatory letter to the readers:* By Girolamo Ruscelli: "L'onorato M. Melchior Sessa havendosi posto in animo di non perdonare" (4 pages).
 Note on the orthography by Ruscelli (9¼ pages).

*First poem, first lines:* By Angelo di Costanzo: "Alpestra, e dur selce, onde il focile / D'Amor, trasse quel foco, ove ha sett'anni."

*Tavola:*

> Angelo Costanzo, Annibal Caro, Anton Francesco Rainieri, Benedetto Varchi, Bernardino Rota, Bernardino Tomitano, Bernardo Capello, Bernardo Tasso, Cavalier Salvago, Claudio Tolomei, Domenico Veniero, Ferrante Carrafa, Francesco Molza, Giacomo Bonfadio, Giacomo Mocenigo, Giacomo Sannazaro, Gioseppe Leggiadro, Giovanni Andrea Ugoni, Giovanni Antonio Benalio, Giovan Batista Amlteo, Giovan Batista Brembato, Giovam Batista Giraldi, Giovanni Guidiccioni, Giovanni Mozzarello, Girolamo Mutio, Giulio Camillo, Giulio Cesare Caracciolo, Lodovico Domenichi, Lodovico Martelli, Luca Contile, Luigi Alamanni, Luigi Tansillo, Pietro Barignano, Pietro Bembo, Remigio Fiorentino, Sebastiano Errizo, **Veronica Gambara**, Vicenzo Martelli, **Vittoria Colonna**.

*End—printer's colophon:* In Venetia per Giovambvattista, & Marchio Sessa Fratelli. MDLVIII.

## VOLUME 9: THE FIRST AND ONLY EDITION (9). 1560. CASE Y 7184. 7452

The last volume in the series of *Rime diverse* is bound together with volume 8 (*Libro ottimo*).

*Title page:* R I M E / DI DIVERSI / *A U T O R I* / ECCELLENTISS. / LIBRO NONO.

*Printer's elaborate logo, woodcut frames the above title. Logo:* TENTANDA / VIA EST

*Bottom of title page:* IN CREMONA PER VINCENZO CONTI / M D L X [1560]

*Pages:* 334 pages

*Prefatory poem:* By Cesare Donelli Lollio (four sonnets, 2 pages)

*Dedicatory letter:* By Vincenzo Conti (the printer) addressed to Guglielmo Gonzaga, Duca di Mantova. Note that unlike the Giolito volumes, the dedicatory letter is set in roman not italic type (4 pages). It begins: Veramente vano, anzi di niun frutto farebbe stato il desiderio mio, & l'esser'io nato sotto l'ali dell'Illustriss. Casa Gonzaga;. . . ."

*First poem, first lines:* By Traiono Dordoni: "Puon ben Signor, perch'altri u'ami, e pregi / D'Augusto, e Scipio a mille glorie intese / Alzarsi al par ogn' hor le vostre imprese, Per reportarne sempiterni fregi."

*Tavola*:

Annibal Caro, Alessandro Malvagia, Antonio Caggi, Angelo Rinieri, Anton Maria Braccioforte, Alessandro Lionardi, Antonio Borghetti, Antonio Sottile, Alessandrro Bernoni, Baldessar Castiglioni, Bernardin Tomitano, Bernardo Capello, Cesar Malvagia, Cristoforo Serraglio, Carlo Riccio, Cristoforo Guazzoni, Cesar Manzi, Carlo Biolchi, Costanzo Landi, Cavalier Gualtieri, Cristoforo Codebo, Crisippo Selva, Cesar Donelli Lollio, Dario Tuccio, Federico Rossi, Filippo Forteguerra, Filomeno Quistro, Francesco Veggio, Francesco di Rivaldi, Gio. Francesco Fabri, Gio. Francesco Pusterla, Giuseppe Gallani, Gian Andrea Languillara, Guido San Giorgi, Giulio Rangone, Gio. Matteo Faitano, Galeazzo Nuvoloni. Girolamo Fiorelli, Gio. Battista Matelica, Gio. Agostino Arcelli, Gio. Antonio Taglietto, Giuseppe Betussi, Gio. Francesco Arrivabene, Giulio Nuvoloni, Giovanni Offredi, Girolamo Alessandrino, Gio. Battista Mantacheti, Honofrio Bonnontio, Luigi Gonzaga, Luca Contile, Luca Campagna, **Lucia Bertana**, Lodovico Domenichi, Lodovico Riva, Lodovico Tedesco, Luigi Cassola, **Laura Battiferro**, Lelio Capilupo, Monsignor della Casa [Giovanni], Maganza, Mutio, Nicolo Maggi, Nicolo Spadaro, Ottaviano Fodri, Paolo Golfi, Petronio Gessi, Pietro Mercante, Panfilo Ferri, Paolo Ferrari, Silvio Pontevico, Scipione Gonzaga, Traiano Dordoni, **Virginia Salvi**, Ubertino Sala.

*Last page—printer's colophon:* IN CREMONA / PER VINCENZO CONTI / M D L X

## VOLUME 10: ONE EDITION, TWO COPIES

Lodovico Domenichi's anthology of fifty-three women poets, the *Rime diverse d'alcune nobilissime, et virtuosissime donne*, published in 1559 by Vincenzo Budragho in Lucca. As far as I know, there are only two copies of the edition in the United States: one at the Beinecke Library at Yale University, which I own a microfilm of; and the other at the University of Iowa. We are especially indebted to Sid Huttner, curator of Special Collections at Iowa, who sent their copy to us at the Newberry Library on loan, and we treasured the opportunity to hold the physical book in our hands and examine it directly.

Domenichi's *Rime diverse delle donne* is not always considered as part of the Giolito poetry anthology set. Not to treat it as such is, I believe, a mistake. Domenichi, who was the originator of the Giolito series and the editor of all three editions of volume 1, designed his women's anthology so that it resembled the rest of the volumes in the set in every way possible. He may have intended his all-women anthology to be welcomed as the missing volume 8, as Bongi has noted. See my rather long note to volume 8 in appendix A on the question of how bibliographers have seen the 1559 Busdragho volume as fitting into the series.

The following description is applicable to both the Beinecke and the Iowa imprints.

**Title page (note that only Giolito's** Libro primo **in the series has the title** Rime diverse**):**
RIME / D I V E R S E / *D'ALCUNE NOBILISSI* / ME, ET VIRTUOSISSIME / DONNE, / *RACCOLTE PER M. LODO* / *VICO DOMENICHI, E IN-* / *TITOLATE AL SIGNOR* / GIONNOTO CASTIGLIO / NE GENTIL'HVOMO / MILANESE / ★★
Printer's crest, an oval frame with curly flourishes; inside the frame a winged dragon; no motto.
Bottom of title page: *In Lucca per Vincenzo Busdragho.* / M D L I X. [1559]

**Pages:** 238 pages paginated on both sides of each sheet.

**Dedicatory letter:** By Lodovico Domenichi addressed to Gionnoto Castiglione "MOLTO MAGNIFICO, ET NOBILISSIMO SIGNOR MIO." The type of the dedicatory letter is roman (whereas Giolito's dedicatory letters are always in italics). It begins: "Sono gia molti anni passati, ch'essendo Io con l'animo, & con l'opere tutto volto a celebrare quanto per mesi poteva allhora, la nobilta, &eccellentia delle Donne; laqual cosa Io ridussi poi in un giusto volume; si come il pensier mi guidava, mi posi in un medesimo tenpo raunare cio che mi pareva potere procurar loro gloria, e honore. Cosi con laiuto d'alcuni amorevolimiei, & grande mente affettionati al valor Donnesco, raccolsi da piu parti assai ragioneuole quantita di rime composte da Donne." Domenichi also pays tribute in this letter to other women who appear to be patrons of the volume: **Signora Lavinia Sanvitale**, other Signore in Pavia such as **Signora Contessa Paola di Beccaria, Signore Livia** her daughter, and **Signora Ottavia Baiarda**. Also the honorable subject of this anthology, **Signora Lucia Sauli**, Also **Signora Lucia Bertana**. (3 pages)
Note the *praeteritio* in this dedicatory letter.

**A second dedicatory letter, this one in italic type:** By the publisher Vincenzo Busdragho addressed to "AL NOBILE E VORTUOSO M. GE / RARDO SPADA GENTILHVO/MO LUCCHESE, / E SVO OSSER- / VANDISSIMO." The complete letter text follows:

Il nuovo volume, de le rime di diverse eccellenti Donne, da M. Lodovico Domenichi raccolte, quale hora per le miei stampe viene in luce (il mio M. Gherardo Magnifico) si per diverse honorate cagioni, come ancora per esser voi sempre stato sollecito & invitto defensore de l'eccellenza de la donne, a voi piu d'ogn'altro si dovea, cosi a me, e parso ragionevole farvene dono, anzi per meglio dire. Effetturare parte di quanto la nobilta de l'animo vostro da perse stessa gia gran tempo fa s'havea meritato: & insiememente inanimare gl' altri che gia sono incaminati a le virtuose attioni, a piu caldamente accendersi, di que desiderii che fanno altrui aquistare la perpetuita del nome: aquali ancora non manchera occasione far chiaro con l'opere, l'affetto del cuor mio: voi adonque, come da me non possiate riciever maggior ricompensa de meriti vostri e del molto che vi debbo, accetterete

il poco che col cuore vi offero, e bacio le mani. Di Lucca il di primo Giugno del
MDLIX.

Affettionatissimo, Vincenzo Busdragho

Errata page follows on the verso, page 8.

*First poem, first author, first lines of volume:* Mad. Aurelia Petrucci, Sanese: "Dove sta
il tuo valor, Patria mia cara; / Poiche il giogo servil, misera, scordi; / Et solo nutri in
Te pensier discordi, / Prodiga del tuo mal, del bene avara?"

*"Tavola de nomi delle donne descritte in questo libro"* (names followed by page numbers):

Aurelia Petrucci, 9 (two sonnets, no addressees)

Anna Golfarina, 54 (one poem)

Athalanta Sanese, 77 (one sonnet)

Alda Torella Lunata, 129, 236–37 (one sonnet addresses Anton Francesco Rinieri,
  another sonnet and two short poems have no addressees)

Berenice G., 13–16 (one canzone)

Cassandra Petrucci, 23 (nine sonnets, one canzone, one short poem, two sonnets
  on the death of Aurelia Petrucci)

Clarice de Medici and de gli StrozziFiorentina, 31 (one poem)

Claudia dalla Rovere, Signora di Vinovo di Piemonte, 32 (two sonnets, one addressed to Mons. Marescial di Brisacho)

Candida Gattesca de gli Alluminati, Pistolese, 34 (one sonnet)

Cornelia Brunozzi de' Villani Pistolese, 38–39 (three sonnets, two of them addressed to Maria Martelli de' Panciatichi)

Catherina Pellegrina, 41 (one sonnet responding to sonnet by Ottaviano della
  Ratta to her)

Diamante Dolfi, 42–43 (two sonnets, one with no adressee, one to Signora Livia
  Pia Poeta)

Ermellina Arringhieri de Cerretani Sanese, 33 (one poem)

Egeria da Canossa, 46–50 (one long canzone, one sonnet to Signora Lucia Bertana)

Fausta Tacita, 50–53 (three sonnets; one long canzone)

Fiorenza G. Piemontese, 35–36 (one canzone addressed to S. Anton Galeazzo Bentivoglio)

Francesca [da] B[aldi] Sanese, 234 (one sonnet with no address, one sonnet addressed to Girolamo Popponi, a sonnet by Popponi to Francesca B.)

Giulia Braccali de Ricciardi Pistolese, 37 (two sonnets, one addressed to Mad.
  Cornelia Villani)

Gentile Dotta, 42 (one sonnet)

Gaspara Stampa 56–58 (five sonnets, one addressed to M. Giovan Iacopo
  Bonetti)

Suor Girolama Castellana, 61–68 (nine sonnets: one addressed to Leonora da Este, one addressed to Antonio Gaggi, seven sonnets with no addressee; and one long canzone)

Gostanza D'Avala, Duchessa d'Amalfi, 69–71 (five sonnets)

Honorata Pecci Sanese, 72 (two sonnets)

Hortensia [or Ortensia] Scarpi, 75–76 (two different sonnets, each responding to Pia Bichi's sonnet)

Hippolita Mirtilla, 78–85 (six sonnets, four of these addressed to Gaspara Stampa, and two canzoni)

Isabella Riaria de Pepoli, Contessa de Riarii, 55 (one sonnet)

Isabella di Morra, 86–99 (ten sonnets, three long canzoni)

Livia Torniella Bonromea, 12 and 229 (ten sonnets and a response to her: two to Domenichi, Domenichi's sonnet to her, five sonnets to Giuseppe Betussi, two to Leonora Falletta, one to Agostino Rocchetta)

Laudamia da Sangallo, 17–18 (two sonnets and a response to her: one sonnet to Domenichi, one from him to her, one to Gio. Iacopo Bonetti)

Lucretia Figliucci, 19–22 (six sonnets and a response: one to Cassandra Petrucci; a response from Cassandra to Lucretia, and five additional sonnets by Lucretia)

Leonora Falletta da San Giorgio, 73, 218–28 (twenty-two sonnets in all by Fallett: one to Domenichi, followed by a response from him, one with no addressee, two sonnets to Livia Torniella Bonromea, a a response to M. Agostino Rocchetta, sixteen more sonnets without addressee by Falletta, and one last sonnet addresed to Giuseppe Betussi)

Lucretia di Raimondo, 100–101 (one poem in octaves)

Laudomia Forteguerri, 102–4 (six sonnets: one without an addressee, four addressed to Madama Margherita d'Austria, another addressed to S. Alda Torella Lunata)

Lisabetta da Cepperello Fiorentina, 105–8 (four sonnets: one addressed to Duca Alessandro de'Medici and the other three with no addressee; one long canzone with no addressee)

Livia Poeta, 109 (four sonnets, one of these addresses Signor Gio. Galeazzo Rosci)

Lucia Bertana, 111–18 (a suite of sixteen sonnets: one sonnet to Lodovico Domenichi and a response form him to her, one jointly addressed to Vittoria Colonna and Veronica Gambara, one to Signora Silvia Contessa di Scandiano, one to Gherardo Spini with a response from him, two more addressed to Veronica Gambara, another to Mad. Gostanza Castalda, another to Francesco Castaldo, another to Don Gabrielo Franceschi with a response from him, another to Gherardo Spini with a response from him, another to Domenichi with a response from him)

Maddalena Pallavicina de Marchesi di Ceva, 31 (one sonnet to her father, Giulio Cesare)

Maria Langosca Solera, Pavese, 33 (one sonnet addressed to M. Agostino Rocchetta)

Maria Martelli de Panciatichi Fiorentina, 39–40 (two sonnets addressed to Madama Cornelia Villani)

Maria da Sangallo, 59–60 (three sonnets: one to Signora Bianca Rangona Contessa di Bagno, one to Donna Silvia di Somma, Contessa di Bagno, one to Signora Lavinia Colonna)

Maria Spinola, 119–20 (three sonnets with no addressees)

Narda N. Fiorentina, 121–27 (six poems: one sonnet addressed to Giovan Iacopo Bonetti, three to Damon, two canzoni, and one short poem)

Olimpia Malipiera, 130–48 (thirty-four poems: thirty-two sonnets, including responses from Lodovico Domenichi, and two additional poems)

Mad. P. S. M., 44–45 (four sonnets)

Pia Bichi, 75 (one sonnet)

Reina di Navarra, 11 (two sonnets: one to God, one to the Marchesa di Pescara, Vittoria Colonna)

Silvia di Somma, Contessa di Bagno, 10 (two sonnets: one with no addressee, one addressed to Signora Lavinia Colonna)

Selvaggia Braccali de Bracciolini, 40 (one sonnet addressed to Maria Martelli de Panciatichi)

Silvia Marchesa de Piccolomini, 76 (one sonnet)

Virginia Gemma de Zuccheri da Orvieto, 128 (two sonnets, no addressees)

Veronica Gambara da Correggio, 149–62 (twenty-four poems: two sonnets to Vittoria Colonna, each with a response, eighteen other sonnets, and two additional poems)

Virginia Martini de Salvi Sanese (also known as Virginia Salvi), 162 (sonnets and canzoni addressed to Cardinal Farnese, Marguerite de Navarre, the Count Annibal d' Elci, the members of the Accademia Fiorentina, Cavalier Saracini, Deserto Intronato, Lattantio Benucci, Cardinal Trivultio, Cardinal Vitelli, the kind of France, Archbishop Verallo, the Carndinal of Nabples, Vittoria Colonna Marchese di Pescara [206–17]—twenty-four sonnets)[7]

The Iowa imprint of Domenichi's *Rime d'alcune diverse nobilissime, et virtuosissime donne* (Lucca: Busdragho, 1559) resembles the Beinecke edition in every way, except that it has some water damage and its page order has been disturbed. In the Iowa copy the page order is: 226, 229, 230, 231, 232, 227, 228, 237, *tavola*, 233, 234, 235, 236, *tavola*, colophon.[8]

# Chronology of Events

1492 Birth of Vittoria Colonna at Marino.

1500 Birth of Charles V in Ghent, grandson of Holy Roman Emperor Maximilian I.

1502 Birth, on Ischia, of Giovanna d'Aragona and of Alfonso d'Avalos, Marchese del Vasto.

1503 Birth of Maria d'Aragona on the island of Ischia. The French fleet lays siege to the castle of Ischia. Costanza d'Avalos, chatelaine of the castle, drives them off.

1508 Future literary leader and bishop, Alessandro Piccolomini (descendent of Pope Pius II) born in Siena on June 13.

1509 Marriage of Vittoria Colonna and Ferrante Francesco d'Avalos on Ischia.

1510–36 Ischia salon led first by Costanza d'Avalos and Vittoria Colonna and, later, Maria d'Aragona and Giovanna d'Aragona Colonna; participating poets: Jacopo Sannazaro, Galeazzo di Tarsia, Girolamo Britonio, Jacopo Campanile, Giano Anisio, Cosimo Anisio, Paolo Giovio, Marcantonio Flaminio, Minturno, Bernardo Tasso, Luigi Tansillo, Angelo di Costanzo, Bernardino Rota.

1513 Birth of Giulia Gonzaga at Gazzuola, near Mantua.

1515 Birth of the poet Laudomia Forteguerri in Siena.

1517 Pope Clement VII (Giulio de' Medici) succeeds Leo X as pope.

Luther sends his ninety-five theses to Archbishop Albrecht von Brandenburg questioning the selling of indulgences and challenges the authority of the pope in Germany.

1519 Nineteen-year-old Charles V unanimously elected Holy Roman Emperor.

1520 October. Coronation of Charles V as Holy Roman Emperor at Aix-la-Chappelle.

1521 Diet of Worms. Emperor Charles V demands that Martin Luther disavow his writings against the papacy. Luther refuses, is excommunicated, and is declared an outlaw.

Brother of Vittoria Colonna, Ascanio Colonna, marries Giovanna Aragona in Rome.

1525 An anthology of Luther's writings translated into Latin and published in Venice by Zoppino; six more editions published in the ensuing thirty years.

February 24. Battle of Pavia, most decisive battle in the Valois wars between Francis I, king of France, and the Italian cities under the emperor Charles V. The French lost perhaps twelve thousand men; imperial losses numbered in the hundreds; Francis I is taken prisoner.

Vittoria's husband Ferrante Francesco d'Avalos dies after Battle of Pavia of tuberculosis.

1526 Marriage of Giulia Gonzaga and Vespasiano Colonna, Duke of Traetto and Count of Fondi, at Paliano.

1527 Sack of Rome by Charles V's troops. Pope Clement VII is taken prisoner.

1528 Giulia Gonzaga's husband Vespasiano Colonna dies in his camp of old war wounds.

The Genovese mercenaries, hired by France sack Naples. They fire and sink Charles's fleet in the bay of Naples. Ascanio Colonna and Alfonso d'Avalos survive the bloody sea battle.

1529–34 January 19, 1529, Giulia Gonzaga's opens her salon at Fondi. Poets and reform thinkers gather. Among regular attendees are Vittoria Colonna, Bernardo Tasso, Marcantonio Flaminio, Duke Ferrante Sanseverino di Salerno, Cardinal Ippolito de'Medici, Gandolfo Porrino (then her secretary), Annibal Caro, Claudio Tolomei, Luigi Tansillo, Camillo Capilupi, Francesco Maria Molza, Isabella Bresegna, the d'Aragona sisters.

1530 Peace of Cambrais signed. Coronation repeated at Bologna: Clement VII officially recognizes Charles V as Holy Roman Emperor and king of Naples, Sicily, Sardinia, Spain. Charles V places Siena under his rule; installs Spanish troops and a Spanish governor in Siena.

Peace of Augsburg signed; German princes declare Protestant faith.

Antonio Brucioli's vernacular translation of the Bible with commentaries is printed in Venice.

1531 Juan de Valdés enters the court of Pope Clement VII.

1532 Death of Luigi Gonzaga, brother of Giulia Gonzaga and husband of her stepdaughter Isabella Colonna; Vittoria Colonna is first introduced to the teachings of Valdés when she is in Rome that year.

1533 Vittoria Colonna and Caterina Cibo join forces to save the Capuchin Order from expulsion from the Church. Pope Clement VII (Cibo's uncle) is persuaded to keep the order and makes Ochino its general.

1533–34 Vittoria Colonna presides over her salon at the Convent of San Silvestro in Capite in Rome. Caterina Cibo, Ochino, Valdés, Cardinal Reginald Pole, and Cardinal Giovanni Morone attend. Colonna is already a literary celebrity: Ariosto cites her in the *Orlando furioso*, book 37; the poet Bernardo Tasso eulogizes her; Castiglione leaves his *Il cortegiano* for her to critique; Bembo and Giovio attend her.

1534 First edition of Luther's translation of the Bible.

August 9. The Turks led by the corsair and admiral, Barbarossa (Khair-ed-Din), sack and burn Fondi. Giulia Gonzaga flees before they arrive. Girolamo Muzio publishes the *La ninfa fuggiva* fictionalizing Gonzaga's escape from Barbarossa's clutches.

September 25. Pope Clement VII dies at the age of fifty-six. Paul III (Alessandro Farnese) is elected pope.

1535 August 10. Cardinal Ippolito de' Medici dies at the age of twenty-four, possibly of poison, at his estate at Itri. Giulia Gonzaga is at his side when he succumbs. He had vowed to give up his cardinalate to marry Gonzaga.

Valdés meets Giulia Gonzaga in Naples.

November 25. Charles V's triumphal entrance into Naples, flanked by his two captains, Alfonso d'Avalos and Ascanio Colonna. They return as the victors in the battle of Tunis, where Charles and his captains vanquished eighty thousand Turkish troops. During the festivities and for the next six months, Charles stays at the Castel Novo in Naples. A series of balls and games are held to celebrate the victors. Charles remains at the Naples court until March 22, 1536.

Giovanna d'Aragona leaves her husband, Ascanio Colonna, taking her six children with her; she takes up residence at the d'Avalos *castello* on Ischia.

Valdés leaves Rome and comes to Naples in the service of Charles V. Abandoning Charles's service, Valdés acquires a villa on the Riviera di Chiaia and gathers disciples around him, Giulia Gonzaga among them. Naples becomes the epicenter of the religious reform movement in Italy, with Giulia Gonzaga and Valdés collaborating as leaders. Friendships tighten among the Colonna-d'Avalos women and the reform thinkers.

1535–36 Giovanna d'Aragona stays with Costanza d'Avalos in the Castel dell'Ovo in Naples, and together they attend Valdés's lectures at his house in Chiaia, Giulia's salon at the convent of San Francesco delle Monache in Naples, and Ochino's Lenten sermons at San Giovanni Maggiore in Naples.

1536 Giulia Gonzaga gets papal authorization to move into the convent of San Francesco delle Monache, situated in the center of Naples. As financier of the community, she resides in the convent and receives numerous visitors. Attendees of her convent salon include poets, the local elite, and disciples of Valdés, among whom are Isabella Bresegna, Costanza d'Avalos, Maria d'Aragona, Giovanna d'Aragona, Clarissa Orsini, Caterina Cibo, Ferrante Sanseverino, Pietro Carnesecchi, Marcantonio Flaminio, Bernardino Ochino, Pietro Martire Vermigli, Marcantonio Flaminio, Marco Antonio Magno, Bernardo Tasso, Annibal Caro, Benedetto Varchi, Gondolfo Porrino.

Calvin publishes first edition of his *Institutes of the Christian Religion*.

1537 Vittoria Colonna follows Ochino north on his speaking tour to Ferrara. She stays at the Este palace and takes part in the religious reform circle initiated by Duchess Renée de France.

The Sienese writer Marcantonio Piccolomini's reform *Dialogo* circulates but is never published. The dialogue features three Sienese women interlocutors: Laudomia Forteguerri, Girolama Carli de'Piccolomini, wife of the allegedly heretical writer Bartolomeo Carli de'Piccolomini, and Frasia Marzi.

Pope Paul III (Alessandro Farnese) imposes a salt tax on his vassals in the papal states. Ascanio Colonna, Vittoria Colonna's brother, and the vassals meet and move to boycott the tax.

1538 Vittoria Colonna's *Rime* is published by Antonio Viotti in Parma marking the first solo edition of a woman's collected poetry.

In January, Charles V names Alfonso d'Avalos del Vasto governor of Milan. Maria d'Aragona, now the mother of seven children, inaugurates her court in Milan. While she remains, her correspondence with such Naples Valdesians as Ochino and Carnesecchi, in Milan she gathers around her the writers Bernardo Capello, Girolamo Muzio, Niccolò Franco, Pietro Aretino, Bernardino Spina, Paolo Giovio, and Luca Contile. She commissions work from Titian.

1540 February. The people of Perugia protest the pope's new salt tax. They demonstrate before the papal envoy, Cardinal Jacobazzi, but with no success. In May, Pope Paul III marshals an army of ten thousand Spanish and Italian mercenaries. On July 4 the pope's troops enter Perugia and confiscate its weapons and bullion.

Ochino publishes his reform tract *Dialogi sette* "con privilegio" with Zoppino in Venice.

1540–46 Antonio Brucioli's vernacular translation of the Bible with commentaries printed many times and read at the courts and the homes of merchants and laborers in Venice, Florence, Urbino, Mantua, and Ferrara.

1541   Gabriel Giolito (fl. 1538–78) opens, in Venice, what will be the most commercially successful publishing business in Italy. The firm's first publication under the name Gabriel Giolito is Nicolò Franco's *Dialoghi piacevoli*. Under Giolito's direction, the press publishes mostly secular poetry, drama, history, and fiction.

February. The Salt War begins. Ascanio Colonna and his vassals refuse to pay Pope Paul III's new salt tax. Colonna obstructs the passage of travelers going into Rome. He makes raids on the papal cattle at Ostia. The pope demands that Colonna appear before him; he refuses and withdraws to his fortress at Genazzano with two thousand men; he soon moves his men to Paliano.

March 6–8. Salt War continues. Ascanio's sister, the poet Vittoria Colonna, intervenes from Rome to try to head off an armed conflict. Sends letters to Ascanio and to Charles's ambassadors.

March 15. The pope's army arrives at the gates of Paliano. Ascanio's wife Giovanna d'Aragona Colonna leaves Rome and takes refuge at Ischia with her children. Vittoria Colonna, acting as her brother's secretary of state, guides his actions from Rome. In mid-March she abandons her home at the convent of San Silvestro in Rome and flees to safety in Orvieto, where she takes up residence in the monastery of San Paolo d'Orvieto.

The Salt War continues through April and into May. On April 8, Giovanna writes a clemency appeal herself to the pope begging him to take pity on the poor people living on their lands. Vittoria Colonna sends the pope a pair of sonnets telling him to end the war.

On May 9, Ascanio's troops surrender at Paliano and the war ends. The pope's troops raze Ascanio's fortifications at Marino, Rocca di Papa, and finally, in January 1543, at Paliano.

Early in August, Valdés dies. His will bequeaths all his papers and writings to Giulia Gonzaga granting her the right to edit and publish or not to publish his works, as she wishes.

1541–44   Cardinal Reginald Pole, Vittoria Colonna, and others establish a circle of reform thinkers at Viterbo. The circle includes Flaminio and Carnesecchi. Gonzaga takes part by letter.

1541   Alessandro Piccolomini gives a public lecture on a sonnet by Laudomia Forteguerri, which comes out in a printed edition later that year: *Lettura del Alessandro Piccolomini Infiammato fatta nelli Accademia degli Infiammati* (Bologna: Bartolomeo Bonardo & Marc'Antonio da Carpi, 1541). It is the first work of literary criticism of a woman's poetry ever published.

1542   July 4. Pope Paul III (Alessandro Farnese) inaugurates the Inquisition and the Counter-Reformation with his bull *Licet ab initio*.

Alessandro Piccolomini dedicates his major work *De la Institutione di tutta la vita de l'huomo nato nobile* (On the conduct of a nobleman's life [Venice: Scoto, 1542]) to the poet Laudomia Forteguerri.

1543 Giulia Gonzaga negotiates the publication of the first edition of the anonymous *Trattato utilissimo del beneficio di Giesu Cristo crocifisso* with the Venetian publisher Bernardino de' Bindoni. The *Beneficio* (as the book is known) is an immediate success. Forty thousand copies of the book are sold in the first six years after its publication, despite the Church's banning of the work.

1543–49 Ascanio remains banished from his lands until the death of Paul III.

1544 Summer. Vittoria Colonna leaves Viterbo and returns to Rome where she moves to the Convent Sant' Anna de' Funari.

Giuseppe Betussi's publishes his dialogue *Raverta* (Venice: Giolito, 1544), featuring the celebrated poet and courtesan Francesca Baffo in conversation with the nobleman Ottaviano Raverta and Lodovico Domenichi.

The battle of Ceresole Alba. Charles's governor of Milan, Alfonso d'Avalos del Vasto, loses twelve thousand men to the French; the next year Charles withdraws his support from d'Avalos.

1545 The Council of Trent opens (convened by Pope Paul III) to respond to demands for reform and to reconsider questions of doctrine raised by Luther and the Protestant Reformation in northern Europe. It will meet in three sessions: December 1545–January 1548 in Bologna; May 1551–April 1552 at Trent; January 1562–December 1563 at Trent. Its members consisted primarily of bishops and cardinals. The continuation of the Inquisition (inaugurated in 1542) and the promulgation of Indexes of Prohibited Books grew out of its sessions and its recommendations.

The *Rime diverse*, the first edition of the first volume of Giolito poetry anthology series is published in Venice, edited by Lodovico Domenichi; women poets Francesca Baffo, Vittoria Colonna, and Veronica Gambara are included.

Giulia Gonzaga negotiates the publication of Valdés's *Alfabeto cristiano* with the printer Nicolò Bacarini in Venice. Marco Antonio Magno, Giulia's secretary, translated it from the Spanish into Italian.

1546 The second edition of the Giolito poetry anthologies, *Rime diverse*, book 1, is published in Venice, edited again by Domenichi, with women poets Baffa, Colonna, Gambara, and two new additions: Laudomia Forteguerri and Laura Terracina.

Death of Martin Luther.

On March 31, Alfonso d'Avalos del Vasto dies at Vigevano. Charles names Ferrante Gonzaga as governor of Milan. Maria d'Aragona moves her court out of the ducal palace to Pavia where she inaugurates her new salon and opens the academy Chiave d'Oro.

The poet Isabella di Morra is murdered in Favale in the kingdom of Naples by her brothers. Her complete oeuvre will be published five times in the next thirteen years: in the four Giolito poetry anthology series edited by Dolce (1551–52, 1552, 1555, 1556) and in Domenichi's anthology of fifty-three women produced by the printer Busdragho in Lucca in 1559.

1546–49 Betussi in the service of Gaspara Stampa's lover Collalto di Collaltino.

1547 The widow Maria d'Aragona d'Avalos and her sister Giovanna d'Aragona Colonna return to Ischia and Naples with their literary protégées Contile and Muzio. The Sereni and Ardenti academies in Naples unite under Maria d'Aragona's patronage.

On 25 February, Vittoria Colonna dies in Rome with Flaminio and Pole at her bedside.

The first edition of volume 2 of the Giolito poetry anthology series, *Rime di diversi nobili huomini*, book 2, comes out; no editor is named and Giolito himself writes the dedicatory letter. The women poets Giulia (no last name) and Veronica Gambara are included.

On May 13, the popular leader Cesare Mormillo spurs the people to a rebellion; the nobility supports the revolt. Widespread rioting and bombardment of the city ensues. Charles's viceroy, Pedro di Toledo, closes the academies and enforces a Spanish-style Inquisition. The d'Aragona sisters and salon withdraw to Ischia. Her courtiers, Contile and Muzio, return to Milan to serve Governor Ferrante Gonzaga and they join the academy of the Fenici.

Tullia d'Aragona publishes both *Rime* and *Dialogo* with Giolito in Venice.

1548 On July 12, three bales of heretical books of Antonio Brucioli's are publicly burned in the Piazza San Marco in Venice. He is fined 50 ducats and exiled for two years. He pays the fine, returns in 1549 to Venice, and resumes printing.

Giolito publishes the first edition of the *Rime* of Laura Terracina, edited by Domenichi.

The second edition of volume 2 of the Giolito poetry anthology series, *Rime di diversi nobili huomini*, book 2, is published in Venice. No editor is named; dedication letter by Giolito. The same two women as in the first edition of volume 2 are included.

1549 In Florence, an edict in November orders all owners of Protestant books to present them to the vicar within fifteen days under penalty of 100 scudi and ten years in the galleys; in particular books by Ochino and Vermigli are mentioned.

The Venetian Council of Ten orders Vincenzo Valgrisi to publish an index of prohibited books (*catalogo*). It bans the *opera omnia* of forty-seven authors, including Ochino, Vermigli, and Giulio della Rovere, and includes a hundred individual titles. This *catalogo* is the first to prohibit Valdes's *Alfabeto* and the anonymous *Beneficio di Christo*. It prohibits all anonymous works printed since 1525. In June 1549, this *catalogo* is suppressed. There still exists no papal index.

Death of Paul III (Alessandro Farnese); the election of Julius III (Gian Maria del Monte).

1549–50  The new pope, Julius III, restores Ascanio's estates in the Castelli Romani to him, officially pardons him, and presents him with a large commemorative bowl from the Forum excavations.

1549  The third edition of the first volume of the Giolito poetry anthology series, *Rime diverse*, book 1, edited by Domenichi comes out, with the same five women poets included as in the second edition.

1550  Flaminio dies at Pole's house in Rome.

The only edition of the third volume of the Giolito-style poetry anthology series comes out, *Delle rime di diversi nobilissimi . . . autori*, edited by Andrea Arrivabene. It includes only two women poets, Colonna and Gambara. The publisher this time is Bartolomeo Cesana in Venice.

Valdes's *Le centodieci divine considerazioni* is finally published for the first time in Basel by Celio Secondo Curione (Italian exile, professor at the University of Basel, and friend of Isabella Bresegna). Giulia Gonzaga preserves the manuscript in Spanish and negotiates the contract for its translation and publication with Curione in Basel in 1550.

1550, 1551  Giolito publishes the first two editions of Terracina's *Discorso*. Valvassori publishes the *Discorso* the same year.

1551  Volume 4 of the Giolito-style poetry anthology series comes out, edited by Hercole Bottigaro and published by Anselmo Giaccarello in Bologna. Women poets Giulia Aragona, Lucia Bertana, Gieronima Castellana, Vittoria Colonna, Veronica Gambara, Marguerite de Navarre, Virginia Salvi, and Faustina Vallentina are included.

The Accademia dei Dubbiosi in Venice issues a formal decree that there should be a literary "temple" constructed to praise and honor principally Giovanna d'Aragona and that such a temple is already underway for Maria d'Aragona by the editor Girolamo Ruscelli (Venice: Griffio, 1552).

1551–52, 1552  Two new editions of volume 5 of the Giolito poetry anthology series come out, *Rime di diversi illustri signori napoletani*, both edited by Lodovico Dolce. A new woman poet is introduced: Isabella di Morra of Favale in the kingdom of Naples. Di Morra's *canzoniere* will be published five times in a period of thirteen years: in the three editions of book 5 of the Giolito poetry anthologies edited by Dolce, a fourth time in Giolito's book 7 in 1556, and the fifth time in Domenichi's all-women anthology published by Busdragho in Lucca in 1559.

1552 *Rime* of Vittoria Colonna published by Giolito and edited by Dolce.

Giolito's senior editor Domenichi is convicted of heresy and sentenced to life in the *fortezza* in Pisa for publishing the *Nicomediana* of Calvin and Sleidan's *Commentarii*. Duchess of Ferrara, Renée of France, obtains his release from prison several months later.

The Sienese revolt against Spanish rule. The Florentines and Spanish troops under Charles V begin a siege outside the walls of Siena that lasts three years and ends in 1555 with the Sienese surrender. Laudomia Forteguerri commands a company of a thousand women in the construction of fortifications for the defense of the city. The French fight on the side of the Sienese against the troops of Cosimo de' Medici and the imperial army of Charles V.

Ruscelli's *Lettura sopra un sonnetto dell' Marchese del Vasto . . . alla divina signora marchesa del Vasto* (Venice: Griffio) is published containing a landmark appendix advertising the names of 259 distinguished women from thirty-five Italian cities.

Giuseppe Betussi publishes his dialogue *Leonora* (Lucca: Busdragho) dedicated to the learned elite woman Leonora Ravoira-Falletti of Savona.

1553 A papal order of August 12 condemns all Talmuds to burning. In Rome and Venice, massive burnings of the Talmud are carried out. Hundreds of thousands of Hebrew books are burned this year across Italy. Cardinal Cristoforo Madruzzo, Cardinal of Trent, founds and patronizes a Hebrew press at Riva di Trento that thrives from 1558–62 in response to the forced closings of Hebrew presses in Venice.

Gaspara Stampa (1523–54) makes her debut in print in volume 6 of the Giolito-style poetry anthology series edited by Girolamo Ruscelli, *Il sesto libro rime di diversi eccellenti autori* (Venice: Giovam Maria Bonelli, Al Segno del Pozzo). This volume contains more women writers than the previous Venetian anthologies: Tullia d'Aragona, Vittoria Colonna, Veronica Gambara, Ippolito Mirtilla, Coletta Pasquale, Virginia Salvi, and Maria Spinola, in addition to Gaspara Stampa.

1554 Gaspara Stampa dies unexpectedly in April at age thirty-three. The printer Pietrasanta in Venice, who produces Ruscelli's poetry anthologies and lives in his house, publishes Gaspara Stampa's collected *Rime* posthumously. Her sister, Cassandra Stampa, edits the collection.

Ascanio Colonna loses Charles V's support. The viceroy of Abruzzo arrests him and transports him to Naples, where he is imprisoned in the Castelnuovo for the rest of his life.

Giolito publishes two more editions of Terracina's *Rime*, both edited by Domenichi.

1554–55 Giolito publishes the 1554–55 index of prohibited books. This new index bans new titles, including Marsilio of Padua's *De defensor pacis*, the complete works of Pier Paolo Vergerio, Dante's *De monarchia*, Lorenzo Valla's *De falso donatione Constantini*, his *De libero arbitrio,* the *omnia opera* of Occam, Erasmus's works, Lucian, the Talmud, and many works of Savonarola.

1555 Death of Pope Julius III. Marcello II (Marcello Cervini) elected pope; dies that year.

Pope Paul IV (Gian Pietro Carafa) elected pope. He vastly expands the Inquisition and the powers of the grand inquisitor, the fanatic Michele Ghislieri, who conducts sessions on heresy twice a week with the pope attending every session.

Paul IV makes laws curbing Jews' freedom in Italy. Only one synagogue is allowed per city; the Jews must wear a yellow headdress; they are not permitted to own real estate or hire Christians. They may not use any language except Latin and Italian to draw up contracts. False converts are to be publicly burned.

The third edition of volume 5 of the Giolito poetry anthology series, *Libro quinto delle rime di diversi illustri signori napoletani*, edited by Dolce, comes out with Morra again as the only woman poet represented.

December 31. When Paul IV moves against Spain, Naples, and the Colonna towns and properties in the Castelli Romani, Giovanna Colonna flees Rome in disguise, leading her family to safety in Tagliacozzo.

The publication of Girolamo Ruscelli's multilanguage poetry anthology *Del tempio all divina signora donna Giovanna d'Aragona* (Venice: Pietrasanta).

Chiara Matraini's *Rime e prose* is published in 1555 by the printer Vincenzo Busdragho in Lucca.

Charles V abdicates to his son Philip II of Spain.

1556 Volume 7 of the Giolito poetry anthology series comes out: *Rime di diversi signori napoletani*, book 7, edited by Dolce. The women poets included are Chiara Matraini, Isabella di Morra, Caterina Pellegrina, Lucretia di Raimondo, and Laura Terracina.

The siege of Siena ends with Florentine/Spanish victory and the city's surrender.

Betussi publishes his dialogue *Le imagini del tempio di Giovanna d'Aragona* (Florence: Torrentino), which contains his thoughts on the fall of Siena. The *Imagini* features an allegorical temple with statues that represent famous literary women and their male "conservators."

Terracina's *Rime* edited by Domenichi at Giolito in Venice.

1557 Longtime reform activist Caterina Cibo dies in Florence.

Betussi publishes the second edition of his *Imagini del tempio* (Venice: de' Rossi).

Cardinal Morone is arrested and taken to the Castel Sant' Angelo. A former inquisitor, he is considered above reproach. Officials seize his books and belongings. He languishes in prison until Paul IV's death.

Control over Siena officially transferred by Philip II of Spain to Cosimo de' Medici.

March 24. Ascanio Colonna dies in the Castel Novo in Naples, after three years in prison there. In September, Pope Paul IV pardons Giovanna and son Marcantonio Colonna, who had been excommunicated by Pope Paul III.

1558 September 21. Death of Charles V at the monastery in Yuste, Spain.

Leading reform thinker Cardinal Pole dies in an outbreak of an epidemic in England.

On August 22, fifty-seven men of the presses subpoenaed by the Venetian Holy Office; they are forbidden to print the Bible in any vernacular. A new index is circulated in draft.

Volume 8 of the Giolito-style poetry anthology series comes out, *I fiori delle rime de' poeti illustri*, edited by Ruscelli and published by Sessa in Venice. The women poets included are Vittoria Colonna and Veronica Gambara. The Busdragho press in Lucca publishes Terracina's *Sesto rime.*

1559 "Volume 10" of the Giolito-style poetry anthology series comes out, edited by Domenichi but published in Lucca by Vincenzo Busdragho: the *Rime diverse d'alcune nobilissime et vituosissime donne.* This is the first anthology ever devoted almost exclusively to women poets; fifty-three Italian women writers are represented in this volume.

January meeting called in Giunti's store in Venice by the bookmen's guild. They reject the pope's orders and refuse to print the index or submit inventories.

On Saturday, March 18, ten to twelve thousand volumes are publicly burned in Venice. Public book burnings staged throughout Italy.

April. Paul IV fights publishers and booksellers with economic sanctions. The contents of Venetians' bookstores in the papal states are seized. Venetian booksellers and publishers are barred from book fairs in the papal states. The Venetian booksellers' united front disintegrates.

A new index, published in Rome by Pope Paul IV, condemns the *opera omnia* of 550 authors. Among the works condemned are Rabelais, Machiavelli, Aretino, Francesco Berni, Giovanni Della Casa, Poggio, Boccaccio's *Decameron,* sixty editions of the vulgate Bible and all vernacular editions of it. All anonymous books are banned.

Domenichi is hired by Cosimo to work on an official history of Medici rule in Florence.

Giolito's third edition of Terracina's *Discorso* published.

August 18. Pope Paul IV dies. The people rush to the buildings of the Inquisition and destroy them. They tear down Paul's statue and mutilate it. Pius IV (Giannangelo de' Medici) is elected pope.

July 8. The Venetian government accepts Paul IV's index and authorizes its publication. On August 11 the Holy Office punishes fine publishers Zernaro, Valgrisi, Bosello, Valvassori, and Varisco. Tommaso and Giovanni Naria Giunti, Gabriel Giolito, Michele Tramezzino, Marchi Sesso, Francesco Biundoni, and Andrea Arrivabene; the priors of the booksellers guild present their inventories before the Venetian tribunal together with the forbidden books.

1560  Volume 9 of the Giolito-style poetry anthology series is published in Cremona and edited by Vincenzo Conti: *Rime di diversi autori eccellentissimi,* including the women poets Laura Battiferra, Lucia Bertana, and Virginia Salvi.

The new pope, Pius IV, restricts power of the Holy Office to matters of faith only, not simony, blasphemy, and sodomy. The fanatic Cardinal Ghislieri remains grand inquisitor.

Farri in Venice prints Terracina's *Sesto rime, rime quinte, Discorso.* The publisher Amato in Naples prints the *Sesto rime.*

Giovanna d'Aragona returns to the Colonna palace in Rome after fifteen years in exile.

1561  Carnesecchi travels to Naples to edit Pole's works for publication with Giulia Gonzaga. Gonzaga moves out of her convent at San Francesco delle Monache in Naples and into the hotel Borgo delle Vergini, where both she and Carnesecchi stay until the work is completed.

1563  Closing of the Council of Trent in December. The council's decrees accepted on December 6 by representatives of the emperor Ferdinand I, the kings of Poland and Portugal, the dukes of Savoy and Florence, and the Republic of Venice.

1564  A commission established by the Council of Trent issues a new, authoritative Index of Prohibited Books, banning all books forbidden by previous papal and Council Indexes, all works by authors deemed heretical by the Church, all obscene and lascivious writings, and all writings on astrology, magic, and divination.

The death of Bernardino Ochino, who fled from Italy to Switzerland and was expelled from Zurich as a heretic at the age of seventy.

The death of Lodovico Domenichi, the producer of the first anthology of women poets, in Pisa.

1566 The death of Giulia Gonzaga in Naples.

The death of the editor of many women poets, Girolamo Ruscelli.

1567 Under the increasing presures of the Index of Prohibited Books of 1564 and the Inquisition, the Giolito press shifts its emphasis to producing principally religious books.

October 1. Giulia Gonzaga's longtime collaborator and friend Pietro Carnesecchi is beheaded and he is burned as a heretic.

1568 The death of Maria D'Aragona in Naples.

1571 The death of the Sienese poet Virginia Martini de' Salvi in Rome.

1575 Giovanna d'Aragona Colonna dies after son Marcantonio's official triumphal entry is celebrated in Rome following his victory at Lepanto. She is buried at Paliano in the same tomb with her husband Ascanio.

The death of Renata di Francia, Duchess of Ferrera and leader of a religious reform circle, in France.

1577 The death of Isabella Bresegna, the protégée of Giulia Gonzaga and Juan de Valdés, in exile in Chiavenna.

1589 The death of the poet Laura Battiferra in Florence.

# Biographical-Bibliographical Index of
# Authors, Patrons, Popes

ARAGONA, GIOVANNA D', DUCHESS OF TAGLIACOZZO, 1502–75. Born on Ischia.
Granddaughter of King Ferrante of Naples. Marries Vittoria Colonna's brother
Ascanio Colonna, 1521. Abandons Ascanio, 1535. Dedicatee of Girolamo Ruscelli, ed., *Del tempio all divina signora donna Giovanna d'Aragona* (Venice: Pietrasanta,
1555) and of Giuseppe Betussi, *Le imagini del tempio della Signora Donna Giovanna
d'Aragona* (Florence: Torrentino, 1556; Venice de' Rossi, 1557). Hosts poetry salons Ischia, Naples, Milan, Pavia, Rome with sister Maria d'Aragona. Attends
Giulia Gonzaga's salons. Publications in manuscript: letters to Pope Paul III,
Cardinal Alessandra Farnese.

ARAGONA, MARIA D', MARCHESA DEL VASTO, 1503–68. Born on Ischia. Granddaughter of King Ferrante. Marries Alfonso d'Avalos. Leads salons on Ischia and
Naples with Costanza d'Avalos and Vittoria Colonna. Attends Giulia Gonzaga's
salons. Inaugurates literary salons in Milan and Pavia, 1538–46. Reinaugurates
salons in Naples and Ischia, 1547. Supporter of academies: the Chiave d'Oro in
Pavia, the Fenici in Milan; the Sereni and Ardenti in Naples. Publications in
manuscript: six letters to reform thinker Cardinal Seripando.

ARAGONA, TULLIA D', 1510–56. Born in Rome. Poet, singer, courtesan. Married
Silvestro Guicciardi, 1543 in Siena. Moves to Florence, 1545, where Varchi serves
as her protector. In 1548, she makes her final move, to Rome. Publications: *Rime*
(Venice: Giolito, 1547); *Dialogo della infinità di amore* (Giolito, 1547); Giolito Poetry
Anthology Series, vol. 6 (1553); *Il Meschino altramente detto il Guerrino* (Venice:
Sessa, 1560).[1]

ARETINO, PIETRO, 1492–1556. Born in Arezzo. Educated in Perugia; Rome 1517.
Moves to Gonzaga court, 1523. Presents himself to Francis I, king of France.

BELPRATO, GIOVANNI VINCENZO, CONTE DI AVERSA. Born ca. 1505 near Naples; date of death unknown. Religious reform leader and activist. Patron of Laura Terracina. Publications: GPAS 5a (1552), 5b (1555); *Libro della historia de' Romani di Sesto Ruffo* (Florence: Torrentino, 1550); *Solino delle cose marvigliose del mondo* (Venice: Giolito, 1557).

BEMBO, CARDINAL PIETRO, 1470–1547. Publications: GPAS 1a (1545), 1b (1546), 1c (1549), 4 (1551), 8 (1558); *Asolani.*

BERTANA, LUCIA DELL'ORO, 1521–67. Born in Bologna. Poet, scholar, critic. Marries Gurone Bertani of Modena; she is listed among the illustrious women in Betussi's sculpture forum in his *Imagini del tempio della Signora Giovanna d'Aragona* (Florence: Torrentino, 1556; Venice: de' Rossi, 1557). Publications: GPAS 4 (1551), 9 (1560), 10 (1559); included in *Rime di diversi in morte della Signora Irene delle Signore di Spilimbergo* (1561); and in *Rime in lode di Lucrezia Gonzaga* (1562).

BETUSSI, GIUSEPPE, 1512–73. Born in Bassano. Poet, dialogue writer. In service of a succession of soldiers: Camillo Caula, Gian Luigi Vitelli, Alfonso d'Avalos, Vicino Orsini, Collaltino Collalto. Publications: the dialogues *Raverta* (Venice: Giolito, 1544) and *Leonora* (Lucca: Busdragho, 1557); *Imagini del tempio della Signora Donna Giovanna d'Aragona Colonna* (Florence: Torrentino, 1556; Venice: de' Rossi, 1557); GPAS 1a (1545), 1b (1546), 1c (1549), 9 (1560), 10 (1559); translator of Boccaccio, *De claris mulieribus,* published as *Libro di Gio: Boccaccio delle donne illustri* (Venice: Al Segno del Pozzo, Andrea Arrivabene, 1545).

BONELLI, GIOVANNI MARIA, active as printer in Venice, 1546–89. Published with Al Segno del Pozzo.

BONROMEA (BORROMEO), LIVIA TORNIELLA, fl. ca. 1554. Born in Novara. She is listed among the illustrious women in Betussi's sculpture forum, *Imagini del tempio della Signora Giovanna d'Aragona* (Florence: Torrentino, 1556; Venice: de' Rossi, 1557). Publication: GPAS 10 (1559).

BRACCALI DE BRACCIOLINI, SELVAGGIA DE, fl. 1550. Born in Pistoia. Marries Guglielmo Bracciolini. Publication: GPAS 10 (1559).

BRACCALI, GIULIA DE RICCIARDI PISTOLESE, fl. ca. 1550. Publication: GPAS 10 (1559).

BRESEGNA, ISABELLA. 1510–77. Born probably in Spain. Reform circles of Valdés and Gonzaga in Naples, ca. 1536. Lifelong reform activist and protégée of Giulia Gonzaga. Marries García Manrique, 1527. Moves to Piacenza where Manrique is named governor in 1548. Flees Italy to Tubingen, 1557, and later Zurich; never returns to Italy. Celio Curione dedicates his edition of the complete works of Olimpia Morata to Bresegna, 1558. Moves to Chiavenna, 1559. Dies there.

BRUNOZZI, CORNELIA DE VILLANI, fl. ca. 1550. Publication: GPAS 10 (1559).

BUSDRAGHO, VINCENZO, 1524–1601. Born in Lucca. Reform circles. Publisher and editor of modest means. His firm becomes stable in 1549. Publishes Laura Terracina, *Le seste rime* (1558); the works of Chiara Matrini (see Matraini); Domenichi's anthology of women (see Domenichi).

CANOSSA, EGERIA DA, fl. ca. 1560. Member of the academy of the Accesi in Reggio. Publication: GPAS 10 (1559).

CARAFA, FERRANTE, MARCHESE DI SAN LUCIDO; CONTE D'ARCHI, DUKE OF MONDRAGONE, 1509–87. Born in Naples. Soldier under Charles V. Taught by poet Antonio Minturno. Member of Maria d'Aragona's salons in Naples and Neapolitan academies: the Sereni, Ardenti, and Incogniti. Appointed deputy of the city of Naples. Recommends publication of Naples poets to L. Dolce in Venice in Ruscelli, ed., *Il tempio alla Diva Giovanna d'Aragona*. Publications: GPAS 5 (1551–52), 5a (1552), 5b (1555), 6 (1553), 7 (1556), 8 (1558).

CARNESECCHI, PIETRO, 1505–67. Born in Florence. Protonotary in the Church. Attends religious reform circles of Giulia Gonzaga in Naples in late 1530s, of Cardinal Pole in Viterbo, 1541–42, and of Caterina Cibo and Ochino in Florence. Protected by Cosimo I de' Medici and Giulia Gonzaga. Edits Pole's writings with Gonzaga after Pole's death. Convicted of heresy and executed by beheading in Rome after Gonzaga's death.

CARO, ANNIBAL, 1507–66. Born at Civitanova Marche da Giambattista. Poet and courtier. Gaddi and Guidiccioni are his protectors in Rome until their deaths in 1543. Caro next serves Cardinal Farnese. Publications: *Lettere familiari*; GPAS 1a (1545), 1b (1546), 1c (1549), 2a (1547), 2b (1548), 3 (1550), 4 (1551), 5 (1551–52), 5a (1552), 5b (1555), 6 (1553), 8 (1558), 9 (1560).

CASTELLANA, SUOR GIROLAMA, fl. 1560. Born in Bologna. Nun in convent of San Giovanni, Bologna. Publications: GPAS 4 (1551), 10 (1559).

CASTIGLIONE, BALDESAR, 1478–1529. Born in Casanatico near Mantua. Educated in Milan. Served Duke of Milan, later Duke of Urbino. Publications: *Il cortegiano* (The book of the courtier; 1521); GPAS 1a (1545), 1b (1546), 1c (1549), 3 (1550), 6 (1553), 9 (1560).

CATHERINE DE' MEDICI, QUEEN OF FRANCE, 1519–89. Born in Florence. Marries Henry II, king of France in 1547; queen until Henry's death in 1559. First cousin of Cosimo I de' Medici; niece of Caterina Cibo.

CEPPARELLO, LISABETTA DA FIORENTINA, fl. 1535. Born in Florence. Publication: GPAS 10 (1559).

CERRETANI, ERMELLINA ARRINGHIERI DE. Publication: GPAS 10 (1559).

CEVA, MADDALENA PALLAVICINA DE, MARCHESA. Publication: GPAS (1559).

CHARLES V, HABSBURG HOLY ROMAN EMPEROR AND KING OF SPAIN, 1500–1558. Born in Ghent. Crowned emperor in Aix-la-Chappelle in 1520. Pope Clement VII officially crowns Charles emperor again in Bologna, 1530. The noble Naples families d'Aragona, Colonna, and d'Avalos served Charles V as clients and led his armies. Charles crushes eighty thousand Turks in Tunisia, 1535; makes triumphal entry into Naples, 1535; lays siege with Florentines to Siena and defeats Sienese republicans, 1555. Abdicates his rule to son Philip II. Dies in Spain.

CIBO (CYBO), CATERINA, DUCHESS OF CAMERINO, 1501–57. Born in Ponzano near Florence. Granddaughter of Lorenzo (*Il magnifico*) de' Medici. Educated in classical literature and philosophy; reads Greek, Latin, and Hebrew fluently. Marries Giovanni Maria da Varano, Duke of Camerino in 1520. Supports reform preacher and Capuchin friar Bernardino Ochino and the Capuchins and participates in reform circles of Gonzaga and Valdés. Excommunicated by Pope Paul III and forced to abdicate from duchy, 1536. Flees to Florence. Chief interlocutor in several of Ochino's *Dialogi sette* (Venice: Zoppino, 1540). Recipient of letters written to her by reform theologian Marcantonio Flaminio. Leader of women's circles in 1540s–50s in Florence. Eulogized on her death by Laura Battiferra in four sonnets.

CLEMENT VII (Giulio de' Medici, 1478–1534). Pope, 1523–34.

COLLALTO, COLLALTINO DI, 1523–69. Poet and career military man who serves under the kings of France, Francis I and Henry II, the king of England, Henry VIII. Betussi serves him as secretary, 1545–49. Lover of Gaspara Stampa. Publications: GPAS 1a (1545), 1b (1546), 1c (1549).

COLONNA, ASCANIO, DUKE OF TAGLIACOZZO AND PALIANO, ca. 1490–1557. Born in Marino. Marries Giovanna d'Aragona in 1521. She leaves him in 1535. Fights Pope Paul III's troops when they attack him at Paliano, Rocca di Papa, Genazzano, and other Colonna strongholds in the so-called Salt War of 1541. He loses the war. Paul III confiscates all his lands and excommunicates him. His properties are restored by Pope Giulio III in the early 1550s. In 1554, accused of seeking an alliance with France against Charles V and is arrested and incarcerated in the Castelnuovo in Naples, where he dies in prison in 1557.

COLONNA, LIVIA. Ward and niece of Ascanio Colonna. She is raped and murdered in 1554 by Marzio Colonna. Francesco Cristiani edits and publishes anthology of poems that memorializes her life and death, *Rime di diversi ecc. Autori in vita e in morte dell' ill. S. Livia Colonna* (Rome: Antonio Barré, 1555). Publication: GPAS 10 (1559).

COLONNA, VESPASIANO, DUKE OF FONDI, ca. 1490s–1528. Soldier in the service of Charles V. Marries Giulia Gonzaga in 1526. Dies in his camp of wounds sustained in war. Leaves Giulia as his sole heir so long as she remains unmarried.

COLONNA, VITTORIA, MARCHESA DI PESCARA, ca. 1490–1547. Born in Marino. Granddaughter of Duke of Urbino, Federico da Montefeltro. Marries Ferrante Francesco d'Avalos, Marchese di Pescara, 1509; is widowed, 1525. Participates in leadership of Ischia salon, 1509–30. Inaugurates convent salon at San Silvester in Capite, Rome, 1531. Ariosto praises her in canto 37 of the *Orlando furioso*. Follows Ochino north to Ferrara, Verona, Lucca, 1537. Acts as Ascanio Colonna's secretary of state in Salt War from Rome, 1541. In Orvieto, March–August 1541. Joins Pole's *cenacolo* in Viterbo, 1541–42. Returns to Rome. Moves into convent of Santa Anna, 1542–47. Publications: *Rime* (Parma: Viotti, 1538); *Rime* (Florence: Zoppino, 1539); *Rime* (Venice: Zoppino, 1540); *Rime* (Venice: Imperador & Vinetiano, 1540, 1544); *Rime* (Venice: Valvassori, 1546); *Rime* (Venice: Comino da Trino, 1548); her *Rime* are also included in GPAS 1a (1945), 1b (1546), 1c (1549),

3 (1550), 4 (1551), 6 (1553), 8 (1558), 10 (1559); selected letters by Colonna published in G. Ruscelli, ed., *Lettere di diversi autori* (Venice: Ziletti, 1556); see also Rinaldo Corso, *Dichiaratione fatta sopra la seconda parte delle rime della divina V. Colonna* (Bologna: de Phaelli, 1543), the first extended literary critical study of a woman's poetry.

CONTILE, LUCA, 1505–74. Born in Cetona near Siena. Educated at Siena and Bologna. In the service of Maria d'Aragona d'Avalos in Milan, 1543–46. Follows d'Aragona to Naples in 1546 and is fired by her in 1548. Memberships in the Fenici in Milan and the Chiave d'Oro in Pavia. Enters Ferrante Gonzaga's service in Milan in 1548. Publications: *Delle lettere di Luca Contile* (Pavia: Girolamo Bartoli, 1564); GPAS 6 (1553), 8 (1558), 9 (1560).

COSIMO I DE' MEDICI, DUKE OF FLORENCE, 1519–74. Born in Florence. Marries Eleonora di Toledo in 1539. Becomes duke of Florence and Siena with his conquest of Siena in 1555. Pope Pius V crowns him grand duke of Tuscany in 1569 after he surrenders Carnesecchi to the Inquisition in 1567. Opens his court to reform thinkers in the late 1540s and early 1550s. In the 1560s he collaborates zealously with the Roman Inquisition. Patron of the poets Tullia d'Aragona, Varchi, Domenichi, and Laura Battiferra, the painters Vasari and Michelangelo, and the sculptors Bartolomeo Ammannati and Giambologna. Institutes a new academy in Florence, the Fiorentina, and brings the Flemish publisher Torrentino to Florence to promote book culture.

DELLA CASA, GIOVANNI, 1503–56. Born in Mugello near Florence. Studied law at Bologna. Cleric and poet; authored the first *catalogo* of forbidden books for the Roman Holy Office in 1549. His own poetry was criminalized in the *catalogo* of 1559. A member of Gaspara Stampa's salon in Venice. Publications: *Rime* (1558); his famous conduct book *Galateo* (1558); his Latin treatise on friendship (*De officiis inter potentiores et tenuiores*); GPAS 1a (1545), 1b (1546), 1c (1549), 4 (1551), 6 (1553), 9 (1560).

DOLCE, LODOVICO, 1508–68. Born in Venice. Editor, playwright, and poet. Publishes a total of 358 books during his thirty-year career as the Giolito press. Member of the academy of the Fratta at Rovigo and the Infiammati in Padua. Publications: editor and poet in GPAS 1a (1545), 1b (1546), 1c (1549), 2a (1547), 2b (1548), 5 (1551–52), 5a (1552), 5b (1552), (1555), 7 (1556); *Osservazioni nella volgar lingua*, in four books (Venice: Giolito, 1552, 1556, 1558, 1560); translation of Ovid's *Metapmorphoses*, titled *Trasformazioni*; tragedies *Tieste* (1543), *Troiane* (1567), *Ifigenia* (1551), and *Medea* (1557); one of the principal editors of Vittoria Colonna; responsible for the publication of the poets of the Naples academies and Maria d'Aragona's salons.

DOLFI, DIAMANTE, fl. ca. 1560. Publications: anthologized in Dionigi Atanagi, ed., *Rime di diversi nobilissimi et eccentissimi autori in morte della signora Irene delle signore di Spilimbergo* (Venice: Domenico & Giovanni Battista Guerra, 1561); GPAS 10 (1559).

DOMENICHI, LODOVICO, 1515–64. Born in Piacenza. Editor, translator, writer. Publishes a total of 172 books during his career. Educated at Padua and Pavia. Receives his laureate at Padua in law. Comes to Venice under protection of Aretino in 1541. Joins Ortolani academy in Piacenza with Anton Francesco Doni. Joins Giolito firm in Venice in 1545. Transfers to Florence in 1546 in service of Cosimo I de' Medici. Opens small press with Doni. Joins Florentine firm of Torrentino. Participates in religious reform circles. Convicted of heresy and imprisoned in Pisa, 1552; released later that year. Named official historian by Cosimo de' Medici, 1559. Publications: editor and inaugurator of the Giolito poetry anthology series (GPAS) *Rime diverse di molti eccellentissimi auttori*: 1a (1545), 1b (1546), 1c (1549), 2a (1547), 2b (1546), and 10—the first anthology of women poets ever, *Rime diverse d'alcune nobilissime, et virtuosissime donne* (Lucca: Busdragho, 1559); *La nobiltà delle donne* (Venice: Giolito, 1549); translates Polybius's *Histories* (Venice: Giolito, 1546).

DONI, ANTON FRANCESCO, 1513–74. Born in Florence. Writer, printer, editor. Protégée of Aretino in Venice. Works for Giolito and Marcolini presses, 1545–53. Opens press with Domenichi in Florence, 1546. Publications: *Le lettere* (1544); *I Marmi* (Venice 1553); GPAS 1a (1545), 1b (1546), 1c (1549), 2a (1547), 2b (1548), 5 (1551–52), 5a (1552), 5b (1555).

ELEONORA DI TOLEDO, DUCHESS OF FLORENCE AND SIENA, 1522–62. Born in Spain. Daughter of Viceroy of Naples Pedro di Toledo. Marries Cosimo I de' Medici, 1539. Patron of Tullia d'Aragona, Laura Battiferra, Giorgio Vasari, and others. Inaugurates poetry academy in Florence, the Elevati. Supported the Jesuits and the founding of Jesuit College in Florence in 1547.

ESTE, ISABELLA D', MARCHESA OF MANTUA, 1474–1539. Born in Ferrara. Marries Marchese Francesco Gonzaga, 1490. Patron and friend of many artists and poets: Michelangelo, Titian, Mantegna, Costa, Boiardo, Ariosto, Castiglione, and Equicola.

FALLETTA, LEONORA RAVOIRA, PRINCESS OF MELAZZO, fl. ca. 1550 in Monferrato. Marries Gioirgio Falletti. Principal interlocutor of Betussi's dialogue *Eleonora* and listed among the illustrious women in Betussi's sculpture forum in his *Imagini del tempio della Signora Giovanna d'Aragona* (Florence: Torrentino, 1556; Venice: de' Rossi, 1557). Publication: GPAS 10 (1559).

FARNESE, CARDINALE ALESSANDRO, 1520–89. Papal nephew. Poet, patron of art, architecture, and literature. Publication: GPAS 10 (1559).

FIGLIUCCI, LUCRETIA, fl. ca. 1550. Publication: GPAS 10 (1559).

FLAMINIO, MARCANTONIO, 1498–1550. Born at Serravalle in the Veneto. Educated at Padua. Humanist, poet, Aristotelian scholar, theologian, cleric. Publications: *Carminum libri VIII* (Lyons, 1548); *Carmi* (Florence: Torrentino, 1549); *Della nova scelta di lettere du diversi nobilissimi huomini et eccellentissimi ingegni*, ed. B. Pino (Venice, 1582); believed to be author or coauthor of the *Beneficio di Cristo* (Venice: Bernardo de' Bindoni, 1543); translation and commentary on book 12 of Aristotle's *Metaphysics*, titled *Paraphrasis* (Venice: Tacuino, 1536).

FORTEGUERRI, LAUDOMIA, 1515–55? Born in Siena. Marries Giulio di Alessandro Colombini 1537; has three children; widowed 1542. Marries Petruccio Petrucci 1544. One of three protagonists with Girolama Carli de' Piccolomini and Frasia Marzi in Marcantonio Piccolomini's unpublished *Dialogo* (ca. 1537). Commands a thousand women in building of fortifications during siege of Siena, 1552–53. Celebrated in Monluc's (also known as Montluc) *Commentaires* of Blaise de Monluc. Listed among the illustrious women in Betussi's sculpture forum in his *Imagini del tempio della Signora Giovanna d'Aragona* (Florence: Torrentino, 1556; Venice: de' Rossi, 1557). Publications: her sonnet *Ora ten va' superbo, or corri altero* (Bologna: da Carpi, 1541); GPAS 1b (1546), 1c (1549); 10 (1559) contains Forteguerri's suite of five poems dedicated to Charles V's daughter, Margaret of Austria.

FRANCIS I, 1494–1547. King of France, 1515–47. Brother of Marguerite de Navarre. Invades Milan in 1515; defeated and ousted from Italy, Battle of Pavia, 1525. Patron of the arts and poets; his court is a center for Italian poets and intellectuals in exile: Collalto, Carnesecchi, and such pro-French Neapolitan nobles as Isabella di Morra's father. Patron of studies in astrology, alchemy, and the Kabbalah.

FRANCIS II, 1544–60. King of France, 1559–60. Marries Mary, queen of Scots. French court still offers refuge to Italian intellectuals and fugitives from the Roman Inquisition such as Duchess Renée of Ferrara and her former courtiers.

GÀMBARA, VERONICA, 1485–1550. Born in Pratoalboino near Brescia. Humanist education. Marries Giberto X. Signor of Correggio in 1509. Widowed in 1518. Client of Charles V. Circle of Bernardo Tasso, Aretino, Bembo. Friend and role model for Vittoria Colonna. Publications: no sixteenth-century solo edition but she is anthologized and published in sixty-eight collected poetry books; 129 of her letters published (Chiapetti 1879); GPAS 1a (1545), 1b (1546), 1c (1549), 2a (1547), 2b (1548), 3 (1550), 4 (1551), 6 (1553), 8 (1558), 10 (1559).

GIOVIO, PAOLO, 1486–1552. Born in Como. Medical degree at Pavia, 1511. Bishop, historian, biographer, physician to Pope Clement VII. Publication: *Elogia doctorum vivorum* (1546); *Historiarum sui temporis libri* (1550–51).

GOLFARINA, ANNA, fl. ca. 1555. Publications: anthologized in *Del tempio alla Divina Signora Donna Giovanna d'Aragona*, ed. G. Ruscelli (Venice: Pietrasanta, 1555); GPAS 10 (1559).

GONZAGA, GIULIA, DUCHESS OF FONDI, 1513–66. Born at Gazzuolo near Mantua. Marries Vittoria Colonna's cousin Vespasiano Colonna, 1526. Inaugurates salon at Fondi, 1529. Flees Barbarossa and his marauding sailors at Fondi, 1534. Moves into convent of San Francesco delle Monache in Naples. Publications: she negotiates contract for the printing of the anonymous *Beneficio di Cristo*, generally thought to be Marcantonio Flaminio's revision of a treatise by the friar Benedetto da Mantova, (Venice: Bernardo de' Bindoni, 1543), which sells out in forty-five thousand copies between 1543 and 1549; also negotiates contract and may have coauthored Juan de Valdés's *Alfabeto Cristiano*, trans. Marco Antonio Magno (Venice: Bacarini, 1545), twenty-three editions of which published,

1543–97, all contraband after 1549; author of thousands of letters not collected in a sixteenth-century or modern edition.

HENRY II, 1519–59, King of France, 1547–59. Marries Catherine de' Medici, 1533. Patron of artists and poets. French court still offers refuge to Italian intellectuals fleeing the Roman Inquisition or Aragonese hegemony in Naples.

JULIUS III (Giovanni Maria Ciocchi del Monte, 1487–1555). Pope, 1549–55.

LEO X (Giovanni de' Medici, 1475–1521). Pope, 1513–21.

LUNATA, ALDA TORELLA, fl. ca. 1550 in Pavia. Listed among the illustrious women in Betussi's sculpture forum in his *Imagini del tempio della Signora Giovanna d'Aragona* (Florence: Torrentino, 1556; Venice: de' Rossi, 1557); GPAS 10 (1559).

MALIPIERA, OLIMPIA, ?–1559. Born in Venice of elite parents. Publication: GPAS 10 (1559).

MARGUERITE OF ANGOULÊME, QUEEN OF NAVARRE, 1492–1549. Marries Charles, duc d'Alençon, 1509; widowed in 1525. Marries Henri d'Albret, king of Navarre. With her brother Francis, becomes a supporter of the Reformation. Corresponds with Vittoria Colonna, 1538. Publications: *Histoires des Amans fortunez . . .* (sixty-seven tales from the *Heptaméron* without linking discussions), ed. Pierre Boiastuau (Paris: Gilles Robinot, 1558); *L'Heptaméron des nouvelles de très illustre et très excellente Princesse Marguerite de Valois, Royne de Navarre . . .* (seventy-two tales in the standard order and format), ed. Pierre Gruget (Paris: J. Caveillier, 1559); GPAS 4 (1551), 10 (1559).

MARTELLI, MARIA DE PANCIATICHI. Publication: GPAS 10 (1559).

MATRAINI, CHIARA, 1515–1604? Born in Lucca. Marries Vincenzo Contarini in 1531; widowed in 1542. Bartolomeo Graziani and, later, Cesare Coccopani are her lovers. Commissioned portrait of herself for chapel of Santa Maria Forisportam in Lucca, 1576. Counter-Reformation ideology in later works. Publications: *Rime e prose di madonna Chiara Matraini* (Lucca: Busdragho, 1555); *Meditazioni spirituali di madonna Chiara Contarini de' Matraini* (Lucca: Busdragho, 1581); *Considerazioni sopra i sette salmi penitenziali* (Lucca: Busdragho, 1566); *Breve discorso sopra la vita e laude della Beatiss. Verg. E Madre del Figliuoli di Dio* (Lucca: Busdragho, 1590); *Lettere con la prima e secondo parte delle Rime* (Venice: Moretti, 1597); GPAS 7 (1556).

MIRTILLA, IPPOLITA, fl. ca. 1550. Venetian poet. Close friend of Gaspara Stampa and member of her salon. Publications: GPAS 6 (1553), 10 (1559).

MORATA, OLIMPIA, 1526–55. Born in Ferrara. Marries German Lutheran physician Andreas Grunthler, 1549. Moves to Germany. Publications: *Olympiae Fulviae Moratae mulieris omnium eruditissimae Latina et Graeca, quae haberi potuerunt, monumenta* (Basel: Petrum Pernam 1558, 1562, 1570), published posthumously by Secondo Curione and dedicated to Isabella Bresegna.

MORRA, ISABELLA DI, 1520–45. Born in Favale, kingdom of Naples. Poet classically educated in Latin literature, Roman history. Murdered by her brothers. Protégée of published poet and Florentine academy member Don Diego Sandoval de Castro. Publications: GPAS 5 (1551–52), 5a (1552), 5b (1555), 7 (1556), 10 (1559).

MUZIO, GIROLAMO, 1496–1576. Born in Padua. Member of salons of Duchess Renée and Duke Ercole of Ferrara, 1537–38, of Maria d'Aragona in Milan and Pavia, 1539–46, and of the d'Aragona salons in Naples and Ischia, 1547. Protector of Tullia d'Aragona. Publications: GPAS 1a (1545), 1b (1546), 1c (1549), 2a (1547), 2b (1548), 8 (1558), 9 (1960).

OCHINO, BERNARDINO, 1487–1564. Born in Siena. Head of Capuchin order of friars. Protégé of Vittoria Colonna and Caterina Cibo. Leading figure in *spirituali* reform circles in Naples and northern cities. Delivers Lenten sermons at San Giovanni Maggiore in Naples, 1536. Lecture tour in Verona, Bologna, Pisa, Ferrara. Flees from Inquisition to Geneva, 1542. Publications: *Dialogi sette* (Venice: Zoppino, 1540), with Caterina Cibo as chief interlocutor; *Prediche di mess. Bernardino Ochino* (Basel: n.p., n.d. [ca. 1549, 1551]).

PASQUALE, COLETTA, fl. ca. 1550. Publication: GPAS 6 (1553).

PAUL III (Alessandro Farnese, 1468–1549). Pope, 1534–49.

PAUL IV (Gian Pietro Carafa, 1476–1559). Pope, 1555–59.

PECCI, HONORATA, fl. ca. 1550. Born in Siena. Publication: GPAS (1559) 10.

PETRUCCI, AURELIA, 1511–42. Born in Siena. Publication: GPAS (1559) 10.

PETRUCCI, CASSANDRA, fl. ca. 1550. Publication: GPAS (1559) 10.

PICCOLOMINI, ALESSANDRO, 1508–78. Born in Siena. Educated, Padua at University. Academy member of the Sienese Intronati and the Paduan Infiammati. Circle of Varchi, Aretino, Tomitano, Speroni, Dolce. Publications: *La Raffaella*, also titled. *De la bella creanza de le donne* (Venice: Curzio Navo, 1539); *Lettura* on a sonnet of Laudomia Forteguerri (Bologna: da Carpi, 1541), delivered as a presentation at the academy of the Infiammati; also, dedicated to Laudomia Forteguerri his *De la sfera del mondo: Libri quatro in lingua Toscana* (Venice: Bevilaqua, 1561); *De la institutione di tutta la vita de l'huomo nato nobile* (Venice: Scoto, 1542); *In lode delle donne* (Venice: Giolito, 1545); and, published in manuscript only, his edited *La Tombaiad* (1540), a collection of Sienese women's and men's sonnets; translation of Xenophon's *Oeconomicus* (Venice: Al Segno del Pozzo, 1540); Piccolomini's letters are included in Bernardino Pini, *Della nuova scielta di lettere di diversi nobilissimi huomini . . .* (Venice: n.p., 1574).

PICCOLOMINI, SILVIA, MARCHESA, fl. ca. 1550, Siena. Publication: GPAS (1559) 10.

PIETRASANTA, PLINIO, fl. 1553–59, in Venice. Printer. Lives in Ruscelli's house for a time. Books printed: Alessandro Piccolomini's comedy *L'amor costante* (1554); Gaspara Stampa's *Rime* (1554), posthumously; Girolamo Ruscelli's, *Del tempio alla divina Signora Donna Giovanna d'Aragona* (1555); Varchi's *Sonetti* (1555).

PIUS IV (Giovanni Angelo de' Medici, 1499–1565). Pope, 1559–65.

PIUS V (Michele Ghislieri, 1504–72). Inquisitor general; afterward, pope, 1566–72.

POLE, CARDINAL REGINALD, 1500–1558. Born in England of royalty. Papal ambassador to Viterbo. Leads a reform circle there with Vittoria Colonna. With Carnesecchi and Flaminio, Pole becomes major leader of the Valdesian or *spirituali* movement in Italy. Corresponds with Vittoria Colonna, Giulia Gonzaga, and

Caterina Cibo, all leaders in the reform movement in Italy. Dies in England, under suspicion of heresy. Publications: reform writings such as his *Defense of the Unity of the Church* (originally published in Rome as *De unitate* in 1539 by Blado); *Reformatio Angliae* (The Reformation of England, n.d.).

RENÉE DE FRANCE (RENATA DI FRANCIA), DUCHESS OF FERRARA, 1510–75. Born in France. Princess and daughter of King Louis XII. Marries Ercole II d'Este in 1528. Inaugurates her religious reform salon in 1537 in Ferrara. Receives Vittoria Colonna and Ochino in 1537 as her guests. Patron of Olimpia Morata and other Protestants. Duke Ercole puts her under house arrest, 1554. Returns to France when Duke Ercole dies, 1559.

ROTA, BERNARDINO, 1508–75. Born in Naples. Member, Naples and Ischia salons and academies. Publications: GPAS 5 (1551–52), 5a (1552), 5b (1555), 6 (1553), 7 (1556), 8 (1558).

RUSCELLI, GIROLAMO, 1504–66. Born in Viterbo. Hellenist, linguist, humanist. Editor. Publishes 125 books in the course of his career. Educated at Padua. Founder and member of the academy of the Sdegno in Rome. Publications: *Lettura sopra un sonnetto alla divina signora marchesa del Vasto . . .* (Venice: Griffio, 1552); editor, *Il sesto libro delle rime di diversi eccellenti autori* (Venice: Al Segno del Pozzo, 1553); editor, *Del tempio alla divina Signora Donna Giovanna d'Aragona* (Venice: Pietrasanta, 1555); GPAS 5 (1551–52), 5a (1552), 5b (1555), editor of 6 (1553), 8 (1558); edition and translation of Plato's *Timaeus* and Ptolemy's *Geography*; editor of posthumous edition of Vittoria Colonna's *Rime* (Venice: Sessa, 1558); *Lettere di diversi autori eccellenti* (Venice: Ziletti, 1556).

SALVI, VIRGINIA MARTINI DE', ?–1571, fl. in Siena. Moves to Rome, 1555, after sack of Siena. Listed among the illustrious women in Betussi's sculpture forum in his *Imagini del tempio della Signora Giovanna d'Aragona* (Florence: Torrentino, 1556; Venice: de' Rossi, 1557); GPAS 4 (1551), 6 (1553), 9 (1560), 10 (1559).

SANDOVAL DE CASTRO, DIEGO, ca. 1505–46. Friend and alleged lover of Isabella di Morra. Murdered by Morra's brothers near Favale, kingdom of Naples, in 1546. Member of Cosimo's Accademia Fiorentina in Florence. Publications: *Canzoniere* (Venice, 1542; Rome: Valerio Dorico & Loigi fratelli, 1542).

SANGALLO, LAUDAMIA DA, fl. ca. 1555. Publication: GPAS 10 (1559).

SANGALLO, MARIA DA, fl. ca. 1555. Publication: GPAS 10 (1559).

SANVITALE, LAVINIA, fl. ca. 1555. Publication: GPAS 10 (1559).

SAULI, LUCIA, fl. ca. 1555. Publication: GPAS 10 (1559).

SCARPI, HORTENSIA, fl. ca. 1555. Born in Genoa. Publication: GPAS 10 (1559).

SOMMA, SILVIA DI, CONTESSA DI BAGNO, fl. ca. 1555. Publication: GPAS 10 (1559).

SPINOLA, MARIA, fl. ca. 1550. Born in Genoa. Publication: letter to Aretino (1540); GPAS 6 (1553), 10 (1559).

STAMPA, GASPARA, 1523–54. Born in Padua. Poet and musician. Moves to Venice. Member of the academy of the Dubbiosi in Venice. Initiates a salon with her mother and sister, Cassandra Stampa: their circle includes her brother, Baldassarre

Stampa, Monsignor Giovanni Della Casa, Girolamo Parabosco, Varchi, Speroni, Francesco Sansovino, Aretino, and her lover Collalto Collaltino. Publications: GPAS 6 (1553), 10 (1559); *Rime* (Venice: Pietrasanta, 1554); a solo edition of her poems posthumously published and edited by her sister Cassandra.

TACITA, FAUSTA, fl. 1550. Publications: anthologized in *Del tempio alla divina Signora Donna Giovanna d'Aragona*, ed. G. Ruscelli (Venice: Pietrasanta, 1555); GPAS 10 (1559).

TANSILLO, LUIGI, 1510–68. Born at Tenosa, in the kingdom of Naples. Lyric poet. In service of Viceroy of Naples, Pedro di Toledo. Later serves Maria d'Aragona. Named governor of Gaeta, 1561. Publications: *Stanze a Bernardino Martirano* (1540); *La balia* (1552); *Le lagrime di San Pietro* (1585); GPAS 5 (1551–52), 5a (1552), 5b (1555), 6 (1553), 7 (1556), 8 (1558).

TASSO, BERNARDO, 1493–1569. Born in Venice. Marries Porzia de' Rossi. Serves Ferrante Sanseverino, prince of Salerno. Father of Torquato Tasso. Publications: *Amadigi* (1560); *Ragionamento della poesia* (1562); GPAS 1a (1545), 1b (1546), 1c (1549), 2a (1547), 2b (1548), 3 (1550), 5 (1551–52), 5a (1552), 5b (1555), 8 (1558).

TERRACINA, LAURA BACIO, 1519–77. Born in Chiaia, Naples. Member of the Incogniti academy in Naples. Marries Polidoro Terracina, 1537. Publications: *Prime rime* (Venice: Giolito 1548, 1549, 1550, 1553, 1554, 1556, 1565); *Prime rime* (Venice: Domenico Farri, 1560; Naples: Bulifon, 1692); *Discorso* (1550, 1567); *Rime seconde* (Florence: Giunti, 1549); Doni, ed., published her *Discorso* after his *Libraria*; *Le quarte rime* (Venice: Valvassorio, 1550; Domenico Farri, 1560); *Le quinte rime* (Venice: Valvassorio, 1552); *Le seste rime* (Lucca: Busdragho, 1558; Naples: Raimondo Amato, 1694; Bulifon, 1694; *Le settime rime* (Florence: Giunti, 1604); Terracina was also anthologized in GPAS 1b (1546), 1c (1549), 7 (1556).

VALDÉS, JUAN DE, 1509?–41. Born in Cuenca, Spain of *converso* family. Force him to flee Spain because of his religious views. Arrives in Rome and enters service of Pope Clement VII, 1531. Serves Charles V in Naples, 1535. Theologian, writer. Publications: *Alfabeto Cristiano*, with a dedicatory letter to Giulia Gonzaga, trans. Marco Antonio Magno (Venice: Bacarini, 1545)—twenty-three editions, 1543–97, all contraband after 1549; *Le cento e dieci divine considerazioni*, ed. Celio Secundo Curione (Basel, 1550).

VALLENTINA, FAUSTINA, fl. ca. 1550. Born in Naples. Publication: GPAS 4 (1551).

# NOTES

## INTRODUCTION

The epigraph to the introduction is from Adrian Johns, *The Nature of the Book: Print and Knowledge in the Making* (Chicago: University of Chicago Press, 1998), 3. An underlying theme in my discussions of women and men's printed books in sixteenth-century Italy in the chapters that follow concerns the mediated nature of printed texts. Unlike the manuscript book, which arrived in its reader's hand almost without changes other than the author's own revisions, the early modern author's work underwent so many alterations between its original submission in manuscript and the final printed book that its connection to a prior author was never unproblematic. The submitted work was corrected, abridged, edited, its dialect "impurities" purged, translated, posthumously edited and reprinted—and in the process of typesetting the work was invariably published with new errors. Publishing, then, was always a collaborative project and a highly mediated one, both for male and female authors.

1.  The abridged edition of Eisenstein's volume is *The Printing Revolution in Early Modern Europe* (Cambridge and New York: Cambridge University Press, 1983). See also Eisenstein, *The Printing Press as an Agent of Change: Communications and Cultural Transformations in Early-Modern Europe*, 2 vols. (Cambridge: Cambridge University Press, 1979); Johns, *The Nature of the Book*; Brian Richardson, *Printing, Writers and Readers in Renaissance Italy* (Cambridge: Cambridge University Press, 1999); Richardson, *Print Culture in Renaissance Italy: The Editor and the Vernacular Text, 1470–1600.* (Cambridge: Cambridge University Press, 1994); Roger Chartier, ed., *The Culture of Print: Power and the Uses of Print n Early Modern Europe,* trans. Lydia G. Cochrane (Princeton, NJ: Princeton University Press, 1987). Susan Broomhall's recent *Women and the Book Trade in Sixteenth-Century France* (Oxford and Burlington, VT: Ashgate Press, 2002) is a welcome exception to the absence of women as a category in studies in book history and will, I'm sure, lead the way to more such studies.

2.  Joan DeJean, *Tender Geographies: Women and the Origins of the Novel in France* (New York: Columbia University Press, 1991).

3.  Broomhall, *Women and the Book Trade,* 1.

4.  Carlo D. Dionisotti, "La letteratura italiana nell'età del Concilio di Trento," in *Geografia e storia della letteratura italiana* (Turin: Einaudi, 1967), 187–92. Dionisotti's states

that there had always been individual women geniuses in Italian literary history but that only between 1540 and 1560—and neither before nor since during the early modern period—did women writers constitute a group: "Soltanto nella letteratura del medio cinquecento le donne fanno gruppo. Non prima nè poi" (191).

5. Ibid.: "La prima, abiusiva, raccolta a stampa delle *Rime* di Vittoria Colonna apparve nel 1538, poveramente e fuori mano, a Parma. Era, salvo errore, la prima raccolta a stampa apparsa in Italia di rime d'una donna, col suo propria nome, e fu come una scintilla caduta nella paglia" (191–92).

6. See Axel Erdmann, *My Gracious Silence: Women in the Mirror of Sixteenth-Century Printing in Western Europe* (Luzern: Gilhofer & Rauschberg, 1999), 201–23.

7. For a list of the "Giolito" poetry anthology series books and their publishers, see my app. A.

8. It is still a trope among scholars of early women to observe that public speech and publication were forbidden to virtuous women in early modern Italy. Yes, Leonardo Bruni and Francesco Barbaro's pronouncements on the subject support such a view. But in fact there was a strong tradition of learned fifteenth-century women writers in Italy, whose names were above reproach and who eagerly sought publication, whether through the circulation of their works in manuscript or in printed editions—among them Isotta Nogarola, Laura Cereta, and Cassandra Fedele. See my and Margaret King's editions of these women. But there are many more such women writers: see Margaret L. King and Albert Rabil, Jr., *Her Immaculate Hand: Selected Works by and about the Women Humanists of Quattrocento Italy* (Binghamton, NY: Medieval and Renaissance Texts and Studies, 1980); and see also the recent fifty-odd-volume series of early modern European women writers, edited by King and Rabil and published by the University of Chicago Press under the series title the Other Voice in Early Modern Europe.

9. Girolamo Ruscelli, *Lettura di Girolamo Ruscelli sopra un sonetto . . . alla divina signora Marchesa del Vasto* (Venice: Giovan Griffio, 1552).

10. Lodovico Domenichi, *La nobiltà delle donne* (Venice: Gabriel Giolito, 1549).

11. Ann Rosalind Jones, *The Currency of Eros: Women's Love Lyric in Europe, 1540–1620* (Bloomington and Indianapolis: Indiana University Press, 1990), 4. On a more metacultural plane, I find Jones's negotiatory perspective useful because it is inconsistent with any notion of ideologies as monolithic. In the Gramscian sense that Stuart Hall (whom Jones cites as a source) defines the term, "there is never any one, single, unified and coherent 'dominant ideology' which pervades everything. . . . The object of analysis is therefore not the single stream of 'dominant ideas' into which everything and everyone has been absorbed, but rather the analysis of ideology as a differentiated terrain, of the different discursive currents, their points of juncture and break and the relations of power between them" (Stuart Hall, *Critical Dialogues in Cultural Studies*, ed. David Morley and Kuan-Hsing Chen [New York and London: Routledge, 1996], 433–34). Hall's Foucauldian keywords "discourse" and "discursivity" (discursive currents, etc.) are especially relevant to my project since the term "discourse" subtends

both speech and action, both writing and performance, as forms of articulation that must be studied not separately but as moving parts on a continuum.

12. E. Goldsmith, "Publishing the Lives of Hortense and Marie Mancini," in *Going Public: Women and Publishing in Early Modern France*, ed. E. Goldsmith and Dena Goodman (Ithaca, NY, and London: Cornell University Press, 1995), 41.

13. Joan B. Landes, *Women and the Public Sphere in the Age of the French Revolution* (Ithaca, NY, and London: Cornell University Press, 1988), 23. Landes makes the point that in France the salon was "displaced in part with the creation of a modern publishing apparatus, as a mode of cultural production."

14. Joan DeJean, *Tender Geographies: Women and the Origins of the Novel in France* (New York: Columbia University Press, 1991), esp. 17–42.

15. Jones, *The Currency of Eros*.

16. The gratitude for such subventions and grants was noticeably and copiously acknowledged by editors or authors in the prefaces to their books.

17. On the phenomenal productivity of such Venetian editors as Domenichi, Dolce, Ruscelli, and others, see Claudia Di Filippo Bareggi, *Il mestiere di scrivere* (Rome: Bulzoni, 1988); and Ronnie H. Terpenning, *Lodovico Dolce, Renaissance Man of Letters* (Toronto: University of Toronto Press, 1997). Domenichi published a total of 172 books in the course of his career at the presses; some of these books were other authors' works that he edited, some translations, and others were his own original works; his colleague Lodovico Dolce (for the sake of comparison) was by far and away the top producer during these years, publishing a total of 358 books in the course of his thirty-six years of steady work at the Giolito press (Terpenning, *Dolce*, 12); Ruscelli's total output numbered 125 books and Betussi's was thirty-two books.

    The interruptions in the received tradition of early women writers is the point hammered home in Pamela Joseph Benson and Victoria Kirkham, eds., *Strong Voices, Weak History: Early Women Writers and Canons in England, France and Italy* (Ann Arbor: University of Michigan Press, 2005); and in Deanna Shemek's important essay on Domenichi's 1559 anthology in that volume, "The Collector's Cabinet: Lodovico Domenichi's Gallery of Women," 239–62. It was not, in fact, Domenichi's anthology itself that would be known to posterity since its print run was small. Without the title of Lodovico Domenichi's *Rime d'alcune nobilissime et virtuossime donne* (Lucca: Busdragho, 1559) ever crossing his lips, Antonio Bulifon, a successful publisher and editor with a taste for women's writings, printed a line-for-line copy of Domenichi's anthology under a new title: *Rime di cinquanta illustri poetesse* (Naples: Bulifon, 1695). The Bulifon volume was widely disseminated, and without it many of the women poets who would not otherwise have survived entered the canon. Subsequent large-scale women-only anthologies have included the following: Luisa Bergalli, ed., *Componimenti delle più illustri rimatrici di ogni secolo*, 2 vols (Venice: Morra, 1726).; Jolanda De Blasi, *Le scrittrici italiane dalle origini al 1800* (Florence: Nemi, 1930); and Laura Anna Stortoni, ed., *Women Poets of the Italian Renaissance: Courtly Ladies and Courtesans,* trans. Laura Anna Stortoni and Mary Prentice Lillie (New York: Italica Press, 1996).

18. Harriette Andreadis's brilliant and highly nuanced study, *Sappho in Early Modern England: Female Same-Sex Literary Erotics, 1550–1714* (Chicago: University of Chicago Press, 2001), has shown that a tradition of same-sex love poetry began to emerge among women writers in sixteenth-century England.

    Agnolo Firenzuola drew the comparison between the Sienese poet Laudomia Forteguerri and Sappho in a dialogue he titled *On the Beauty of Women*, which was published in 1541, before Domenichi's women's anthology, but he clearly knew Forteguerri's poems from a book Alessandro Piccolomini had published earlier in 1541: *Lettura del S. Alessandro Piccolomini Infiammato fatta nell'Accademia degli Infiammati* (Bologna: Bonardo & Marc'Antonio da Carpi, 1541), a critical appraisal of Forteguerri's work, which had also been presented at the academy of the Infiammati in Padua. Firenzuola puts the remark referred to in the mouth of his dialogue's only male character, Celso. For this reference to Firenzuola's *On the Beauty of Women*, I am indebted to Konrad Eisenbichler, "Laudomia Forteguerri Loves Margaret of Austria," in *Same Sex Love and Desire among Women in the Middle Ages*, ed. Francesca Canadé Sautman and Pamela Sheingorn (New York: Palgrave, 2001), 277–80. Firenzuola "links" but does not identify Forteguerri with Sappho, as I explain in chapter 5.

19. Girolamo Ruscelli, *Del tempio alla divina signora donna Giovanna d'Aragona* (Venice: Plinio Pietrasanta, 1555); the work included poems in Latin, ancient Greek, and Spanish as well as in Italian. Giuseppe Betussi's *Le imagini del tempio della signora donna Giovanna Aragona* was published first in Florence by Cosimo I de' Medici's official printer Lorenzo Torrentino (1556); the work was published again in 1557 by Giovanni de' Rossi in Venice.

20. As Virginia Cox notes in her "Women Writers and the Canon in Sixteenth-Century Italy," in *Strong Voices, Weak History*, ed. Benson and Kirkham, 14–31, at 24, Rinaldo Corso's commentaries on Colonna's *Rime spirituali* and her complete collected poetry are the first large-scale critical assessments of a woman's writings ever published. Abigail Brundin notes in her forthcoming biography of Vittoria Colonna that Corso's initial commentary, *Dichiaratione fatta sopra la secondo parte delle Rime delle Divina Vittoria Collonna. . . [sic]*, was first published in 1543 (Bologna: Gian Battista de Phaelli).

    The critical essay on Laudomia Forteguerri's work that I cite above in n. 18, titled *Lettura . . . nell'Accademia degli Infiammati*, contains a text, a close reading, and an analysis of one of Forteguerri's sonnets, whereas Corso's work addresses Colonna's oeuvre in its entirety.

21. Salvatore Caponetto, *The Protestant Reformation in Sixteenth-Century Italy*, trans. Anne C. Tedeschi and John Tedeschi (Kirksville, MO: Thomas Jefferson Press, 1999), 83.

    Head of Cosimo's Florentine academy now, *Benedetto Varchi*, who had agreed to give two lectures a month on literary topics, delivered a sermon in 1549 on Good Friday that had so much material from already criminalized *Beneficio di Cristo* that it amounted to a public reading of the book combined with a promotional lecture on it. The anonymously authored *Beneficio di Cristo*, whose contract Giulia Gonzaga had negotiated with the printer Bindoni in Venice in 1543, sold roughly 40,000 copies in the first six years after it came out. It was considered the most dangerous Protestant book in circulation.

22. Ochino's *Dialogi sette* (without the *h* in *dialoghi*) was published by Zoppino in Venice in 1540. Of the seven dialogues, the first and the second name *Duchessa* and *Bernardino* (Cibo and Ochino) as the two interlocutors; the fourth and seventh dialogues name *Huomo* and *Donna* as interlocutors (a man and a woman); the third names as speakers *Maestro* and *Discepolo*; the fifth, *Christo* and *Anima*; and the sixth *Angelo custode* and *Anima peregrina*.

   The two letters from Flaminio, which I discuss in chapter 6 are dated and February 25, 1547 and May 4, 1549; the letter texts are in Marcantonio Flaminio, *Lettere*, ed. Alessandro Pastore (Rome: Edizioni dell' Ateneo & Bizzaro, 1978), 156–58; 171–73. I am indebted to Gabriella Zarri for calling my attention to Dario Marcatto's edition and commentary on Flaminio's letters in Marcantonio Flaminio, *Apologia del Beneficio di Cristo* (Florence: Olschki, 1996), 211–17: Marcatto demonstrates that Flaminio sent the same letter also dated May 4, 1549, almost verbatim, to Giulia Gonzaga.

23. Tullia D'Aragona's *Dialogo* was published by Gabriel Giolito in Venice in 1547. See Tullia d'Aragona, *Dialogue on the Infinity of Love*, ed. and trans. Rinaldina Russell (Chicago: University of Chicago Press, 1997).

24. Speroni's *Dialogo d'amore* featuring "Tullia" as an interlocutor was first published by Aldo Manuzio in Venice in 1542.

25. On Varchi's reputation as a sodomizer and his liaisons with boys, see Umberto Pirotti, *Benedetto Varchi e la Cultura del suo Tempo* (Florence: Olschki, 1971), 46–56. On the draconian laws against sodomy and their enforcement in Florence in the 1540s and 1550s, see Michael Rocke, *Forbidden Friendships: Homosexuality and Male Culture in Renaissance Florence* (Oxford: Oxford University Press, 1996), esp. 231–35.

26. Laura Battiferra, *Il primo libro dell' opere toscane* (Florence: Giunti, 1560). See also Laura Battiferri degli Ammannati, *Il primo libro delle opere toscane* (Urbino: Accademia Raffaello, 2000); a bilingual edition of Battiferra, edited and translated by Victoria Kirkham, is forthcoming from the University of Chicago Press's the Other Voice in Early Modern Europe series.

27. When I speak of the fifteen volumes in the so-called Giolito poetry anthology series as an ensemble of texts (as I will throughout this book), I am following Giolito's great biographer and bibliographer Salvatore Bongi in his treatment of these books as a series of texts that must be regarded as a group or a suite of books: Bongi, *Annali di Gabriel Giolito de' Ferrari*, 2 vols. (Rome: I Pincipali Librai, 1890, 1895).

CHAPTER ONE

1. I take the term "cultural hegemony" from Stuart Hall's readings of Gramci in Hall's, "Gramsci's Relevance for the Study of Race and Ethnicity," 411–40, and his "What Is This 'Black' in Black Popular Culture?" 465–75, both in *Critical Dialogues in Cultural Studies*, ed. David Morley and Kuan-Hsing Chew (London and New York: Routledge, 1996). A passage from the latter essay sums up the sense in which I'm using the term: "Cultural hegemony is never about pure victory or pure domination (that's not what

the term means); it is never a zero-sum cultural game; it is always about shifting the balance of power in the relations of culture; it is always about changing the dispositions and the configurations of cultural power, not getting out of it." (468).

2. On the reform movement in Italy, see Thomas F. Mayer, *Reginald Pole: Prince and Prophet* (Cambidge: Cambridge University Press, 2000); John Martin, *Venice's Hidden Enemies: Italian Heretics in a Renaissance City* (Berkeley, Los Angeles, and London: University of California Press, 1993); Massimo Firpo, *Dal Sacco di Roma all'Inquisitione: Studi su Juan Valdés e la Riforma italiana* (Turin: Edizioni dell'Orso, 1998); Caponetto, *The Protestant Reformation*; Delio Cantimori, *Eretici italiani del Cinquecento: Ricerche storiche* (Florence: Sansoni, 1977); José C. Nieto, *Juan de Valdés and the Origins of the Spanish and Italian Reformation* (Geneva: Librairie Droz, 1970); Elizabeth G. Gleason, *Gasparo Contarini: Venice, Rome, and Reform* (Berkeley: University of California Press, 1993); Gleason, "On the Nature of Sixteenth-Century Italian Evangelism: Scholarship, 1953–1978," *Sixteenth-Century Journal* 9, no. 3 (1978): 3–25; Gleason, *Reform Thought in Sixteenth-Century Italy* (Chico, CA.: Scholars Press, 1981); Gigliola Fragnito, *La Bibbia al rogo: La censura ecclesiastica e i volgarizzamenti della Scrittura (1471–1605)* (Bologna: Il Mulino, 1997); Anne J. Schutte, *Pier Paolo Vergerio: The Making of an Italian Reformer* (Geneva: Droz, 1977); Barry Collett, *A Long and Troubled Pilgrimage: The Correspondence of Marguerite D'Angoulême and Vittoria Colonna, 1540–1545* (Princeton, NJ: Princeton Theological Seminary, 2000). When I speak of the reform movement, or species of reform, in which Vittoria Colonna, Costanza d'Avalos, Giovanna and Maria Aragona, Giulia Gonzaga, and others who were followers of Valdés participated, I follow Thomas Mayer and others in using the label *spirituali*.

3. On relations between Charles V, Naples, and Rome, 1500–1560, see Thomas James Dandelet, *Spanish Rome: 1500–1700* (New Haven, CT: Yale University Press, 2001); and Ludwig Pastor, *The History of the Popes from the Close of the Middle Ages,* ed. and trans. Ralph Francis Kerr (St. Louis: B. Herder, 1923), vol. 14. Fabrizio Colonna marched into Naples with King Charles VIII in February 1495 and took the city, but by October the French were forced to withdraw, and the Aragonese King Ferdinando II (reigned 1495–96) returned to the throne of Naples. The next brief occupation of Naples by the French occurred in 1502, soon after Fabrizio Colonna's defection to King Federico d'Aragona, the successor of Ferdinando II.

4. Claudio Mutini, "Avalos, Costanza d'," in *Dizionario biografico degli Italiani* (hereafter *DBI*), 63 vols. (Rome: Istituto della Enciclopedia italiana, 1962), 4:621–22; see also Suzanne Therault, *Un cénacle humaniste de la Renaissance autour de Vittoria Colonna châtelaine d'Ischia* (Florence: Sansoni, 1968); Alfredo Reumont, *Vittoria Colonna, vita, fede, poesia,* trans. Giuseppe Müller and Ermanno Ferrero (Turin: Loescher, 1883); Vittoria Colonna, *Carteggio,* ed. Ermanno Ferrero and Giuseppe Müller, 2d ed. (Turin: Loescher,1892). D'Avalos was born ca. 1460, the daughter of Iñigo I d'Avalos and Antonella d'Aquino. In 1483 she married Federico del Balzo and was widowed soon afterward. She took control of the duchy of Francavilla in 1501 and followed her brother Iñigo II to Ischia the same year, assuming regency over the island after he defected to France (according to Donata Chiomenti Vassalli, *Giovana d'Aragona: Fra*

*baroni, principi, e sovrani del Rinascimento* [Milan: Mursia, 1987], 17; Mutini doesn't mention his defection); he died in 1503. Charles named her Principessa of Francavilla but not until 1541, the year she died. Her nephew Ferrante Francesco d'Avalos (1489–1525), Marchese di Pescara, married Vittoria Colonna in 1509. She was also the aunt of Alfonso d'Avalos, Marchese del Vasto (1502–46) and Costanza d'Avalos (1503–75), Duchess of Amalfi, who was married to Duke Alfonso Piccolomini. Therault relies principally on Amalia Giordano, *La dimora di Vittoria Colonna a Napoli* (Naples: Melfi & Joele, 1906).

5. Vittoria Colonna's grandfather was Federico da Montefeltro, Duke of Urbino; her cousin Pompeo Colonna was Viceroy of Naples, 1530–32.

6. The authoritative biographies are Chiomenti Vassalli, *Giovanna d'Aragona*; Giuseppe Alberigo, "Aragona, Giovanna d'," *DBI* (1961), 3:694–96; Alberigo, "Aragona, Maria d'," *DBI* (1961), 3:701–2; see also Gaspare de Caro, "Avalos Alfonso d'," *DBI* (1962), 3:612–16; and Dandelet, *Spanish Rome.*

7. Therault, *Un cénacle humaniste*, 344–45. Therault notes that historians have also specu-lated that during the siege of Naples in 1528, Gonzaga might have taken refuge in Ischia, joining her sisters there.

8. Therault's *Un cénacle humaniste*, the inspiration for this chapter, is a fascinating piece of detective work in its tracing of Vittoria Colonna's influence through the works of her circle on Ischia across two decades.

9. Therault (ibid.) dates the first of two periods of the d'Avalos salon on Ischia to the years 1509–25, led by the poet Sannazaro et al.; and the second, to 1527–36, headed by Giovio, Tasso, Tansillo, et al.

10. See my app. A for a list of the poetry anthologies of the forties and fifties that were launched by the Giolito press in Venice; app. A also includes a list of the women poets published in the anthologies. See app. B for an alphabetical index of the participating poets, female and male, the editors, and the dedicatees of the volumes.

11. Therault, *Un cénacle humaniste*, 224–25, reproduces the sonnet cited by Giordano, *La dimora di Vittoria Colonna*, as sonnet 30. This unpublished sonnet, among others that Galeazzo dedicated to Vittoria Colonna, is preserved in F. Bartelli, *Note Biografiche: Galeazzo di Tarsia* (Cosenza: A. Trippa, 1906), 204.

12. Therault, *Un cénacle humaniste*, 209: "A l'aria dolce, al suon de le parole, / Invido Phoebo dal balcon suo dice, / Che debbio far s'in terra è un altro sole? / Più aver l'usato affanno omai non lice / Poichè via più ch'io splendo, splender suole / Questa al mondo, gentil nova Phenice." (Jealous Phoebus from his balcony responds to the sweet air and the sound of her words: "What should I do if there is another sun on earth? Having the old jealous pangs is no longer right, because this gentle new Phoe-nix is much more used to shining in the world than I" [my translation].)

13. On the depiction of poetic works as mausoleums or temples as suggested in the graphic design of title pages, see Cic. De orat.1.201; Cic. Inv. 1.1; Cic. Off. 1.156; Hor. 3.30; Liv. Pr. 6; Virg. A. 3.102; 8.312; V. Max. 8.7.4.

14. Girolamo Ruscelli, *Del tempio* (Venice: Pietrasanta 1555); and Giuseppe Betussi, *Le imagini del tempio* (Venice: De'Rossi, 1557).

15. Therault, *Un cénacle humaniste*, 213 and 453, reports that this text is in Giordano, *La dimora di Vittoria Colonna*, 53.

16. Therault, *Un cénacle humaniste*, 453n38, notes that this passage from Capanio's *Tempio* appears to be extant in print only in Benedetto Croce, *Aneddoti di varia letteratura*, 3 vols. (Bari: Laterza, 1953–54), 1:326.Croce found the verses in the Biblioteca Nazionale of Naples (Cod. Misc. 13. G. 42). Therault also reports that both Croce and Giordano note that the verses were plagiarized by Niccolò Franco in a dialogue he published in Venice in 1536.

17. On Petrarch's sonnet 128 from the *Rime sparse* and the trope, see Margaret Brose, "Petrarch's Beloved Body: 'Italia mia,'" in *Feminist Approaches to the Body in Medieval Literature*, ed. Linda Lomperis and Sarah Stansbury (Philadelphia: University of Pennsylvania Press, 1993), 1–20.

18. Therault, *Un cénacle humaniste*, 218 and 454n61, notes that her source for the text of this sonnet is Giordano, *La dimora di Vittoria Colonna*, 51.

19. Marino Sanuto, *I diarii di Marino Sanuto, 1496–1533*, 58 vols., ed. F. Stefani, G. Berchet, and Nicolò Berozzi (Venice: Visentini, 1897), 46:664–70.

    Paolo Giovio, *Opera*, vol. 1, *Epistolarum Pars Prior*, ed. Giuseppe Guido Ferrero (Rome: Istituto Poligrafico dello Stato, 1956), 118–23—page numbers given in the text are to this work; Suzanne Therault writes at length about the tragic naval battle at the Capo d'Orso, in *Un cénacle humaniste* (349–66); Chiomenti Vassalli, *Giovanna d'Aragona*, 63–64, mentions it in passing. Therault quotes excerpts from Giovio's letter in French translation but does not give the Italian text. I am indebted to Therault and Chiomenti Vassalli for the notion that Costanza's guests might possibly have heard and seen traces of the battle, which was miles away. They certainly heard of its outcome immediately.

20. Paulo Giovio, *Opera*, 1:118–23.

21. I have estimated the day of Giovio's departure from Ischia from his remark in his letter that Moncado's corpse remained unburied for two days and from the letter's dateline: "in calende di Magio 1528."

22. The Genoese and their admiral Filippino Doria (referred to as *il Conte*) and their eight ships are the unnamed lead ship referred to as the *capitana*, the *Pellegrina*, the *Donzella*, the *Serena*, the *Fortuna*, the *Mora*, the *Patrona* (or *di Nettuno*), and the *Signora*. The six ships from the emperor Charles V's fleet commanded by the Spanish admiral Ugo di Moncada (referred to as *don Ugo*) are the *Gobba*, the *Secames*, the *Perpignana*, the *Calabrese*, an unnamed ship referred to only as *la di don Bernardo*, and the unnamed *capitana* or lead ship commanded by Moncada. Giovio uses the generic term *galea* to encompass the warships in his narrative; and it is not clear whether he means the low-slung "galleys" used in naval warfare, which would have been propelled by oarsmen rather than sails, or whether we should understand the term *galea* to mean "galleon," the larger, square-rigged sail-driven ship that sat high in the water.

23. According to his dedicatory letter to *Il Cortignano*, when Castiglione finished writing that work in 1516, he gave Vittoria Colonna a copy of it to read. The work was first

printed by Aldus Minutius in Venice in 1528, but it circulated widely in manuscript well before that date.

24. Republic 3.398a; 10.595 ff., 605b, 607a.

25. The Venetian poetry anthologies are the subject of chapter 2.

26. See Therault, *Un cénacle humaniste*, 234–44, where she describes Tasso's increased output and participation in the island circle in the 1530s.

27. Ibid., 233–34; Alessandro Pastore, *Marcantonio Flaminio: Fortune e Sfortune di un Chierico nell'Italia del Cinquecento* (Milan: Franco Angeli, 1981), says nothing about the humanist's relations with the Ischia circle, and Tasso is only mentioned in passing.

28. Therault, *Un cénacle humaniste*, 233; we have no evidence that Flaminio himself visited the island except twice—1514 when he was six and then in 1538.

29. On Gonzaga's presence in Naples, see Giorgio Patrizi, "Colonna, Vittoria," *DBI* (1962), 27:449.

30. Colonna's biographers and editors disagree about these early dates (1530–34): see Colonna, *Carteggio*; Patrizi, "Colonna, Vittoria"; Reumont, *Vittoria Colonna*; Collett, *A Long and Troubled Pilgrimage*; Roland H. Bainton, *Women of the Reformation in Germany and Italy* (Minneapolis: Augsburg Publishing, 1971); Suzanne Therault, *Un cénacle humaniste*.

31. On Caterino Cibo, see B. Feliciangeli, *Notizie e documenti sulla vita di Caterina Cibo-Varano* (Camerino: Tipografico Savini, 1891); Franca Petrucci, "Cibo, Caterina," in *DBI* (1981), 25:237–41; Maria Teresa Guerra Medici, *Famiglia e potere in una signoria dell'Italia centrale: I Varano di Camerino* (Camerino: Universita degli Studi di Camerino, 2002); Cesare Vasoli, "Caterina Cibo Varano," in *Civitas Mundi: Studi sulla cultura del Cinquecento.Raccolta di Studi e Testi* 194 (Rome: Edizioni Storia e Letteratura, 1996), 121–38; Bainton, *Women of the Reformation*; Caponetto, *The Protestant Reformation*.

32. Regarding Colonna's letter to Cardinal Contarini, see Patrizi, "Colonna, Vittoria," 450; and Colonna, *Carteggio*, 93–96.

33. On Cibo's flight north, see Petrucci, "Cibo, Caterina," 238–40; and Guerra Medici, *Famiglia e potere*, 51–53. Paul's vengeance was diasastrous for Cibo. When Cibo betrothed her daughter Giulia da Varano to the future Duke of Urbino (Guidobaldo della Rovere) in 1528, Pope Paul III in 1534 forbade the marriage. He was determined to prevent so powerful an alliance as a wedding between the heirs to the duchies of Camerino and Urbino would represent, right in his own backyard. But on October 11, 1534, Guidobaldo and Giulia were married, after which Paul excommunicated Cibo, her daughter, and her new husband; he also expelled Cibo from her duchy, investing Ercole Varano di Ferrara as Duke of Camerino with the promise that the duchy would be restored to the pope's nephew Ottavio Farnese (Guerra Medici, *Famiglia e potere*, 63). See esp. Petrucci on Cibo's repeated need to take up arms against neighboring lords who attempted to seize Camerino after her husband's death in 1528. Cibo, like Gonzaga and the princess of Francavilla of Ischia, belongs to the sixteenth-century caste of amazons I mention earlier.

34. See Nieto, *Juan de Valdés and the Origins*; Caponetto, *The Protestant Reformation*, 64–79; on Valdés's thought, see Giovanni di Valdés, *Alfabeto Cristiano: Dialogo con Giulia Gonzaga* (Venice, 1545; composed ca. 1535), ed. Benedetto Croce (Bari: Laterza, 1938).

35. Giulia Gonzaga was born near Mantua in Gazzuolo in 1513, a granddaughter of Gianfrancesco Gonzaga, Lord of Sabbioneta. She came to her marriage with Vespasiano Colonna with a dowry of twelve thousand gold ducats in 1526. Educated in classical literature and history alongside her brothers, like Colonna and the d'Aragona sisters, she carried on an extensive correspondence with the leading intellectuals of her time. The basic bio-bibliographical sources on her are Oliva, *Giulia Gonzaga Colonna*; Guido Dall'Olio, "Gonzaga, Giulia," in *DBI*, 57:783–87; Bruto Amante, *Giulia Gonzaga e il movimento religioso femminile* (Bologna: Zanichelli, 1896); Ireneo Affò, "Vita di donna Giulia Gonzaga" in *Raccolta ferrarese di opuscoli scientifici e letterari di chiarissimi autori italiani*, 8 (Venice, 1780), 145–88; Oddone Ortolani, *Pietro Carnesecchi* (Florence: Felice Le Monnier, 1963); Siro Mulli, *Giulia Gonzaga* (Milan: Treves, 1938); Pasquale d'Ercole, *Il cardinale Ippolito de' Medici* (Terlizzi: Giannone, 1907); Giuseppe Moretti, "Il cardinale Ippolito dei Medici," *Archivio Storico Italiano*, vol. 2 (1940); Therault, *Un cenacle humaniste*. Some of Gonzaga's letters are contained in Müller and Ferrero's edition of Vittoria Colonna's *Carteggio*; others are contained Giuseppe Paladino, ed., *Opuscoli e lettere di Riformatori Italiani del Cinquecento* (Bari: Laterza & Figli, 1913); and Massimo Firpo and Dario Marcatto, eds., *I processi inquisitoriali di Pietro Carnesecchi, 1557–1567* (Vatican City: Archivio Vaticano, 1998–2000), 4 vols.

36. Chiomenti Vassalli, *Giovanna d'Aragona*, 80–82, gives a step-by-step description of Charles's triumphal entry and the processions, banquets, and balls that followed his arrival.

37. Giulia was actually in double mourning. Her only surving brother Luigi Gonzaga (1500–1532), had died of wounds he sustained in the battle of Ancona; meanwhile Ippolito de' Medici (1511–35) renounced his cardinalate in order to marry Giulia Gonzaga. The plan was that he would marry Giulia and become Duke of Florence, crowned by Charles V. He had proposed to Giulia and she had already accepted in July 1535 (Oliva, *Giulia Gonzaga Colonna*, 197–98; Oliva does not give the exact date), just weeks before he died on August 10; Ippolito believed he had been poisoned.But had Gonzaga gone through with the marriage she would have been forced to relinquish her title, lands, and rents—everything her late husband Vespasiano Colonna had left her, with the proviso that she not remarry.

38. Oliva (ibid., 114–20) lists the "regulars" at Fondi.

39. For both stories, see Dall'Olio, "Gonzaga, Giulia," 783; Affò, "Vita di donna Giulia Gonzaga," 145–88.

40. Oliva, *Giulia Gonzaga Colonna*, 163–71.

41. See Nieto, *Juan de Valdés and the Origins*, 143. Nieto, the leading authority on Valdés, observes that no one knows why the theologian left Rome for Naples but he notes that some scholars believe it was because he was identified with the friends of Clement and that when Paul III, who was an enemy of Clement, came to the papal throne Valdes's position at court suddenly became untenable.

42. Nieto (ibid., 145) notes that he was given the title "veedor de los castillos" (inspector of castles) while in Charles's service.

43. Ibid., 147; see also Ortolani, *Pietro Carnesecchi*, 163: according to Carnesecchi, Valdés customarily provided Ochino with an outline and notes that he (Ochino) would use as the basis for his sermon the following day in church.

44. The list is verbatim from a footnote in Oliva, *Giulia Gonzaga Colonna*, 221. Oliva does not give the source of his anonymous list but comments only that he assumes it is much reduced from the number of actual visitors to her salon. The source could have been one of her two secretaries: Magno or Flaminio.

45. Ibid., 236.

46. Valdés's own dedicatory letter addressed to Giulia Gonzaga in the published preface to the *Alfabeto cristiano* (Venice: Bacarini, 1545) makes clear that he meant the dialogue to accurately report the contents of their conversation; Valdés's letter is reproduced in its entirety in Croce's modern edition of Valdés's *Alfabeto*, 4–6. Nieto, *Juan de Valdés*, does not cite this dedicatory letter but comments that the *Alfabeto* was reproduced from conversations "which had actually taken place between Giulia and Valdés" (191).

47. The 1545 Bacarini edition of the *Alfabeto* is extremely rare. I have not yet seen it. Paul F. Grendler, *The Roman Inquisition and the Venetian Press, 1540–1605* (Princeton, NJ: Princeton University Press, 1977), 81n, notes that the Cambridge University Library holds a copy of this edition. He also says that Bacarini published twenty-three editions of the work between 1543 and 1597 (all contraband after 1549). The British Library Catalogue lists only one edition of the dialogue unter the title *Alphabeto Christiano, che insegna la vera via d'acquistare il lume dello Spirito Santo* (trans. M. A. Magno from the Spanish of Juan de Valdés), 76 fols. ([Venice?], 1546). No publisher is named.

48. Gonzaga's secretary Marco Antonio Magno's dedicatory letter is addressed to "Giulia Gonzaga sua patrona." The letter is reprinted in Croce, ed., *Alfabeto*, 3. In this suggestive prefatory letter, Magno asks Giulia to check to see whether he's succeeded in channeling her "voice" somehow in his translation: "in the way hat the composer of the work has led her to the Holy Spirit with equally divine arguments" ("E cosí a V.S. Illustrissima mando la effigie di sé medesima, accioché vegga se io ho cosí ben saputo farla ragionare in lingua sua, come il compositore dell'opra l'ha indutta con cosí divini ragionamenti allo amore dello Spirito Santo.") The analogy itself introduces ambiguity and as does the term *compositore* since Magno himself is now in a sense the *compositore* of the work. But none of this constitutes an argument for or against Gonzaga's co-authorship.

49. Croce, ed., *Alfabeto*, in the appendix, 173–78, prints the whole text of Valdés's *Testamento*.

50. According to Oliva, *Giulia Gonzaga Colonna*, Gonzaga as much as admitted to having been the translator of Valdés's *Considerazioni,* the original (Spanish language) manuscript of which she preserved (237). But see Caponetto below who credits the authorship of the *Considerazioni* to Flaminio.

51. Grendler, *The Roman Inquisition*, 77–78; the *Catalogo* (index) of 1549 prohibited the publication and distribution of Valdés's *Alfabeto* and the anonymous *Beneficio di Christo* by title (86). See also Oliva, *Giulia Gonzaga Colonna*, 236: it was also Gonzaga herself

who negotiated the contract to publish the *Beneficio* with the Venetian printer Bernardo de' Bindoni in 1543.

52. See Oliva, *Giulia Gonzaga Colonna*, 190–208, for an unsentimental and superbly researched portrait of their relationship.

53. In addition to Caponetto, on Valdés and Valdesian thought in Ochino, Colonna, and others, see also Elizabeth G. Gleason, "The Capuchin Order in the Sixteenth Century," in *Religious Orders of the Catholic Reformation, In Honor of John C. Olin*, ed. R. L. DeMolen (New York: Fordham University Press, 1994), 31–67; Gleason, "On the Nature of Sixteenth-Century Italian Evangelism: Scholarship, 1953–1978," *Sixteenth-Century Journal* 9, no. 3 (1978): 3–25; Collett, *A Long and Troubled Pilgrimage*, esp. 66–104; Massimo Firpo, *Inquisizione romana e controriforma: Studi sul Cardinal Giovanni Morone e il suo processo d'eresia* (Bologna: Il Mulino, 1992); Roland H. Bainton, *Bernardino Ochino esule e riformatore senese del Cinquecento 1487–1563* (Florence: Sansoni, 1940); Bainton, *Women of the Reformation*; Colonna, *Carteggio*.

54. On the genre of epistolary self-consolation, see George W. McClure, *Sorrow and Consolation in Italian Humanism* (Princeton, NJ: Princeton University Press, 1991).

55. Vittoria Colonna, *Rime* (Parma: Viottis, 1538).

56. Vittoria Colonna, *Rime*, ed. Lodovico Dolce (Venice: Giolito, 1552).

57. Colonna, *Carteggio*, 238–39. For the full text of the letter, see p. 33 of this chapter.

58. Reumont, *Vittoria Colonna*, 168. I follow Reumont and Ferrero and Müller, eds., *Carteggio*, in assigning dates throughout.

59. According to Reumont, *Vittoria Colonna*, 162, Colonna stayed at the Este palace; he speaks of Colonna's "soggiorna nella sua residenza," meaning the duke's residence.

60. Ibid., 167.

61. On Renata di Francia, see Bainton, *Women of the Reformation*, 235–54; Massimo Firpo, *Inquisizione romana*; Collett, *A Long and Troubled Pilgrimage*.

62. John Calvin, *Instituzione della religione christiana di Messer Giovanni Calvino*, trans. Giulio Cesare Pascali (Geneva: J.Burgese, A. Davodeo, F. Iacchi, 1557).

63. Thirteen more editions of her poetry would be published by 1586, all but one in Venice. Special Collections in the Regenstein Library at the University of Chicago has a copy of the beautiful 1538 Parma edition.

   Colonna's biographers have traditionally treated half of these editions separately, titled the *Rime spirituali*, as signally expressive of the spiritual awakening she experienced in Naples and Ferrara. Rinaldina Russell, in her article "The Mind's Pursuit of the Divine: A Survey of Secular and Religious Themes in Vittoria Colonna's Sonnets," *Forum Italicum* 26 (1992): 14–27; and Collett, *A Long and Troubled Pilgrimmage*, 69–70, caution against this artificial distinction between her amatory and religious poetry, arguing that her *rime amorose* and *rime spirituali* taken together respresent a single journey whose end is the soul's ascent to God.

64. Caponetto, *The Protestant Reformation*, 235.

65. Ibid., 235.

66. Ibid., 242–43; Olimpia Morata, *The Complete Writings of an Italian Heretic*, ed. and trans. Holt N. Parker (Chicago: University of Chicago Press, 2003). Morata (1526–55),

daughter of the Vicenza university professor Fulvio Pellegrino Morato, married the German Lutheran physician Andreas Grunthler in 1549, and together they fled to Schweinfurt in 1554. She died of tuberculosis in that city at twenty-nine.

67. Pope Paul III's pretext for invading and occupying towns and feudatories in the papal states, such as Ascanio Colonna's, was failure to pay the salt tax. The papal threats began in 1538 and the disastrous invasions commenced in 1540, first of Perugia and next the Colonna lands and towns. See chapter 3 on the Salt War.

68. Collett, *A Long and Troubled Pilgrimage*, 112, identifies this "reverendissimo di Ferrara" as the Suffragan Bishop of Ferrara, Ottaviano de Castello. Müller and Ferrero, the editors of Colonna's *Carteggio*, do not have a footnote identifying the reference, which is unusual for them.

69. *Matthew* 20:1–16. The parable of the vineyard fits well. Pietro Bembo (1470–1547), poet, critic, historian, was born into Venetian patriciate. He decided very late in life to become a priest, but he was not ordained until 1539, when he was almost seventy.

70. Domenico Tordi, "Vittoria Colonna in Orivieto durante la Guerra del Sale," *Bollettino della società umbra di Storia Patria*, vol. I (Perugia: Boncampagni, 1895), 473–533, at 489, notes that Vittoria Colonna arrived at the gates of the monastery of San Paolo in Orvieto on March 17, 1541, and she lived there until August 9, 1541, when she left to return to Rome (510).

71. Francesco Gui, "Il papato e i Colonna al tempo di Filippo II," in *Atti del convegno internazionale di studi storici del IV centenario della morte di Filippo II, 5–7 Novembre 1998* (Cagliari: AM&D Edizioni, 1999), 9–77, has linked the Colonna's involvement in the reform movement to their resistance to Pope Paul II's territorial aggression. Donata Chiomenti Vassalli, *Giovanna d'Aragona Colonna* put forward the same thesis. Colonna probably followed Pole to Viterbo in September, although her first letter with a dateline from Viterbo in Ferrero and Müller, eds., *Carteggio*, is her letter of December 8, 1541, to Giulia Gonzaga. See text and translation of the letter on pp. 33–34.

72. Valdés is thought to have died at the end of July or beginning of August 1541; Costanza d'Avalos died a few months earlier that year.

73. Mayer, *Reginald Pole*, 119, calls the *Beneficio* (the *Trattato utilissimo del beneficio di Giesu Cristo crocifisso verso i Cristiani* is its full title), "the most celebrated product of Pole and Flaminio's relationship amd of the Italian Reformation."

74. My narrative in the pages that follow is indebted not only to Guido Dall'Olio's biography of Giulia Gonzaga as cited above but also to the biographies and bibliographies of Giovanna and Maria d'Aragona by Giuseppe Alberigo, Vittoria Colonna by Giorgio Patrizi, Marcantionio Flaminio by Alessandro Pastore, and Pietro Carnesecchi by Antonio Rotondò in the *DBI*, 3:694–96; 3:701–2; 27:448–57; 48:282–88; and 20:466–76, respectively. For Pole's role in Viterbo in the early 1540s I am indebted to Mayer, *Reginald Pole*.

75. On Valdés, Valdesian thought, and the doctrine of justification through faith alone, see Nieto, *Juan de Valdés and the Origins*, esp. 130–34; and Caponetto, *The Protestant Reformation*, 78–81.

76. The quote is taken from Nieto, *Juan de Valdés and the Origins,* 162; Pole's oath of allegiance to the pope was delivered on his deathbed in 1558—clearly as a last ditch effort to appear in no way heterodox.

77. Ibid., 155–59. Nieto takes Giulia's and Carnesecchi's rejection of the pope as the vicar of Christ as having come from Valdés's teaching, though Valdés's writings are suggestively silent on the matter. He neither refutes nor supports papal authority.

78. On the correct appellation for the Valdesians, Collett, *A Long and Troubled Pilgrimage,* 47–104, is excellent. He distinguishes the Valdesian *spirituali* and the Calvinistic *évangéliques* from other groups of Protestants, heterodox thinkers, and Counter-Reformation proponents.

79. On the importance of Calvin's *Institutes* for the *spirituali* movement in Italy, see Caponetto, *The Protestant Reformation,* 40, 84, 105, 124, 222, 224; and Mayer, *Reginald Pole,* 84 ff.

80. Mayer, *Reginald Pole,* 157. Pole's warning to Colonna comes from Carnesecchi's recollections many years later at his trial in 1567, in Giacomo Mansoni, ed., "Il processo Carnesecchi," *Miscellanea di storia italiana* 10 (1870): 268, as cited by Mayer, *Reginald Pole,* 123.

81. The citation comes from Caponetto, *The Protestant Reformation,* 57, on Carnesecchi's third trial by the Roman Inquisition in 1566.

82. Mayer's observation in his *Reginald Pole,* more complex: he states that for Pole and many of his circle "poetic *lusus* was as important as religion" (123).

83. Ferrero and Müller, eds., *Carteggio,* 42:240, note that the work Colonna refers to in this letter to Gonzaga is Valdés's *Commentarii o declaracion breve y compendiosa sobre la epsitola de S. Pablo apostel à los Romanos* (Venice, 1556).

84. Ferrero and Müller, eds., *Carteggio,* 42:238–40. Vittoria Colonna to Giulia Gonzaga, December 8, 1541.

85. On the manuscript Gonzaga brought to Venice, see Mayer, *Reginald Pole,* 120–21; the authorship of the *Beneficio* is disputed, but I have no reservations in following Mayer's assessment of it as Pole's and Flaminio's joint composition. Mayer argues for the authorship of Pole as the principal writer of the work, noting the many similar passages between the *Beneficio* and Pole's earlier work, the *De unitate* (120).

    Many scholars hold that the anonymous *Beneficio* was a heavily redacted treatise composed by the Benedictine monk, Benedetto da Montova (a.k.a. Benedetto Fontanini), who had been a disciple of Valdés in Naples; in the late 1530s, Benedetto, so the story goes, traveled north to Mantua bringing his manuscript with him.

86. On the immense popularity of the *Beneficio* with all social classes, see esp. John Martin, *Venice's Hidden Enemies: Italian Heretics in a Renaissance City* (Berkeley, Los Angeles, and London: University of California Press, 1993).

87. Dall'Olio, "Gonzaga, Giulia," 784. On the testimony of Apollonio Merenda, another member of Pole's Viterbo circle, see *I processi inquisitoriali,* ed. Massimo Firpo and Marcatto; L. Amabile, *Il S. Officio della Inquisitione in Napoli,* I (Citta di Castello, 1892) as cited in Dall'Olio, "Gonzaga, Giulia," 786–87.

88. See, on Ochino's flight to the north, Patrizi, "Colonna, Vittoria," 452: Patrizi says the book Ochino sent her was probably the *Prediche* (his sermons). The Newberry Library owns a copy of this work: Bernardino Ochino, *Prediche* (Venice: n.p., 1541).

89. For an important consideration of Gonzaga's and Valdés's influence on Vittoria Colonna's writing and thought during the Viterbo and post-Viterbo years (1541–46), see Rinaldina Russell, "L'ultima meditazione di Vittoria Colonna e l'"Ecclesia Viterbiensis,'" *La Parola del testo* 4, no. 1 (2000): 151–66. Russell finds in poems Colonna wrote during her residence in Viterbo the expression of *spirituali* concepts not found in her earlier work.

90. On Maria d'Aragona and Alfonso d'Avalos, see, principally, Francesco Fiorentino, "Maria d'Aragona, Marchesa del Vasto," in *Studi e Ritratti della Rinascenza*, ed. Luisa Fiorentino (Bari: Laterza, 1911), 157–91. See also the authoritative biographies previously cited: Alberigo, "Aragona, Giovanna" and "Aragona, Maria d'"; Caro, "Avalos, Alfonso d'"; see also Claudio Mutini, "Contile, Luca," *DBI* (1962), 28:495–502; Abd-el-Kader Salza, *Luca Contile: Uomo di lettere e di Negozi del Secolo XVI. Contributo alla storia della vita di corte e dei poligrafi del 500* (Florence: G. Carnesecchi, 1903). See also Chiomenti Vassalli, *Giovanna d'Aragona;* Oliva, *Giulia Gonzaga Colonna;* see also Maria d'Aragona's correspondence with Seripando in "Donna Maria d'Aragona marchesa del Vasto," in *Studi e Ritratti*, ed. Fiorentino.

91. Benedetto Nicolini, *Studi cinquecenteschi*, vol. 1, *Ideali e passioni nell'Italia religiosa* (Bologna: Tamari, 1968), 76–83.

92. Ibid., 78.

93. Fiorentino, ed., *Studi e Ritratti*, 170.

94. *Delle lettere di Luca Contile* (Pavia: Girolamo Bartoli, 1564). Henceforth cited in text as *Lettere*.

95. Salza, *Luca Contile*, 42. Salza cites a letter in which Contile reports that on March 27 there were fourteen thousand infantry and seven hundred cavalry in Milan.

96. Contile, *Lettere*, 1:110, to Orlando Marescotti, as cited in Fiorentino, ed., *Studi e Ritratti*, 174. Fiorentino, "Maria d'Aragona," 170, notes the participation of a number of women friends of Maria's in the daily activities of the court; among these he names the Marchesa di Sonzino, Isabella Brivio, Luigia Visconti, and Cavaliera Visconti.

97. On the uprising in Naples in 1547 led by Cesare Mormillo, see Salza, *Luca Contile*, 55–56. Salza observes that Mormillo and his popular movement anticipated Masaniello by a century but the issues were the same.

98. Salza, *Luca Contile;* and Fiorentino, ed., *Studi e Ritratti*, list Giambattista d'Azzia (the Marchese della Terza), Ferrante Carrafa, Angelo di Costanza, Bernardino Rota, Bernardo Spina, Antonio Minturno, and Luigi Tansillo among the returning members of Costanza d'Avalos's Ischia salon.

   In 1548, Maria d'Aragona fired Luca Contile; his offense was having written and dedicated a work of fifty *rime* to her sister Giovanna.

99. Carolyn Lougee Chappell, "Salons," in *The Encyclopedia of the Renaissance*, ed. Paul F. Grendler (New York: Scribners, 1999), 388–89: The salon was the site of sociability,

as Carolyn Lougee Chappell has observed, "whose roots stretched back to medieval and Renaissance courts" (388); but Lougee Chappell also notes that the term "salon" was not coined until the nineteenth century, although it is associated most commonly with seventeenth- and eighteenth-century French culture. See Lougee Chappell, *Le paradis des femmes: Women, Salons, and Social Stratification in Seventeenth-Century France* (Princeton, NJ: Princeton University Press, 1976).

100. For the notion of the "itinerant" salon woman, I am indebted to Elizabeth C. Goldsmith, "Publishing the Lives of Hortense and Marie Mancini," in *Going Public: Women and Publishing in Early Modern France*, ed. Elizabeth C. Goldsmith and Dena Goodman (Ithaca, NY, and London: Cornell University Press, 1995), 41.

101. Natalie Zemon Davis, in the essay "City Women and Religious Change" in her *Society and Culture in Early Modern France: Eight Essays* (Stanford, CA: Stanford University Press, 1965), critiques the speculations about the appeal Protestantism and other forms of religious reform had for sixteenth-century women. She discusses, and for the most part dismisses, the hypotheses of Max Weber, Lawrence Stone, Robert Mandrou, and others. French working women who had enough education to read the Scriptures for themselves, she concludes, were often, like our Italian salon women, simply too estranged from their parish priests not to question the religion of their fathers.

102. Joan B. Landes, *Women and the Public Sphere in the Age of the French Revolution* (Ithaca, NY, and London: Cornell University Press, 1988), 23. Landes makes the point that in France the salon was "displaced in part with the creation of a modern publishing apparatus, as a mode of cultural production."

CHAPTER TWO

1. See my apps. A and B. Here I provide detailed descriptions and a complete author index for all fifteen of the volumes that Giolito's biographer and bibliographer Bongi, *Annali di Gabriel Giolito*, considered part of the "Giolito" anthology set. Louise George Clubb and William G. Clubb, in "Building a Lyric Canon: Gabriel Giolito and the Rival Anthologists, 1545–1590," *Italica* 68, no. 3 (1991): 332–44, give a wonderful introduction to the sixteenth-century phenomenon of the anthologies in Italy and the place of the Giolito's volumes in relation to other anthologists:

> Almost overnight Giolito's two volumes had set the pattern for the most explosive flowering in history of the genre "lyric poetry anthology." Between 1545 and 1590 alone there are more than a hundred anthologies, each containing several hundred poems, about which exact data are available, but how many more remain neglected and uncatalogued in institutional and private libraries may never be determined. . . . It is beyond discussion that poets of the Ecole lyonnaise and the Pléiade, lyricists of the Siglo de Oro and countless Elizabethans supplemented their *Rime sparse* and *Sonetti e Canzoni* with one or another of Giolito's and of his rivals' anthologies. (332–33)

In recent years, the Giolito anthologies have been the subject of a number of excellent studies: see, now, Shemek, "The Collector's Cabinet," 239–62; Elena Strada,

Beatrice Bartolomeo, Franco Tomasi, Paolo Zaja, and Monica Bianco's essays in *"I più vaghi e i più soavi fiori": Studi sulle antologie di lirica del Cinquecento*, ed. Monica Bianco and Elena Strada (Padua: Orso, 2001); María Luisa Cerrón Puga, "Materiales para la construcción del canon petrarquista: Las antologías de Rime (libri I–IX)," *Critica del testo*, 2, no. 1 (1999): 249–90; Marie-Françoise Piejus, "La première anthologie des poèmes féminins: L'écriture filtrée et orientée," in *Le pouvoir et la plume: Incitation, contrôle et répression dans l'Italie du XVIe siècle* (Paris: Université de la Sorbonne Nouvelle, 1982), 193–213; Piejus, "Le poetesses Siennoises entre le jeu et l'écriture," in *Les femmes écrivains en Italie au Moyen Age et à la Renaissance* (Aix-en-Provence: l'Université de Provence, 1994), 312–32. My chapter on the anthologies focuses on the political and cultural contexts of the anthologies rather than on either their formal features or their place within the Petrarchan tradition.

2. On Domenichi's 1559 anthology of women poets, *Rime diverse d'alcune nobilissime, et virtuosissime donne*, see, above all, Shemek, "The Collector's Cabinet"; and Piejus, "La première anthologie des poèmes féminins."

3. Salza, *Luca Contile*, esp. 32–57; Francesco Fiorentino, *Studi e ritratti della Rinascenza: Donna Maria d'Aragona, Marchesa del Vasto* (Bari: Laterza & Figli, 1911).

4. On the Naples academies, see Michele Maylender, *Storia delle Accademie d'Italia*, 5 vols. (Bologna: Cappelli, 1926–30), see esp. 1:304–5; 2:332–33; 3:202–3; 5:190–92; on Maria Aragona's Academy of the Fenici in Milan, 2:356–361; and for comparison's sake, see also Maylender on the Infiammati in Padua, 3:266–70. See also Tobia R. Toscano, "Un'orazione latina di Bernardino Rota, 'principe' dell'accademia dei Sereni di Napoli," *Critica letteraria* 23 (1995): 81–109.

5. Salza, *Luca Contile*, 55, notes that the popular leader of the revolt was Cesare Morillo (who led the popular uprisings in Naples in 1528) and the leader of the dissident noble faction was "one" Caracciolo, the abbot of Bari (not to be confused.with the archbishop of Bari, Girolamo Sauli, who was Varchi's patron in 1544: see Deana Basile, "Fasseli gratia per poetessa," in *The Cultural Politics of Duke Cosimo I de'Medici*, ed. Konrad Eisenbichler (Aldershot: Ashgate, 2001), 138.

6. Pedro di Toledo and his wife were born in Spain, yet their children married into the Italian nobility. Their daughter Eleonora (who was also born in Spain) married Cosimo I de'Medici; their son García married Vittoria (the niece of the poet Victoria Colonna), who was the daughter of Giovanna d'Aragona and Ascanio Colonna. The amicable relations between the Neapolitans and the Spanish-Italian bureaucracy was far from being the case in Florence and Siena as we shall see in chaps. 4 and 5, where citizens were deeply suspicious of and hostile to the Spanish.

7. Salza, *Luca Contile*, 55; but note that Contile's own letters, published in *Delle lettere di Luca Contile: Primo volume diviso in due libri* (Pavia: Girolamo Bartoli,1564), contain much more relevant detail than Salza provides in his descriptions of them.

8. Contile to Bernardo Spina, May 15, 1547 (*Delle lettere*, vol. 1, fols. q3–4).

9. Contile to Spina, July 15, 1547 (*Delle lettere*, vol. 1, unnumbered fols. q4–4v).

10. Paola. Farenga, "Di Costanzo, Angelo," *DBI* (1991), 30:742–47; Gaspare de Caro, "Carafa, Ferrante," *DBI* (1976), 19:543–45.

11. Fiorentino, *Studi e ritratti*, 179.

12. This excerpt from Ferrante's *stanze* celebrating d'Aragona's return appears in ibid., 178.

13. Paul F. Grendler, *The Roman Inquisition and the Venetian Press, 1540–1605* (Princeton, NJ: Princeton University Press, 1977), 82–88.

14. *Catalogo di diverse opere, compositioini, et libri, li quali come heretici, sospetti, impii & scandalosi si dichiarono dannati, & prohibiti in questa inclita citta di Vinegia* (Venice: Vincenzo Valgrisi, 1549).

15. Gonzaga was the widow of Vespasiano Colonna, the first cousin of Giovanna d'Aragona's husband Ascanio Colonna. Gonzaga negotiated the contract with the Venetian printer Bernardo de' Bindoni to publish the anonymous *Beneficio* in 1543; and in 1545 she herself set the terms under which another Venetian publisher, Nicolò Bacarini, produced the *Alfabeto*, which she probably cowrote with Valdés. Both works sold thousands of copies and were immensely influential in Italy. It's important to note that Gonzaga not only was related by marriage to the Aragona sisters but was Vittoria Colonna's cousin-in-law as well.

16. The Italian academies typically took names that were full of self-mockery; the Dubbiosi (the dubious or uncertain ones), the Intronati (those who are dumbstruck), the Infiammati (the inflamed, the excited ones), the Pellegrini (the wanderers, the pilgrims), the Incogniti (the unrecognized, the unknowns), and the Ardenti (the impatient, the ones who burn with desire) were all fraternities whose members publicly staked out positions on current issues of a literary, philosophical, or religious sort that were both serious and entertaining.

17. Michele Maylender, *Storia delle Accademie d'Italia* (Bologna and Trieste: Liccinio Cappelli, 1927), 2:224–26; see also Francesco Saverio Quadrio, *Storia e ragione d'ogni poesia* (Brescia, 1739), 1:59. See also Lucia N. Bassani, *Il polyirafo Veneto: Giuseppe Betussi* (Padua: Antenore, 1992) on the Intronati and Infiammati academies.

18. Ercole Bentivoglio (1507–73; born in Mantua), for example, who does not figure prominently in this study, belonged to four academies in addition to the informal "Accademia del Giolito": the Elevati and Filareti in Ferrara, the Pellegrini in Venice, and the Infiammati in Padua. His work appears in most of Giolito's popular poetry anthologies. Giolito's two most senior editors, Lodovico Dolce and Lodovico Domenichi, were affiliated, each of them in turn, with the Fratta in Rovigo, the Ortolani in Piacenza, the Fiorentina in Florence, the Pellegrini in Venice, and the Infammati in Padua.

19. Girolamo Ruscelli, ed., *Del tempio alla divina signora donna Giovanna d'Aragona, fabricato da tutti i più gentili Spiriti, & in tutte le lingue principali del mondo* (Venice: Plinio Pietrasanta, 1555), 23–27.

20. *Lettura di Girolamo Ruscelli sopra un sonnetto dell'illustrissimo signor marchese della Terza alla divina signora Marchesa del Vasto* (Venice: Giovan Griffio, 1552). See the text of the Dubbiosi's Decree in Ruscelli, ed., *Del tempio alla . . . Giovanna d'Aragona*, 25–27: here the Dubbiosi explain why they have rejected the proposal of a joint tribute to the two sisters and have decided to consecrate their *tempio* as a monument for Giovanna

d'Aragona alone; Maria d'Aragona, they said, had already had her due in Ruscelli's *Lettura*. The Marchese della Terza was the Neapolitan poet Giovambattista d'Azzia who courted Maria after the death of her husband. Other works of his appear in the Giolito antholgies, vols. 5a, 5b, and 6 (see my appendixes to this chapter).

21. For a complete description of all the Naples anthologies, see my apps. A and B. On Giolito's editions of the Naples poets edited by Dolce, see also Angelo Nuovo and Christian Coppens, *I Giolito e la stampa nell'Italia del XVI secolo* (Geneva: Droz, 2005), 161–69. Nuovo notes that Giolito was especially eager to corner the Naples market because it represented one of the most populous and potentially profitable urban centers in Italy and that this might have driven the publication of the Naples poets. She also observes that these poets' works (some of them at any rate) came into Dolce's hands via the Naples bookseller Marcantonio Passero (162), whom Dolce cites as his source in his dedicatory letter to the 1556 edition (*Rime di diversi signori napoletani . . . Libro settimo* [vol. 7]). But it's important to note that in Dolce's three prior Naples anthologies of vol. 5 (1551/52; 1552; 1555), he never once mentions Passero as his source; and since all four editions are different from one another and contain different poets (as well as four different dedicatory letters), it is safe to assume that while some poems indeed came from Passero, others are likely to have come to Dolce from other sources.

22. David Abulafia, "The South," in *Italy in the Age of the Renaissanc, 1300–1550*, ed. John M. Najemy (Oxford: Oxford University Press, 2004), 208–25. Coining phrase "the Italian South" to demarcate the kingdom of Naples and Sicily from the cities in central and northern Italy, Abulafia usefully shows how different and yet how like Renaissance Naples was to the rest of the peninsula during the same period.

23. See my app. B.

24. For complete descriptions of all three editions of what I call vol. 5, see my app. B.

25. On the last of Dolce's *Rime di diversi napoletani*, see my app. B.

26. Lodovico Domenichi, ed., *Rime diverse d'alcune nobilissime, et virtuosissime donne* (Lucca: Busdragho, 1559). See my app. B, for a detailed description of the history, author rosters, and dedicatory letters for all fifteen editions that Salvatore Bongi, Giolito's nineteenth-century bibliographer, considered part of the so-called Giolito poetry anthology set. Domenichi's 1559 anthology of women poets (my vol. 10), though published by Busdragho in Lucca, is treated in app. B as part of the set. See Bongi's two-volume edition of the *Annali di Gabriel Giolito*. Busdragho's 1559 edition of Domenichi's *Rime diverse d'alcuni nobilissime . . . donne* is an extremely rare volume and must have had a relatively small print run. The British Library does not own a copy. In the United States, the volume is, as far as I have been able to learn, only held by two university libraries: the Beinecke at Yale University and the University of Iowa (Iowa City), Special Collections. I have seen both libraries' editions and I compare them in app. B.

27. Women authors are listed in boldface in my app. A, "An Index of Authors, Editors, Patrons, and Printers of the Giolito Anthology Series"; women are also listed in boldface in the author rosters in my app. B.

28. Girolamo Ruscelli, *Il sesto lbro delle rime di diversi eccellenti autori* (Venice: Al Segno del Pozzo, 1553). Ruscelli's vol. 6 of the anthology series is described in my app. B.

29. Sheryl E. Reiss and David G. Wilkins, eds., *Beyond Isabella: Secular Women Patrons of Art in Renaissance Italy* (Kirksville, MO: Truman State University Press, 2001), contains a spectacular array of essays on elite women patrons of the visual arts from the fourteenth to the sixteenth centuries. See also Kate Lowe, "The Progress of Patronage in Italian Renaissance Art," *Oxford Art Journal* 18 (1995):149.

30. The design practices of the early printed anthologies were the subject of a paper I presented at the Newberry Library ("The Woman in the Text: Selling Books and Celebrity in the Venetian Book Trade [1545–1560]," May 21, 2004); I am indebted to the library for the reproduction of the images in figs. 2–11.

31. Ruscelli's *Lettura* was published by Giovan Griffio in Venice in 1552; the lists are in an index, 62–72.

32. Only thirteen women were listed from Siena and eleven from Florence. The eleven women listed for Parma includes Charles V's daughter Margaret of Austria, wife of Duke Ottavio Farnese, no doubt a patron or prospective patron.

33. Domenichi published numerous other of his works with several other printers, but this time his publisher was Giolito. His catalog of famous modern women and their cities is found at the end of bk. 5 of the *Nobiltà delle donne*, fols. 244–74v.

34. On Colonna and Gambara's patronage of artists, see Marjorie Och, "Vittoria Colonna and the Commission for a *Mary Magdalene* by Titian," 192–223; and Katherine A. McIver, "Two Emilian Noblewomen and Patronage Networks in the Cinquecento," 159–76—both in *Beyond Isabella*, ed. Reiss and Wilkins.

35. See Shemek's rich and nuanced analysis of the *Discorso* in "Getting a Word in Edgewise: Laura Terracina's Discorsi on the *Orlando furioso*" in her *Ladies Errant: Wayward Women and Social Order in Early Modern Italy* (Durham, NC, and London: Duke University Press, 1998), 126–57.

36. For a description of the contents of the first, as well as the other volumes in this series, see my app. B.

37. There are a few exceptions: Vittoria Colonna (the Marchesa di Pescara) and Alfonso d'Avalos (the Marchese del Vasto) are sometimes listed in the rosters by their titles.

38. The driving forces of the Inquisition in 1553 were two future popes: Cardinal Gian Pietro Carafa (soon to be elected Pope Paul IV; reigned 1555–59); and Fra (later Cardinal) Michele Ghislieri (Pope Pius V; reigned 1566–72). At the time of the mass burnings of the Talmud, the sitting pope was Julius III (Gian Maria Del Monte; reigned 1550–55), a nonentity, according to Grendler, "who vacillated between reform and frivolity" (*The Roman Inquisition*, 96).

39. Ibid., 39–47. The Republic of Venice created the Venetian Inquisition on April 22, 1547; a new magistracy, called the *Tre Savii*, consisting of three nobles from the highest echelons of government, was instituted to meet regularly with delegates representing the papacy. This signified Venice's independence from Rome. The Venetian government was always eager to stamp out heresy and happy to rid Venice of the Jewish press, but it was unwilling to ban or burn books that had nothing to do with heresy.

40. Ibid., 92.

41. Ibid., 92–93; Brian Pullan, *The Jews of Europe and the Inquisition of Venice, 1550–1670* (London and New York: I. B. Tauris, 1997), 82–83. Cristoforo Madruzzo, Cardinal of Trent and the presiding officer of the Council of Trent, founded a Jewish publishing business at Riva di Trento that survived the Inquisition and flourished 1558–62 (Grendler, *The Roman Inquisition*, 93).

42. *Cathalogus librorum haereticorum* . . . (Venice: Gabriele Gioloto, 1553); Grendler, *The Roman Inquisition*, 95–96.

43. *Index auctorum, et librorum, qui ab officio S. Rom. & universalis Inquistionis caveri ab omnibus et singulis in universa Christiana Republica mandantur* . . .(Venice: Girolamo Giglio, 1559).

44. Grendler, *The Roman Inquisition*, esp.118–19. At the same time, Grendler points out that while Giolito (and no doubt other Venetian publishers) made a show of complying with the Holy Office's orders to hand over forbidden books to them for destruction and burning, the publisher didn't do it, handing in instead only a selection of some Prostestant book and none of the banned Italian titles (125).

45. I say "staged" because both Ludwig Pastor (*History of the Popes*, vol. 14) and Grendler (*The Roman Inquisition*) suggest that the burning of books functioned as a theater of cruelty to intimidate and threaten.

46. Grendler, *The Roman Inquisition*, 120.

47. On Domenichi's 1559 anthology of women, see, esp., Shemek, "The Collector's Cabinet"; and Piejus, "La première anthologie des poèmes féminins."

48. Angela Piscini, "Domenichi, Lodovico," *DBI*, 40:595–600.

49. John Tonkin, "Johannes Sleidanus," in *Encyclopedia of the Renaissance*, ed. Paul F. Grendler, 6 vols. (New York: Scribners, 1999), 6:42–43. John Sleidan (1506–56), who was born in Germany, studied law in Orléans, and was secretary to the Cardinal Jean du Bellay, was considered a moderate among Protestants. He kept in close touch with Bucer, Melanchthon, and Calvin. See Piscini, "Domenichi, Ludovico," 596. Domenichi and Torrentino, the Fleming who was Cosimo I's official printer, finally sneaked Sleidan's *Commentarii* and the anonymous *Nicodemiana* (attributed to Calvin) past the Holy Office, publishing them in 1557.

50. Again: for a complete description of vol. 1 in its three editions see my app. B. See app. A for an index of all authors in the Giolito anthology set; women's names are in boldface.

51. On Muzio, see Bongi, *Annali di Gabriel Giolito*, 1:xxvii and xlii: characterizing Muzio as one of Giolito's *clienti*, he also notes that Muzio was one of small group of intellectuals who frequented the publisher's home as though it were an academy or salon.

   Colonna's publishers were Viotti (1538), Zoppino (1539a; 1539b; 1540), Imperador and Vinetiano (1540; 1544), Valvassori (1546), and Comino da Trino (1548).

52. On Terracina, see Claudio Mutini, "Bacio Terracina, Laura," *DBI* (1963), 5:61–63; Bongi, *Annali di Gabriel Giolito*, 1:227–32; 355; 455 (on Terracina); see also Nancy Dersofi, "Laura Terracina," in Rinaldina Russell, ed., *Italian Women Writers: A Bio-Bibliographical Sourcebook* (Westport, CT: Greenwood Press, 1994), 423–40.

53. Grendler, *The Roman Inquisition*, 286–93. Grendler argues also that while the Inquisition and interdiction of books lasted into the eighteenth century, what he calls "the high Counter-Reformation" only prevailed "for a few decades" (1550–70?) in sixteenth-century Italy.

54. Romeo De Maio, "Belprato, Vincenzo," *DBI* (1966), 8:49.

55. D. Caccamo, "Bonifacio, Giovanni Bernardino," *DBI* (1970), 12:197–201.

56. Caccamo (ibid., 198) reports that Bonifacio took out a volume of Ovid's *Tristia* and made a show of reading it during the saying of mass and, after mass, refused the priest's blessing of holy water.

57. Domenichi, *La nobiltà delle donne*. Bongi, *Annali di Gabriel Giolito*, 1:246–49, discusses the work, its publication, its antecedents, the history and tradition of writings on the women question by ancients and moderns, and the dedicatory letters that accompany the work. Also bound with the copy of the work I've used in the Newberry Library is a separate volume: Domenichi's translation from the French of Agrippa's treatise, *La nobiltà delle donne*; but there is no attribution to Agrippa as the work's author; accompanying Domenichi's translation of Agrippa's treatise is Alessandro Piccolomini's *In lode delle donne* (Venice: Giolito 1549).

58. In the first of two epilogues to his dialogue, this one in the form of a letter to Bartolomeo Gottifredi, Domenichi acknowledges his debt Agrippa et al. (as named above). It's odd that he doesn't mention Boccaccio's *De claris mulieribus,* published in a bestselling translation as *Libro di M. Gio: Boccaccio delle donne illustri*, with an addition of modern women's lives by Domenichi's colleague and friend Giuseppe Betussi (Venice: Al Segno del Pozzo, Andrea Arrivabene, 1545).

59. See my app. B for a complete description of the volume. It is also useful to take into account Domenichi's frenzied attempt in the last years of his life (1559–64) to work simulataneously on all burners: during this period his somewhat farflung employers assumed he was virtually under contract and available to them on a quotidian basis; by "employers" I mean Giolito in Venice, Cosimo I de'Medici in Florence, and Vincenzo Busdragho in Lucca, where he also had old friends in the Turini and della Barba families as well as the Busdraghi. During this period, he hammered out a series of translations of the classics for Giolito, from Pliny's *Natural History* (1561) and *Plutarch's Lives* (1560) to Polybius's *Histories* (1563), in addition to a series of eight satirical dialogues that Giolito also published of his in 1562, among them *D'Amore* (On love), *Della Corte* (On princely courts), and *Della Stampa* (On the publishing house).

60. On the arrangement of the poems, see Shemek, "The Collector's Cabinet"; and Piejus, "La première anthologie des poèmes féminins." On the miniature *canzoniere* form, see Erika Milburn, *Luigi Tansillo and Lyric Poetry in Sixteenth-Century Naples* (Leeds: Maney Publishing for the Modern Humanisties Research Association, 2003), 84–103.

61. See Piejus, "La première anthologie de poèmes féminins," 203 ff., on the *réseau*.

62. Ibid., 203. Victoria Kirkham, "Laura Battiferra degli Ammannati's First Book of Poetry: A Renaissance Holograph Comes Out of Hiding," *Rinascimento* 36 (1996): 351–91.

63. I've provided the first lines of each of the poets' poems to make it easier for the reader to follow my discussion when we get to my texts and translations of the *réseau* poems. The numbers in parenthesis correspond to Domenichi's pagination.

64. The formulation "high Counter-Reformation" (as opposed to the high Renaissance) is Grendler's (*The Roman Inquisition*, 293).

65. Harriette Andreadis highly nuanced and persuasive study, *Sappho in Early Modern England: Female Same-Sex Literary Erotics, 1550–1714* (Chicago: University of Chicago Press, 2001) has made me want to rethink these (the poetry between women in Domenichi's anthology) and other sixteenth-century Italian women's poetry and letters addressed to women. It's now clear to me that there was a substantial tradition in Europe of female same-sex literary erotics. As I note in chap. 5, on Laudomia Forteguerri's suite of poems for Margaret of Austria, Konrad Eisenbichler has also written suggestively on the subject: "Laudomia Forteguerri Loves Margaret of Austria," in *Same-Sex Love and Desire among Women in the Middle Ages*, ed. Francesca Canadé Sautman and Pamela Sheingorn (New York: Palgrave, 2001), 277–304.

66. See, for example, Victoria Kirkham, "Poetic Ideals of Love and Beauty," and David Brown, introduction to *Virtue and Beauty: Leonardo's Ginevra de' Benci and Renaissance Portraits of Women*, ed. David Brown (Princeton, NJ: Princeton University Press, 2001), 49–62; 11–23.

67. Bergalli, ed., *Componimenti delle più illustri rimatici*; and Maria Bandini Buti, ed., *Poetesse e scrittici*, Enciclopedia biografica e bibliografica "italiana," ser. 6 (Rome: Istituto Editoriale Italiano, B.C. Tosi, 1941–42), 2 vols. There's nothing in the *DBI* on these women either.

68. I am very much indebted to Deanna Shemek for her suggestions on the texts and translations that follow.

69. *Quadrella*, a rare poetic image for *le quadrelle d'Amore* (the darts of Cupid). The *Grande Dizionario della lingua italiana*, ed. Salvatore Battaglia, vol. 15 (Turin: Editrice Unione, 1990), cites the sixteenth-century poet Cariteo, 13. Again I am indebted to Letizia Panizza and Deanna Shemek for their translation suggestions.

70. Solon warned Croesus that no man should be called happy until he dies, so uncertain is the life of men. Croesus repeated Solon's warning when Cyrus condemned him to death and Cyrus, much moved, realized that even the wealthiest man on earth wasn't happy, and thus he spared his life. The implication is that Cyrus let Croesus live as long as he found him useful and when he grew bored with him, he ordered his execution.

71. See Ovid *Fasti* 5.195–96: Flora the Italian woodland goddess of flowers, was once the girl Chloris. She was pursued by Zephyr and raped, but as consolation she was made goddess of the spring and flowering meadows. She is feted in the festival of Floralia by women every spring with ritual dancing and songs. The Flora story is, of course, an appropriate reference since Maria herself is a Florentine. Botticelli painted in the popular tale of Flora in his *Primavera*.

72. Milburn, *Luigi Tansillo and Lyric Poetry*, 84–103.

73. Ibid., 84—though Milburn doesn't mention the canzonieri of Colonna and Terracina.

74. On Virginia Martini de' Salvi (b.?–d. 1571? [the date of her last composition), see Salvi and the other Siennese poets Domenichi published in his 1559 anthology in Marie-Françoise Piejus, "Les poetesses Siennoises entre le jeu et l'écriture," in *Les femmes écrivains en Italie au Moyen Age et à la Renaissance* (Aix-en-Provence: l'Université de Provence, 1994), 312–32. Salvi's poems were also published in the Giolito anthologies, volumes 4 (Bologna: Giaccarrello, 1551), 6 (Venice: Arrivabene,1553), and 9 (Cremona: Conti, 1560); and in Dionigi Atanagi's funeral anthology for Irene di Splilimbergo (1561); finally, Celio Magno published a canzone and two sonnets by Salvi: *La bella e dotta canzone la vittoria dell'armata della santissima lega, nuovamente seguita contra la turchesca* (Venice, 1571); and *Due Sonetto di due Gentildonne Senesi, Madre, & Figliuola* (Venice, 1571).

75. For a list of individual women's appearances in the Giolito series, see my app. A.

76. The story of the vibrant women's literary community in Siena and Cosimo's siege and sack of the city is told in chap. 4.

77. Without a shred of acknowledgment of the existence of Domenichi's *Rime d'alcune nobilissime, et virtuosissime donne* (Lucca: Busdragho 1559), Antonio Bulifon published a line-for-line copy of Domenichi's anthology under a new title: *Rime di cinquanta illustri poetesse* (Poems by fifty illustrious poetesses [Naples, 1695]). The Busdragho volume had an exceptionally small print run, and if Bulifon had not republished the 1559 anthology in 1695 in a volume of his own that was widely disseminated, many of Domenichi's women poets would never have been republished.

78. The solo editions comprise the following: Parma: Viotti, 1538; Venice: Zoppino, 1539; Venice: Imperador & Vinetiano, 1540, 1544; Venice: Valvassori, 1546; Venice: Comino da Trino, 1548 ; Venice: Giolito, 1552, 1559.

79. Gaspara Stampa, *Rime*, ed. Cassandra Stampa (Venice: Plinio Pietrasanta, 1554).

80. I discuss Laudomia's mini-*canzoniere* at length in chap. 4. Texts are provided of all her sonnets dedicated to Margaret of Austria.

81. The relevant documents and studies of the case are in Benedetto Croce, *Isabella Morra e Diego Sandoval de Castro con l'edizione delle "Rime" della Morra e una scelta di quelle del Sandoval* (Bari: Laterza, 1929), which reprints a detailed synopsis of the account of the Morra murders titled *Familiae nobilissimae historia a Marco Antonio de Morra* (Naples: Giovanni Domenichi Roncalioli, 1629), written by Marco Antonio de Morra, the son of Isabella's youngest brother Camillo, who was away from home at military camp at the time of the homicides; see also Giovanni Caserta, *Isabella Morra e la società meridionale del Cinquecento* (Matera: Mela, 1976); Domenico Bronzini, *Isabella di Morra con l'edizione del canzoniere*, Edizione riveduta e accresciuta (Matera: Montemurro, 1975); Juliana Schiesari, "The Gendering of Melancholia: Torquato Tasso and Isabella di Morra," in *Refiguring Woman: Perspectives on Gender and the Italian Renaissance*, ed. Marilyn Migiel and Juliana Schiesari (Ithaca, NY: Cornell University Press, 1991), 231–62.

82. Giolito vol. 5 (three printings: 1551–52, 1552, and 1555) and Giolito vol. 7 (1556). See my app. B for a full description. These Naples/Giolito volumes are known as 5, 5a, 5b, and 7 in my appendixes.

83. Diego Sandoval di Castro, *Rime* (Rome: Valerio Dorico e Loigi fratelli, 1542).

84. The modern edition of Sandoval's *canzoniere* is *Rime*, ed. Tobia R. Toscano (Rome: Salerno Editrice, 1997).

85. Again I am indebted to Erika Milburn's suggestive discussion of Tansillo's miniature *canzoniere* in her *Luigi Tansillo and Lyric Poetry*, esp. 84–97, for remarks about Morra's *rime*.

86. I've numbered the poems following the order in which they appear in the 1559 anthology. Recently a number of excellent studies and editions of Morra's work have come out: Bronzini, *Isabella di Morra*; Caserta, *Isabella di Morra*; Schiesari, "The Gendering of Melancholia"; J. Schiesari, "Isabella di Morra (c. 1520–1545)," in *Italian Women Writers: A Bio-Bibliographical Sourcebook*, ed. Rinaldina Russell (Westport, CT, and London: Greenwood Press, 1994), 279–85; Valeria Finucci, "Isabella di Morra," in *An Encyclopedia of Continental Women Writers*, ed. Katharina Wilson, 2 vols. (New York: Garland, 1991), 2:876–77; Rinaldina Russell, "Intenzionalità artistica della 'disperata,'" in *Generi poetici medievali: Modelli e funzioni letterarie* (Naples: Società editrice napoletana, 1982), 163–82; all are indebted to the Benedetto Croce's pioneer studies, *Isabella di Morra e Diego Sandoval de Castro con l'edizione delle "Rime" della Morra e una scelta di quelle del Sandoval* (Bari: Laterza, 1929), and "Sulle prime stampe delle rime d'Isabella di Morra," in *Aneddoti di varia letteratura* (Bari: Laterza, 1953).

87. The order of the poems in the early editions can't be attributed to di Morra since they were published posthumously from a manuscript no longer extant. Nor can the order be attributed to Domenichi since in his 1559 Busdragho anthology of women he's published di Morra's first eight sonnets in exactly the same order in which they appear in Dolce's 1552 (Venice: Giolito) and 1555 editions (Venice: Giolito).

88. Domenichi's prefatory letter to his *Rime diverse d'alcune nobilissime et virtuosissime donne* (Lucca: Busdragho, 1559) bears the date June 1, 1559; the Holy Office's infamous *Index auctorum, et librorum* published in Venice by Girolamo Lilio (or Giglio) is dated July 21, 1559.

89. That she would have been tried for heresy had she lived is the opinion of her biographer of record, Patrizi, "Colonna, Vittoria," 27:448–57.

90. Grendler, *The Roman Inquisition*, 286–93.

## CHAPTER THREE

1. I rely on Vittoria Colonna, *Carteggio*, for the dating of her travels. Abigail Brundin, whose critical biography of Vittoria Colonna is forthcoming at Ashgate Press, observes that little is known about Colonna's seven-month stay in Lucca.

2. The narrative of the pope's invasion of Perugia is from Pastor, *The History of the Popes*, 11:328–47.

3. On the escalating conflict between Colonna and Paul III see also Franca Petrucci, "Colonna, Ascanio," *DBI* (1982), 27:271–75; and Chiomenti Vassalli, *Giovanna d'Aragona*, 93–99.

4. Colonna, *Carteggio*, 217–18.

5. The quoted material can be found in ibid., 217.

6. In response to the pope's occupation of Perugia, Ascanio plundered the papal herd of cattle in Ostia, which became the pretext for the pope's siege of the Colonna *fortezze*.

7. "Signor the Marchese" refers to Manrique de Lara Marchese d'Aquilar, the ambassador of Charles V. *Estaranno preparati*: they will stand ready meaning Charles's troops. Here Colonna overestimates Charles's interest in intervening. By *in tutti i lochi* I take it that Colonna means all Colonna's fortifications at Paliano, Rocca di Papa, Gennazzano, and so on.

8. *Il matrimonio con Francia*: she refers here to the marriage negotiations between Pope Paul III's niece, Vittoria Farnese, daughter of Pier Luigi Farnese, and the French Duke d'Aumale, son of Claudio, Duke of Guisa, which seemed to have been successfully concluded. With Pope Paul masterminding a new alliance via a marriage contract with the French royal family—presumably over against Charles V (and remember that it was Pope Clement VII's secret alliance with the French king that had prompted the emperor's sack of Rome in retaliation)—the emperor might want to punish the pope again by fighting on Ascanio's side in the salt tax dispute. So reasoned Colonna. In any case, the marriage contract fell through and Vittoria Farnese did not marry the French duke; she married the Duke of Urbino, Guidobaldo II, in 1548.

9. Colonna, *Carteggio*, 217–18.

10. Colonna refers here again to Paul III's supposed arranging of a marriage alliance with France as detailed in n. 8 above.

11. Conciano is the emperor's ambassador.

12. Colonna, *Carteggio*, 214–17.

13. Dandelet, *Spanish Rome*, 45–52.

14. Colonna, *Carteggio*, 219–20.

15. Valanzola was secretary to the emperor's ambassador, the Marchese d'Aquilar. I've retained the various different spellings of the secretary's name found in Colonna's letters: Valanzola (130), Valenzuola (131), Valensuola (134).

16. Note the specialized language in Vittoria Colonna's transmission of Aquilar's secretary's (Valanzola) report of the emperor's guarantees regarding the pope's future conduct toward Ascanio and his lands Marino and Nemi. The following terms and phrases are formulaically repeated in Colonna's letters to Ascanio as if they carried legal force: *partito* or *partiti*—the proposed plan or proposals; *ultimo* or *questo ultimo*—the final proposal; *dare in potere*—the transfer of property from one party to another, in this case from Ascanio to the pope's representatives and vice versa; and the *ordine dell'imperadore*—the command issued by the emperor to sanction the concluding of a pact; *in scrittis*—the legal form, *in writing*, in which the emperor's order had to be articulated.

17. Ferrero and Mueller's notes to the *Carteggio* identify the duke as Pier Luigi Farnese, Duke of Castro and nephew of Pope Paul.

18. Editor Ferrero, one of the editors of Colonna, *Carteggio*, 220, identifies Camillo as the lord of Zagarolo, brother of the archbishop Francesco Zagarlo. The monastery referred to in this letter is l'abbazia di Subiaco.

19. Colonna, *Carteggio*, 219–20.

20. See, for comparison sake, the portraits of Ascanio Colonna in Chiomenti Vassalli, *Giovanna d'Aragona*; and Petrucci, "Colonna, Ascanio."

21. Colonna, *Carteggio*, 220–21.

22. Ibid., 222–24.

23. Ibid. (March 7 or 8, 1541), 222. The ambiguous pronoun *suo* (*suo servitio*) seems to cast blame in two directions: Colonna's remark could be heard as "Suo servitio" (the emperor's responsibility) or "suo servitio" (meaning Aquilar's service to Charles).

24. Ferrero's note (*Carteggio*) identifies the man referred to as "Pietro Paulo" as "perhaps" Pietro Paolo Santorio, a *cameriere* of Ascanio's.

25. I'm assuming the man referenced as merely "Marchese" is the Marchese d'Aquilar.

26. Del Vasto is Maria d'Aragona's husband and the nephew of Vittoria Colonna's husband (Ferdinando d'Avalos, died 1526), who was also a soldier in Charles V's army.

27. Ferrero, ed., Colonna, *Carteggio*, 221, identifies this man as Pietro Paolo Santorio, a servant of Ascanio.

28. Vittoria Colonna to Ascanio Colonna, in Colonna, *Carteggio*, "7 or 8 March, 1541," say the editors (221–22). Note that I've placed this letter after the one dated March 8. To me this letter dated March 7 or 8 respresents the last straw and the last offer, particularly in response to Aguilar's proposal, supposedly from Charles, that Charles give the Colonna stronghold (Rocca di Papa) to Farnese.

29. The dates of Colonna's stay in Orvieto come from Domenico Tordi, "Vittoria Colonna in Orvieto," in *Bollettino della società umbra di Storia Patria*, vol. I (Perugia: Boncompagni, 1895), 473–533.

30. Colonna, *Carteggio*, 224–25.

31. See her correspondence with Guidiccioni in Girolamo Ruscelli, ed., *Lettere di diversi autori* (Venice: Ziletti, 1556); and V. Colonna, *Carteggio*, CXXVI, 211–13.

32. Guidiccioni, *Lettere inedite di Monsignor Giovanni Guidiccioni da Lucca* (Lucca: Tipografia di Giuseppe Giusti, 1855), 209–12.

33. Ibid., 197–98.

34. Ibid., 204–5: see text below.

35. Ibid., 204–5.

36. A formulation evocative of Anchises' famous exhortation to his son in *Aen.* 6.851–53.

37. See Aragona's letter in Alfredo Reumont, "Di Vittoria Colonna: a proposito dell'operetta Vittoria Colonna, par J. Lefevre Deumier," *Archivio storico italiano*, n.s. 5, *Giornale storico degli Archivi Toscani* (Firenze: Vieussuex, 1857), 143–44.

38. Marino, where Colonna was born, was one of the Colonna towns under siege during the war.

39. Vittoria Colonna, *Rime*, ed. Alan Bullock (Rome and Bari: Laterza 1982), 214. The sonnet reproduced here is referred to, though not by number or title, in Patrizi, "Colonna, Vittoria," 451.

40. Guidiccioni, *Lettere inedite*, letters 78–85, 222–41.

41. Ibid., letter 82, 232–34.

42. Ibid., letter 81, 230–32.

43. Ibid., letter 85, 238–39: Twenty infantrymen came down from the citadel to report that two companies were already in favor of surrendering to Farnese. The next day the mutiny was fully under way in the upper town.

44. Ibid., letter 86, 240–41.

45. Paliano had enormous significance for this branch of the Colonna family. Giulia Gonzaga (married to Vespasiano Colonna, Ascanio and Vittoria's cousin) was married there, and Giovanna and Ascanio Colonna would be buried there in a single marble tomb. On their marriage and burial rites at Paliano, see Oliva, *Giulia Gonzaga Colonna*, 26–28; and Chiomente Vassalli, *Giovanna d'Aragona*, 171.

46. Guidiccioni, *Lettere*, 243.

47. Ibid., 243–44. According to Guidiccioni, the agreement to surrender was not reached without a violent struggle among the Colonna men still remaining in the citadel of Paliano. In this letter, the commissary tells of the sounds of clashing arms and blood-curdling screams of "Kill! Kill!" coming from the upper town throughout the night.

48. Chiomenti Vassalli, *Giovanna d'Aragona*, 112. The next pope, Julius III (1549–55), pardoned Ascanio, gave him back all the lands he had previously held, and restored his feudatory titles and rights; see also Petrucci, "Colonna, Ascanio," 271–75. Thus rehabilitated, Ascanio hoped to win back his wife Giovanna. When she refused, he sold off his fiefs at Nemi and Genzano and refused to pay his daughter Vittoria's dowry, though he had no objection to her betrothal to Garcìa di Toledo, who was the son of the Spanish viceroy of Naples and brother of Eleonora di Toledo, Cosimo I de' Medici's wife. There is an illustration of an alchemy lab in a sixteenth-century Italian palazzo that is supposedly like Ascanio's (Chiomenti Vassalli, *Giovanna d'Aragona*, 97 ff.).

49. Vittoria Colonna, *Rime* (Venice: Bartolomeo l'Imperador & Francesco Vinetiano, 1544); Colonna, *Rime* (Venice: Valvassore, 1546); Colonna, *Rime spirituali* (Venice: Valgrisi, 1546); Colonna, *Dichiaratione fatta sopra la seconda parte della rime della divina V. Colonna da Rinaldo Corso* (Bologna: G. B. de Phaelli, 1543), which also contains her text. She had already published four editions of her *Rime* before the Salt War: the first edition by Antonio Viotti in Parma in 1538; three in 1539; and one in 1540.

## CHAPTER FOUR

1. Pastor, *History of the Popes*, 14:92–93.

2. After the death of the Farnese pope, Paul III, in 1550, the new pope Giulio III restored all the lands, towns, and the fiefs to Ascanio Colonna that Paul had seized at the end of the Salt war.

3. Paul IV (Gian Piero Carafa), seventy-nine when he was elected to the papal throne on May 23, 1555, came from an ancient Neapolitan family who were not pro-Spanish (unlike the Colonna) and who had always seen the Spanish as the wrongful oppressors of Naples and Milan.

4. On the Carafa war see, above all, Dandelet, *Spanish Rome*; and Pastor, *History of the Popes*, 14:64–180, for their portraits of Paul IV, and to Pastor for his blow-by-blow account of the Carafa war against Spain and the Colonna family.

5. On the details of Giovanna's escape, see Chiomenti Vassalli, *Giovanna d'Aragona*, 136; on the early hostility between the Colonna family and Paul IV, see also Alessandro Andrea, *Della guerra di Campagna di Roma nel Pontificato di Paolo IV: L'anno MDLVI e LVII.* (Naples: Giovanni Gravier, 1769).

6. As news of the escape reached Pope Paul IV, he ordered the execution of the guard at the Porta di Lorenzo who had waved Giovanna and her entourage through.

7. Chiomenti Vassalli, *Giovanna d'Aragona*, 148; Salza, *Luca Contile*.

8. The title page of Ruscelli's *Tempio* bears the date 1555 (no month); but Ruscelli's dedicatory letter to the volume is dated December 15, 1554. From this date we can conjecture a print date of two to eight months later, between February and September 1555.

9. See, on Betussi, Bassani, *Il poligrafo veneto*; G. Zonta, "Note betussiane," in *Giornale storico della letteratura italiana* 52 (1908): 321–66; and Claudio Mutini, "Betussi, Giuseppe," *DBI* (1971), 13:779–81.

10. Dandelet, *Spanish Rome*, 55.

11. The banning of books on grounds of lewdness is described by Grendler, *The Roman Inquisition*, 116.

12. Ibid., 116. Though the gathering, sorting, researching, and judging being done for Paul IV's new index was already underway with a vengeance early in 1556, the work didn't go to the printers in Rome until January 1559.

13. Ibid., 116–17, 125; and see my index of poets, publishers, and dedicatees in my app. A.

14. Grendler, *The Roman Inquisition*, 117. On the papal lists of prohibited books, see also, esp., Caponetto, *The Protestant Reformation*, 270–306; Pastor, *The History of the Popes*, 14:259–88.

15. Grendler, *The Roman Inquisition*, 93: the Hebrew press Madruzzo, founded in 1558, stayed open until 1562. Information on suppression of classic literature can also be found in Grendler, *The Roman Inquisition*, 116. For a list of Ruscelli's poetry anthologies and their patrons in the Giolito series, see my app. A.

16. Gaspara Stampa (1523–54), her widowed mother, and her sister Cassandra conducted a salon in Venice attended by such scholars, artists, and musicians as her Padua-educated brother Baldessare (who was also a poet), Girolamo Parabosco, Francesco Sansovino, Ortensio Lando, Varchi, Domenichi, Sperone Speroni, and Giovanni Della Casa, among others. See Fiora Bassanese, *Gaspara Stampa* (Boston: Twayne, 1983); Ann Rosalind Jones, "Surprising Fame: Renaissance Gender Ideologies and Women's Lyric," in *The Poetics of Gender*, ed. Nancy K. Miller (New York: Columbia University Press, 1986); and A. R. Jones, "New Songs for the Swallow: Ovid's Philomela in Tullia d'Aragona and Gaspara Stampa," in *Refiguring Women: Gender Studies and the Italian Renaissance*, ed. Marilyn Migiel and Juliana Schiesari (Ithaca, NY: Cornell University Press, 1991). While Abd-el-kader Salza, "Madonna Gasparina Stampa secondo nuove indagine," *Giornale storico della letteratura italian* 62 (1913): 1–101, long ago argued that Stampa was a courtesan, most scholars now characterize her as a *virtuosa* or professional singer and not a prostitute or courtesan; the case was briefly reopened by Antonio Barzaghi, *Donne o cortegiane? La prostituzione a Venezia: Documenti di costume dal XVI al XVI secolo* (Verona: Bertani, 1980). For editions of her work, see *Rime di Gaspara Stampa e di Veronica Franco*, ed. Abd-el-kader Salza (Bari: Laterza, 1913); in English translation with Italian text, see *Gaspara Stampa: Selected Poems*, ed. and trans. Laura Anna Stortoni and Mary Prentice Lillie (New York: Italica, 1994). Jane Tylus is

currently preparing to publish a new English translation with the Italian text on the facing page.

17. Ruscelli, ed., *Tempio alla divina signora*, 3r (but the folios of this prefatory letter are not numbered).

18. Terracina, *Rime* (Venice: Giolito, 1548, 1554, 1556); *Rime . . . una diceria d'amore* (Venice: Valvassori, 1550); *Quinte rime* (Venice: Valvassori, 1552); *Il discorso sopra tutti i primi canti di 'Orlando Furioso* (Venice: Giolito, 1549, 1550, 1551); *Il discorso* (Venice: Valvassori, 1550).

19. See Caponetto, *The Protestant Reformation*, 295; and see my chap. 1. Torrentino had been in trouble before. In 1552 he was known as a Protestant sympathizer and was found guilty of having published Calvin and the Lutheran Johann Sleidan under the title *Nicomediana* in collaboration with his editor Lodovico Domenichi, who was sent to prison for a year for his hand in the work.

    Betussi, *Le imagini del tempio*. The dedicatory letter by Betussi is dated May 10, 1556, from Rome. Mutini, "Betussi, Giuseppe," 9:780, notes that Betussi first published this work in Florence in 1556.

20. See also Francesco Cristiani, ed., *Rime di diversi, ecc. autori in vita e in morte dell'ill. S. Livia Colonna* (Rome: Antonio Barre, 1555), in honor of the young Livia Colonna, a ward and kinswoman of Ascanio Colonna, who after being abducted and married by Marzio Colonna, was strangled to death in her own bed by Pompeo Colonna in 1554. The details of the abduction and murder are in Chiomenti Vassalli, *Giovanna d'Aragona*, 131.

21. See Margaret L. King, *The Death of the Child Valerio Marcello* (Chicago: University of Chicago Press, 1994), for a prototype of the genre. On Atanagi's anthology for Spilimbergo, see Anne Jacobson Schutte, "Irene di Spilimbergo: The Image of a Creative Woman in Late Renaissance Italy," *Renaissance Quarterly* 1 (1991): 42–61; see D. Atanagi, ed., *Rime di diversi nobilissimi et eccellentissimi autori in morte della signora Irene delle signore di Splilimbergo* (Venice: Domenico & Giovanni Battista Guerra, 1561).

22. The text from *Odes* 3.30 is "exegi monumentum aere perennius." The only Italian precedent I know in which a book of encomia is figured as a temple is Girolamo Parabosco's *Il tempio della fama in lode d'alcune gentildonne venetiane* (Venice: Comin da Trino, 1548). But this tiny book containing only a few stanzas and consisting of a mere twenty-six folios, four of which are a panegyric to Venice, has nothing in common with the *tempio* books of Ruscelli and Betussi which are major projects centered on the honor of one woman and the rehabilitation of her family name.

23. Its dedicatory letter is addressed to Cardinal Cristoforo Madruzzo of Trent, who was an active and effective opponent of Paul IV's repressive policies. I am grateful to Paul Gehl for his suggestion that the publication of the *Tempio* amounted to the Venetian book men's "firing of a first shot across the bow at the pope."

24. Betussi's statement—"io stesso ho voluto divenire un'altro Ulisse, per chiarimi del vero"—appears on the last (but unpaginated) folio of the *Imagini del tempio* in an afterword addressed "Alle illustri et virtuose donne." Zonta, "Note betussiane," 345, also cites and comments on the passage.

25. For the gatherings Betussi went to, the term is *veglia* or soiree or evening party, used by the writer Celio Malespini, *Ducento Novelle* (Venice: al segno dell'Italia, 1609) of the "evenings" he attended in Siena. I am grateful for the reference to Deana Basile's brilliant Toronto University dissertation (1999): "*Specchio delle rare e virtuose donne*: The Role of the Female Interlocutor in Sixteenth-Century Dialogues on Love," 186 and to Albert Rabil for calling my attention to Basile's dissertation. On the subject of Betussi being a society journalist, Zonta (344) is scathing in his characterization of "questa moderna forma giornalistica."

26. Boccaccio, *Libro di Gio: Boccaccio delle donne illustri, tradotto per Messer Giuseppe Betussi, con una additione fatta dal medesimo delle donne famose dal tempo di M. Giovanni fino ai giorni nostri* . . . (Venice: Andrea Arrivabene, Al Segno del Pozzo, 1545). See the new English translation of Boccaccio's *De mulieribus*: Giovanni Boccaccio, *Famous Women*, ed. and trans Virginia Brown (Cambridge, MA: Harvard University Press, 2001.)

    So far I have found little on Ruscelli (b. in Viterbo 1504; d. 1566). He's an elusive figure: a productive editor but beyond that we know little. Claudia Di Filippo Bareggi counts thirty-five new titles among the books he edited and/or published between 1550 and 1566, and thirty-one reprints of works he had previously published, coming to a total for those years of sixty-six editions credited to his name. I checked through the indexes of vols. 12–16 of Pastor's *History of the Popes* for any mention of Ruscelli and there were zero. Zero again in the *Cambridge History of Italian Literature* (ed. Peter Brand and Lino Pertile [Cambridge: Cambridge University Press, 1996]); nothing in Grendler's *The Roman Inquisition*, except one citation of a publication with Pietrasanta in 1554: *Il capitolo delle lodi del fuso* (10). Brian Richardson, *Print Culture in Renaissance Italy. The Editor and the Vernacular Text, 1470–1600* (Cambridge: Cambridge University Press, 1994), has a number of citations on Ruscelli, the most interesting of which is that in 1553–55 Ruscelli put the printer Plinio Pietrasanta up in his house and also paid him a salary (9). He appears among the lists of Venetian *poligrafi* and their works in Di Filippo Bareggi's *Il mestiere di scrivere*.

27. Of Siena, the city of Laudomia Forteguerri and many other Sienese women he admired, Betussi wrote in the *Imagini*, fol. 30: "Ah infelice, & lacrimosa Citta, come teco sforzata sono piangere le adversita tue, poiche di cosi fiorita, & piena do tutte le delitie, sei cosi venuta in uggio a' Fati, che io ti veggio nelle mani di genti Barbare, et oltremontane."

28. On Betussi see Bassani, *Il poligrafo veneto*; Zonta, "Note betussiane"; and Mutini, "Betussi, Giuseppe."

29. Claudio Mutini, "Caula, Camillo," *DBI* (1979), 22:540–42. Caula also wrote poetry and frequented Giolito's business in San Apollinaire near the Rialto in Venice or spent time at the house of Collalto.

    Orsini, lord of Montorotondo, was also well connected in the literary world; he was a nephew of Leone Orsini, Principe of Italy's most influential academy in 1540–41, the *Infiammati* in Padua, and was a frequent guest at Giolito's house on the Rialto in Venice (Bassani, *Il poligrafo veneto*, 11–15). His work appeared in the first edition of vol. 1 of Giolito's poetry anthology series, as did Betussi's.

30. Mutini, "Betussi, Giuseppe," 779–81; Zonta, "Note betussiane," 343–47.

31. G. Fontanini, *Biblioteca dell'eloquenza italiana* (Parma: Per li fratelli Gozzi a spese di L. Mussi, 1803–4). Ruscelli's work as a linguist is described in Di Filippo Bareggi, *Il mestiere di scrivere*, 290–91, where he is characterized as "un sistematore e un teorizzatore della lingua e della letteratura volgare. È vero che la somma della opere appartementi al settore letterario aggiunte a quelle retorico-linguistico ci porta a quasi il 66% di tutti in suoi titoli."

32. Praise for Ruscelli's work in the classics is documented in Di Filippo Bareggi, *Il mestiere di scrivere*, 80. On Ruscelli's excoriation of Dolce's works, see Bongi, *Annali di Gabriel Giolito*, 1:101, 354, 363. In his *Tre discorsi* (Venice: Per Plinio Pietrasanta, 1553), Ruscelli tore into Dolce's editions of the *Decameron*, his *Metamorfosi*, and his book titled *Osservazioni*. Bongi makes the point repeatedly that at first Ruscelli wanted to give Dolce his criticisms privately, but that it was Dolce who blew the whole thing up into a public fight. In addition to Ruscelli's battering Dolce black and blue for his sloppy translations of Ovid's *Metamorphoses*, he charged that Dolce had plagiarized passages from Vives in his *Dialogo della institution delle donne*.

33. The full title is *Lettera di Girolamo Ruscelli, sopra un sonetto dell'illustriss: Signor Marchese della Terza alla divina Signora Marchesa del Vasto: Ove con nuove et chiare ragioni si pruova la somma perfettione delle donne; & si discorrono molte cose intorno alla scala Platonica dell'ascendimento per le cose create alla contemplatione di Dio: Et molte intorno alla vera bellezza, alla gratia, & alla lingua Volgare: Ove ancora case occasione di nominare alcune Gentildonne delle più rare d'ogni terra principal dell'Italia* (Venice: Giovan Griffio, 1552).

34. Ruscelli's list of "illustrious" (*più rare*) women is remarkable for its length: it fills almost twenty-two pages (= 10 + folio pages: 63r–72v). The author of the sonnet, Marchese della Terza, is the poet Giovambattista d'Azzia. A suitor of Maria d'Aragona after the death of her husband (Alfonso d'Avalos, a.k.a Marchese del Vasto), d'Azzia's poems appear in the 2d and 3d editions of vols. 5a, 5b, and 6 of Giolito's anthology series.

35. Colonna, *Rime* (Venice: Sessa, 1558).

36. Regarding Ruscelli's collaboration with Spadafora, see Caponetto, *The Protestant Reformation*, 346 ff: Ruscelli published Spadafora's orations in 1552 and 1554. Ruscelli's *Lettere di diveri autori* was published in Venice by Giordano Ziletti in 1556.

37. Bassani, *Il poligrafo veneto*, 79. Claudio Mutini, "Baffo, Franceschina," *DBI*, 5:163. Baffo (also known as Francesca Baffa), whose exact dates are unknown, flourished in Venice in the decade 1543–52. She was so famous for her learning that travelers came from all over Europe to hear and converse with her. Her poems were published in three successive editions of the Giolito anthologies: 1545, 1546, 1549 (see my app. A); Betussi's *Raverta*, which features Baffa in conversation with Lodovico Domenichi, was published in 1544 by Giolito. Giuseppe Betussi, *La Leonora: Ragionamento sopra la vera bellezza* (Lucca: Vincenzo Busdragho, 1557).

38. On the doctrine of *angeli* or *demoni*, see Betussi, *La Leonora*, fols. 23–24; cf. Proc. *In Timaeum Comment* 1.341, 3.126, 3.192; Proc. *Repub. Comment*. R. 2.243; Iamblichus *Myst.* 2.6.

39. I'm thinking of Christine de Pizan's (1365–1430?) decidedly gendered depiction of her allegorical personae, for example, in *The Book of the City of Ladies*; but Betussi and his Italian contemporaries seem not to have known Christine: she is not cited by sixteenth-century Italian writers and her works did not appear in print in France until the late eighteenth century. There was, however, an English translation made of Christine's *City of Ladies* a century after her death: *The Boke of the Cyte of Ladyes*, trans. Brian Anslay (London: Imprinted by Henry Pepwell, 1521).

40. Compare Bassani, *Il poligrafo Veneto*, 83: arguing the opposite, Bassani sees the the *imagini* as following medieval models rather than humanist ones.

41. Both *Veritas* and *Fama* are often personified in Latin literature. For personifications of *Veritas*, see Gell. 12.11.7: "Alius quidam veterum poetarum, cuius nomen mihi nunc memoriae non est, Veritatem Temporis filiam esse dixit." (Aulus Gellius also said that "Truth is the daughter of Time".) On *Veritas*, see also Hor. *Carm.* 1.24.7; Mart. 10.72.11; Apul. *Met.* 8.7. On *Fama* as a mythological character, see Verg. *Aen.* 4.174; Luc. 4.574; Mart. 7.6.4 and 7.12.10; Stat. *Theb.* 4.32; Hor. *Carm.* 2. 28; Prop. 2.34.94.

42. The emperor Constantine (A.D. 285–337) gave the ancient city of Byzantium its new name—Constantinople—when he made it the new capital of the Roman Empire.

43. The common enemy being the Turks who in 1453 sacked and took Constantinople, the great metropolis that was regarded as the last outpost of European Christendom in the East. From the mid-fifteenth century on references to the Turks' sack of Constantinople and the call to arms to take back the ancient capital becomes a trope among the Italian humanists.

44. "La misera Italia" is an echo of Petrarch's *Rime sparse* 128: "Italia mia, ben che 'l parlar sia indarno / a le piaghe mortali," which deals, two hundred years earlier, with the same themes—the wars between Italian lords in which Italians kill one another; the quest for foreign wealth at the expense of domestic happiness; the barbarian threat beyond Italy's borders; and the underlying problems of human greed and ambition.

45. Gaius Caesar (*Gai*, the Gaiuses), known as Caligula, was emperor of Rome (A.D. 37–41); Nero, the Roman emperor (A.D. 54–68) famous for his madness and brutality; Mezentius is the cruel tyrant in the *Aeneid* who, with Turnus, fights Aeneas; Attila, the famously arrogant and savage king of the Huns (A.D. 434–53), who sacked numerous Italian cities; Brennus, the king of the Gauls, who captured and sacked Rome in 390 B.C.

46. The coupling "numero et ombra" (number and shade) are typical ways in Latin poetry to talk about rhythm or poetic meter and metaphorical shading, coloring, or portrayal whether in painting or poetry.

47. Plato, *The Republic*, trans. Paul Shorey, in *The Selected Dialogues of Plato*, ed. Edith Hamilton and Huntington Cairns (Princeton, NJ: Princeton University Press, 1978).

48. Chiomenti Vassalli, *Giovanna d'Aragona*, 139–40.

49. This is almost a verbatim quote from Hor. *Odes* 3.30.1.

50. Betussi, fol. 9r of the *Imagini del tempio*, uses the Italian word *simulacro* here for his representation of Giovanna, denoting the sense that he is dealing only in likenesses, semblances, or traces of the human spirits he portrays, suggesting that he will never be able to capture the living essences of those he describes.

51. Betussi omits the most interesting part of Pliny's anecdote: Zeuxis, to the horror of the Crotonians, had insisted that the girls pose naked. The ancient Greek painter Zeuxis (397–400 B.C.) is perhaps the most frequently cited ancient painter in the Renaissance. He is best known for his use of shading: his grapes, writes Pliny, were so realistic that the birds pecked at them. Pliny says Zeuxis's painting was of Penelope not Venus but notes that in his painting of Penelope for the Crotonians he represented virtue (*pinxisse mores*). See Plin. *Nat. Hist.* 35.65–66. Cicero (*De Invent.* 2.1.1) writes that the Crotonians ordered Zeuxis to paint a Helen for their temple; but Pliny (*Nat. Hist.* 35.66) writes that Zeuxis's painting of Helen was in Rome in the Porticoes of Philippus; elsewhere Cicero mentions Zeuxis in passing (*Brut.* 18.70; *De orat.* 3.7.26).

52. One of the most popular of these catalogs in sixteenth-century Italy was Giovanni Boccaccio's *De claris mulieribus* (ca. 1345), which was translated into Italian by Giuseppe Betussi (Venice: Andrea Arrivabene, Al Segno del Pozzo, 1545); see the new edition and translation in Latin and English: Boccaccio, *Famous Women,* ed. and trans. Brown.

53. For lists of the publishers of popular poetry anthologies and the men and women published in them, for the years 1540–60, see my chap. 2 and app. A.

54. I assume that the remaining women, whose names I've not yet found in poetry anthologies of the period, are also patrons or writers.

Betussi spells Forteguerri's name *Laodamia*; I've changed the spelling to conform to the more common spelling of her name to avoid confusion.

55. Every woman on this list was published in Domenichi's subsequent anthology of fifty-three women poets (Lucca: Busdragho, 1559). See chap. 1 on the seventeenth- and eighteenth-century anthologies by Antonio Bulifon and Luisa Bergalli in which the same authors appear again.

56. See my alphabetical index of writers, editors, publishers, and dedicatees in the Giolito poetry anthology series in app. A.

57. Bongi, *Annali di Gabriel Giolito,* 1:xxvii–xxviii.

58. Ibid., 1:xxvii.

59. Maylender, *Storia delle Accademie d'Italia,* 2:356–61.

60. Also praised in this section of the dialogue is a supporting cast of twenty-five other women writers and patrons, whose names and hometowns are designated as follows: Angelica Vallari Cane, Casalasca; Anna Cappona, Astignana; Anna Bentivoglia Simonetta, Bolognese; Buona Contessa di Bene, Piemontese; Buona Maria Soarda di San Giorgio, Casalasca; Caterina dal Carretto, Savonese; Camilla Capriuola Stanga, Bresciana; Collaltina Collalta Treccha, Vinetiana; Camilla Pallavicina da Corte, Maggiore; Camilla Valente dal Verme, Mantovana; Claudia Arconata, Francese; Donnetta de' Marchesi di Ceva; Girolama Rochetta Ferrera, Savonese; Hortensia Colloretta Mont'Albana di Friuli; Isabella di Scalengo, Piemontese; Isabella Grimaldi Genovese; Isabella Sforza, Melanese; Lucretia Veretta, Savonese; Madama di Raconigi, Piemontese; Maddalena Pallavicina, Pavese; Madama d'Oneglia, Genovese; Margherita Salvi Contessa d'Elci, Sanese; Thomasina Rochetta dal Carretta dal Carretto, Savonese.

61. On the marriage, see, esp., Petrucci, "Colonna, Ascanio," *DBI*, 27:271–75. The mis-
understandings and estrangement between Giovanna d'Aragona and her husband
Ascanio, though interesting, are outside the scope of my narrative. The couple had
lived apart since the mid-1530s, they had seven children together, and in the end they
were buried together in a single mausoleum in Paliano. In the 1550s, Ascanio began to
behave in a bizarre fashion. When his eldest son Marcantonio Colonna married Felice
Orsini, a great-granddaughter of Paul III, in 1552, Ascanio disinherited both his son
and his wife Giovanna. Marcantonio tried to get one of his father's servants to accuse
him of sodomy with boys and of playing both the active and passive roles in the act.
In 1554, he was arrested by Charles V's agents for treason and charged with having
defected to the French king. He was incarcerated in the Castelnuovo in Naples. He
in turn accused Giovanna and Marcantonio of forging the letters that were used to
incriminate him, and as a consequence he disinherited Giovanna and their eldest son
He died in prison on March 23, 1557.

62. Giovanna's return to Rome and reconciliation with the new pope, Pius IV, are de-
scribed in an official notice and a contemporary diary: *Avvisi*, Fondo Urbinate 1039,
Rome; A. Massarelli, *Diaria* (Freiburg: Harder, 1911), 7:346, as cited in Chiomenti
Vassalli, *Giovanna d'Aragona*, 152–53, 155.

63. See the full text of Giovanna Colonna's letter to Pope Paul III in chap. 3, 96–97.

CHAPTER FIVE

1. Giuseppe Betussi, *Le imagini del tempio della signora donna Giovanna Aragona, Dialogo di
M. Giuseppe Betussi: Alla illustrissima signora donna Vittoria Colonna di Tolledo* (Venice:
Giovanni de'Rossi, 1557). Betussi had originally published the work under the title *Le
immagini . . .* in Florence in 1556 with Cosimo I de' Medici's official printer Lorenzo
Torrentino. An afterword (not paginated), titled "Alle illustri et virtuose donne"
signed by Betussi, is found at the very end of the book after the Tavole (indexes of
names and subjects). It is signed "di Siena" but is undated. Betussi's here apologizes
to the women he has eulogized because it has taken him so long to get the work out:
"Alle illustri et virtuose donne, Il Betussi. Non spiaccia a molte di voi, o generossime
Donne, che meritareste un mare di lode, & sarebbe ancho poco, di vedervi da me ris-
trette in cosi angusto, & povero termine, la dove (forse) aspettavate in iscambio le Vite
vostre gia tanto fa da me a voi promesse, ampiamente, & riccamente descritte, hog-
gimai deversi publicare." [O you most generous of women, who merit a sea of praise
(and even that would be too little), I hope that most of you will not be displeased to
see yourselves confined by me to so poor and slender a venue nor that you will be
displeased to have to see yourselves published finally now, when you have waited so
long for the encomia I already promised you and described so elaborately and fully.]
The introductory dedicatory letter (addressed to Vittoria di Toledo and positioned as
a foreword to the book) is dated by Betussi May 10, 1556, and signed "di Roma."

Betussi was in Florence when he composed his dialogue *La Leonora* in 1557 (published that year by Busdragho in Lucca). Mutini, "Betussi, Giuseppe," 13:779–81,
says of the peripatetic Betussi that between 1555 and 1558 he sojourned in Pavia with

Ippolito Gonzaga, the Borromeo family, and the Madruzzo family and with Vicino Orsini in Rome, where he also saw Vittoria di Toledo and Giovanna d'Aragona, and that he finished *La Leonora* in 1557 as the guest of Varchi in a villa, La Topaia, which Cosimo had given as a gift to Varchi. Betussi's dedicatee, Vittoria di Toledo, of course had close ties with Florence since her husband Garcia di Toledo was the brother of Cosimo's wife Eleonora di Toledo. On Betussi, see also Bassani, *Il poligrafo veneto*; and Zonta, "Note betussiane," 321–66. I am grateful to Konrad Eisenbichler for his suggestions in this chapter.

2. Estimates of the number of survivors left in Siena by the end of the siege vary: there is general aggreement that before the war there were around thirty thousand people living in the city; at the end of the war estimates of the remaining population range between six thousand and ten thousand.

3. All Italian and Latin translations are mine except where otherwise noted. I have retained the orthography of the sixteenth-century editions with the exception of j/i, &/e, and the diacriticals, which have been modernized for readability.

4. Alessandro Sozzini, *Diario delle cose avvenute in Siena dai 20 luglio 1550 ai 28 giugno 1550 scritto da Alessandro Sozzini con altre narrazioni e documenti relativi alla caduta di quella repubblica* (Florence: Pietro Vieusseux Editore, 1842), 1:399. The passage is referred to in passing without Italian text or translation in Simon Pepper and Nicholas Adams, *Firearms and Fortifications: Military Architecture and Siege Warfare in Sixteenth-Century Siena* (Chicago: University of Chicago Press, 1986), 138.

5. I am indebted to Pepper and Adams, *Firearms and Fortifications*, 138, for the reference to the war memoir of Roberto Cantagalli, *La guerra di Siena, 1552–1559* (Siena: Accademia senese degli Intronati, 1962), 386: "Un soldato del Bentivoglio scrivera giusto in quei giorni (24 Febbraio) in una sua corrispondenza con Lucca che per 10 miglia intorno a Siena non c'era piu un muro in piedi e che la campagna era infestata di cani che divoravano i cadaveri."

6. Ibid.; see the eyewitness description of the siege in Blaise de Monluc [a.k.a. Montluc], *Commentaires de Blaise de Monluc, Maréchal de France*, ed. Paul Courteault (Paris: Libraire Alphonse Picard & Fils, 1913), 2:86–87.

7. Betussi, *Le imagini del tempio*, fol. 31r. I have retained Betussi's capitalization of the names of the women he celebrates and of the virtue they embody, in Forteguerri's case *Fama*. See also Betussi in his role as *Verità* praising Forteguerri in a Petrarchan sonnet. Laodamia's image represents Fame or Glory (*Fama*) in his temple book for Giovanna d'Aragona Colonna, fols. 32r–32v.

8. Ibid., fols. 31r–32v.

9. The marshal's description of Forteguerri's leadership in the defense of Siena is in Monluc, *Commentaires*, 2:86–87:

> Tous ces pauvres habitans, sans monstrer nul desplaisir ny regret de la ruyne de leurs maisons, mirent les premiers la main a l'oeuvre, chascun accourt a la besogne. Il ne fust jamais qui'il n'y eust plus de quatre mil ames au travail; et me fust montre par des gentils-hommes sienois un grand nombre de gentil-femmes portans des paniers sur leur teste pleins de terre. Il ne sera jamais, dames siennoises, que je

n'immortalize vostre nom tant que le livre de Monbtluc vivra; car, a la verite, vous estes dignes d'immortelle louange, si jamais femmes le furent. Au commencement de la belle resolution que ce peuple fit de deffendre sa liberte, toutes les dames de la ville de Sienne se despartirent en trois bandes: la premiere estoit conduicte par la signora Forteguerra, qui estoit vestue de violet, et toutes celles qui suivoient aussi, ayant son accoustrement en facon d'une nymphe, court et monstrant le brodequin; la seconde estoit la signora Picolhuomini, vestue de satin incarnadin, et sa truppe de mesme livree; la troisiesme estoit la signora Livia Fausta, vestue toute de blanc, comme aussi estoit sa suitte, avec son enseigne blanche. Dans leurs enseignes elles avoient de belles devises; je voudrois avoir donne beaucoup et m'en resouvenir. Ces trois escadrons estoient composez de trois mil dames, gentil-femmes ou bourgeoises; luers armes estoient des pies, des palles, des hotes, et des facines. Et en cest equipage firent leur monstre et allerent comnmencer les fortifications. Monsieur de Termes, qui m'en a souvent faict le compte (car je n'estois encor arrive), m'a asseure n'avoir jamais veu de sa vie chose si belle que celle-la. Je vis leurs ensignes despuit. Elles avoient faict un chant a l'honneur de la France, lorsqu'elles alloient a leur fortification; je voudrois avoir donne le meillur cheval que j'aye et l'avoir pour le mettre icy.

10. *The Commentaries of Messire Blaize de Monluc, Mareschal of France* (London: Printed by Andrew Clark for Henry Brome, 1674), bk. 3, 141–42. Sienese eyewitness Sozzini, *Diario delle cose avvenute in Siena dai 20 Luglio 1550 ai 28 Giugno 1555*, 279, also mentions the women's participation in the siege works; he says that *gentildonne*, shopkeepers, and even *contadini* came into the city center to work on the fortifications and kept working through the night until 3 A.M.; he quotes Montluc's description in full, in French, explaining that the French general himself had sent him the relevant pages.

11. Girolamo Bargagli, *Dialogo de' giuochi che nelle vecchie sanesi si usano di fare: Del materiale Intronato* (Siena: Luca Bonetti, 1572). A modern edition of this dialogue is available under the title *Dialogo de' giuochi che nelle vegghie sanesi. . .*, ed. P. D'Incalci Ermini, with an introduction by R. Bruscagli (Siena: Accademia Senese degli Intronati, 1982), 57, as cited in Marie-Françoise Piejus, "Varietà: L'orazione in *Lode delle donne* di Alessandro Piccolomini," *Giornale storico della letteratura italiana* 170, no. 4 (1993): 524–51.

12. Alessandro Piccolomini, *Della sfera del mondo: Libri quatro in lingua Toscana* (Venice: Nicolo Bevilacqua, 1561), 2. This passage comes from the dedicatory letter to Laudomia Forteguerri, but it is signed and dated from the Villa di Valzanzibio, August 10, 1539. For this reference I am indebted to Konrad Eisenbichler, "Laudomia Forteguerri Loves Margaret of Austria," in *Same-Sex Love and Desire among Women in the Middle Ages,* ed. Francesca Canadé Sautman and Pamela Sheingorn (New York: Palgrave, 2001), 277–304.

13. See R. Bruscagli's introduction to Bargagli, *Dialogo de' giuochi*; see also Piejus, "Varietà," 524–51.

14. The passage is from Bargagli, *Dialogo de' giuochi*, 197–98; see also Adriana Mauriello, "Cultura e società nel Siena del Cinquecento," *Filologia e letteratura* 17 (1971): 26–48; the passage I cite is in Marie-Françoise Piejus, "Les poetesses Siennoise entre le jeu

et l'escriture" in *Les femmes écrivains en Italie au Moyen Age et à la Renaissance* (Aix-en-Provence: Université de Provence, 1994), 315–32, quote on 319.

15. Celio Malespini, *Ducento novelle* (Venice: al segno dell'Italia, 1609), fol. 86v. I am indebted to Deana Basile, "*Specchio delle rare e virtuose donne*: The Role of the Female Interlocutor in Sixteenth-Century Dialogues on Love" (Ph.D. diss, University of Toronto 1999), 186, for calling attention to this passage.

16. Marc'Antonio Piccolomini (1505–79), despite his conviction as a murderer in Siena in 1545, served as a secretary to several prelates, though he did not take holy orders himself until 1570. Rita Belladonna discovered the manuscript of Piccolomini's dialogue bound together with an obscene political satire in the Biblioteca Communale ("Gli Intronati, le donne, Aonio Paleario e Agostino Museo in un dialogo inedito di Marcantonio Piccolomini, Il Sodo Intronato (1538)," *Bullettino senese di storia patria* 99 (1994): 48–90.

17. Ibid. The date of the women's real-time conversation was All Saints' Day (October) 1537, according to Belladonna (52).

18. On Battiferri's membership in the Sienese Intronati, see Conor Fahy, "Women and Italian Cinquecento Literary Academies," in *Women in Italian Renbaissance Culture and Society,* ed. Letizia Panizza (Oxford: Legenda, 2000), 438–52. Fahy also notes that the date of Battiferri's supposed induction must be suspect since in 1557 the academy was still closed as a result of the siege and occupation of Siena. See also L. Sbaragli, "I 'Tabellioni' degli Intronati," *Bullettino senese di storia patria,* ser. 3, 1 (1942): 177–213, 238–67.

19. On the documentary dialogue, see Virginia Cox, *The Renaissance Dialogue: Literary Dialogue in Its Social and Political Contexts, Castiglione to Galileo* (Cambridge: Cambridge University Press, 1992), 9–10. I find Cox's ironic use of the term "documentary dialogue" especially useful since here invented speeches are put into the mouths of persons whose reputations and names were unassailable in order to support and supposedly "document" certain views as though they were factual transcripts of real speech.

20. Valerio Marchetti and Rita Belladonna, "Carli Piccolomini, Bartolomeo," *DBI,* 20:194–96.

On Paleario's heresy trial, see Valerio Marchetti, *Gruppi ereticali Senesi del cinquecento* (Florence: La Nuova Italian Editrice, 1975), 46–49: Paleario was arraigned and questioned by the officers of the Inquisition on December 12, 1542, but he was absolved and released.

21. On the relationship between Bartolomeo Carli and Paleario, see Belladonna, "Gli Intronati," 49; and Marchetti and Belladonna, "Carli Piccolomini, Bartolomeo," 194–96. On the *Alfabeto,* see my chap. 2. The *Alfabeto,* which did not appear in print until 1546 though it circulated widely in manuscript after 1535, should probably be considered the product of the combined efforts of the Neapolitan reform thinkers Juan de Valdés and Giulia Gonzaga, who acted as Valdés's editor, translator, and agent with the Venetian presses.

22. Belladonna, "Gli Intronati," 52.

23. Regarding the heresy accusations against Intronati members, see Ibid., 52; Capo-netto, *The Protestant Reformation*, 112–16, 315–16 ff., includes a fascinating biography of Aonio Paleario, who with others led the heretical Erasmianism that raged like a forest fire among intellectuals in Siena, Perugia, and Padua and was linked to the academies in those cities from 1531, with the publication of Erasmus's *Enchiridion militis Christiani*, to around 1544.

24. See Belladonna's text of Piccolomini's previously unpublished *Dialogo* in "Gli Intronati," 78–79.

25. Ibid., 82–84.

26. Here I essentially recap Belladonna's conclusions (ibid., 57–58), though I go a step further in suggesting the inextricability of the connection in Piccolomini's project between perpetrating a more flattering image of the women of the Sienese *veglie* and of the religiocultural politics of the *Intronati*.

27. On A. Piccolomini (1508–79) the best source is Florindo Cerreta, *Alessandro Piccolomini: Letterato e filosofo Senese del cinquecento* (Siena: Accademia Senese degli Intronati, 1960), 6. Alessandro, whose family seems to have destined him at birth for a career in the Church, had already received a number of church benefices when he was a nine-year-old boy, which were conferred on him by another clan member, Cardinal Giovanni Piccolomini in Siena. Piccolomini was intensely involved all his life with literature (especially Greek), moral philosophy, and science, about which he wrote extensively; while he showed no interest in theology or issues of doctrine. He studied for a short period at the University of Bologna; he spent four years at the University of Padua (1538–42), where he studied the works of Aristotle and played leading roles in both the academies of the Intronati in Siena and the Infiammati in Padua. He promptly left Siena when the emperor Charles V and Cosimo I de'Medici launched a war on the city, occupied it, and incorporated it officially in Cosimo's expanding kingdom. Piccolomini's career in the Church appears to have been strictly opportunistic. His other benefices included the rectorship of the church of San Giorgio in Siena, conferred on him in 1540 and the archbishopric of Patrasso to which he was also appointed in 1540; in 1541 he was named coadjutor of the archbishop of Siena. He published two successful comedies, two books on conduct (one of them a comic dialogue), two books on astronomy and cosmography, and numerous Italian translations of Latin and Greek works (including Xenophon's *Oeconomicus*), and numerous sonnets and letters. He died in Siena in 1579.

28. Piccolomini's Italianized title of the orginal Greek *Oikonomikos* is *La oeconomica* (Venice: Al Segno del Pozzo, 1540); I'm going to refer to the work throughout the chapter by its Latinized title, *Oeconomicus*, in keeping with the Anglo-American tradition.

29. Alessandro Piccolomini, *In lode delle donne* (Venice: Giolito 1545); Piccolomini, *De la bella creanza de le donne* (Venice: Curzio Navo & fratelli, 1539). The *De la bella creanza* is usually cited as the *Raffaella*.

30. Piejus, "Varietà," 525. Piejus makes here a convincing for moving the date of the *Lode* back to 1538 on the basis of an allusion in the *Lode* to a passage in the *Raffaella*.

NOTES TO PAGES 137–139 · 308

31. See Ronnie H. Terpening, *Lodovico Dolce: Renaissance Man of Letters* (Toronto: University of Toronto Press, 1997), 19, on Dolce's connection with the Infiammati; he was also a member of the Accademia Frattegiana and the Pellegrini.

32. Henricus Cornelius Agrippa's *Dialogo . . . delle donne* was first published in 1529, in Latin. It was almost immediately translated into French, English, Italian, and German. In 1544 Dolce edited the first Italian edition of the work (translated from the French by Francesco Coccio) for Giolito. On Giolito's combined edition of the two works—Piccolomini's *In lode delle donne* and Agrippa's *Dialogo della institutione delle donne*, which came out in 1545 and was edited by Dolce—see Bongi, *Annali di Gabriel Giolito*, 1:77, 94–95.

33. Betussi would soon translate the work into Italian himself under the title *Libro di M. Giovanni Boccaccio delle donne illustri* (Venice: Andrea Arrivabene, Al Segno del Pozzo, 1545); see also Boccaccio, *Famous Women*, ed. and trans. Brown.

    My comments on Piccolomini's *In lode delle donne* are indebted to Piejus's edition and critique of the work in her "Varietà," 524–51.

34. *Repub.* 5.456 ff. Compare Piejus's edition of Piccolomini's treatise on women in "Varietà," 548.

35. See Piccolomini's letters to Varchi in Florindo Cerreta, "An Account of the Early Life of the Accademia degli Infiammati in the Letters of Alessandro Piccolomini to Benedetto Varchi," *Romanic Review* 48 (1957): 249–64.

36. Cerreta, *Alessandro Piccolomini*, 32–33. By the fifteenth century, pilgrimmages to the tomb of Petrarch had become, says Cerreta, "a mania." Poets were inspired to publish collections of poetry on their visits to this tomb. Bernardo Bembo, Antonio Brocardo, Girolamo Malipiero, and Varchi had all done this. Cerreta notes that over time the practice of writing commemorative lyrics degenerated into satire writing that was anti-Petrarchan.

37. Cerreta, *Piccolomini*, 34n3.

38. Cerreta, *Alessandro Piccolomini*, 32–34, doesn't cite a particular date on which the sonnets on Petrarch's tomb were presented at an academy meeting but they must have been performed there since this collection of sonnets by women and men, as he notes, was initiated by Piccolomini but was completed by the members of the Infiammati as an an academy project (33). The collection was later referred to as the *Tombaide*. Cerreta has published all five of the women's *rime* in an appendix to the above book, 241–46; the women's *rime* include his own *rime* answering each of the women's works.These *rime* were first published in F. Cerreta, "*La Tombaide*: Alcune rime inedite sur un pelegrinaggio petrarchesco ad Aqua," *Italica* 35 (September 1958): 162–66.

39. Biblioteca Nazionale, Florence, Cod. Pal. 228, II, I, sec. 5, fols. 71v–72r, as noted in Cerreta, *Piccolomini*, 32–34; 241–48. See also Cerreta's brief note, "La Tombaide," 162–66.

40. Cerreta, *Piccolomini*, 241–48.

41. The prolific Sienese poet Virginia di Matteo Salvi is not to be confused withVirginia de Achille Salvi, also of Siena, notes Cerreta, *Alessandro Piccolomini*, 34n5.

42. Cod. Pal. 288, c. 65v, as edited in Cerreta, *Piccolomini*, 241.

43. Cod. Pal. 288, c. 65r, as edited in Cerreta, *Piccolomini*, 242.

44. Cod. Pal. 288, c. 66v, as edited in Cerreta, *Piccolomini*, 242.

45. Alessandro Piccolomini, *Raffaella* (Venice: Curzio Navo,1539; 1540; Venice: Grifio, 1557; Venice: Meda Fratelli, 1558; Milan 1560; Venice: Domenico Farri, 1574; Venice: Grifio, 1574).

46. See nn. 29 and 45. I am very much indebted to the excellent articles of Piejus, "Varietà," 524–51; and "Venus Bifrons: Le double ideal feminin dans *La Raffaella* d'Alessandro Piccolomini," in *Images de la femme dans la litterature Italienne de la Renaissance prejuges misegynes et aspirations nouvelles*, ed. Andre Rochon (Paris: Universitaire de la Sorbonne Nouvelle, 1980), 81–131.

47. The characterization of *Raffaella* as bawdy comes from Eisenbichler, "Laudomia Forteguerri Loves Margaret of Austria," 295.

48. Pius II circulated his *De duobus amantibus* (ca. 1444), before he became pope. See Piejus, "Venus Bifrons," 86.

49. The dates given for the births of Forteguerri's children and her marriages are from C. Zarrilli's article on Forteguerri in the *DBI*, 49:153–55. The title page of the *Institutione* seems to indicate a considerable gap in time between the work's completion or partial completion in manuscript and its first printing. According to Zarrilli (153) and the Archivio di Stato di Siena (see fol. 419r for the birth dates of Forteguerri's children), Forteguerri's son Alessandro was born in1539. The title page reads: *De la institutione di tutta la vita de l'huomo nato nobile, e in citta libera, libri X in lingua toscana. Dove e peripateticamente e platonicamente, intorno a le cose de l'ethica, economica, e parte de la politica, e raccolta la somma di quanto principalmente puo concorrere a la perfetta e felice vita di quello. Composti dal S. Alessandro Piccolomini, a beneficio del nobilissimo fanciullino Alessandro Colombini, pochi giorni innanzi nato; figlio de la immortale Mad. Ladomia Forteguerri al quale (havendolo egli sostenuto a battesmo) secondo l'usanza dei compari, dei detti libri fa dono. Venetiis: apud Hieronymum Scotum, 1542.* Therefore from the inscription on the title page we know that Piccolomini completed the manuscript of the book in 1539, a few days before the birth of Laudomia's son, that he had held the baby at his baptism, and that he presented the book for the education of the boy probably in manuscript at the time of the baptism, and again in its published form fresh from the printers' in 1542, three years after the first draft was completed.

50. While the publication date on the title page of the *Institutione* is 1542 and Ottaviano Scotto's dedicatory letter to the Marchese and Marchesa del Vasto (Alfonso d'Avalos and his wife Maria d'Aragona d'Avalos) is dated March 16, 1542, the second dedicatory letter to Forteguerri, which was written by Piccolomini himself, is dated January 1, 1540, and in that letter he describes the occasion of the baptism of Forteguerri's son "just this past autumn." If we accept the composition date for the *Institutione* suggested in Piccolomini's dedicatory letter, we have to imagine that between 1538 and 1539 Piccolomini was preparing at least four different book manuscripts for publication. When he handed Forteguerri the newly dedicated work on the day of the baptism—or if he did so—perhaps the manuscript consisted only in the title page, the table of contents, the dedicatory letter, and sketches for chapters.

51. As far as I know, there is no English translation in print of Piccolomini's *Institutione*.

52. Alberti's *De familia* was not known in the sixteenth century and would have to wait another hundred years for its rediscovery.

53. For the comparison to Alberti, I am again indebted to Piejus, "Varietà," 530. On the *Institutione*, see also Alessandra Del Fante: "Amore, famiglia e matrimonio nell' 'Institutione' di Alessandro Piccolomini," *Nuova rivista storica* 68 (1984): 511–26.

54. The *Insitutione* was published in fourteen editions before 1600: Venice: H. Scotum 1542, 1543, 1545; Venice: G. M. Bonelli, 1552; Venice: Francesco dell'Imperadori, 1559; Venice: G. Ziletti, 1560, 1561, 1569; Venice: Imperadori, 1569; Venice: n.p., 1575; Venice: Ziletti, 1575, 1582, 1583; Venice:Ugolino, 1584. After Trent in 1560 Piccolomini revised the work substantially deleting all references to love theory.

55. Alessandro Piccolomini, *Institutione di tutta la vita de l'huomo nato nobile, e in citta libera* . . . (Venetia: apud Hieronymum Scotum, 1542), bk. 10, chap. 2, fols. 217v–218, 219.

56. Piejus, "Varietà," 540.

57. Piccolomini, *Institutione*, bk. 10, chap. 2, fol. 218v: "Essendo dunque questo verissimo dico, che parimente l'affetto e la benevolenza, che a la consorte e a i figli si porta . . . , i quali più tosto charità filiali, e matrimoniale, che Amore si de chiamare."

58. Ibid., fols. 218–218v.

59. Ibid., chap. 4, fol. 222.

60. Ibid., fol. 223.

61. Marsilio Ficino, *Commentary on Plato's Symposium on Love*, trans. and ed. Sears Jayne, 3d ed. (Woodstock, CT: Spring Publications, 1994), speech 5, esp. 84–95; cf. Plato, *Symp.* 210–11.

62. Piccolomini, *Institutione*, bk. 9, chap. 4, fol. 192v.

63. Alessandro Piccolomini, *Lettura del S. Alessandro Piccolomini Infiammato fatta nell'Accademia degli Infiammati* (Bologna: Bartolmeo Bonardo & Marc'Antonio da Carpi, 1541); and Lodovico Domenichi, ed., *Rime diverse* (Venice: Giolito, 1546); a third edition of the *Rime diverse* came out with Forteguerri's sonnet included in 1549.

64. Cerreta, *Alessandro Piccolomini*, see esp. 23–31 on Piccolomini's role in the *Infiammati*. See also Zarrilli, "Forteguerri, Laudomia," in *DBI*, 49:153–55; Piejus, "Venus Bifrons," 81–131; Piejus, "Varietà," 524–51; Eisenbichler, "Laudomia Forteguerri Loves Margaret of Austria," 277–304.

65. Two similar letters from Piccolomini to Dolce are printed in Bernardino Pini, ed., *Della Nuova Scielta di Lettere di diversi nobilissimi huomini et eccell. ingegni* (Venice: n.p., 1574). Here are excerpted passages from one of these letters, 178–79:

> Il ritratto della vostra cortesia, che profondissimamente mi s'impresse nell'animo in quel brevissimo spatio di tempo, ch'io stetti con voi & insieme ancora *l'affetto ardentissimo*, et la devuta riversa. . . m'han tutto, ingannando mi col desio, sperare di giorno in giorno di haver qualche occasione di potere in presentia mostrarvi quella piu parte . . . della *calda affettione* mia verso di voi. . . . Questo so bene, che di *caldezza d'affetto* punto inferior non vi sono, come che per essere il mio affetto devuto, venga a farsi per questo minore. Communque si sia, m'e stata sommamente cara *l'amorevolissima vostra lettera*: nella quale non le vostre parole, ma la

mente vostra istessa veggio & contemplo, *calda di quell'amore verso di me, che la natural vostra cortesia le accende dattorno.*

I have italicized the erotically charged language for easy access. Note that I cite the same letters below in my discussion of patronage language in the sixteenth century.

66. See my chap. 1 and app. B for the list of anthologies.

67. This was a translation of the first six books, to be more precise; the volume was titled *I sei primi libri dell'Eneide di Virgilio* (Venice: Comin da Trino, 1540).

68. Piccolomini, *Lettura*, 3–4 (my pagination) contain his prefatory letter to the president of the academy, Leone Orsino, which describes how Forteguerri's sonnets came into his hands.

69. On women's attendance and involvement at the meetings and activities of the Infiammati, see Piccolomini's letters to Benedetto Varchi in Florindo Cerreta, "An Account of the Early Life of the Accademia," *Romanic Review* 48 (1957): 249–64. In Piccolomini's letter of June 9, 1541, he tells Varchi of the visit of Giovanna Malatesta and Lucretia Pia to the academy (259). See also Landoni, ed., *Lettere all'Aretino*, vol. 2, pt. 1, 235 ff., as cited by Cerreta (254), on the Infiammati's activities involving a collection of sonnets composed by a number of "gentildonne sanesi."

70. Two years later, Rinaldo Corso would publish the first large-scale critical essay on a woman's collected poetry in his review of Vittoria Colonna's work titled *Dichiaratione fatta sopra la seconda parte delle Rime della Divina Vittoria Collonna [sic] Marchesana di Pescara . . .* (Bologna: Gian Battista de Phaelli, 1543).

71. See n. 65 above on the *Lettura*.

72. The *Rime diverse*, Giolito's first anthology of contemporary poets, was issued again in a third edition in 1549. Giolito, the most prestigious of the Venetian publishing houses, as noted in chap. 1, with its multiple editions and successful marketing of a series of anthologies of new poets, was able to produce a standard list of contemporary writers whose names soon became widely known and whose works would be reanthologized throughout that and the next century.

73. Forteguerri's six extant sonnets (five addressed to Margaret of Austria, and one to Alda Torella Lunata) were to constitute an important component in Lodovico Domenichi's anthology of fifty-three women poets titled *Rime diverse d'alcune nobilissime, et virtuosissime donne*, 102–4. See also chap. 2, n. 77. Two of Forteguerri's sonnets to Margaret were published again in Bergalli, ed. *Componimenti poetici*, 76: "Ora ten vai superbo, or corri altero" and "Lasso, chel mio bel sole i santi rai," as emended by Bergalli.

74. Piccolomini, in his introduction to Forteguerri's sonnet (*Lettura*, 11; the pages are not numbered in the edition so this my own pagination for easy reference), gives the following chronology: they first met in 1535 and they saw each other again in Siena "due anni sono" (two years ago), which would have been in 1538 or 1539.

75. On Charles's entrance into Siena and his early policies there, see Sozzini, *Diario*, 1:21–87.

76. This marriage alliance shows how Charles V tended to try to cover all the bases, even at the expense of betraying his own vassals. In marrying Margaret to the pope's grandson, Ottavio Farnese, whose father Pier Luigi Farnese, the pope's top military

man, would personally savage the Colonna towns and lands in the Salt War, Charles insulted Ascanio Colonna, long one of the mainstays of his regime in Italy.

77. Piccolomini, *Lettura*, 1. Regarding my belaboring the point that the eroticized vocabulary in Piccolomini's account of Laudomia's meeting with Margaret is ambiguous: it may or may not suggest to readers that Forteguerri's literary pursuit of the emperor's daughter had a sexual component (however "platonic"). I only bother to demonstrate that such language was standard in the courtship/patronage letters of clients to their patrons (or hoped-for patrons) as a supplement to Konrad Eisenbichler's suggestive article, "Laudomia Forteguerri Loves Margaret of Austria," in which he argues that Piccolomini's characterization (in the *Lettura*) of the relationship between the two women is evidence of a rare instance in the Renaissance of the explicit account of a platonic love affair between women.

78. As I noted above, similarly impassioned language is found in two letters from Alessandro Piccolomini to Dolce: see Pini, *Della nuova scielta di lettere di diversi nobilissimi huomini*, 178–79.

79. Eisenbichler, "Laudomia Forteguerri Loves Margaret of Austria," 277–80. The dialogue under discussion in Eisenbichler's article is Firenzuola's *On the Beauty of Women*.

80. Plato *Symposium* 189d–192c.

81. Eisenbichler, "Laudomia Forteguerri Loves Margaret of Austria," 277.

82. Harriette Andreadis, *Sappho in Early Modern England: Female Same-Sex Literary Erotics, 1550–1714* (Chicago: University of Chicago Press, 2001), has shown that in sixteenth- and seventeenth-century England a tradition of same-sex literary erotics begins to emerge among women writers. Within this tradition she documents a wide spectrum of literary affectivity between women, including both women writers who were flamboyantly transgressive in representing their sexuality and women whose writings portrayed intimate friendships with other women but "who wished to dissociate themselves from transgression." These women, writes Andreadis, who were "not willing to flout social mores developed an erotically charged yet shadowed language of female same-sex friendship" (103).

83. In a provocative essay, Eisenbichler, "Laudomia Forteguerri Loves Margaret of Austria," 277–304, argues that Forteguerri's poems represent a rare instance of same-sex female platonic love in the Renaissance, but his argument is well contextualized in Agnolo Firenzuola's contemporary dialogue *On the Beauty of Women* (1541), in which Forteguerri and Margaret of Austria are depicted as "lascivious" lovers like Sappho. "This type of woman," wrote Firenzuola, "by nature spurns marriage and flees from intimate conversation with us men" (277).

84. Domenichi, ed., *Rime diverse d'alcune nobilissime*.

85. On Andreadis's work, see n. 82 above. For examples of the tradition in Italy, see the following collections of women's *rime*: the anthology of fifty-three women poets edited by Domenichi, *Rime diverse d'alcune nobilissime*, which I discuss in chap. 2.

86. All the poems exchanged among women that I mention here are in Domenichi, ed., *Rime diverse d'alcune nobilissime*, and Bulifon, ed., *Rime di cinquanta illustri poetesse*.

87. The translations are mine, as throughout the chapter.

88. Piccolomini, *Lettura*, 26, calls attention to this metaphor noting that Forteguerri cannot have meant that the Tiber had bathed the skirt of the lady, having called her "il mio sole." Nor is it fitting to say that the "gonna del Sole" is bathed. Citing Quintilian's advice, Piccolomini suggests simply letting the metaphor go without bringing in the image of the sun again. To me it made sense to have the "sun" bathing the Tiber banks since the theme of the poem is that Forteguerri's "sun" (*il mio sole*) is enriching the Tiber (i.e., Rome) by her presence.

89. My text retains the spelling of the first edition of her sonnet, *Lettura del S. Alessandro Piccolomini Infiammato: va . . . corre*. But see Domenichi, ed., *Rime d'alcune nobilissime: va . . . corri*; Bulifon, ed., *Rime di cinquanta illustri poetesse: vai . . . corri*; Bergalli, ed., *Componimenti poetici: vai . . . corri*; and Eisenbichler, "Laudomia Forteguerri Loves Margaret of Austria," 299: *vai . . . corri*.

90. Domenichi, ed., *Rime diverse d'alcune nobilissime*, 102, has substituted *vede* for *mostran* in line 13.

    At line 14, a number of variants are found in the editions subsequent to Piccolomini's: *può* (Domenichi, Bulifon, Bergalli); *pote* (Eisenbichler).

91. Note that I have decided to follow the order in which the poems are published in their first edition: Domenichi, ed., *Rime diverse d'alcune nobilissime*; the same order is preserved in Bulifon, ed., *Rime di cinquanta poetesse*.

92. Piccolomini, *Lettura*, 22.

93. Piccolomini, *Lettura*, 13.

94. Robert M. Durling, ed., *Petrarch's Lyric Poems: The "Rime sparse" and Other Lyrics* (Cambridge, MA: Harvard University Press, 1997), sonnet 180.

95. It's important to note that Piccolomini's connections extended far beyond Siena. When war bore down on Siena from its neighbor to the east, the bishop decided to remain in Rome after 1549. He dedicated his collected poetry, *Cento sonnetti* (Rome: Vincenzo Valgrisi, 1549), to Vittoria Colonna di Toledo, the dedicatee of Betussi, Girolamo Ruscelli, and a number of other prominent poets. Vittoria di Toledo was the daughter of Giovanna d'Aragona (of the *Tempio* fame), and Betussi was quick to name both Giovanna and her estranged husband Ascanio Colonna in his preface to Piccolomini's *Sonnetti*.

96. Piccolomini, for example, was never tried as a religious heretic, but in 1560 the Roman Holy Office forced him to purge his best-selling conduct book, the *Institutione*, of most occurrences of the word *amore* and of all other references in the book to extramarital relations between the sexes.

97. Domenichi, ed., *Rime diverse d'alcune nobilissime*, 234, includes a poem by one "Francesca B. Sanese" in his all-women anthology. I'm assuming that Domenichi's "Francesca B" and Betussi's "Francesca de' Baldi Sanese" are one and the same woman.

## CHAPTER SIX

1. My translation from Cornelius Firmano, *Diarium*, extracts 35–47; the Latin text is in Pastor, *The History of the Popes*, 17:401–2; see also Domenico Orano, *Liberi pensatori*

*bruciati in Roma* (Livorno: Bastogi, 1971). The execution is also described in Oddone Ortolani, *Pietro Carnesecchi: Con estratti dagli Atti del Processo del Santo Officio* (Firenze: Felice le Monnier, 1963), 153–67.

2. On Cibo in Florence in the 1540s and 1550s, see now Gabriella Zarri, "La spiritualità di Caterina Cibo: Indizi e testimonianze," in *Caterina Cybo duchessa di Camerino (1501–1557)*, ed. Pierluigi Moriconi, Atti del Convegno, Camerino, Auditorium S. Caterina, 28–30 ottobre 2004 (Camerino: Tipografia "La Nuova Stampa," 2005), 313–31. On Cibo's life, see Maria Teresa Guerra Medici, *Famiglia e potere in una signoria dell'Italia centrale: I Varano di Camerino* (Camerino: Università degli Studi di Camerino, 2002); Cesare Vasoli, "Caterina Cibo Varano," in *Civitas Mundi: Studi sulla cultura del cinquecento,* Raccolta di Studi e Testi 194 (Rome: Edizioni Storia & Letteratura, 1996), 121–38; B. Feliciangeli, *Notizie e documenti sulla vita di Caterina Cibo-Varano* (Camerino: Tipografico Savini, 1891); Franca Petrucci, "Cibo, Caterina," in *DBI*, 25:237–41; Bainton, *Women of the Reformation*; Caponetto, *The Protestant Reformation.*

On Gonzaga's life, see Oliva, *Giulia Gonzaga Colonna*; Dall'Olio, "Gonzaga, Giulia," 783–87; Amante, *Giulia Gonzaga*; Affò, "Vita di donna Giulia Gonzaga," 145–88.

On Carnesecchi's life and trial, see Ortolani, *Pietro Carnesecchi*; Mulli, *Giulia Gonzaga*; d'Ercole, *Il cardinale Ippolito de'Medici*; Moretti, "Il cardinale Ippolito dei Medici"; Firpo and Marcatto, eds., *I processi inquisitoriali di Pietro Carnesecchi.*

3. Oliva, *Giulia Gonzaga Colonna*, 219–21; Nieto, *Juan de Valdés and the Origins.*

4. An account of the regular attendees can be found in Oliva, *Giulia Gonzaga Colonna*, 221n5. This list of frequent attendees seems to have come from Magno's notes. Also in Magno's list are Costanzo d'Avalos, Princess of Ischia and aunt of Vittoria Colonna's deceased husband, the sisters Maria and Giovanna d'Aragona, the ubiquitous Roman scholar and writer, Annibal Caro, and the poet Bernardo Tasso, among others. Vittoria Colonna's name does not appear on this list, but I added her to the group since in the 1530s she generally went everywhere her in-laws the Aragona sisters and Costanza d'Avalos went.

On Bernardino Ochino and Valdesian thought in Ochino and the Valdesians, see Caponetto, *The Protestant Reformation*; Gleason, "The Capuchin Order," 31–67; Elizabeth Gleason, "On the Nature of Sixteenth-Century Italian Evangelism," 3–25; Collett, *A Long and Troubled Pilgrimage*, esp. 66–104; Firpo, *Inquisizione romana*; Bainton, *Bernardino Ochino*; and Bainton, *Women of the Reformation.*

5. Marcantonio Flaminio, *Paraphrasis* (Venice: Tacuino, 1536). Pastore, *Marcantonio Flaminio*; Flaminio, *Lettere*; A. Pastore, "Flaminio, Marcantonio," *DBI*, 48:282–88.

6. It was in 1542–43 that Flaminio, working with Cardinal Pole, probably composed the *Beneficio di Cristo* (the *Trattato utilissimo del beneficio di Giesu Cristo crocifisso verso i Cristiani* is its full title), the key manifesto of the Italian reform movement, which was published anonymously by Bindoni in Venice in 1543. Thomas F. Mayer, *Reginald Pole, Prince and Prophet* (Cambridge: Cambridge University Press, 2000), 119, argues convincingly that the anonymous was not only the work of Flaminio and Pole, but that it was "the most celebrated product of Pole and Flaminio's relationship and of the Italian Reformation."

On Vittoria Colonna's role as a leader and participant in Valdesian reform circles in the late 1530s and 1540s, see her *Carteggio*, ed. Ermanno Ferrero, Domenico Tordi, and Giuseppe Müller (Turin: Leoscher, 1889–92); Reumont, *Vittoria Colonna*; Patrizi, "Colonna, Vittoria," 448–57.

7. Antonio Rotondò, "Carnesecchi, Pietro," in *DBI*, 20:466–76. Carnesecchi went to trial with unanimous witnesses to his innocence, by Giovanni Della Casa among others and the active intervention of Cosimo I de' Medici, who wrote on his behalf to Cardinal Juan Alvarez, the Commisario of the Inquisition Office, Cardinal Giovanni Salviati, and the imperial ambassador to Rome, Juan de Vega. The trial ended with Pope Paul III granting Carnesecchi absolution. After the trial he stayed on in Rome where he visited Vittoria Colonna for the last time before she died.

8. Cosimo's mother, Maria Salviati, and Caterina Cibo were the daughters of the sisters Lucrezia and Maddalena de'Medici; Lucrezia and Maddalena were both daughters of Lorenzo (Il magnifico) de'Medici and Clarice Orsini. Giulia Gonzaga's lover, Cardinal Ippolito de'Medici, was also a first cousin of Salviati and Cibo. He was the natural son of Giuliano de'Medici, a brother of Maddalena and Lucrezia de'Medici.

9. Oliva, *Giulia Gonzaga Colonna*, 260–61.

10. Ibid., 259–62; Ortolani, *Pietro Carnesecchi*, 106–17.

11. Dall'Olio, "Gonzaga, Giulia," 783–87.

12. My account of this "payoff"—the pope's coronation of Cosimo I as Grand Duke of Tuscany—is left for the end of the chapter. While I've stripped my account of the event down to bare bones, Roberto Cantagalli, *Cosimo I de'Medici, granduca di Toscana* (Milan: Mursia, 1985), 282–90, is fascinatingly cinematic: he leads the reader slowly, step by step through the ritual. Earlier, Cantagalli (271–82) had convincingly made the case that Cosimo knew that the surest means to getting Pius V to crown him Grand Duke of Tuscany was to surrender Carnesecchi. Pius V (the religious fanatic Michele Ghislieri), formerly the presiding officer of the Roman Inquisition before becoming pope had been determined to nail Carnesecchi at least since 1561. Cosimo was finally crowned grand duke by the Pope in Rome on March 5, 1570, but only after the duke had succumbed to a steady stream of requests by Ghislieri to hand over alleged "heretics." It was the by far the ugliest chapter in Cosimo's not exactly principled rise to power.

13. On Cibo's life, see Zarri, "La spiritualità di Caterina Cibo"; Medici, *Famiglia e potere*; Vasoli, "Caterina Cibo Varano"; Feliciangeli, *Notizie e documenti sulla vita di Caterina Cibo-Varano*; =Petrucci, "Cibo, Caterina," 237–41; Bainton, *Women of the Reformation*; Caponetto, *The Protestant Reformation*.

14. The *Dialogi* (note the idiosyncratic spelling of Ochino's work without the *h*) were composed while Ochino was still in the order, but the work did not come out in print until after he had left Italy and the Capuchins. On Flaminio, see Pastore, *Marcantonio Flaminio*; Flaminio, *Lettere*.

15. The *Alfabeto* was published by Nicolo Bacarini in Venice in 1545. Oliva, *Giulia Gonzaga*, p. 236, notes that it was translated and edited for publication after the death of Valdés in 1541. Oliva thinks the dialogue could have been drafted as early as 1536,

in response to the death of the man Gonzaga promised she would marry, Ippolito de'Medici.

The original translation of the *Alfabeto* from the Spanish into Italian was done by Giulia Gonzaga's secretary Marco Antonio Magno, when Valdés died in 1541, bequeathing all his papers and writings to her. But this early translation was no doubt edited by Gonzaga herself before she took the manuscript to the printer, Nicolo Bacarini, inVenice in 1545 for its publication. See my discussion of Gonzaga's coauthorship of the *Alfabeto* above in chap. 1, 18–19.

16. Speroni's *Dialogo d'amore* was published in 1542; Tullia d'Aragona was one of the principal interlocutors in it. Betussi's *Raverta,* featuring the celebrated Venetian courtesan Francesca Baffa as a central character, was published in 1544; and Betussi's *Leonora* (1557) puts Leonora Falletta, who was a noblewoman in real life and a patron of Betussi's, in the main role and gives her all the long, learned philosophical speeches in the dialogue, relegating the male speakers around her to playing the sidekicks to her Socrates.

17. The first edition of Ochino's *Dialogi sette* was published by Zoppino in Venice in1540; Zoppino reprinted the *"Dialogi"* in 1542. All citations in this chapter are from Bernardino Ochino, *I "Dialogi Sette" e altri scritti del tempo della fuga,* ed. Ugo Rozzo (Turin: Claudiana, 1985). Hereafter, this work will be cited in the text.

18. Ficino, *Commentary on Plato's Symposium on Love*; a Latin and an Italian version of Ficino's *Commentary* were written and distributed in manuscript in 1469 and 1474, respectively. The first printed edition of the work was produced in 1484 in Venice as part of Ficino's Latin translation of the complete works of Plato: *Opera Platonis.*

19. Ficino, *Commentary on Plato's Symposium on Love,* see esp. 141–45, 170–71. Over thirty works influenced by Ficino's commentary were published between 1469 and 1585, including the subsequently influential dialogues by Ebreo, Equicola, Bembo, Castiglione, Speroni, Betussi, Sansovino Gottifredi, Tullia d'Aragona, and Varchi. Among these, the most influential disseminators of Neoplatonic love theory were Leone Ebreo's *Dialoghi d'amore* (1501; followed by eleven editions) and Castiglione's *Il cortignano* (1519; followed by sixteen editions).

20. *I "Dialogi Sette."* Rozzo's note tells us this passage comes from 1 Tim. 6:15–16: "King of kings, Lord of lords; who only hath immortality, dwelling in the light which no man can approach."

21. Oliva, *Giulia Gonzaga Colonna,* 236. All citations from the *Alfabeto* will be from Giovanni di Valdés, *Alfabeto Cristiano: Dialogo con Giulia Gonzaga,* introduction by B. Croce (Bari: Laterza, 1938).

22. Oliva, *Giulia Gonzaga Colonna,* 221.

23. The concept of *conveniens, convenientia,* that which is suitable, fitting, or appropriate is a key term in Cicero's philosophical works: see *Fin.* 3.21; *Nat. D.* 3.28; *Div.* 2.34; *Off.* 1.40.144.

24. On Crates, a fourth century Athenian philosopher, see Cicero *Acad.* 1.9.34; the others Ochino lists are well-known ancient philosophers and standard humanist fare.

25. Ochino, *I "Dialogi Sette,"* ed. Rozzo, 62: "L'ho cerca nella scientia e nella eloquentia, nelle virtù morali, in speculare la verità e contemplare Dio, in gustare tutte le cose,

massime Dio; e finalmente ho esperimentato tutto e trovato miserie dove io pensavo fusse la felicità."

26. The so-called academy was not a formal institution but an informal circle of Florentine intellectuals, artists, churchmen, and other leading men, at whose center was the Neoplatonist philosopher and translator of Plato, Marsilio Ficino (see Arthur Field, *The Origins of the Platonic Academy* [Princeton, NJ: Princeton University Press, 1988]).

27. Ochino, *I "Dialogi Sette,"* ed. Rozzo, 64: "Però disse Platone: quello esser felice il quale non pendea se non solo da Dio. La nostra cupidità è infinita e sempre a nuove cose."

28. On Cosimo's literary patronage, see esp. Antonio Ricci, "Lorenzo Torrentino and the Cultural Programme of Cosimo I de'Medici," in *Cultural Politics of Duke Cosimo de' Medici*, ed. Konrad Eisenbichler, 135–48; and Basile, *"Fasseli gratia per poetessa,"* 103–20. See also Claudia Di Filippo Bareggi, "In nota alla politica culturale di Cosimo I: L'Accademia Fiorentina," *Quaderni storici* 23 (1973): 627–74; Umberto Pirotti, *Benedetto Varchi e la cultura del suo tempo* (Florence: Olschki, 1971); Eric Cochrane, *Florence in the Forgotten Centuries, 1527–1800: A History of Florence and the Florentines in the Age of the Grand Dukes* (Chicago: University of Chicago Press, 1973); Judith Bryce, "The Oral World of the Early Accademia Fiorentina," *Renaissance Studies* 9, no. 1 (1995): 77–103.

29. See chap. 5. Piccolomini's critical essay on Forteguerri's sonnet *Hora te'n va superbo* was published in Bologna by Bartolomeo Barnardo and Marc'Antonio da Carpi in 1541. But Piccolomini's essay dealt only with a single work. I am indebted to Abigail Brundin's for calling my attention to Monica Bianco's article about Rinaldo Corso's commentaries on Vittoria Colonna's collected poetry: "Le due redazioni del commento di Rinaldo Corso alle rime di Vittoria Colonna," *Studi di filologia italiana* 56 (1998): 271–95. Corso's *Dichiaratione fatta sopra la seconda parte delle Rime . . .* (Bologna: Gian Battista de Phaelli, 1543) was the first critical assessment of the collected works of any author—male or female. See Vittoria Colonna, *Sonnets for Michelangelo: A Bilingual Edition*, ed. and trans. Abilgail Brundin (Chicago and London: University of Chicago Press, 2005). Brundin's critical biography of Colonna is forthcoming.

See my chap. 5 on Varchi's friendship with Piccolomini and his interest in Piccolomini's literary relationship with Forteguerri. It's my assumption both Varchi's connections in Bologna and his encouragement of Piccolomini, who was at an earlier stage of his career at the time, were instrumental in getting Piccolomini's lecture on Forteguerri's poetry published in Bologna.

30. For a physical description of the edition *Polibio historico greco tradotto per M. Lodovico Domenichi: Con due fragmenti me i quali si ragiona delle Reppubliche, & della grandezza di Romani* (Venice: Gabriel Giolito, 1545), see S. Bongi, *Annali di Gabriel Giolito,* 1:91–92, 117, 387.

31. On Doni's publishing connections with Domenichi and Giolito, see my index of anthology poets in app. A. See also Paul F. Grendler, *Critics of the Italian World, 1530–1560: Anton Francesco Doni, Nicolò Franco, and Ortensio Lando* (Madison: University of Wisconsin Press, 1969).

32. On Torrentino, see Grendler, *Critics of the Italian World,* 56.

33. See ibid., 133; Caponetto, *The Protestant Reformation,* 295. The books Domenichi was charged with having translated and published were Calvin's *Nicomediana* and Sleidan's *Commentarii,* printed in a pirate edition, says Piscini, "Domenichi, Lodovico," 40:599–600.

34. See Piscini, "Domenich, Lodovico," 40:598–600. With Domenichi's assistance, Cosimo's printer Torrentino had already published forbidden texts by Contarini, Carnesecchi, Morone, Valdés, and Erasmus—all authors forbidden by the index of 1549 published by the Roman Holy Office. For some reason, Cosimo did not intervene to protect Domenichi, though he must have done so for Torrentino; the Medici printer was never charged. Fortunately for Domenichi, the notoriously pro-Protestant Duchess of Ferrara, Renata di Francia, secured his release in May 1553. Piscini notes twice in that article that Cosimo embraced a very rigid religious politik after 1550 and that, for this reason, Domenichi distanced himself more often from Florence. Piscini also notes that in 1554 Domenichi was in Lucca exploring the idea of setting up an independent press with the backing of the Turini family, the Della Barba family, and the publisher Vicenzo Busdragho.

35. D'Aragona no doubt read Greek in Latin or vernacular translations; there is no reason to think she may have read Greek philosophy in the original Greek.

36. On Isabella d'Este (1474–1539) and her patronage, see Deanna Shemek, "In Continuous Expectation: Isabella d'Este's Epistolary Desire," in *Phaethon's Children: The Este Court and Its Culture in Early Modern Italy,* ed. Dennis Looney and Deanna Shemek (Tempe, AZ: Medieval and Renaissance Texts and Studies, 2005), 269–300; Alessandro Luzio and Rodolfo Renier, *Mantova e Urbino: Isabella d'Este ed Elisabetta Gonzaga nelle relazioni familiari e nelle vicende politiche* (Turin: Roux & Co., 1893); Rose Marie San Juan, "The Court Lady's Dilemma: Isabella d'Este and Art Collecting in the Renaissance," *Oxford Art Journal* 14, no. 1 (1991): 67–78.

37. Bongi, *Annali di Gabriel Giolito,* 1:166–67.

38. D'Aragona published her sonnet to Ochino in the 1547 Giolito edition of her *Rime.* It became a notorious piece brought out again in the second and third editions of her *Rime* that Giolito produced in 1549 and 1560. As far as we know, Ochino never responded to d'Aragona's poem.

39. Tullia d' Aragona, *Rime della Signora Tullia di Aragona et di diversi a lei* (Venice: Gabriel Giolito, 1547).

40. The 1842 edition of Sozzini, *Diario delle cose avvenute in Siena,* is the modern edition of the *Diario,* vol. 1.

41. The list of Tullia d'Aragona's dedicatees and addressees in the 1547 Giolito edition of her *Rime* make it clear that her close friends were Noveschi partisans (the brothers Emilio and Ottaviano Tondi, for example). But the 1545 revolt would prove to be only the first act of the much bloodier citizens' revolt against their subsequent Spanish overlords, a revolt that brought Charles V and Cosimo to the gates of Siena in 1551. As we saw in the preceding chapter, in 1555, after almost four years under siege and bombardment the Sienese surrendered, Spanish and Florentine forces entered the

city, Spanish colonial rule was reestablished in the city, and in 1560 Siena was officially absorbed into the duchy of Cosimo I de' Medici.

42. Bongi, *Annali di Gabriel Giolito*, 1:173–74, provides a transcription of the record from the Archivio di Stato in Siena of Tullia d'Aragona's marriage to Silvestro Guicciardi of Ferrara in Siena on January 8, 1543. Bongi also notes that, while nothing is known concerning the precise reasons for Tullia's marriage, nor is anything whatsoever known about Guicciardi beyond the fact of his marriage to Tullia, we do know from Vecellio and other sixteenth-century writers that courtesans and prostitutes often married to acquire legal protection exempting them from having to comply with laws governing prostitutes, such as the sumptuary law.

43. Ibid., 1:175.

44. On this, see ibid., 177–85; see also d'Aragona, *Rime della signora Tullia di Aragona*, fol. 9; Bongi is very good at describing her alliances, the *tumulto*, or popular uprising, of 1546, the role of the *noveschi,* the expulsion of the Spanish from Siena, the dangers she faced in the small city. Deana Basile's account of d'Aragona's move to Florence in "*Fasseli gratia per poetessa*" (135–48) is interesting for its inferences drawn from Bongi's account of the incidents referred to above and the accompanying documents. Basile argues that it's d'Aragona's ties with the Sienese-expelled *noveschi* (the Spanish-supporting *noveschi*) that clinch, among other factors, Cosimo and Eleonora's decision to protect the poet.

45. Bongi, *Annali di Gabriel Giolito*, 1:180, says that Pedro di Toledo helped d'Aragona with her letter of appeal to Eleonora; he provides the texts of the correspondence with Eleonora, and identifies Pedro di Toledo as the duchess's nephew.

46. Basile, "*Fasseli gratia per poetessa,*" 135–48.

47. *Cronaca fiorentina, 1537–1555*, ed. Enrico Coppi (Florence: Olschki, 2000), at 25: "In mano d'una barbara spagnola et nimica alla patria del suo marito," as cited by Chiara Franceschini, "*Los scholares son casa de su excelentia como lo es toda la Compañia*: Eleonora di Toledo and the Jesuits," in *The Cultural World of Eleonora di Toledo*, ed. Konrad Eisenbichler (Aldershot and Burlington, VT: Ashgate, 2004), 181–206, at 185n14.

48. The citation of the document containing Cosimo's instructions and the English translation of his words come from Deana Basile, "*Fasseli gratia per poetessa,*" 135–47; Basile notes that four words written in Cosimino's hand were enough to legitimate d'Aragona's status as an author of note with the Florentine authorities: "Fasseli gratia per poetessa" (grant her leniency as a poet). According to Salvatore Bongi, "Il velo giallo di Tullia d'Aragona," *Rivista critica della letteratura italiana* 3, no. 4 (1886): 86–95, the document is still extant in the Archivio di Stato in Florence (as cited in Basile, "*Fasseli gratia per poetessa,*" 136).

49. Basile, "*Fasseli gratia per poetessa,*" 138–41.

50. Julia L. Hairston, "Out of the Archive: Four Newly-Identified Figures in Tullia d'Aragona's *Rime della Signora Tullia di Aragona et di diversi a lei (1547),*" *Modern Language Notes* 118 (2003): 257–63, calls d'Aragona's 1547 *Rime* a "choral anthology." Noting that Victoria Kirkham, "Laura Battiferra degli Ammannati's First Book of Poetry: A Renaissance Holograph Comes Out of Hiding," *Rinascimento* 36 (1996): 351–91, was

the first to use the term (at 353), Hairston distinguishes the "choral anthology" (which consists of one principal poet with many poets responding to her with their own poems) from the "lyric anthology" (which consists of an editor and many contributing poets). In its format, the choral anthology resembles the typical fifteenth-century letterbook in its assembling by the author of a number of shortish works addressed to her by her friends and her shortish works addressed in response to them.

51. These names include all d'Aragona's dedicatees and addressees in her *Rime*.

52. Pirotti, *Benedetto Varchi*, 46–56. On the criminalization of homosexual sodomy in Florence in the 1540s and 1550s, see Rocke, *Forbidden Friendships*, 233–35. Active partners in the act of sodomy, regardless of age or status, were to be sentenced to forced labor on the galleys for life; for adults playing the passive role in sodomy, the punishment was death by public burning.

53. I am indebted to Julia Hairston for calling my attention to Lisa Curtis-Wendlandt's "Conversing on Love: Text and Subtext in Tullia d'Aragona's *Dialogo della Infinità d'Amore*," *Hypatia* 19, no. 4 (Fall 2004): 75–96, esp. 91; see notes 54 and 56 (below) for a list of studies of d'Aragona's works.

54. Curtis-Wendlandt, "Conversing on Love," doesn't touch on d'Aragona's omission of the trope. See also the important studies of Fiora A. Bassanese, "Selling the Self; or, The Epistolary Production of Renaissance Courtesans,"in *Italian Women Writers from the Renaissance to the Present*, ed. Maria Ornella Marotti (University Park: Pennsylvania State University Press, 1999), 69–82, at 78; and see Ann Rosalind Jones, *The Currency of Eros: Women's Love Lyric in Europe, 1540–1620* (Bloomington: Indiana University Press, 1990), 103–17. Both Bassanese and Jones (in d'Aragona's *Rime*) foreground d'Aragona's highly successful strategy of appropriating the Neoplatonic language, idioms, and tropes.

55. Letizia Panizza, "Review Article: Ann Rosalind Jones, *The Currency of Eros: Women's Love Lyric in Europe, 1540–1620*," *Italian Studies* 47 (1992): 80–84, at 84.

56. On Tullia d'Aragona's *Dialogo*, see also Deana Basile, "*Specchio delle rare e virtuose donne*: The Role of the Female Interlocutor in Sixteenth-Century Dialogues on Love" (Ph. D. Thesis, University of Toronto, 1999); and d'Aragona, *Dialogue on the Infinity of Love*. Both Basile and Russell, in her introduction to the *Dialogue*, emphasize the influence of Leone Ebreo's *Dialoghi d'amore* (1501) as the first instance of a Renaissance love dialogue in which the female role is equal in importance to the male. As Basile points out, until recently doubts about d'Aragona's authorship of the *Dialogo* haunted its reception. Benedetto Croce, *Poeti e scrittori del pieno e del tardo Rinascimento* (Bari: Laterza, 1945); and John Charles Nelson, *Renaissance Theory of Love: The Context of Giordano Bruno's "Eroici furori"* (New York: Columbia University Press, 1958) assumed that at least parts of the dialogue were written by Varchi or Girolamo Muzio. But in addition to Russell's study of the *Dialogue*, other recent scholarship has dispelled such doubts as groundless, such as that by Fiora Bassanese, "Private Lives and Public Lies: Texts by Courtesans of the Italian Renaissance," *Texas Studies in Literature and Languages* 30 (1988): 295–319; and Bassanese, "What's in a Name? Self-Naming and Renaissance

Women Poets," *Annali d'italianistica* 7 (1989): 104–15; Ann Rosalind Jones, "Enabling Sites and Gender Difference: Reading City Women and Men," *Women Studies: An Interdisciplinary Journal* 19, no. 2 (1991): 239–49; Janet L. Smarr, "A Dialogue of Dialogues: Tullia d'Aragona and Sperone Speroni," *Modern Language Notes* 113 (1998): 204–12; and Gloria Allaire, "Tullia d'Aragona's *Il Meschino altramente detto il Guerino* as Key to a Reappraisal of Her Work," *Quaderni d'italianistica* 16 (1995): 33–50.The largest troves of primary sources in print on d'Aragona are still contained in Guido Biagi, "Un'etera romana: Tullia d'Aragona," *Rivista critica della letteratura italiana* 3, no. 4 (1886): 655–711; and Bongi, *Annali di Gabriel Giolito,* 1:150–99.

57.  On the public's familiarity with Cibo and Gonzaga, see chap. 1.

58.  On her legendary flight from Barbarossa when the Turks sacked Fondi in 1535, see chap. 1. Francesco Maria Molza and other poets wrote about Gonzaga's supposed kidnapping. In reality, Gonzaga had received plenty of advance warning. She packed her things and left Fondi with her entourage, arriving safely in another of the Colonna castles hours before the Turks had even reached Fondi.

59.  On Cibo see the numerous biographies above in n. 2. After successfully defending her duchy against the Varano clan and marrying off her daughter Giulia to Guidobaldo delle Rovere, who would later be Duke of Urbino, Pope Paul III excommunicated Cibo, her daughter, and her daughter's husband and confiscated the duchy of Camerino, ultimately giving it to Ercole Varano. It was at that point, in 1535, that Cibo fled to Florence.

60.  See Cathy Santore, "Julia Lombardo, 'Somtuosa Meretrize': A Portrait of Property," *Renaissance Quarterly* 41, no. 1 (1988): 44–87.

61.  D'Aragona, *Dialogue on the Infinity of Love,* ed. and trans. Russell and Merry, 55. All English text of Tullia d'Aragona's *dialogue* in this chapter are from this edition and hereafter are cited in the text as *Dialogue,* ed. and trans. Russell and Merry. Italian text is taken from Giuseppe Zonta, ed., *Trattati d'amore del Cinquecento* (Bari: Laterza, 1912), 185–248, and is hereafter cited in the text as Zonta, ed., *Trattati.*

62.  D'Aragona, *Dialogue,* ed. and trans. Russell and Merry, 63n. See also Ficino, *Commentary on Plato's Symposium,* 141 ff, for a list of sixteenth-century love dialogues.

63.  Russell, in d'Aragona, *Dialogue,* ed. and trans. Russell and Merry, 63, notes that the topos of the greater nobility of the beloved over the lover in the God's eyes goes back to Plato (*Symposium* 179b–180b) and that in this passage d'Aragona appears to be indebted to Ebreo's *Dialoghi d'amore.*

64.  Jon R. Snyder, *Writing the Scene of Speaking: Theories of Dialogue in the Late Renaissance* (Stanford, CA: Stanford University Press, 1989), has shown that the Renaissance dialogue never seems to proceed directly toward its supposed goal (of answering the question about the duration and nature of love) but winds circuitously like the labyrinth Tullia's friend Speroni describes in his love dialogue: it is a "pleasant labyrinth" (*un piacevole labirinto*). According to Snyder, Speroni's *Dialogo d'amore* is structured as a series of games; one game is enclosed within another. Deana Basile (*Specchio delle rare e virtuose donne,* 145 ff.) notes that images of hunting, trapping, and trickery also predominate in

Tullia's *Dialogo*: to this end d'Aragona employs the colorful verbs *aggirare* (surround, trap), *ingarbugliare* (entangle, trick), *carrucolare* (flatter, fool with bribery; literally, to lift up with a pulley), and *uccellare* (to cheat, trick, deceive; literarily, to snare, as in bird catching). Basile also notes that, in d'Aragona's use of game imagery, there is constant talking of winning and losing, and we find such terms as *tornare a bomba* (to go back to home base), being "caught" (*colto*, as in a game of tag), and *come la ronfa del Valera* (to end the game in a tie). Basile follows Virginia Cox in theorizing that, with a newly literate reading public, the woman in the text, in this case Tullia, plays the second, less learned fiddle to Varchi's first violin. But this is not exactly true. The character Tullia, as d'Aragona portrays her, is always on top. She's never at a loss for more than a minute. Both characters play the game, and both know the rules. The unusual thing about this dialogue in contrast to the love dialogues of her contemporaries is its heavy reliance on Aristotelian terms and methodology.

65. I'm quoting Bongi here who says that she was "pushing forty" ("doveva oggimai avvicinarsi alla quarantina") when she arrived in Florence (Bongi, *Annali di Gabriel Giolito*, 1:178).

66. Pirotti, *Benedetto Varchi*, 46–56. On the harsh sentences mandated in Florence for convicted sodomists, see Michael Rocke, *Forbidden Friendships*.

67. Curtis-Wendlandt, "Conversing on Love," 82–83.

68. Scholars disagree as to whether Penelope was d'Aragona's daughter or sister. Chronologically, it seems unlikely that Penelope could have been anything but Tullia's daughter. Penelope was born in 1535, when Tullia, who is believed to have been born either in 1505 or 1510, was either 30 or 25. Whatever the biological relationship, the important point is that Tullia d'Aragona acted as her mother and took responsibility for her care and upbringing.

69. Franceschini, "*Los scholares son casa*," 181–206.

70. Penelope died in Rome soon after their arrival. D'Aragona continued to publish her poetry until her death in 1556: her *Rime* after the 1547 edition was published again by Giolito in 1549 and 1560; her *Dialogo della infinità di amore* was published after the 1547 edition only once again in 1552; see also n. 71 just below on her publication in Ruscelli's 1553 anthology. In 1560 her major work, the epic poem *Il Meschino, altramente detto il Guerrino*, was published posthumously by Sessa in Venice.

71. Ruscelli's 1553 anthology (*Rime di diversi*), in which d'Aragona's poems appear with those of Colonna, Veronica Gambara, Virginia Salvi, and other elite women, is known as bk. 6 in the Giolito-inspired poetry anthology series. Ruscelli edited this volume and negotiated its publication with the printer Giovanni Maria Bonelli at Al Segno del Pozzo in Venice. See my app. A, which lists the participating poets, editors, and dedicatees in the poetry anthology series that Giolito inaugurated in Venice in 1545. See n. 70 above for the dates of the reprintings of the collected *Rime* and her dialogue after she left Florence.

72. Some critics have doubted d'Aragona's authorship of the *Meschino* based on its stylistic differences from her other works. Gloria Allaire, however, in "Tullia d'Aragona's *Il Meschino*," argues convincingly for the work's authenicity. Allaire believes that

d'Aragona wrote or first drafted the *Meschino* between 1543 and 1546, before her arrival in Florence. I am indebted to Julia Hairston for calling my attention to Allaire's article.

73. On Cibo in Florence, see now Zarri, "La spiritualità di Caterina Cibo," 313–31.

74. On Gonzaga's evenings at Fondi and Naples, see Oliva, *Giulia Gonzaga Colonna*, 221n5, where there is a list of those who visited her lodgings in Naples in the years 1536–45 when she opened an office in a convent in Naples where she and her secretaries managed her business affairs and a personal correspondence Oliva describes as "vast." The categories listed for her frequent visitors were *Gentildonne* (Constanza d'Avalos, Maria d'Aragona, Giovannia d'Aragona Colonna, Caterina Cibo, and others); *Gentiluomini* (Juan de Valdes and Ferrante Sanseverino, il principe di Salerno); *Ecclesiastici* (Carnesecchi and others); *Letterati* (Flaminio, Bernardo Tasso; Annibal Caro, and Benedetto Varchi, among others); and *Predicatori di passaggio* (Ochino and Pietro Martire Vermigli).

75. Morone's trial by the Roman Holy Office opened May 31, 1557; the cardinal was vindicated of all charges on March 13, 1560. Firpo and Marcatto, eds., *Il processo inquisitoriale del Cardinal Giovanni Morone*, 266–67. Petrucci, "Cibo, Caterina," cites the same description of Cibo from the Morone trial.

76. Pirotti, *Benedetto Varchi*, 59; Varchi, *De sonetti di m. Benedetto Varchi*, pt. 1 (Florence: Apresso M. Lorenzo Torrentino, 1555), 258, as cited by Pirotti. The translation that follows and all others are mine unless otherwise noted.

77. Cosimo's major domo, Riccio, in fact, owned the only known manuscript of the *Beneficio*, older than the first edition of the *Beneficio* of 1543. See Caponetto, *The Protestant Reformation*, 85–87. Caponetto also notes that Riccio's *Beneficio* manuscript was contained in a codex of other writings on the doctrine of *giustificazione*, including a manuscript of Valdés's own treatise on the subject, the contraband *Della medesima giustificazione*.

78. Oliva, *Giulia Gonzaga Colonna*, 236, notes that it was Giulia Gonzaga who negotiated the contract with Bindoni to publish the *Beneficio* (it will be recalled that she did the same for Valdés's posthumous *Alfabeto* in 1545). For the best description of the authorship and printing of the *Beneficio* (published under the title *Trattato utilissimo del beneficio di Gesu christo crocifisso verso i christiani*) and the storm its publication produced, see Caponetto, *The Protestant Reformation*. No stranger to controversial choices, Bindoni was also the printer who had published Savonarola's *Prediche*. Caponetto, 70–73, seems to accept without question the conclusion arrived at by some scholars that Flaminio almost single-handedly produced the *Beneficio*, by heavily redacting and rewriting a treatise composed by a Benedictine monk named don Benedetto Fontanini of Mantua. More recently, Mayer, *Reginald Pole*, 119 ff., has observed that many scholars now believe that Flaminio and Pole wrote the *Beneficio* together, with Pole as the major architect of the work.

79. See Caponetto, *The Protestant Reformation*, 78–79: in answer to the question, of what must one do to be saved, the *Beneficio* explained that "faith itself justifies, meaning that God receives as just, all those who truly believe that Jesus has redeemed us from

sin. However, just as the light is not separable from the flame which burns of itself alone, so good works cannot be separated from faith, which justifies of itself alone."

80. Ibid., 85.

81. Ibid., 84. Saint Jerome (347–419 A.D.), famous for having produced the translation of the Bible into the vulgate, is Flaminio's addressee.

82. See n. 78 above.

83. Caponetto, *The Protestant Reformation*, 79.

84. It's relevant to recall that even Lorenzo de' Medici's chancellor, Bartolomeo Scala, had educated his daughter, Alessandra Scala (1475–1506), as a Hellenist and she had performed Sophocles' *Antigone* in Florence before a group of family friends and fellow Greek scholars.

85. I have tried to select texts for commentary that, for the most part, are not discussed in Bainton, *Women of the Reformation,* 187–98; my translations are based on the original Italian texts in Flaminio, *Lettere*, 156–58, 171–73. See also Pastore, *Marcantonio Flaminio*. Flaminio sent the same letter to Giulia Gonzaga; see n. 88 below.

86. Luke 9:23, Mark 8:34; Matt. 16:24.

87. Phil. 3:14.

88. Flaminio, *Lettere*, to Caterina Cibo (May 4, 1549), 171–73. I am indebted to Gabriella Zarri for calling my attention to Marcantonio Flaminio, *Apologia del "Beneficio di Cristo" e altri scritti*, ed. Dario Marcatto (Florence: Olschki, 1996), 210–17; here Marcatto shows that Flaminio sent essentially the same letter to Giulia Gonzaga; some passages in Flaminio's letter toGonzaga are replicated almost verbatim in the May 4 letter to Cibo.

89. Bainton, *Women of the Reformation*, 198, suggests that Flaminio's mention of his "vision" might have linked him in the eyes of the Roman Holy Office with the Illuminists.

90. John 11:26.

91. Pastore, *Lettere*, Flaminio to Cibo (February 25, 1547), 157–58.

92. Battiferra (1523–89) was born the illegimitate daughter of the Urbinese priest Giovanni Antonio Battiferri; he refused to recognize Laura as his daughter until she was twenty years old. She was briefly married to the court organist at Urbino, Vittorio Serenio, who died in 1549; she married Bartolomeo Ammannati in 1550. Recent studies of Battiferra offer conflicting views of Battiferra's political-religious orientation. See Enrico Maria Guidi's introduction to *Il primo libro delle opere toscane* by Laura Battiferri degli Ammannati (Urbino: Accademia Raffaello, 2000); Victoria Kirkham, "Creative Partners: The Marriage of Laura Battiferra and Bartolomeo Ammannati," *Renaissance Quarterly* 55, no. 2 (2002): 498–558; Kirkham, "Laura Battiferra degli Ammannati benefattrice dei Gesuiti fiorentini," in "Committenza femminile," ed. Sara Matthews-Grieco and Gabriella Zarri, special issue *Quaderni storici* 104, no. 35 (2000): 331–54; Kirkham, "Dante's Phantom, Petrarch's Specter: Bronzino's Portarit of the Poet Laura Battiferra," in *Visibile Parlare: Dante and the Art of the Italian Renaissance*, ed. Deborah Parker, special issue, *Lectura Dantis*, nos. 22–23 (1998): 63–139; Victoria Kirkham, "Laura Battiferri degli Ammannati's 'First Book' of Poetry. A Renaissance Holograph Comes out of Hiding," *Rinascimento* 36 (1996): 351–91; and see, currently,

Kirkham's introduction to *Laura Battiferra and Her Literary Circle: An Anthology*, ed. and trans. Victoria Kirkham (Chicago: University of Chicago Press, 2006). See also Giovanna Rabitti, "Laura Battiferri Ammannati (1523–1589)," in *Italian Women Writers*, ed. Rinaldina Russell, 44–49; Enzo Noe Girardi, "Battiferri, Laura," in *DBI*, 7:242–44.

93. Pastor, *History of the Popes*, 14:482 (Cardinal Ghislieri to Inquisitore Girolamo d'Genova, dated March 31, 1559, from Rome): "Firenze è vero che è mal provista d'Inquisitori, ma il duca zelantissimo dà ogni favore a questo santo officio."

94. On Bronzino and Battiferra's circle in Rome and Florence, see Deborah Parker, *Bronzino: Renaissance Painter as Poet* (Cambridge: Cambridge University Press, 2000).

95. Paola Tinagli, "Eleonora and Her 'Famous Sisters': The Tradition of 'Illustrious Women' in Paintings for the Domestic Interior," in *The Cultural World of Eleonora di Toledo*, ed. Eisenbichler, 119–35, at 122.

96. Giuseppe Betussi published his translation of Boccaccio's catalog of famous women, the *Delle donne illustri*, in 1545 with the printer Andrea Arrivabene under the logo Al Segno del Pozzo in Venice. At the end of his translation, Betussi appended an addendum with fifty modern women's lives, including the Duchess Renata di Francia of Ferrara, Vittoria Colonna, Duchess Eleonora Gonzaga of Urbino, Marguerite de Navarre, and Isabella d'Este, among others. Giulia Gonzaga, of course, was not a native of Naples but she spent almost her entire life there and is associated with city rather than Sabbioneta, where she was born. The Eleonora d'Aragona Betussi writes about (he calls her Leonora d'Aragona) was the celebrated daughter of King Ferrante of Naples (1458–94), the wife of Duke Ercole I d'Este of Ferrara (1471–1505), and the mother of Isabella d'Este.

97. Ilaria Hoppe, "A Duchess' Place at Court: The Quartiere di Eleonora in the Palazzo della Signoria in Florence," in *The Cultural World of Eleonora di Toledo*, ed. Eisenbichler, 98–118, at 110–11; Hoppe draws attention to a mid-fifteenth-century example of the employment of a famous-women cycle: Francesco Sforza's architect Filarete's *Trattato di architettura* mentions that Duchess Bianca Maria Visconti of Milan requested that her suite of rooms in the Castello be decorated with such *donne illustri* as Judith, Artemisia, and Marzia, all icons of heroism in Boccaccio's *De claris mulieribus*.

98. Tinagli, "Eleonora and Her 'Famous Sisters,'" 127.

99. Hoppe, "A Duchess' Place at Court," 111.

On Eleonora's choice of figures for her program, see Tinagli, "Eleonora and her 'Famous Sisters,'" 120; and Pamela J. Benson, "Eleonora di Toledo among the Famous Women: Iconographic Innovation after the Conquest of Siena," in *The Cultural World of Eleonora di Toledo*, ed. Eisenbichler, 136–56, at 137–41. The role of Eleonora in the actual planning of the program for the rooms in her apartment has long been contested; but examining Vasari's correspondence with Eleonora and Cosimo closely, both Tinagli and Benson argue convincingly that Eleonora was fully involved in the design and execution of the famous-women programme. Benson (148) makes the point that the four women Eleonora selected for her program (Penelope, Hersilia, Ester, and Gualdrada), whose images surrounded her in her living quarters and with whom she presumably identified, were peacemakers who stepped in to settle the quarrels of men.

100. Bruce L. Edelstein, "La fecundissima Signora Duchessa: The Courtly Persona of Eleonora di Toledo and the Iconography of Abundance," in *The Cultural World of Eleonora di Toledo*, ed. Eisenbichler, 71–97, at 92, has suggested that Ammanati's images of Eleonora as Ceres may allude to the duchess's highly profitable monopoly over the local grain market, which brought her a substantial yearly income and assured her financial independence.

101. Benson, "Eleonora di Toledo among the Famous Women," 138, argues against the assumption that a noble woman's quarters in Florence were not public and would not have had political content in their decor.

102. Guidi, introduction to *Il primo libro*, 12 ff. Laura Battiferra, *I sette salmi penitenziali del santissimo profeta Davit* (Florence: I Giunti, 1564).

103. See Zarri, "La spiritualità di Caterina Cibo"; she discusses there, among other things, Cibo's correspondence with Ochino long after he had left Italy and settled in Geneva.

104. Kirkham, "Laura Battiferra degli Ammannati benefattrice," 331–54.

105. Petrucci, "Cibo, Caterina," observes that the Holy Office of Rome defined her as "haeretica, sectatrix haereticorum et doctrix monialium haereticarum." The quotation comes from the proceedings of the trial in Rome of Cardinal Morone in 1557 (see Firpo and Marcatto, eds., *Il processo inquisitoriale del cardinale Giovanni Morone*, vol. 1).

106. All texts by Battiferri in this chapter are from Laura Battiferri degli Ammannati, *Il primo libro dell'opere toscane*, ed. Enrico Maria Guidi, hereafter cited as *Il primo libro*, ed., Guidi, in the text. A beautiful copy of the first edition of this her poetic oeuvre is conserved in the Newberry Library; it was published under the same title in 1560 by the Giunti press in Florence. See *Laura Battiferra and Her Literary Circle*, ed. and trans. Kirkham.

107. "Benedetto" and "Cibo" are both capitalized in the original 1560 Giunti edition of Battiferra; but cf. Guidi, ed., *Il primo libro*, 90 (sonnet 86a). Guidi, in this modern edition, capitalizes "Cibo" but not "benedetto."

108. Regarding her meetings with women at convents, see Zarri, "La spiritualità di Caterina Cibo."

109. This phrase is straight out of Petrarch, *Canz.* 146.5–6: "O fiamma. O rose sparse in dolce falda/ di viva neve in ch' io mi specchio et tergo."

110. See Cantagalli, *Cosimo I de' Medici*, 277–78; Carnesecchi had been invited to dine with Cosimo as the guest of honor the night his arrest took place, perhaps to ensure (Cantagalli observes) that Carnesecchi would be on hand when the Ghislieri's men arrived.

111. Ibid., 288–90, provides pages of desciptive details capturing every gesture, every garment worn, every exchange of ritual objects at the ceremony performed.

EPILOGUE

1. The number of plague victims is disputed. Brian Pullan, *Rich and Poor in Renaissance Venice* (Oxford: Blackwell, 1971), 315, reports that between fifty and fifty-one thousand died in Venice in the plague of 1575–77, one-third of the population; John

Martin, *Venice's Hidden Enemies: Italian Heretics in a Renaissance City* (Berkeley: University of California Press, 1993), 200, estimates that forty thousand succumbed to the plague.

2. The following numbers per year are random tabulations I made from Salvatore Bongi, *Annali di Gabriel Giolito*: year 1553, forty-five editions produced; year 1554, thirty-seven editions; year 1557, twenty-seven editions, year 1558, thirty-seven editions.

3. On the overall decline in productivity at the Giolito press after 1571, see Bongi, *Annali di Gabriel Giolito*, vol. 2. During the 1560s and early 1570s, Giolito's numbers were still relatively high: twenty-five editions in 1567; twenty-two in 1568; thirteen in 1569; seventeen in 1570; and twenty-four in 1571–72. The deep slide began in 1573, with seven editions; Giolito never experienced a real recovery after that year.

4. In 1570, Venice's colony Cyprus fell to the Turks. After Venice, Naples, and their Spanish allies defeated the Turkish fleet at Lepanto, Venice and Spain went to war again to recover Cyprus. Unable to drive the Turks out and with the war's expenses mounting daily, Venice signed a separate peace treaty with the Turks in 1573 and withdrew from the island.

5. In table 2, I have provided a list of women's works published in Italy during the years 1564–1654. See S. Bongi, *Annali*, 2: 268–269; the Giolito volumes of Battiferra's work are collected editions of the seven penitential psalms and other poems titled *Salmi penitentiali do diversi eccellenti autori*.

6. The Lucchese poet Chiara Matraini (1519–1604) stands apart from the other women poets treated in this book. Although Matraini was a contemporary of Stampa, Colonna, Terracina, Tullia d'Aragona, Forteguerri, and Battiferra and while she wrote poetry, too, she did not belong either to an urban literary group or to a religious reform cell. Her works were not produced in a solo edition by any of the Venetian presses until 1597. What was worse, when the small printing shop in Lucca run by Vincenzo Busdragho did publish Matraini's collected poems in 1555, the Venetian editor Lodovico Dolce simply vacuumed her eighty-four sonnets, assorted canzoni, sestinas, and octaves into his own volume 7 of the Giolito poetry anthology series, effectively burying her and her work under his title "Poems by Various Neapolitan Gentlemen and Others" (*Rime di diversi signori napoletani e d'altri . . .*). All but one of Matraini's six major works were published between 1581 and 1602, and four of those works were devotional writings.

7. Both Fonte's and Marinella's works have been published in the University of Chicago Press series the Other Voice in Early Modern Europe: Moderata Fonte (Modesta Pozzo), *The Worth of Women*, ed. and trans. Virginia Cox (1997) and Lucrezia Marinella, *The Nobility and Excellence of Women and the Defects and Vices of Men*, ed. and trans. Anne Dunhill, with an introduction by Letizia Panizza (1999).

8. See now the University of Chicago Press's modern editions in the Other Voice in Early Modern Europe series of three fifteenth-century women letter writers: Isotta Nogarola's *Complete Writings* [ca. 1462], ed. and trans. Margaret King and Diana Robin (2004); Cassandra Fedele, *Letters and Orations*, ed. and trans. Diana Robin (1999); Laura Cereta, *The Collected Letters of a Renaissance Feminist*, ed. and trans. Diana Robin (1997).

9. Cinquecento males continued to publish their correspondence without a break (Aretino, Contile, Giovio, Caro, Bembo, etc.). Elite sixteenth-century women such as Vittoria Colonna and Giulia Gonzaga left vast letter collections, but Colonna's letters (cited frequently in this book) were first published as a collection in the late nineteenth century and Gonzaga's letters still await publication.

## APPENDIX A

The volumes I list here are those that Salvatore Bongi, editor of *Annali di Gabriel Giolito de' Ferrari da Trino di Monferrato*, and subsequent bibliographers have considered as belonging to the so-called Giolito set of poetry anthologies. The numbers and letters (in the case of multiple editions of a volume) in parentheses after the edition number are shorthand labels for the fifteen editions I refer to hereafter.

1. No surname is given and the author has not been identified.
2. On the three editions of vol. 5, see Bongi, *Annali di Gabriel Giolito*, 1:356–57, 365–66, 466–67: Giolito labeled the first edition of vol. 5 *Libro terzo* (my 5), not realizing at first that other presses (Al Segno del Pozzo in Venice and Giaccarello in Bologna) had already published a *Libro terzo* and *Libro quarto*. To avoid the confusion that was affecting sales, Giolito in 1552 brought out a second edition titled *Libro quinto* (my 5a). In 1555, Giolito brought out a third edition also titled *Libro quinto* (my 5b).
3. The publication date given on the title page is 1552, but in accord with the date on Dolce's dedicatory letter, I refer to it as 1551–52 to distinguish the volume from its second edition, which is dated 1552.
4. Bongi, *Annali di Gabriel Giolito*, 1:466: notes that the dedicatory letter is by Arrivabene but that Ruscelli was the editor.
5. In ibid. (1:487–88), Bongi notes, following Dolce's dedicatory letter to Montenero, that the poems for vol. 7 were originally collected by Marc'Antonio Passero at various times and that he sent them to Dolce, who then reorganized them for publication under the title *Libro settimo*.
6. On the disputes surrounding the so-called vol. 8 in the Giolito anthology series Bongi (ibid., 1:487–88) wrote:

> One of the great mysteries of Italian bibliography concerns the so-called "Libro Ottavo" of the *Rime Diverse*. Since . . . the ninth and last volume published in Cremona by Vincenzo Conti came unmediated after Volume VII, it seems clear that Conti . . . and the buyers of the "Giolito" set thought that Volume VIII [whatever happened to it] had to be some book published between 1556 and 1560. Among the most reasonable of the various conjectures put forward were: that the missing book was the *Rime delle virtuosissime Donne* published in 1559 by Domenichi; or that the lost volume was really the *Fiori delle Rime de' Poeti illustri* edited by Ruscelli in 1558 for Sessa. Apostolo Zeno believed the latter was the case.

Bongi goes on to say that he believed the missing vol. 8 was really the *De le rime di diversi eccellentissimi autori nuovamente raccolte, Libro primo* (Lucca: Vincenzo Busdragho, 1556). But Francesco Quadrio, according to a note written by Dr. Giacomo Soranzo in the edition of vol. 8 owned by the Newberry, believed that the purported vol. 8 "never saw the light of day."

7. "Book 10" is my designation. Bibliographers disagree on the connection of Lodovico Domenichi's *Rime diverse* (Lucca: Busdragho 1559) to the anthology series begun by Giolito. See note 6 above on Bongi's thoughts on the opinion on Domenichi's anthology of women.

8. All those listed in the index are poets unless otherwise designated. All those listed as dedicatees are patrons or prospective patrons.

9. Betussi, *Le imagini del tempio della Signora Giovanna d'Aragona* (Venice: de' Rossi, 1557), gives the full name of the Sienese poet Francesca de' Baldi. See chap. 4.

10. Volume 7 (published in 1556) contains eighty-two pages of Matraini's poems. On this and her other publications, see my note on Matraini in the epilogue (327). In addition to Vincenzo Busdragho's solo edition of her collected *Rime e prose* in Lucca in 1555, her poems were also included in an anthology published in Lucca in 1556 by Busdragho's collaborator, Vincenzo Pippi. The Busdragho press may have decided not to include Matraini in its 1559 all-women anthology in order to avoid overexposure of the same author's works within so short a period.

11. Morra was also published in *Rime di Diversi*, ed. Vincenzo Pippi (Lucca: Busdragho, 1556).

12. Bongi (*Annali di Gabriel Giolito*, 1:487–88), reading Dolce's dedicatory letter, notes that Passero collected the poems for vol. 7 and sent them to the vol. editor, Lodovico Dolce.

## APPENDIX B

Maria Luisa Cerrí Cerrón Puga, "Materiales para la construcción del canon petrarquista: Las antologías de *Rime* (libri I–IX)," *Critica del testo* 2, no. 1 (1999): 249–90, also contains detailed physical descriptions of editions of the Giolito anthologies, which she examined in libraries in Paris, Venice, Milan, and Florence. Puga's study does not, however, include Domenichi's 1559 anthology of women poets among the volumes she describes. In this appendix, I not only compare two different copies of Domenichi's last anthology but I have also added my observations on the unique Newberry Library editions (to which the case numbers included refer) of the entire Giolito set and the marginalia of interest in those volumes signed by scholars dating back to the eighteenth century.

1. Both editions of volume 2 are bound together in the modern Newberry binding.

2. Bongi, *Annali di Gabriel Giolito*, 1:143, notes that there's no statement of who edited the poems. The dedicatory letter is by Giolito himself; his dedicatee is Signore Sigismondo Fanzino dalla Torre; Bongi doesn't identify Fanzino or tell us why Giolito dedicates the volume to him. *Libro secondo* came out in only two editions, says Bongi. He also notes here that the third volume (*Libro terzo*) of the *Rime diverse* was published not by Giolito but by Bartolomeo Cesano in Venice in 1550 and that a fourth volume (*Libro quarto*) was published in Bologna by Anselmo Giaccarello in 1551. Why Giolito didn't publish the latter volumes is not explained by Bongi. He says only that Giolito

tried in vain to convince himself of the merit of doing another *Rime diverse* anthology but wound up deciding to leave the work to other presses, presumably because it wasn't as successful as *Libro primo*.

3. Two editions in one binding; volume 6 is the first these.

4. This is in the same binding as the above (vol. 6 or *Libro sesto*) and is a continuation of the nine-book series entitled *Rime diverse*.

5. In this note on Giovan Bonelli's *Libro sesto*, Bongi (*Annali di Gabriel Giolito*, 1:466) states that *Libro settimo* was published by Giolito in 1556. In his article on the *Libro settimo* of the *Rime diverse* (1:487–88), he notes that the poems for this volume were originally collected and edited by Marc'Antonio Passero at various times and that he sent them to Lodovico Dolce, who then reorganzied them in order to publish them with the title *Libro settimo*. Dolce then dedicated them to the Genovese gentleman Matteo Montenero. This book was never republished/reprinted, thus giving it a reputation of being very rare.

6. Two books of *Rime diverse* are bound together in this modern Newberry Library binding. The first of these is volume 8. See my long note on this edition in app. A.

7. Francesco Quadrio, *Lettere, e sonetti di Virginia Salvi a Celio Magno, colle risposte* (Venice, 1571), 259, found three women poets bearing this name: (1) Virginia Martini Salvi, Sanese, fl. ca. 1550, lived in Rome with her family; (2) Virginia Venturi Salvi, Sanese, wife of Matteo Salvi; Lodovico Domenichi speak of her in bk. 5 of *Della nobiltà . . . delle donne*; and (3) Virginia Luti Salvi, wife of Achille Salvi.

8. The Iowa binding is vellum; it has been recently rebound and is tight. The bottom of the inside front cover has an addressogram label stuck to it: that of Kurt L. Schwarz / Bookseller / Beverly Hills, California. On the top of the front inside cover, written in pencil, is the sales price of the volume: $50.00. The title page has been glued onto an inserted page at the bottom of which is handwritten "MDLIX." At top of title page "RIME" has been written into old page/new page seam by the same hand as can be seen in the date under the seam at the bottom of the page. On the dedicatory letter (3) there are two water spots not found in the Yale microfilmed copy: one at lines 10–11, the other on the woodcut illustration for the capital *S*. Other water damage spots in the frontmatter seem not to be present in the Yale microfilm copy we have. The errata page in the Iowa copy is identical to that of the Yale.

### APPENDIX D

1. Henceforth, publications in the poetry anthology series inaugurated by the Giolito press in Venice are referenced as GPAS with the volume number in arabic numerals and the year of publication. See apps. A and B for a full description of the volumes listed and their participants.

# BIBLIOGRAPHY

## PRIMARY SOURCES

Aragona, Tullia d'. *Dialogo della infinità d'amore.* Venice: Gabriel Giolito, 1547.

————. *Rime della Signora Tullia di Aragona et di diversi a lei.* Venice: Gabriel Giolito, 1547.

————. "Dialogo della infinità d'amore." In *Trattati d'amore del Cinquecento,* edited by Giuseppe Zonta, 185–248. Bari: Laterza, 1912.

————. *Dialogue on the Infinity of Love.* Edited and translated by Rinaldina Russell and Bruce Merry. Chicago: University of Chicago Press, 1997.

Arrivabene, Andrea, ed. [*Libro terzo*] *delle rime di diversi nobilissimi et eccellentissimi autori nuovamente raccolte.* Venice: Bartolomeo Cesana, Al Segno del Pozzo, 1550.

Atanagi, Dionigi, ed. *Rime di diversi nobilissimi et eccellentissimi autori in morte della signora Irene delle signore di Spilimbergo.* Venice: Domenico & Giovanni Battista Guerra, 1561.

Bargagli, Girolamo. *Dialogo de' giuochi che nelle vecchie sanesi si usano di fare: Del materiale Intronato* [1572]. Edited by P. D'Incalci Ermini with an introduction by R. Bruscagli. Siena: Accademia Senese degli Intronati, 1982.

Battiferri, Laura degli Ammannati. *Il primo libro dell'opere toscane.* Florence: Giunti, 1560.

————. *Il primo libro delle opere toscane.* Edited by Enrico Maria Guidi. Urbino: Accademia Raffaello, 2000.

————. *Laura Battiferra and Her Literary Circle.* Edited and translated by Victoria Kirkham. Chicago: University of Chicago Press, 2006.

Benedetto da Mantova. *Trattato utilissimo del beneficio di Giesù Christo crocifisso verso i christiani.* Venice: Bernardo de' Bindoni, 1543.

Benedetto da Mantova and Marcantonio Flaminio. *Il beneficio di Cristo.* Edited by Salvatore Caponetto. Turin: Claudiana, 1975.

Bergalli, Luisa, ed. *Componimenti più illustri rimactrici di ogni secolo.* 2 vols. Venice: Antonio Mora, 1726.

Betussi, Giuseppe. *Raverta.* Venice: Gabriel Giolito, 1544.

————. *La Leonora: Ragionamento sopra la vera bellezza.* Lucca: Vincenzo Busdragho, 1557.

————. *Le imagini del tempio della signora donna Giovanna Aragona, Dialogo di M. Giuseppe Betussi Alla illustrissima signora donna Vittoria Colonna di Tolledo.* 2d ed. Venice: Giovanni de' Rossi, 1557. First edition: Florence: Torrentino, 1556.

Blasi, Jolanda de'. *Le scrittrici italiane dalle origini al 1800*. Florence: Nemi, 1930.

Boccaccio, Giovanni. *Libro di Gio: Boccaccio delle donne illustri, tradotto per Messer Giuseppe Betussi, con una additione fatta dal medesimo delle donne famose dal tempo di M.Giovanni fino ai giorni nostri* . . . Venice: Andrea Arrivabene, Al Segno del Pozzo, 1545.

———. *Famous Women*. Edited and translated by Virginia Brown. I Tatti Renaissance Library. Cambridge, MA, and London: Harvard University Press, 2001.

Bottrigaro, Hercole, ed. *Libro quarto della rime di diversi eccellentiss autori nella lingua volgare*. Bologna: Anselmo Giaccarello, 1551.

Bulifon, Antonio, ed. *Rime di cinquanta illustri poetesse*. Naples: Bulifon, 1695.

Calvino, Giovanni [John Calvin]. *Instituzione della religione christiana di Messer Giovanni Calvino*. Translated by Cesare Pascali. Geneva: J. Burgese, A. Davodeo, F. Iacchi, 1557.

Cereta, Laura. *Collected Letters of a Renaissance Feminist*. Edited and translated by Diana Robin. Chicago: University of Chicago Press, 1997.

Chiomenti Vassalli, Donata. *Giovanna d'Aragona fra baroni, principi, e sovrani del Rinascimento*. Milan: Mursia, 1987.

Colonna, Vittoria. *Rime de la divina Vittoria Colonna Marchesa di Pescara: Nuovamente stampato con privilegio*. 1st ed. Parma: [Antonio Viotti], 1538.

———. *Rime*. Florence: Zoppino, 1539.

———. *Rime*. Venice: Zoppino, 1540.

———. *Rime*. Venice: Bartolomeo l'Imperador & Francesco Vinetiano, 1544.

———. *Rime*. Venice: Valvassori, 1546.

———. *Rime spirituali*. Venice: Valgrisi, 1546.

———. *Rime*. Edited by Lodovico Dolce. Venice: Gabriel Giolito, 1552.

———. *Rime*. Venice: Sessa, 1558.

———. *Rime*. Edited by Alan Bullock. Rome: Laterza, 1992.

———. *Carteggio*. Edited by Ermanno Ferrero and Giuseppe Müller with a supplement by Domenico Tordi. 2d ed.Turin Loescher, 1892.

———. *Sonnets for Michelangelo: A Bilingual Edition*. Edited and translated by Abigail Brundin. Chicago and London: University of Chicago Press, 2005.

Conti, Vincenzo, ed. *Rime di diversi autori eccellentiss: Libro nono*. Cremona: Vincenzo Conti, 1560.

Contile, Luca. *Delle Lettere di Luca Contile. Primo volume diviso in due libri*. Pavia: Girolamo Bartoli, 1564.

Cristiani, Francesco. *Rime di diversi, ecc. Autori in vita e in morte dell' ill. S. Livia Colonna*. Rome: Antonio Barre, 1555.

Dolce, Lodovico, ed. *Rime di diversi illustri signori napoletani e d'altri nobiliss. intelletti; nuovamente raccolte, et non piu stampate: Terzo libro allo illus. S. Ferrante Carrafa*. Venice: Gabriel Giolito, 1551–52.

———, ed. *Rime di diversi illustri signori napoletani, e d'altri nobiliss. ingegni. Nuovamente raccolte, et con nuova additione ristampate. Libro quinto. Allo illus. S. Ferrante Carrafa*. Venice: Gabriel Giolito, 1552.

———, ed. *[Rime diverse] Libro quinto delle rime di diversi illustri signori napoletani, e d'altri nobilissimi ingegni. Nuovamente raccolte, e con nova additione ristampate, allo illus. S. Ferrante Carrafa*. Venice: Gabriel Giolito, 1555.

————, ed. *Rime di diversi signori napoletani, e d'altri. Nuovamente raccolte et impresse: Libro settimo.* Venice: Gabriel Giolito, 1556.

Domenichi, Lodovico, ed. *Rime diverse di molti eccellentiss. auttori nuovamente raccolte. Libro primo.* 1st ed.Venice: Gabriel Giolito, 1545.

————, ed. *Rime diverse di molti eccellentiss. auttori nuovamente raccolte. Libro primo, con nuova additione ristampato.* 2d ed. Venice: Gabriel Giolito, 1546.

————. *La nobiltà delle donne.* Venice: Gabriel Giolito, 1549.

————, ed. *Rime diverse di molti eccellentiss. auttori nuovamente' raccolte. Libro primo, con nuova additione ristampato.* 3d ed. Venice: Gabriel Giolito, 1549.

————, ed. *Rime diverse d'alcune nobilissime, et virtuosissime donne, raccolte per M. Lodovico Domenichi, e intitolate al Signor Giannoto Castiglione gentil'huomo milanese.* Lucca: Vincenzo Busdragho, 1559.

Fedele, Cassandra. *Letters and Orations.* Edited and translated by Diana Robin. Chicago: University of Chicago Press, 2000.

Ficino, Marsilio. *Commentary on Plato's Symposium.* Translated by Sears Jayne. 3d ed. Woodstock, CT: Spring Publications, 1994.

Firenzuola, Agnola. *On the Beauty of Women* [1548]. Translated by Konrad Eisenbichler and Jacqueline Murray. Philadelphia: University of Pennsylvania Press, 1992.

Flaminio, Marcantonio. *Lettere.* Edited by Alessandro Pastore. Rome: Edizioni dell'Ateneo & Bizzaro, 1978.

Fonte, Moderata [Modesta Pozzo]. *The Worth of Women.* Edited and translated by Virginia Cox. Chicago: University of Chicago Press, 1997.

Giovio, Paolo. *Opera.* Vol. 1: *Epistolarum Pars Prior.* Edited by Giuseppe Guido Ferrero. Rome: Istituto Poligrafico dello Stato, 1956.

Guidiccioni, Giovanni. *Lettere inedite di Monsignor Giovanni Guidiccioni da Lucca.* Lucca: Tipografia di Giuseppe Giusti, 1855.

King, Margaret L., and Albert Rabil, Jr., eds. *Her Immaculate Hand: Selected Works by and about the Women Humanists of Quattrocento Italy.* 2d rev. ed. Binghamton, NY: Medieval and Renaissance Texts and Studies, 1991.

Malespini, Celio. *Ducento novelle.* Venice: Al Segno dell'Italia, 1609.

Marinella, Lucrezia. *The Nobility and Excellence of Women and the Defects of Men.* Edited and translated by Anne Dunhill with an introduction by Letizia Panizza. Chicago: University of Chicago Press, 1999.

Montluc, Blaise, seigneur de Lasseran-Massencome. *Commentaires de Messire Blaise de Monluc, Mareschal de France, 1521–1576.* Paris: Martom Gobert, 1617.

Morata, Olimpia. *The Complete Writings of an Italian Heretic.* Edited and translated by Holt N. Parker. Chicago: University of Chicago Press, 2003.

Nogarola, Isotta. *Complete Writings: Letterbook, Dialogue on Adam and Eve, Orations.* Edited and translated by Margaret L. King and Diana Robin. Chicago: University of Chicago Press, 2004.

Ochino, Bernardino. *Dialogi sette* [sic]. Venice: Zoppino, 1540.

————. *Prediche.* Venice: n.p., 1541.

————. *I "Dialogi sette" e altri scritti del tempo della fuga.* Edited by Ugo Rozzo. Turin: Claudiana, 1985.

Piccolomini, Alessandro. *De la bella creanza de le donne* [=*La Raffaella*]. Venice: Curzio Navo e fratelli, 1539.

———. *Lettura del S. Alessandro Piccolomini Infiammato fatta nell'Accademia degli Infiammati.* Bologna: Bartolomeo Bonardo & Marc'Antonio da Carpi, 1541.

———. *De la institutione di tutta la vita de l'huomo nato nobile, e in città libera, libri X in lingua toscana.* Venice: apud Hieronymum Scotum, 1542.

———. *Della sfera del mondo: Libri quatro in lingua Toscana.* Venice: Nicolò Bevilacqua, 1561.

Pini, Bernardino. *Della Nuova Scelta di Lettere di diversi nobilissimi huomini et eccell. ingegni.* Venice: n.p., 1574.

*Rime di diversi nobili huomini et eccellenti poeti nella lingua thoscana: Libro secondo.* 1st ed. Venice: Gabriel Giolito, 1547. [No editor named.]

*Rime di diversi nobili huomini et eccellenti poeti nella lingua thoscana. Nuovamente ristampate. Libro secondo.* 2d ed. Venice: Gabriel Giolito, 1548. [no editor named.]

[*Rime di diversi*] *Il sesto libro delle rime di diversi eccellenti autori, nuovamente raccolte, et mandate in luce. Con un discorso di Girolamo Ruscelli. Al molto reverendo, et honoratiss. Monsignor Girolamo Artusio.* Venice: Giovam Maria Bonelli, Al Segno del Pozzo, 1553. [Bongi names Ruscelli as the volume editor, but Andrea Arrivabene claims the editorship in his dedicatory letter.]

Ruscelli, Girolamo, ed. *Lettura di Girolamo Ruscelli, sopra un sonnetto dell' illustriss. signor Marchese della Terza alla divina signora Marchesa del Vasto.* Venice: Giovan Griffio, 1552.

———, ed. *Del tempio alla divina signora donna Giovanna d'Aragona, fabricato da tutti i più gentili Spiriti, & in tutte le lingue principali del mondo.* Venice: Plinio Pietrasanta, 1555.

———, ed. *Lettere di diversi autori.* Venice: Giordano Ziletti, 1556.

———, ed. [*Rime diverse*] *I fiori delle rime de' poeti illustri, nuovamente raccolti et ordinati da Girolamo Ruscelli.* Venice: Giovanni Battista & Melchior Sessa Fratelli, 1558.

Sandoval de Castro, Diego. *Rime.* Rome: Valerio Dorico & Louigi fratelli, 1542.

Sozzini, Alessandro. *Diario delle cose avvenute in Siena dai 20 luglio 1550 ai 28 giugno 1550, scritto da Alessandro Sozzini con altre narrazioni e documenti relativi alla caduta di quella reppublica.* Florence: Pietro Vieusseux Editore, 1842.

Stampa, Gaspara. *Rime.* Edited by Cassandra Stampa. Venice: Plinio Pietrasanta, 1554.

———. *Gaspara Stampa–Veronica Franco: Rime.* Edited by Abd-el-Kader Salza. Bari: Laterza, 1913.

———. *Gaspara Stampa: Selected Poems.* Edited and translated by Laura Anna Stortoni and Mary Prentice Lillie. New York: Italica, 1994.

Stortoni, Laura Anna, ed. *Women Poets of the Italian Renaissance: Courtly Ladies and Courtesans.* Translated by Laura Anna Stortoni and Mary Prentice Littlie. New York: Italica Press, 1996.

Terracina, Laura. *Rime.* Venice: Gabriel Giolito, 1548, 1554, 1556.

———. *Il discorso sopra tutti i primi canti di "Orlando Furioso."* Venice: Gabriel Giolito 1549, 1550, 1551.

———. *Il discorso. . .* Venice: Valvassori, 1550.

———. *Quinte rime.* Venice: Valvassori, 1550.

———. *Sovra tutte le donne vedove di questa città di Napoli.* Naples: Cancer, 1561.

Valdés, Juan de. *Alfabeto cristiano*. Translated by Marco Antonio Magno. Venice: Nicolò Bacarini, 1545.

———. *Alfabeto Cristiano, che insegna la vera via d'acquisitare il lume dello Spirito Santo*. Translated by Marco Antonio Magno. 2d ed. Venice: n.p., 1546.

Valdés, Giovanni di [Juan de Valdés]. *Alfabeto Cristiano: Dialogo con Giulia Gonzaga*. Edited by Benedetto Croce. Bari: Laterza, 1938.

SECONDARY SOURCES

Abulafia, David. "The South." In *Italy in the Age of the Renaissance, 1300–1550*, edited by John M. Najemy, 208–25. Oxford: Oxford University Press, 2004.

Affò, Ireneo. "Vita di donna Giulia Gonzaga." In *Raccolta ferrarese di opuscoli scientifici e letterari di chiarissimi autori italiani*, 8:145–88. Venice, 1780.

Allaire, Gloria. "Tullia d'Aragona's *Il Meschino altramente detto il Guerino* as Key to a Reappraisal of Her Work." *Quaderni d' Italianistica* 16 (1995): 33–50.

Alberigo, Giuseppe. "Aragona, Giovanna d'." In *Dizionario biografico degli Italiani*, 3:694–96. Rome: Istituto dell'Enciclopedia Italiana, 1961.

———. "Aragona, Maria d'." In *Dizionario biografico degli Italiani*, 3:701–2. Rome: Istituto dell'Enciclopedia Italiana, 1961.

Amante, Bruno. *Giulia Gonzaga e il movimento religioso femminile*. Bologna: Zanichelli, 1896.

Andrea, Alessandro. *Della guerra di Campagna di Roma nel Pontificato di Paolo IV: L'anno MDVI e LVII*. Naples: Giovanni Gravier, 1769.

Andreadis, Harriette. *Sappho in Early Modern England. Female Same-Sex Literary Erotics, 1550–1714*. Chicago: University of Chicago Press, 2001.

Bainton, Roland H. *Bernardino Ochino esule e riformatore senese del Cinquecento, 1487–1563*. Florence: Sansoni, 1940.

———. *Women of the Reformation in Germany and Italy*. Minneapolis: Augsburg Publishing, 1971.

Basile, Deana. "*Specchio delle rare e virtuose donne*: The Role of the Female Interlocutor in Sixteenth-Century Dialogues on Love." University of Toronto dissertation: 1999.

———. "*Fasseli gratia per poetessa*: Duke Cosimo I De' Medici's Role in the Florentine Literary Circle of Tullia d'Aragona." In *The Cultural Politics of Duke Cosimo I de' Medici*, edited by Konrad Eisenbichler, 135–48. Aldershot: Ashgate, 2001.

Bassani, Lucia Nadin. *Il Poligrafo veneto: Giuseppe Betussi*. Padua: Antenore, 1992.

Barzaghi, Antonio. *Donne o cortegiane? La prostituzione a Venezia: Documenti di costume dal XVI al XVI secolo*. Verona: Bertani, 1980.

Bassanese, Fiora. *Gaspara Stampa*. Boston: Twayne, 1983.

———. "Private Lives and Public Lies: Texts by the Courtesans of the Italian Renaissance." *Texas Studies in Literature and Languages* 30 (1988): 295–319.

———. "What's in a Name? Self-Naming and Renaissance Women Poets." *Annali d' italianistica* 7 (1989): 104–15.

———. "Gaspara Stampa (1523–1554)." In *Italian Women Writers: A Bio-Bibliographical Sourcebook*, edited by Rinaldina Russell, 404–13. Westport, CT, and London: Greenwood Press, 1994.

————. "Selling the Self; or the Epistolary Production of Renaissance Courtesans." In *Italian Women Writers from the Renaissance to the Present*, edited by Maria Ornella Marotti, 69–82. University Park: Pennsylvania State University Press, 1999.

Belladona, Rita. "Gli Intronati, Le Donne, Aonio Paleario e Agostino Museo in un Dialogo Inedito di Marcantonio Piccolomini, Il Sodo Intronato (1538)." *Bullettino senese di storia patria* 99 (1994): 48–90.

Benson, Pamela. *The Invention of Renaissance Woman: The Challenge of Female Independence in the Literature and Thought of Italy and England.* University Park: Pennsylvania State University Press, 1992.

————. "Eleonora di Toledo among the Famous Women: Iconographic Innovation after the Conquest of Siena." In *The Cultural World of Eleonora di Toledo*, edited by Konrad Eisenbichler, 119–35. Aldershot and Burlington: Ashgate, 2004.

Benson, Pamela Joseph, and Victoria Kirkham, eds. *Strong Voices, Weak History: Early Women Writers and Canons in England, France and Italy.* Ann Arbor: University of Michigan Press, 2005.

Biagi, Guido. "Un'etera romana. Tullia d'Aragona." *Rivista critica della letteratura italiana* 3, no. 4 (1886): 655–711.

Bianco, Monica. "Le due redazioni del commento di Rinaldo Corso alle rime di Vittoria Colonna." *Studi di filologia italiana* 56 (1998): 271–95.

Bianco, Monica, and Elena Strada, eds. *I più vaghi e più soavi fiori: Studi sulle antologie di lirica del Cinquecento.* Padua: Orso, 2001.

Bongi, Salvatore, ed. *Annali di Gabriel Giolito de' Ferrari da Trino di Monferrato.* 2 vols. Rome: Principali Librai, 1890, 1895.

Bronzini, Domenico. *Isabella di Morra con l'edizione del canzoniere.* Matera: Motemurro, 1975.

Broomhall, Susan. *Women and the Book Trade in Sixteenth-Century France.* Oxford and Burlington, VT: Ashgate Press, 2002.

Brose, Margaret. "Petrarch's Beloved Body: 'Italia mia.'" In *Feminist Approaches to the Body in Medieval Literature*, edited by Linda Lomperis and Sarah Stansbury, 1–20. Philadelphia: University of Pennsylvania Press, 1993.

Bryce, Judith. "The Oral World of the Early Accademia Fiorentina." *Renaissance Studies* 9, no. 1 (1995): 77–103.

Caccamo, D. "Bonifacio, Giovanni Bernardino." In *Dizionario biografico degli Italiani*, 12:197–201. Rome: Istituto dell'Enciclopedia Italiana, 1970.

Cantigalli, Roberto. *La Guerra di Siena, 1552–1559.* Siena: Accademia senese degli intronati, 1962.

————. *Cosimo I de' Medici, granduca di Toscana.* Milan: Mursia, 1985.

Cantimori, Delio. *Eretici italiani del Cinquecento.* Florence: Sansoni, 1997.

Caponetto, Salvatore. *The Protestant Reformation in Sixteenth-Century Italy.* Translated by Anne C. Tedeschi and John Tedeschi. Kirksville, MO: Thomas Jefferson Press, 1999.

Caro, Gaspare de. "Avalos, Alfonso d'." In *Dizionario biografico degli Italiani*, 4:612–16. Rome: Istituto dell'Enciclopedia Italiana, 1962.

———. "Carafa, Ferrante." In *Dizionario biografico degli Italiani*, 19:543–45. Rome: Istituto dell'Enciclopedia Italiana, 1976.

Caserta, Giovanni. *Isabella Morra e la società meridionale del Cinquecento*. Matera: Mela, 1976.

Cerreta, Florindo. *Alessandro Piccolomini: Letterato e filosofo Senese del Cinquecento*. Siena: Accademia Senese degli Intronati, 1960.

———. "An Account of the Early Life of the Accademia degli Infiammati in the Letters of Alessandro Piccolomini to Benedetto Varchi." *Romanic Review* 48 (1957): 249–64.

———. "La Tombaide: Alcune rime inedite sur un pelegrinaggio petrarchesco ad Arqua." *Italica* 35 (1958): 162–66.

Chartier, Roger, ed. *The Culture of Print: Power and the Uses of Print in Early Modern Europe*. Translated by Lydia G. Cochrane. Princeton, NJ: Princeton University Press, 1987.

Clubb, Louise George, and William G. Clubb. "Building a Lyric Canon: Gabriel Giolito and the Rival Anthologists, 1545–1590." *Italica* 68, no. 3 (1991): 332–44.

Cochrane, Eric. *Florence in the Forgotten Centuries, 1527–1800: A History of Florence and the Florentines in the Age of the Grand Dukes*. Chicago: University of Chicago Press, 1973.

Collett, Barry. *A Long and Troubled Pilgrimage: The Correspondence of Marguerite d'Angoulême and Vittoria Colonna, 1540–1545*. Princeton, NJ: Princeton Theological Seminary, 2000.

Cox, Virginia. *The Renaissance Dialogue: Literary Dialogue in its Social and Political Contexts, Castiglione to Galileo*. Cambridge: Cambridge University Press, 1992.

———. "Women Writers and the Canon in Sixteenth-Century Italy." In *Strong Voices, Weak History: Early Modern Writers and Canons in England, France, and Italy*, edited by Pamela Joseph Benson and Victoria Kirkham, 14–31. Ann Arbor: University of Michigan Press, 2006.

———. "The Single Self: Feminist Thought and the Marriage Market in Early Modern Venice." *Renaissance Quarterly* 48 (1995): 513–81.

Croce, Benedetto. *Isabella Morra e Diego Sandoval de Castro con l'edizione delle "Rime" della Morra e una scelta di quelle del Sandoval*. Bari: Laterza, 1929.

———. *Poeti e scrittori del pieno e del tardo Rinascimento*. Bari: Laterza, 1945.

Curtis-Wendlandt, Lisa. "Conversing on Love: Text and Subtext in Tullia d'Aragona's *Dialogo della Infinità d'Amore*." *Hypatia* 19, no. 4 (Fall 2004): 75–96.

Dall'Olio, Guido. "Gonzaga, Giulia." In *Dizionario biografico degli Italiani*, 57:783–87. Rome: Istituto dell'Enciclopedia Italiana, 2001.

Dandelet, Thomas James. *Spanish Rome, 1550–1700*. New Haven, CT: Yale University Press, 2001.

Davis, Natalie Zemon. *Society and Culture in Early Modern France: Eight Essays*. Stanford, CA: Stanford University Press, 1965.

DeJean, Joan. *Tender Geographies: Women and the Origins of the Novel in France*. New York: Columbia University Press, 1991.

Del Fante, Alessandra. "Amore, famiglia e matrimonio nell'Institutione di Alessandro Piccolomini." *Nuova rivista storica* 58 (1984): 511–26.

De Maio, Romeo. "Belprato, Giovanni Vincenzo." In *Dizionario biografico degli Italiani*, 8:49. Rome: Istituto dell'Enciclopedia Italiana, 1966.

Di Filippo Bareggi, Claudio. *Il Mestiere si Scrivere*. Rome: Bulzoni, 1988.

———. "In nota alla politica culturale di Cosimo I: L'Accademia Fiorentina." *Quaderni storici* 23 (1973): 627–74.

Dionisotti, Carlo D. "La letteratura italiana nell'età del concilio di Trento." In *Geografia e storia della letteratura italiana*, 183–204. Turin: Einaudi, 1967.

Edelstein, Bruce L. "La fecundissima Signora Duchessa: The Courtly Persona of Eleonora di Toledo and the Iconography of Abundance." In *The Cultural World of Eleonora di Toledo*, edited by Konrad Eisenbichler, 119–35. Aldershot: Ashgate, 2004.

Eisenbichler, Konrad. "Laudomia Forteguerri Loves Margaret of Austria." In *Same Sex Love and Desire among Women in the Middle Ages*, edited by Francesco Canadé Sautman and Pamela Sheingorn, 277–80. New York: Palgrave, 2001.

Eisenstein, Elizabeth. *The Printing Revolution in Early Modern Europe*. Cambridge and New York: Cambridge University Press, 1983.

———. *The Printing Press as an Agent of Change: Communications and Cultural Transformations in Early-Modern Europe*. 2 vols. Cambridge: Cambridge University Press, 1979.

Ercole, Pasquale d'. *Il cardinale Ippolito de'Medici*. Terlizzi: Giannone, 1907.

Erdmann, Axel. *My Gracious Silence: Women in the Mirror of Sixteenth-Century Printing in Western Europe*. Luzern: Gilhofer & Rauschberg, 1999.

Fahy, Conor. "Women and Italian Cinquecento Literary Academies." In *Women in Italian Renaissance Culture and Society*, edited by Letizia Panizza, 438–52. Oxford: Legenda, 2000.

———. "Love and Marriage in the *Institutione* of Alessandro Piccolomini." In *Italian Studies Presented to E. R. Vincent*, edited by C. P. Brand, K. Foster, and U. Limentani, 121–35. Cambridge: Cambridge University Press, 1962.

Franceschini, Chiara. "*Los scholares son casa de su excelentia como lo es toda la Cimpañia*: Eleonora di Toledo and the Jesuits." In *The Cultural World of Eleonora di Toledo*, edited by Konrad Eisenbichler, 181–206. Aldershot: Ashgate, 2004.

Farenga, Paola. "Di Costanzo, Angelo." In *Dizionario biografico degli Italiani*, 39:742–47. Rome: Istituto dell'Enciclopedia Italiana, 1991.

Feliciangeli, Bernardino. *Notizie e documenti sulla vita di Caterina Cibo-Varano*. Camerino: Tipografico Savini, 1891.

Field, Arthur. *The Origins of the Platonic Academy*. Princeton, NJ: Princeton University Press, 1988.

Finucci, Valeria. "Isabella di Morra." In *An Encyclopedia of Continental Women Writers*, edited by Katharina M. Wilson, 2:876–77. New York: Garland, 1991.

Fiorentino, Francesco: "Maria d'Aragona, Marchesa del Vasto." In *Studi e Ritratti della Rinascenza*, edited by Luisa Fiorentino, 157–91. Bari: Laterza, 1911.

Firpo, Massimo. *Dal Sacco di Roma all'Inquisitione. Studi su Juan Valdés e la Riforma italiana*. Turin: Edizioni dell'Orso, 1998.

———. *Inquisizione romana e controriforma: Studi sul Cardinal Giovanni Morone e il suo processo d'eresia*. Bologna: Il Mulino, 1992.

Firpo, Massimo, and Dario Marcatto, eds. *I processi inquisitoriali di Pietro Carnesecchi, 1557–1567*. 4 vols. Vatican City: Archivio Vaticano, 1998–2000.

Fragnito, Gigliola. *La Bibbia al rogo: La censura ecclesiastica e i volgarizzamenti della Scrittura (1471–1605).* Bologna: Il Mulino, 1997.

Girardi, Enzo Noe. "Battiferri, Laura." In *Dizionario biografico degli Italiani,* 7:242–44. Rome: Istituto dell'Enciclopedia Italiana, 1965.

Gleason, Elizabeth G. *Gasparo Contarini: Venice, Rome, and Reform.* Berkeley: University of California Press, 1993.

———. "On the Nature of Sixteenth-Century Italian Evangelism: Scholarship, 1953–1978." *Sixteenth-Century Journal* 9, no. 3 (1978): 3–25.

———. *Reform Thought in Sixteenth-Century Italy.* Chico, CA: Scholars Press, 1981.

———. "The Capuchin Order in the Sixteenth Century." In *Religious Orders of the Catholic Reformation, in Honor of John C. Olin,* edited by R. I. DeMolen, 31–67. New York: Fordham University Press, 1994.

Goldsmith, Elizabeth. "Publishing the Lives of Hortense and Marie Mancini." In *Going Public: Women and Publishing in Early Modern France,* edited by Elizabeth Goldsmith and Dena Goodman. Ithaca, NY, and London: Cornell University Press, 1995.

Grendler, Paul F. *The Roman Inquisition and the Venetian Press, 1540–1605.* Princeton, NJ: Princeton University Press, 1977.

———. *Critics of the Italian World, 1530–1560: Anton Francesco Doni, Nicolò Franco, and Ortensio Lando.* Madison: University of Wisconsin Press, 1969.

Guerra Medici, Maria Teresa. *Famiglia e potere in una signoria dell'Italia centrale: I Varano di Camerino.* Camerino: Università degli Studi di Camerino, 2002.

Gui, Francesco. "Il papato e i Colonna al tempo di Filippo II." In *Atti del convegno internazionale di studi storici del IV centenario della morte di Filippo II, 5–7 Novembre 1998,* 9–77. Cagliari: AM & D Edizioni, 1999.

Hairston, Julia L. "Out of the Archive: Four Newly-Identified Figures in Tullia d'Aragona's *Rime della Signora Tullia di Aragona et di diversi a lei* (1547)." *Modern Language Notes* 118 (2003): 257–63.

Hall, Stuart. "Gramsci's Relevance for the Study of Race and Ethnicity." In *Critical Dialogues in Cultural Studies,* edited by David Morley and Kuan-Hsing Chen, 411–40. New York and London: Routledge, 1996.

Hoppe, Ilaria. "A Duchess' Place at Court: The Quartiere di Eleonora in the Palazzo della Signoria in Florence." In *The Cultural World of Eleonora di Toledo,* edited by Konrad Eisenbichler, 98–118. Aldershot: Ashgate, 2004.

Johns, Adrian. *The Nature of the Book: Print and Knowledge in the Making.* Chicago: University of Chicago Press, 1998.

Jones, Ann Rosalind. *The Currency of Eros: Women's Love Lyric in Europe, 1540–1620.* Bloomington and Indianapolis: Indiana University Press, 1990.

———. "Surprising Fame: Renaissance Gender Ideologies and Women's Lyric." In *The Poetics of Gender,* edited by Nancy K. Miller. New York: Columbia University Press, 1986.

———. "New Songs for the Swallow: Ovid's Philomela in Tullia d'Aragona and Gaspara Stampa." In *Refiguring Woman: Gender Studies and the Italian Renaissance,* edited by Marilyn Migiel and Juliana Schiesari, 263–278. Ithaca, NY: Cornell University Press, 1991.

———. "Enabling Sites and Gender Difference: Reading City Women and Men." *Women Studies. An Interdisciplinary Journal* 19, no. 2 (1991): 239–49.

King, Margaret L. *The Death of the Child Valerio Marcello*. Chicago: University of Chicago Press, 1994.

———. *Women of the Renaissance*. Chicago: University of Chicago Press, 1991.

Kirkham, Vittoria. "Laura Battiferra degli Ammannati's First Book of Poetry: A Renaissance Holograph Comes out of Hiding." *Rinascimento* 36 (1996): 351–91.

———. "Poetic Ideals of Love and Beauty." In *Virtue and Beauty: Leonardo's "Ginevra de' Benci" and Renaissance Portraits of Women*, edited by David Alan Brown, 49–62. Princeton, NJ: Princeton University Press, 2001.

———. "Laura Battiferera degli Ammannati benefattrice dei Gesuiti fiorentini." *Quaderni storici* 104, no. 35 (2000): 331–54.

———. "Dante's Phantom, Petrarch's Specter: Bronzino's Portrait of the Poet Laura Battiferra." In *Visibile Parlare: Dante and the Art of the Italian Renaissance*, edited by Deborah Parker, 63–139. *Lectura Dantis* vols. 22–23 (1998).

———. "Creative Partners: The Marriage of Laura Battiferra and Bartolomeo Ammannati." *Renaissance Quarterly* 55, no. 2 (2002): 498–558.

Landes, Joan B. *Women and the Public Sphere in the Age of the French Revolution*. Ithaca, NY, and London: Cornell University Press, 1988.

Lougee Chappell, Carolyn. "Salons." In *The Encyclopedia of the Renaissance*, edited by Paul F. Grendler. New York: Scribners, 1999.

———. *Le paradis des femmes: Women, Salons, and Social Stratification in Seventeenth-Century France*. Princeton, NJ: Princeton University Press, 1976.

Luzio, Alessandro, and Rodolfo Renier. *Mantova e Urbino: Isabella d'Este ed Elisabetta Gonzaga nelle relazioni familiari e nelle vicende politiche*. Turin: Roux & Co., 1893.

Marchetti, Valerio. *Gruppi Ereticali Senesi del Cinquecento*. Florence: La Nuova Italiana Editrice, 1975.

Marchetti, Valerio, and Rita Belladonna. "Carli Piccolomini, Bartolomeo." In *Dizionario biografico degli Italiani*, 20:194–96. Rome: Istituto dell'Enciclopedia Italiana, 1977.

Marino, John. *Pastoral Economics in the Kingdom of Naples*. Baltimore: Johns Hopkins University Press, 1988.

Martin, John. *Venice's Hidden Enemies: Italian Heretics in a Renaissance City*. Berkeley: University of California Press, 1993.

Martines, Lauro. *Power and Imagination: City-States in Renaissance Italy*. New York: Random House, 1979.

Mauriello, Adriana. "Cultura e società nel Siena del Cinquecento." *Filologia e letteratura* 17 (1971): 26–48.

Mayer, Thomas F. *Reginald Pole: Prince and Prophet*. Cambridge: Cambridge University Press, 2000.

Maylender, Michele. *Storia delle Accademie d'Italia*. 5 vols. Bologna: Capelli, 1926–30.

McClure, George W. *Sorrow and Consolation in Italian Humanism*. Princeton, NJ: Princeton University Press, 1991.

McIver, Katherine A. "Two Emilian Noblewomen and Patronage Networks in the Cinquecento." In *Beyond Isabella: Secular Women Patrons of Art in Renaissance Italy*, edited by Sheryl E. Reiss and David G. Wilkins 159–76. Kirksville, MO: Truman State University Press.

Milburn, Erika. *Luigi Tansillo and Lyric Poetry in Sixteenth-Century Naples*. Modern Humanities Research Association. Leeds: Maney Publishing, 2003.

Moretti, Giuseppe. "Il cardinale Ippolito dei Medici." *Archivio Storico Italiano*, vol. 2 (1940).

Mulli, Siro. *Giulia Gonzaga*. Milan: Treves, 1938.

Mutini, Claudio. "Avalos, Costanza d'." In *Dizionario biografico degli Italiani*, 4:621–22. Rome: Enciclopedia italiana, 1962.

———. "Caula, Camillo." In *Dizionario biografico degli Italiani*, 22:540–42. Rome: Istituto dell'Enciclopedia Italiana, 1979.

———. "Betussi, Giuseppe." In *Dizionario biografico degli Italiani*, 13:779–81. Rome: Istituto dell'Enciclopedia Italiana, 1971.

———. "Bacio Terracina, Laura." In *Dizionario biografico degli Italiani*, 5:61–63. Rome: Istituto dell'Enciclopedia Italiana, 1963.

Nelson, John Charles. *Renaissance Theory of Love: The Context of Giordano Bruno's "Eroici furori."* New York: Columbia University Press, 1958.

Nicolini, Benedetto. *Ideali e passioni nell'Italia religiosa*. Studi cinquecenteschi, vol. 1. Bologna: Tamari, 1968.

———. "Contile, Luca." In *Dizionario biografico degli Italiani*, 28:495–502. Rome: Istituto dell' Enciclopedia, 1983.

Nieto, José C. *Juan de Valdés and the Origins of the Spanish and Italian Reformation*. Geneva: Droz, 1970.

Nuovo, Angela, and Christian Coppens. *I Giolito e la stampa nell'Italia del XVI secolo*. Geneva: Droz, 2005.

Och, Marjorie. "Vittoria Colonna and the Commission for *Mary Magdalene* by Titian." In *Beyond Isabella: Secular Women Patrons of Art in Renaissance Italy*, edited by Sheryl E. Reiss and David G. Wilkins, 192–223. Kirksville, MO: Truman State University Press.

Oliva, Mario. *Giulia Gonzaga Colonna tra Rinascimento e Controriforma*. Milan: Mursia, 1985.

Ortolani, Oddone. *Pietro Carnesecchi*. Florence: Felice Le Monnier, 1963.

Paladino, Giuseppe. *Giulia Gonzaga e il movimento valdesiano*. Naples: F. Sangiovanni & Figlio, 1909.

Panizza, Letizia. "Review Article: Anne Rosalind Jones, *The Currency of Eros: Women's Love Lyric in Europe, 1540–1620.*" *Italian Studies* 47 (1992): 80–84.

———, ed. *Women in Italian Renaissance Culture and Society*. Oxford: Legenda, 2000.

Panizza, Letizia, and Sharon Wood, eds. *A History of Women's Writing in Italy*. Cambridge: Cambridge University Press, 2000.

Parker, Deborah. *Bronzino: Renaissance Painter as Poet*. Cambridge: Cambridge University Press, 2000.

Pastor, Ludwig. *The History of the Popes from the Close of the Middle Ages*. Edited and translated by Ralph Francis Kerr. St. Louis, MO: B. Herder, 1923.

Pastore, Alessandro. *Marcantonio Flaminio: Fortune e Sfortune si un chierico nell'Italia del cinquecento.* Milan: Franco Angeli, 1981.

———. "Flaminio, Marcantonio." In *Dizionario biografico degli Italiani,* 48:282–88. Rome: Istituto dell'Enciclopedia Italiana, 1997.

Pepper, Simon, and Nicholas Adams. *Firearms and Fortifications. Military Architecture and Siege Warfare in Sixteenth-Century Siena.* Chicago: University of Chicago Press, 1986.

Petrucci, Franca. "Cibo, Caterina." In *Dizionario biografico degli Italiani,* 25:237–41. Rome: Istituto dell'Enciclopedia Italiana, 1981.

———. "Colonna, Ascanio." In *Dizionario biografico degli Italiani,* 27:271–75. Rome: Istituto dell'Enciclopedia Italiana,1982.

Piejus, Marie-Françoise. "La première antologie des poèmes féminins: L'écriture filtrée et orientée." In *Le pouvoir e la plume: Incitiation, contrôle e répression dans l'Italie du XVIe siècle,* 193–213. Paris: Université de la Sorbonne Nouvelle, 1982.

———. "Le poetesses Siennoises entre le jeu e l'écriture." In *Les femmes écrivains en Italie au Moyen Age et à la Renaissance,* 312–32. Aix-en-Provence: L'Université de Provence, 1994.

———. "Varietà: L'Orazione in *Lode delle Donne* di Alessandro Piccolomini." *Giornale storico della letteratura italiana* 170, no. 4 (1993): 524–51.

———. "Venus Bifrons: Le double ideal feminin dans *La Raffaella* d'Alessandro Piccolomini." In *Images de la femme dans la litterature Italienne de la Renaissance prejuges misegynes et aspirations nouvelle,* edited by André Rochon, 81–131. Paris: Université de la Sorbonne Nouvelle, 1980.

Pirotti, Umberto. *Benedetto Varchi e la Cultura del suo Tempo.* Florence: Olschki, 1971.

Piscini, Angela. "Domenichi, Lodovico." In *Dizionario biografico degli Italiani,* 40:595–600. Rome: Istituto dell'Enciclopedia Italiana, 1991.

Puga, María Luisa Cerrón. "Materiales para construcción del canon petrarquista: Las antologias de *Rime* (libri I–IX)." *Critica del testo* 2, no. 1 (1999): 249–90.

Pullan, Brian. *The Jews of Europe and the Inquisition of Venice, 1550–1670.* London and New York: I. B. Tauris, 1997.

———. *Rich and Poor in Renaissance Venice.* Oxford: Blackwell, 1971.

Rabitti, Giovanna. "Laura Battiferri Ammannati (1523–1589)." In *Italian Women Writers: A Bio-Bibliographical Sourcebook,* edited by Rinaldina Russell, 44–49. Westport, CT: Greenwood Press, 1994.

Reiss, Sheryl E., and David G. Wilkins, ed. *Beyond Isabella: Secular Women Patrons of Art in Renaissance Italy.* Kirksville, MO: Truman State University Press, 2001.

Reumont, Alfredo. *Vittoria Colonna: Vita, fede, poesia nel secolo decimosesto.* Translated by Giuseppe Müller and Ermanno Ferrero. Turin: Ermanno Loescher, 1889–92.

———. "Di Vittoria Colonna" [contains two letters by Giovanna d'Aragona]. *Archivio storico italiano,* n.s. 5, *Giornale storico degli Archivi Toscani,* 143–45. Florence: Vieusseux, 1857.

Ricci, Antonio. "Lorenzo Torrentino and the Cultural Programme of Cosimo I de' Medici." In *The Cultural Politics of Duke Cosimo I de' Medici,* edited by Konrad Eisenbichler, 103–20. Aldershot: Ashgate, 2001.

Richardson, Brian. *Printing, Writers and Readers in Renaissance Italy.* Cambridge: Cambridge University Press, 1999.

———. *Print Culture in Renaissance Italy: The Editor and the Vernacular Text, 1470–1600.* Cambridge: Cambridge University Press, 1994.

Robin, Diana. *Filelfo in Milan. Writings 1457–1477.* Princeton: Princeton University Press, 1991.

Rocke, Michael. *Forbidden Friendships. Homosexuality and Male Culture in Renaissance Florence.* Oxford: Oxford University Press, 1996.

Rotondò, Antonio. "Carnesecchi, Pietro." In *Dizionario biografico degli Italiani*, 20:466–76. Rome: Istituto dell'Enciclopedia Italiana, 1977.

Russell, Rinaldina. "The Mind's Pursuit of the Divine. A Survey of Secular and Religious Themes in Vittoria Colonna's Sonnets." *Forum Italicum* 26 (1992): 14–27.

———. "L'ultima meditazione di Vittoria Colonna e l' 'Ecclesia Viterbiensis.'" La Parola del testo. Semestrale di filologia e letteratura italiana e comparata dal medioevo al rinascimento (2000) 4.1: 151–66.

———. "Laura Terracina." In *Italian Women Writers. A Bio-Bibliographical Sourcebook*, edited by Rinaldina Russell, 423–40. Westport, CT: Greenwood Press, 1994.

———. "Intenzionalità artistica della 'disperata.'" In *Generi poetici medievali: Modelli e funzioni letterarie*, 163–82. Naples: SEN, 1982.

Salza, Abd-el-kader. "Madonna Gasparina Stampa secondo nuove indagini." *Giornale storico della letteratura italiana* 62 (1913): 1–101.

———. *Luca Contile: Uomo di Lettere e di Negozi del Secolo XVI.* Contributo alla storia della vita di corte e dei poligrafi del 500. Florence: G. Carnesecchi, 1903.

San Juan, Rose Marie. "The Court Lady's Dilemma: Isabella d'Este and Art Collecting in the Renaissance." *Oxford Art Journal* 14, no. 1 (1991): 67–78.

Santore, Cathy. "Julia Lombardo, 'Somtuosa Meretrize': A Portrait of Property." *Renaissance Quarterly* 41, no. 1 (1988): 44–87.

Schiesari, Juliana. "The Gendering of Melancholia: Torquato Tasso and Isabella di Morra." In *Refiguring Woman: Perspectives on Gender and the Italian Renaissance*, edited by Marilyn Migiel and Juliana Schiesari, 231–62. Ithaca, NY: Cornell University Press, 1991.

———. "Isabella di Morra (c. 1520–1545)." In *Italian Women Writers. A Bio-Bibliographical Sourcebook*, edited by Rinaldina Russell, 279–85. Westport, CT: Greenwood Press, 1994.

Schutte, Anne Jacobson. *Pier Paolo Vergerio: The Making of an Italian Reformer.* Geneva: Droz, 1977.

———. "Irene di Spilimbergo: The Image of a Creative Woman in Late Renaissance Italy." *Renaissance Quarterly* 1 (1991): 42–61.

Shemek, Deanna. "The Collector's Cabinet: Lodovico Domenichi's Gallery of Women." In *Strong Voices, Weak History: Early Women Writers and Canons in England, France and Italy*, edited by Pamela Joseph Benson and Victoria Kirkham, 239–62. Ann Arbor: University of Michigan Press, 2005.

———. "Getting a Word in Edgewise: Laura Terracina's *Discorsi* on the *Orlando furioso*." In *Ladies Errant: Wayward Women and Social Order in Early Modern Italy*, 126–57. Durham, NC and London: Duke University Press, 1998.

———. "In Continuous Expectation: Isabella d'Este's Epistolary Desire." In *Phaethon's Children: The Este Court and Its Culture in Early Modern Italy*, edited by Dennis Looney and Deanna Shemek, 269–300. Tempe, AZ: Medieval and Renaissance Texts and Studies, 2005.

Smarr, Janet Levarie. "A Dialogue of Dialogues: Tullia d'Aragona and Sperone Speroni." *Modern Language Notes* 113 (1998): 204–12.

———. *Joining the Conversation: Dialogues by Renaissance Women.* Ann Arbor: University of Michigan Press, 2005.

———. "A Female Tradition? Women's Dialogue Writing in Sixteenth-Century France." In *Strong Voices, Weak History. Early Women and Canons in England, France, and Italy*, edited by Pamela Joseph Benson and Victoria Kirkham, 32–57. Ann Arbor: University of Michigan Press, 2005.

Snyder Jon R. *Writing the Scene of Speaking: Theories of Dialogue in the Late Renaissance.* Stanford, CA: Stanford University Press, 1989.

Terpenning, Ronnie H. *Lodovico Dolce, Renaissance Man of Letters.* Toronto: University of Toronto Press, 1997.

Therault, Suzanne. *Un cénacle humaniste de la Renaissance autour de Vittoria Colonna châtelaine d'Ischia.* Florence: Sansoni, 1968.

Tinagli, Paola. "Eleonora and Her 'Famous Sisters': The Tradition of 'Illustrious Women' in Paintings of the Domestic Interior." In *The Cultural World of Eleonora*, edited by Konrad Eisenbichler, 119–135. Aldershot: Ashgate, 2004.

Tordi, Domenico. "Vittoria Colonna in Orvieto durante la Guerra del Sale." *Bollettino della società umbra di Storia Patria*, 1:473–533. Perugia: Boncampagni, 1895.

Toscano, Tobia R. "Un'orazione latina di Bernardino Roto, 'principe' dell'accademia dei Sereni di Napoli." *Critica letteraria* 23 (1995): 81–109.

Turner, James Grantham, ed. *Sexuality and Gender in Early Modern Europe: Institutions, Texts, Images.* Cambridge: Cambridge University Press, 1993.

Vasoli, Cesare. "Caterina Cibo Varano." In *Civitas Mundi. Studi sulla cultura del Cinquecento.* Raccolta di Studi e Testi, 194:121–38. Rome: Ediozioni Storia e Letteratura, 1996.

Weaver, Elissa. *Convent Theatre in Early Modern Italy: Spiritual Fun and Learning for Women.* Cambridge: Cambridge University Press, 2001.

Zarri, Gabriella. "La spiritualità di Caterina Cibo: Indizi e testimonianze." In *Caterina Cybo duchessa di Camerino (1501–1557)*, edited by Pierluigi Moriconi, 313–31. Atti del Convegno, Camerino, Auditorium S. Caterina, 28–30 ottobre 2004. Camerino: Tipografia "L Nuova Stampa," 2005.

———, ed. *Donna, disciplina creanza cristiana.* Rome: Edizioni di Storia & Letteratura, 1996.

Zarrilli, Carla. "Forteguerri, Laudomia." In *Dizionario biografico degli Italiani*, 49:153–55. Rome: Istituto dell'Enciclopedia Italiana, 1997.

Zonta, Giuseppe. "Note betussiane." *Giornale storico delle letteratura italiana* 52 (1908) 321–66.

# INDEX

*Page numbers in italics refer to figures and tables.*